Get the eBooks FREE!

(PDF, ePub, Kindle, and liveBook all included)

We believe that once you buy a book from us, you should be able to read it in any format we have available. To get electronic versions of this book at no additional cost to you, purchase and then register this book at the Manning website.

Go to https://www.manning.com/freebook and follow the instructions to complete your pBook registration.

That's it!
Thanks from Manning!

Functional Programming in C#

Functional Programming in C#

ENRICO BUONANNO

MANNING

SHELTER ISLAND

Manning Publications Co.
20 Baldwin Road
PO Box 761
Shelter Island, NY 11964

Development editor:	Marina Michaels
Technical development editor:	Joel Kotarski
Review editor:	Aleksandar Dragosavljević
Project editor:	Kevin Sullivan
Copyeditor:	Andy Carroll
Proofreader:	Melody Dolab
Technical proofreaders:	Paul Louth, Jürgen Hoetzel
Typesetter:	Gordan Salinovic
Cover designer:	Leslie Haimes
Cartoons:	Viseslav Radović, Richard Sheppard
Graphic illustrations:	Chuck Larson

ISBN 9781617293955
Printed in the United States of America
2 3 4 5 6 7 8 9 10 – DP – 22 21 20 19 18

To the little monkey...

brief contents

contents

ix

preface

Today, functional programming (FP) is no longer brooding in the research departments of universities; it has become an important and exciting part of mainstream programming. The majority of the languages and frameworks created in the last decade are functional, leading some to predict that the future of programming is functional. Meanwhile, popular object-oriented languages like C# and Java see the introduction of more functional features with every new release, enabling a multiparadigm programming style.

And yet, adoption in the C# community has been slow. Why is this so? One reason, I believe, is the lack of good literature:

- Most FP literature is written in and for functional languages, especially Haskell. For developers with a background in OOP, this poses a programming-language barrier to learning the concepts. Even though many of the concepts apply to a multiparadigm language like C#, learning a new paradigm *and* a new language at once is a tall order.

- Even more importantly, most of the books in the literature tend to illustrate functional techniques and concepts with examples from the domains of mathematics or computer science. For the majority of programmers who work on line-of-business (LOB) applications day in and day out, this creates a domain gap and leaves them wondering how relevant these techniques may be for real-world applications.

These shortcomings posed major stumbling blocks in my own path to learning FP. After tossing aside the *n*-th book that explained something known as *currying* by showing how the add function can be curried with the number 3, creating a function that can add 3 to any number (can you think of any application where this would be even remotely useful?), I decided to pursue my own research path. This involved learning half a dozen functional languages (some better than others), and seeing which concepts from FP could be effectively applied in C# and in the kind of applications most developers are paid to write, and it culminated in the writing of this book.

This book bridges the language gap for C# developers by showing how you can leverage functional techniques in this language. It also bridges the domain gap by showing how these techniques can be applied to typical business scenarios. I take a pragmatic approach and cover functional techniques to the extent that they're useful in a typical LOB application scenario, and dispense with most of the theory behind FP.

Ultimately, you should care about FP because it gives you the following:

- *Power*—This simply means that you can get more done with less code. FP raises the level of abstraction, allowing you to write high-level code while freeing you from low-level technicalities that add complexity but no value.
- *Safety*—This is especially true when dealing with concurrency. A program written in the imperative style may work well in a single-threaded implementation but cause all sorts of bugs when concurrency comes in. Functional code offers much better guarantees in concurrent scenarios, so it's only natural that we're seeing a surge of interest in FP in the era of multicore processors.
- *Clarity*—We spend more time maintaining and consuming existing code than writing new code, so it's important that our code be clear and intention-revealing. As you learn to think functionally, achieving this clarity will become more natural.

If you've been programming in an object-oriented style for some time, it may take a bit of effort and willingness to experiment before the concepts in this book come to fruition. To make sure learning FP is an enjoyable and rewarding process, I have two recommendations:

- *Be patient*—You may have to read some sections more than once. You may put the book down for a few weeks and find that when you pick it up again, something that seemed obscure suddenly starts to make sense.
- *Experiment in code*—You won't learn unless you get your hands dirty. The book provides many examples and exercises, and many of the code snippets can be tested in the REPL.

Your colleagues may be less eager to explore than you. Expect them to protest your adoption of this new style and to look perplexed at your code and say things like, "why not just do *x*?" (where *x* is boring, obsolete, and usually harmful). Don't discuss. Just sit back and watch them eventually turn around and use your techniques to solve issues they run into again and again.

acknowledgments

I'd like to thank Paul Louth, who not only provided inspiration through his `LanguageExt` library—from which I borrowed many good ideas—but who also graciously reviewed the book at various stages.

Manning's thorough editorial process ensured that the quality of this book is infinitely better than if I had been left to my own means. For this, I'd like to thank the team that collaborated on the book, including Mike Stephens, development editor Marina Michaels, technical editor Joel Kotarski, technical proofreader Jürgen Hoetzel, and copyeditor Andy Carroll.

Special thanks to Daniel Marbach and Tamir Dresher for their technical insights, as well as to all those who took part in the peer reviews, including Alex Basile, Aurélien Gounot, Blair Leduc, Chris Frank, Daniel Marbach, Devon Burriss, Gonzalo Barba López, Guy Smith, Kofi Sarfo, Pauli Sutelainen, Russell Day, Tate Antrim, and Wayne Mather.

Thanks to Scott Wlaschin for sharing his articles at http://fsharpforfunandprofit.com, and to the many other members of the FP community who share their knowledge and enthusiasm through articles, blogs, and open source.

about this book

This book aims to show how you can leverage functional techniques in C# to write code that is concise, elegant, robust, and maintainable.

Who should read this book

This book is for an ambitious breed of developer. You know the C# language and the .NET framework. You have experience developing real-world applications and are familiar with OOP concepts, patterns, and best practices. Yet, you're looking to expand your arsenal by learning functional techniques so that you can make the most out of C# as a multiparadigm language.

If you're trying or planning to learn a functional language, this book will also be hugely valuable, because you'll learn how to think functionally in a language you're familiar with. Changing the way you think is the hard part; once that's achieved, learning the syntax of any particular language will be relatively easy.

How this book is organized

The book consists of 15 chapters, divided into 3 parts:

- Part 1 covers the basic techniques and principles of functional programming. We'll start by looking at what functional programming is and how C# supports programming in a functional style. We'll then look at the power of higher-order functions, function purity and its relation to testability, the design of types and function signatures, and how simple functions can be composed into complex programs. By the end of part 1, you'll have a good feel for what a program written in a functional style looks like and for the benefits that this style has to offer.

- With these basic concepts covered, we'll pick up some speed in part 2 and move on to wider-reaching concerns, such as functional error handling, modularizing and composing an application, and the functional approach to understanding state and representing change. By the end of part 2, you'll have acquired a set of tools enabling you to effectively tackle many programming tasks using a functional approach.
- Part 3 will tackle more advanced topics, including lazy evaluation, stateful computations, asynchrony, data streams, and concurrency. Each chapter in part 3 introduces important techniques that have the potential to completely change the way you write and think about software.

You'll find a more detailed breakdown of the topics in each chapter, and a representation of what chapters are required before reading any particular chapter, on the inside front cover page.

Coding for real-world applications

The book aims to stay true to real-world scenarios. To do this, many examples deal with practical tasks such as reading configuration, connecting to a database, validating HTTP requests, and so on—things you may already know how to do, but you'll see them with the fresh perspective of functional thinking.

Throughout the book, I use a long-running example to illustrate how FP can help when writing LOB applications. For this, I've chosen an online banking application for the fictitious Bank of Codeland (BOC)—naff, I know, but at least it has the obligatory three-letter acronym. Because most people have access to an online banking facility, it should be easy to imagine the required functionality and plain to see how the problems discussed are relevant to real-world applications.

I also use scenarios to illustrate how to solve typical programming problems in a functional style. The constant back and forth between practical examples and FP concepts will hopefully help bridge the gap between theory and practice—something I found wanting in the existing literature, as I mentioned.

Leveraging functional libraries

A language like C# may have functional features, but to fully leverage these you'll often use libraries that facilitate common tasks. Microsoft has provided several libraries that facilitate programming in a functional style, including these:

- `System.Linq`—Yes, in case you didn't know, it's a functional library! I assume you're familiar with it, given that it's such an important part of .NET.
- `System.Collections.Immutable`—This is a library of immutable collections, which we'll start using in chapter 9.
- `System.Reactive`—This is an implementation of the Reactive Extensions for .NET, allowing you to work with data streams, which we'll discuss in chapter 14.

This still leaves out plenty of other important types and functions that are staples of FP. As a result, several independent developers have written libraries to fill those gaps. To date, the most complete of these is LanguageExt, a library written by Paul Louth to improve the C# developer's experience when coding functionally.[1]

In the book, I don't use LanguageExt directly; instead, I'll show you how I developed my own library of functional utilities, called LaYumba.Functional, even though it largely overlaps with LanguageExt. This is pedagogically more useful, for several reasons:

- The code will remain stable after the book is published.
- You get to look under the hood and see that powerful functional constructs are deceptively simple to define.
- You can concentrate on the essentials: I'll show you the constructs in their purest form, so that you won't be distracted by the details and edge cases that a full-fledged library addresses.

Code conventions and downloads

The code samples are in C# 7, and for the most part are compatible with C# 6. Language features specifically introduced in C# 7 are only used in chapter 10 and beyond (and in a couple of samples in section 1.2 that explicitly showcase C# 7).

You can execute many of the shorter snippets of code in a REPL, thereby gaining hands-on practice with immediate feedback. The more extended examples are available for download at https://github.com/la-yumba/functional-csharp-code, along with the exercises' setup and solutions.

Code listings in the book focus on the topic being discussed, and therefore may omit namespaces, using statements, trivial constructors, or sections of code that appeared in a previous listing and remain unchanged. If you'd like to see the full, compiling version of a listing, you'll find it in the code repository: https://github.com/la-yumba/functional-csharp-code.

Book forum

Purchase of *Functional Programming in C#* includes free access to a private web forum run by Manning Publications where you can make comments about the book, ask technical questions, and receive help from the author and from other users. To access the forum, go to https://forums.manning.com/forums/functional-programming-in-c-sharp. You can also learn more about Manning's forums and the rules of conduct at https://forums.manning.com/forums/about.

Manning's commitment to our readers is to provide a venue where a meaningful dialogue between individual readers and between readers and the author can take place. It is not a commitment to any specific amount of participation on the part of the author, whose contribution to the forum remains voluntary (and unpaid). We suggest you try asking the author some challenging questions lest his interest stray! The

---

[1] LanguageExt is open source and available on GitHub and NuGet: https://github.com/louthy/language-ext.

forum and the archives of previous discussions will be accessible from the publisher's website as long as the book is in print.

About the author

Enrico Buonanno obtained an MS in Computer Science at Columbia University in 2001 and has been working as a software developer and architect since. He's worked on mission-critical projects for prestigious companies in FinTech (including the Bank for International Settlements, Barclays, and UBS) and other technology-driven businesses.

Part 1

Core concepts

In this part we'll cover the basic techniques and principles of functional programming.

Chapter 1 starts by looking at what functional programming is, and how C# supports programming in a functional style. It then delves deeper into higher-order functions, a fundamental technique of FP.

Chapter 2 explains what pure functions are, why purity has important implications for a function's testability, and why pure functions lend themselves well to parallelization and other optimizations.

Chapter 3 deals with principles for designing types and function signatures—things you thought you knew but that receive a breath of fresh air when looked at from a functional perspective.

Chapter 4 introduces some of the core functions of FP: Map, Bind, ForEach, and Where (filter). These functions provide the basic tools for interacting with the most common data structures in FP.

Chapter 5 shows how functions can be chained into pipelines that capture the workflows of your program. It then widens the scope to developing a whole use case in a functional style.

By the end of part 1, you'll have a good feel for what a program written in a functional style looks like, and you'll understand the benefits that this style has to offer.

Introducing functional programming

This chapter covers

- Benefits and tenets of functional programming
- Functional features of the C# language
- Representation of functions in C#
- Higher-order functions

Functional programming is a programming *paradigm*: a different way of thinking about programs than the mainstream, imperative paradigm you're probably used to. For this reason, learning to think functionally is challenging but also very enriching. My ambition is that after reading this book, you'll never look at code with the same eyes as before!

The learning process can be a bumpy ride. You're likely to go from frustration at concepts that seem obscure or useless to exhilaration when something clicks in your mind, and you're able to replace a mess of imperative code with just a couple of lines of elegant, functional code.

This chapter will address some questions you may have as you start on this journey: What exactly is functional programming? Why should I care? Can I code functionally in C#? Is it worth the effort?

We'll start with a high-level overview of what functional programming (FP) is, and how well the C# language supports programming in a functional style. We'll then discuss functions and how they're represented in C#. Finally, we'll dip our feet in the water with higher-order functions, which I'll illustrate with a practical example.

1.1 What is this thing called functional programming?

What exactly is functional programming? At a very high level, it's a programming style that emphasizes functions while avoiding state mutation. This definition is already twofold, as it includes two fundamental concepts:

- Functions as first-class values
- Avoiding state mutation

Let's see what these mean.

1.1.1 Functions as first-class values

In a language where functions are first-class values, you can use them as inputs or outputs of other functions, you can assign them to variables, and you can store them in collections. In other words, you can do with functions all the operations that you can do with values of any other type.

For example, type the following into the REPL:[1]

```
Func<int, int> triple = x => x * 3;
var range = Enumerable.Range(1, 3);
var triples = range.Select(triple);

triples // => [3, 6, 9]
```

In this example, you start by declaring a function that returns the triple of a given integer and assigning it to the variable `triple`. You then use `Range` to create an IEnumerable<int> with the values [1, 2, 3]. You then invoke `Select` (an extension method on IEnumerable), giving it the range and the `triple` function as arguments; this creates a new IEnumerable containing the elements obtained by applying the `triple` function to each element in the input range.

This short snippet demonstrates that functions are indeed first-class values in C#, because you can assign the multiply-by-3 function to the variable `triple`, and give it as an argument to `Select`. Throughout the book you'll see that treating functions as values allows you to write some very powerful and concise code.

---

[1] A REPL is a command-line interface allowing you to experiment with the language by typing in statements and getting immediate feedback. If you use Visual Studio, you can start the REPL by going to View > Other Windows > C# Interactive. On Mono, you can use the `csharp` command. There are also several other utilities that allow you to run C# snippets interactively, some even in the browser.

1.1.2   Avoiding state mutation

If we follow the functional paradigm, we should refrain from state mutation altogether: once created, an object *never* changes, and variables should never be reassigned. The term *mutation* indicates that a value is changed in-place—updating a value stored somewhere in memory. For example, the following code creates and populates an array, and then it updates one of the array's values in place:

```
int[] nums = { 1, 2, 3 };
nums[0] = 7;

nums // => [7, 2, 3]
```

Such updates are also called *destructive* updates, because the value stored prior to the update is destroyed. These should always be avoided when coding functionally. (Purely functional languages don't allow in-place updates at all.)

Following this principle, sorting or filtering a list should not modify the list in place but should create a new, suitably filtered or sorted list without affecting the original. Type the following into the REPL to see what happens when sorting or filtering a list using LINQ's `Where` and `OrderBy` functions.

Listing 1.1   Functional approach: `Where` and `OrderBy` don't affect the original list

```
Func<int, bool> isOdd = x => x % 2 == 1;
int[] original = { 7, 6, 1 };

var sorted = original.OrderBy(x => x);
var filtered = original.Where(isOdd);

original // => [7, 6, 1]
sorted   // => [1, 6, 7]
filtered // => [7, 1]
```

The original list hasn't been affected. → (points to `original // => [7, 6, 1]`)

Sorting and filtering yielded new lists. (points to `sorted` and `filtered`)

As you can see, the original list is unaffected by the sorting or filtering operations, which yielded new `IEnumerables`.

Let's look at a counterexample. If you have a `List<T>`, you can sort it in place by calling its `Sort` method.

Listing 1.2   Nonfunctional approach: `List<T>.Sort` sorts the list in place

```
var original = new List<int> { 5, 7, 1 };
original.Sort();

original // => [1, 5, 7]
```

In this case, after sorting, the original ordering is destroyed. You'll see why this is problematic right away.

NOTE The reason you see both the functional and nonfunctional approaches in the framework is historical: `List<T>.Sort` predates LINQ, which marked a decisive turn in a functional direction.

1.1.3 Writing programs with strong guarantees

Of the two concepts we just discussed, functions as first-class values initially seems more exciting, and we'll concentrate on it in the latter part of this chapter. But before we move on, I'd like to briefly demonstrate why avoiding state mutation is also hugely beneficial, as it eliminates many complexities caused by mutable state.

Let's look at an example. (We'll revisit these topics in more detail, so don't worry if not everything is clear at this point.) Type the following code into the REPL.

Listing 1.3 Mutating state from concurrent processes yields unpredictable results

```
using static System.Linq.Enumerable;          This allows you to call
using static System.Console;                   Range and WriteLine
                                               without full qualification.

var nums = Range(-10000, 20001).Reverse().ToList();
// => [10000, 9999, ... , -9999, -10000]

Action task1 = () => WriteLine(nums.Sum());
Action task2 = () => { nums.Sort(); WriteLine(nums.Sum()); };

Parallel.Invoke(task1, task2);                 Executes both
// prints: 92332970                            tasks in parallel
//         0
```

Here you define nums to be a list of all integers between 10,000 and -10,000; their sum should obviously be 0. You then create two tasks: task1 computes and prints out the sum; task2 first sorts the list and then computes and prints the sum. Each of these tasks will correctly compute the sum if run independently. When you run both tasks in parallel, however, task1 comes up with an incorrect and unpredictable result.

It's easy to see why: as task1 reads the numbers in the list to compute the sum, task2 is reordering that very same list. That's somewhat like trying to read a book while somebody else flips the pages: you'd be reading some well-mangled sentences! Graphically, this can be illustrated as shown in figure 1.1.

What if we use LINQ's OrderBy method, instead of sorting the list in place?

```
Action task3 = () => WriteLine(nums.OrderBy(x => x).Sum());

Parallel.Invoke(task1, task3);
// prints: 0
//         0
```

As you can see, using LINQ's functional implementation gives you a predictable result, even when you execute the tasks in parallel. This is because task3 isn't modifying the

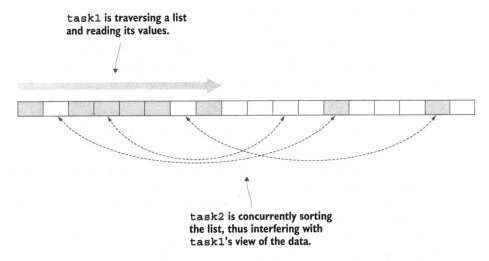

Figure 1.1 Modifying data in place can give concurrent threads an incorrect view of the data

original list but rather creating a completely new "view" of the data, which is sorted—task1 and task3 read from the original list concurrently, but concurrent reads don't cause any inconsistencies, as shown in figure 1.2.

This simple example illustrates a wider truth: when developers write an application in the imperative style (explicitly mutating the program state) and later introduce

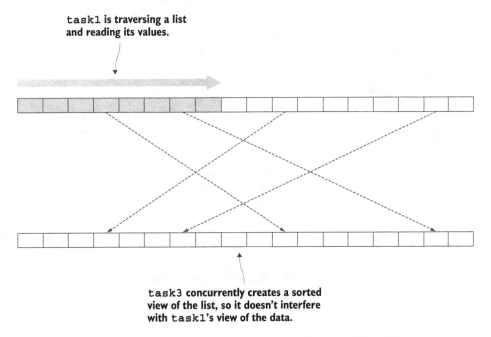

Figure 1.2 The functional approach: creating a new, modified version of the original structure

concurrency (due to new requirements, or a need to improve performance), they inevitably face a lot of work and potentially some difficult bugs. When a program is written in a functional style from the outset, concurrency can often be added for free, or with substantially less effort. We'll discuss state mutation and concurrency more in chapters 2 and 9. For now, let's go back to our overview of FP.

Although most people will agree that treating functions as first-class values and avoiding state mutation are fundamental tenets of FP, their application gives rise to a series of practices and techniques, so it's debatable which techniques should be considered essential and included in a book like this.

I encourage you to take a pragmatic approach to the subject and try to understand FP as *a set of tools* that you can use to address your programming tasks. As you learn these techniques, you'll start to look at problems from a different perspective: you'll start to think functionally.

Now that we have a working definition of FP, let's look at the C# language itself, and at its support for FP techniques.

Functional vs. object-oriented?

I'm often asked to compare and contrast FP with object-oriented programming (OOP). This isn't simple, mainly because there are many incorrect assumptions about what OOP should look like.

In theory, the fundamental principles of OOP (encapsulation, data abstraction, and so on) are orthogonal to the principles of FP, so there's no reason why the two paradigms can't be combined.

In practice, however, most object-oriented (OO) developers heavily rely on the *imperative* style in their method implementations, mutating state in place and using explicit control flow: they use OO design in the large, and imperative programming in the small. So the real question is that of *imperative vs. functional* programming, and I'll summarize the benefits of FP at the end of this chapter.

Another question that often arises is how FP differs from OOP in terms of structuring a large, complex application. The difficult art of structuring a complex application relies on several principles:

- Modularity (dividing software into reusable components)
- Separation of concerns (each component should only do one thing)
- Layering (high-level components can depend on low-level components, but not vice versa)
- Loose coupling (changes to a component shouldn't affect components that depend on it)

These principles are generally valid, regardless of whether the component in question is a function, a class, or an application.

> *(continued)*
> They're also in no way specific to OOP, so the same principles can be used to structure an application written in the functional style—the difference will be in what the components are, and what APIs they expose.
>
> In practice, the functional emphasis on pure functions (which we'll discuss in chapter 2) and composability (chapter 5) make it significantly easier to achieve some of these design goals.[2]

1.2 How functional a language is C#?

Functions are indeed first-class values in C#, as demonstrated in the previous listings. In fact, C# had support for functions as first-class values from the earliest version of the language through the `Delegate` type, and the subsequent introduction of *lambda expressions* made the syntactic support even better—we'll review these language features in the next section.

There are some quirks and limitations, such as when it comes to type inference; we'll discuss these in chapter 8. But overall, the support for functions as first-class values is pretty good.

As for supporting a programming model that avoids in-place updates, the fundamental requirement in this area is that a language have garbage collection. Because you create modified versions, rather than updating existing values in place, you want old versions to be garbage collected as needed. Again, C# satisfies this requirement.

Ideally, the language should also *discourage* in-place updates. This is C#'s greatest shortcoming: everything is mutable by default, and the programmer has to put in a substantial amount of effort to achieve immutability. Fields and variables must explicitly be marked `readonly` to prevent mutation. (Compare this to F#, where variables are immutable by default and must explicitly be marked `mutable` to allow mutation.)

What about types? There are a few immutable types in the framework, such as `string` and `DateTime`, but language support for user-defined immutable types is poor (although, as you'll see next, it has improved in C# 6 and is likely to improve further in future versions). Finally, collections in the framework are mutable, but a solid library of immutable collections is available.

In summary, C# has very good support for some functional techniques, but not others. In its evolution, it has improved, and it will continue to improve its support for functional techniques. In this book, you'll learn which features can be harnessed, and also how to work around its shortcomings.

Next we'll review some language features from past, present, and upcoming versions of C# that are particularly relevant to FP.

---

[2] For a more thorough discussion on why imperatively flavored OOP is a *cause* of, rather than a solution to, program complexity, see *Out of the Tar Pit* by Ben Moseley and Peter Marks, 2006 (https://github.com/papers-we-love/papers-we-love/raw/master/design/out-of-the-tar-pit.pdf).

1.2.1 *The functional nature of LINQ*

When C# 3 was released, along with version 3.5 of the .NET Framework, it included a host of features inspired by functional languages, including the LINQ library (System.Linq) and some new language features enabling or enhancing what you could do with LINQ, such as extension methods and expression trees.

LINQ is indeed a functional library—as you probably noticed, I used LINQ earlier to illustrate both tenets of FP—and the functional nature of LINQ will become even more apparent as you progress through this book.

LINQ offers implementations for many common operations on lists (or, more generally, on "sequences," as instances of IEnumerable should technically be called), the most common of which are mapping, sorting, and filtering (see the "Common operations on sequences" sidebar). Here's an example combining all three:

```
Enumerable.Range(1, 100).
   Where(i => i % 20 == 0).
   OrderBy(i => -i).
   Select(i => $"{i}%")
// => ["100%", "80%", "60%", "40%", "20%"]
```

Notice how Where, OrderBy, and Select all take functions as arguments and don't mutate the given IEnumerable, but return a new IEnumerable instead, illustrating both tenets of FP you saw earlier.

LINQ facilitates querying not only objects in memory (LINQ to Objects), but various other data sources, like SQL tables and XML data. C# programmers have embraced LINQ as the standard toolset for working with lists and relational data (accounting for a substantial amount of a typical codebase). On the up side, this means that you'll already have some sense of what a functional library's API feels like.

On the other hand, when working with other types, C# programmers generally stick to the imperative style of using flow-control statements to express the program's intended behavior. As a result, most C# codebases I've seen are a patchwork of functional style (when working with IEnumerables and IQueryables) and imperative style (everything else).

What this means is that although C# programmers are aware of the benefits of using a functional library such as LINQ, they haven't had enough exposure to the design principles behind LINQ to leverage those techniques in their own designs. That's something this book aims to address.

Common operations on sequences

The LINQ library contains many methods for performing common operations on sequences, such as the following:

- *Mapping*—Given a sequence and a function, mapping yields a new sequence with the elements obtained by applying the given function to each element in the given sequence (in LINQ, this is done with the Select method).

```
Enumerable.Range(1, 3).Select(i => i * 3) // => [3, 6, 9]
```

(continued)

- *Filtering*—Given a sequence and a predicate, filtering yields a new sequence consisting of the elements from the given sequence that pass the predicate (in LINQ, `Where`).

```
Enumerable.Range(1, 10).Where(i => i % 3 == 0) // => [3, 6, 9]
```

- *Sorting*—Given a sequence and a key-selector function, sorting yields a new sequence ordered according to the key (in LINQ, `OrderBy` and `OrderByDescending`).

```
Enumerable.Range(1, 5).OrderBy(i => -i) // => [5, 4, 3, 2, 1]
```

1.2.2 *Functional features in C# 6 and C# 7*

C# 6 and C# 7 aren't as revolutionary as C# 3, but they include many smaller language features that, taken together, provide a much better experience and more idiomatic syntax for coding functionally.

 NOTE Most features introduced in C# 6 and C# 7 offer better syntax, not new functionality. If you're using an older version of C#, you can still apply all of the techniques shown in this book (with a bit of extra typing). However, these newer features significantly improve readability, making programming in a functional style more attractive.

You can see these features in action in the following listing.

Listing 1.4 C# 6 and C# 7 features relevant for FP

```csharp
using static System.Math;

public class Circle
{
    public Circle(double radius)
        => Radius = radius;

    public double Radius { get; }

    public double Circumference
        => PI * 2 * Radius;

    public double Area
    {
        get
        {
            double Square(double d) => Pow(d, 2);
            return PI * Square(Radius);
        }
    }

    public (double Circumference, double Area) Stats
        => (Circumference, Area);
}
```

`using static` enables unqualified access to the static members of `System.Math`, like `PI` and `Pow`.

A getter-only auto-property can be set only in the constructor.

An expression-bodied property

A local function is a method declared within another method.

C# 7 tuple syntax with named elements

IMPORTING STATIC MEMBERS WITH USING STATIC

The using static statement in C# 6 allows you to import the static members of a class (in this example, the System.Math class). As a result, in this example you can invoke the PI and Pow members of Math without further qualification:

```
using static System.Math;

public double Circumference
    => PI * 2 * Radius;
```

Why is this important? In FP, we prefer functions whose behavior relies only on their input arguments because we can reason about and test these functions in isolation (contrast this with instance methods, whose implementation typically interacts with instance variables). These functions are implemented as static methods in C#, so a functional library in C# will consist mainly of static methods.

    using static allows you to more easily consume such libraries, and although overuse can lead to namespace pollution, reasonable use can make for clean, readable code.

EASIER IMMUTABLE TYPES WITH GETTER-ONLY AUTO-PROPERTIES

When you declare a getter-only auto-property, such as Radius, the compiler implicitly declares a readonly backing field. As a result, these properties can only be assigned a value in the constructor or inline:

```
public class Circle
{
    public Circle(double radius)
        => Radius = radius;

    public double Radius { get; }
}
```

Getter-only auto-properties facilitate the definition of immutable types, which you'll see in more detail in chapter 9. The Circle class demonstrates this: it only has one field (the backing field of Radius), which is readonly, so once it's created, a Circle can never change.

MORE CONCISE FUNCTIONS WITH EXPRESSION-BODIED MEMBERS

The Circumference property is declared with an *expression body* introduced with =>, rather than with the usual *statement body* in { }:

```
public double Circumference
    => PI * 2 * Radius;
```

Notice how much more concise this is compared to the Area property!

    In FP, we tend to write lots of simple functions, many of them one-liners, and then compose them into more complex workflows. Expression-bodied methods allow you to do this with minimal syntactic noise. This is particularly evident when you want to write a function that returns a function—something you'll do a lot in this book.

The expression-bodied syntax was introduced in C# 6 for methods and properties, and it was generalized in C# 7 to also apply to constructors, destructors, getters, and setters.

LOCAL FUNCTIONS

Writing lots of simple functions means that many functions are called from one location only. C# 7 allows you to make this explicit by declaring methods within the scope of a method; for instance, the `Square` method is declared within the scope of the `Area` getter:

```
get
{
   double Square(double d) => Pow(d, 2);
   return PI * Square(Radius);
}
```

BETTER SYNTAX FOR TUPLES

Better syntax for tuples is the most important feature of C# 7. It allows you to easily create and consume tuples, and, most importantly, to assign meaningful names to their elements. For example, the `Stats` property returns a tuple of type `(double, double)`, and specifies meaningful names by which its elements can be accessed:

```
public (double Circumference, double Area) Stats
   => (Circumference, Area);
```

Tuples are important in FP because of the tendency to break tasks down into very small functions. You may end up with a data type whose only purpose is to capture the information returned by one function, and that's expected as input by another function. It's impractical to define dedicated types for such structures, which don't correspond to meaningful domain abstractions. That's where tuples come in.

1.2.3 A more functional future for C#?

As I was writing the first draft of this chapter, in early 2016, development of C# 7 was in its early days, and it was interesting to see that *all* the features for which the language team had identified "strong interest" were features normally associated with functional languages. They included the following:

- Record types (boilerplate-free immutable types)
- Algebraic data types (a powerful addition to the type system)
- Pattern matching (similar to a `switch` statement that works on the *shape* of the data, such as its type, rather than just the values)
- Better syntax for tuples

On one hand, it was disappointing that only the last item could be delivered. C# 7 also includes a limited implementation of pattern matching, but it's a far cry from the kind of pattern matching available in functional languages, and it's generally inadequate for the way we'd like to use pattern matching when programming functionally (see section 10.2.4).

On the other hand, these features are still on the table for future versions, and work has been done on the respective proposals. This means we're likely to see record types and a more complete implementation of pattern matching in future versions of C#. So C# is poised to continue in its evolution as a multi-paradigm language with an increasingly strong functional component.

This book will give you a good foundation for keeping up with the evolution of the language and the industry. It'll also give you a good understanding of the concepts and motivations behind future versions of the language.

1.3   *Thinking in functions*

In this section, I'll clarify what I mean by *function*. I'll start with the mathematical use of the word and then move on to the various language constructs that C# offers to represent functions.

1.3.1   *Functions as maps*

In mathematics, a function is a map between two sets, respectively called the *domain* and *codomain*. That is, given an element from its domain, a function yields an element from its codomain. That's all there is—it doesn't matter whether the mapping is based on some formula or is completely arbitrary.

In this sense, a function is a completely abstract mathematical object, and the value that a function yields is determined *exclusively* by its input. You'll see that this isn't always the case with functions in programming.

For example, imagine a function mapping lowercase letters to their uppercase counterparts, as in figure 1.3. In this case, the domain is the set {a, b, c, ...} and the codomain is the set {A, B, C, ...}. (Naturally, there are functions for which the domain and codomain are the same set; can you think of an example?)

How does this relate to programming functions? In statically typed languages like C#, the sets (domain and codomain) are represented with types. For example, if you coded the function above, you could use char to represent both the domain and the codomain. The type of your function could then be written as

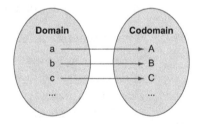

Figure 1.3   A mathematical function is a mapping between the elements of two sets.

```
char → char
```

That is, the function maps chars to chars, or, equivalently, given a char, it yields a char.

The types for the domain and codomain constitute a function's interface, also called its type, or signature. You can think of this as a contract: a function signature declares that, given an element from the domain, it will yield an element from the codomain.[3] This may sound pretty obvious, but you'll see in chapter 3 that in reality, violations of the signature contract abound.

Next, let's look at ways to encode the functions themselves.

1.3.2 Representing functions in C#

There are several language constructs in C# that you can use to represent functions:

- Methods
- Delegates
- Lambda expressions
- Dictionaries

If you're well-versed in these, skip to the next section; otherwise, here's a quick refresher.

METHODS

Methods are the most common and idiomatic representation for functions in C#. For example, the `System.Math` class includes methods representing many common mathematical functions. Methods can represent functions, but they also fit into the object-oriented paradigm—they can be used to implement interfaces, they can be overloaded, and so on.

The constructs that really enable you to program in a functional style are delegates and lambda expressions.

DELEGATES

Delegates are type-safe function pointers. *Type-safe* here means that a delegate is strongly typed: the types of the input and output values of the function are known at compile time, and consistency is enforced by the compiler.

Creating a delegate is a two-step process: you first declare the delegate type and then provide an implementation. (This is analogous to writing an `interface` and then instantiating a `class` implementing that interface.)

The first step is done by using the `delegate` keyword and providing the signature for the delegate. For example, .NET includes the following definition of a `Comparison<T>` delegate.

> **Listing 1.5   Declaring a delegate**

```
namespace System
{
    public delegate int Comparison<in T>(T x, T y);
}
```

As you can see, a `Comparison<T>` delegate can be given two `T`'s and will yield an `int` indicating which is greater.

---

[3] Interfaces in the OO sense are an extension of this idea: a set of functions with their respective input and output types, or, more precisely, *methods*, which are essentially functions, that take `this`, the current instance, as an implicit argument.

Once you have a delegate type, you can instantiate it by providing an implementation, like this.

Listing 1.6   Instantiating and using a delegate

```
var list = Enumerable.Range(1, 10).Select(i => i * 3).ToList();
list // => [3, 6, 9, 12, 15, 18, 21, 24, 27, 30]

Comparison<int> alphabetically = (l, r)            │  Provides an implementation
   => l.ToString().CompareTo(r.ToString());        │  of Comparison

list.Sort(alphabetically);                     ◁──────┐  Uses the Comparison delegate
list // => [12, 15, 18, 21, 24, 27, 3, 30, 6, 9]      │  as an argument to Sort
```

As you can see, a delegate is just an *object* (in the technical sense) that represents an operation—in this case, a comparison. Just like any other object, you can use a delegate as an argument for another method, as in listing 1.6, so delegates are the language feature that makes functions first-class values in C#.

THE FUNC AND ACTION DELEGATES

The .NET framework includes a couple of delegate "families" that can represent pretty much any function type:

- Func<R> represents a function that takes no arguments and returns a result of type R.
- Func<T1, R> represents a function that takes an argument of type T1 and returns a result of type R.
- Func<T1, T2, R> represents a function that takes a T1 and a T2 and returns an R.

And so on. There are delegates to represent functions of various "arities" (see the "Function arity" sidebar).

Since the introduction of Func, it has become rare to use custom delegates. For example, instead of declaring a custom delegate like this,

```
delegate Greeting Greeter(Person p);
```

you can just use the type:

```
Func<Person, Greeting>
```

The type of Greeter in the preceding example is equivalent to, or "compatible with," Func<Person, Greeting>. In both cases it's a function that takes a Person and returns a Greeting.

There's a similar delegate family to represent *actions*—functions that have no return value, such as void methods:

- Action represents an action with no input arguments.
- Action<T1> represents an action with an input argument of type T1.
- Action<T1, T2> and so on represent an action with several input arguments.

The evolution of .NET has been *away* from custom delegates, in favor of the more general Func and Action delegates. For instance, take the representation of a *predicate*:[4]

- In .NET 2, a Predicate<T> delegate was introduced, which is used, for instance, in the FindAll method used to filter a List<T>.
- In .NET 3, the Where method, also used for filtering but defined on the more general IEnumerable<T>, takes not a Predicate<T> but simply a Func<T, bool>.

Both function types are equivalent. Using Func is recommended to avoid a proliferation of delegate types that represent the same function signature, but there's still something to be said in favor of the expressiveness of custom delegates: Predicate<T>, in my view, conveys intent more clearly than Func<T, bool> and is closer to the spoken language.

> **Function arity**
>
> *Arity* is a funny word that refers to the number of arguments that a function accepts:
>
> - A *nullary* function takes no arguments.
> - A *unary* function takes one argument.
> - A *binary* function takes two arguments.
> - A *ternary* function takes three arguments.
>
> And so on. In reality, all functions can be viewed as being unary, because passing *n* arguments is equivalent to passing an *n*-tuple as the only argument. For example, addition (like any other binary arithmetic operation) is a function whose domain is the set of all *pairs* of numbers.

LAMBDA EXPRESSIONS

Lambda expressions, called *lambdas* for short, are used to declare a function inline. For example, sorting a list of numbers alphabetically can be done with a lambda like so.

Listing 1.7 Declaring a function inline with a lambda

```
var list = Enumerable.Range(1, 10).Select(i => i * 3).ToList();
list // => [3, 6, 9, 12, 15, 18, 21, 24, 27, 30]

list.Sort((l, r) => l.ToString().CompareTo(r.ToString()));
list // => [12, 15, 18, 21, 24, 27, 3, 30, 6, 9]
```

If your function is short and you don't need to reuse it elsewhere, lambdas offer the most attractive notation. Also notice that in the preceding example, the compiler not only infers the types of x and y to be int, it also converts the lambda to the delegate type Comparison<int> expected by the Sort method, given that the provided lambda is compatible with this type.

---

[4] A predicate is a function that, given a value (say, an integer), tells you whether it satisfies some condition (say, whether it's even).

Just like methods, delegates and lambdas have access to the variables in the scope in which they're declared. This is particularly useful when leveraging *closures* in lambda expressions.[5] Here's an example.

Listing 1.8   Lambdas have access to variables in the enclosing scope

```
var days = Enum.GetValues(typeof(DayOfWeek)).Cast<DayOfWeek>();
// => [Sunday, Monday, Tuesday, Wednesday, Thursday, Friday, Saturday]

IEnumerable<DayOfWeek> daysStartingWith(string pattern)
   => days.Where(d => d.ToString().StartsWith(pattern));     ◁─────────┐

daysStartingWith("S") // => [Sunday, Saturday]
```

The `pattern` variable is referenced from within the lambda and is therefore captured in a closure.

In this example, `Where` expects a function that takes a `DayOfWeek` and returns a `bool`. In reality, the function expressed by the lambda expression also uses the value of `pattern`, which is captured in a closure, to calculate its result.

This is interesting. If you were to look at the function expressed by the lambda with a more mathematical eye, you might say that it's actually a *binary* function that takes a `DayOfWeek` *and* a `string` (the pattern) as inputs, and yields a `bool`. As programmers, however, we're usually mostly concerned about the function signature, so you might be more likely to look at it as a *unary* function from `DayOfWeek` to `bool`. Both perspectives are valid: the function must conform to its unary signature, but it depends on two values to do its work.

DICTIONARIES

Dictionaries are fittingly also called *maps* (or *hashtables*); they're data structures that provide a very direct representation of a function. They literally contain the association of *keys* (elements from the domain) to *values* (the corresponding elements from the codomain).

We normally think of dictionaries as data, so it's enriching to change perspectives for a moment and consider them as functions. Dictionaries are appropriate for representing functions that are completely arbitrary, where the mappings can't be computed but *must* be stored exhaustively. For example, to map Boolean values to their names in French, you could write the following.

Listing 1.9   A function can be exhaustively represented with a dictionary

```
var frenchFor = new Dictionary<bool, string>
{
    [true] = "Vrai",
    [false] = "Faux",
```

C# 6 dictionary initializer syntax

---

[5] A *closure* is the combination of the lambda expression itself along with the context in which that lambda is declared (that is, all the variables available in the scope where the lambda appears).

```
};

frenchFor[true]
// => "Vrai"
```

> Function application is
> performed with a lookup.

The fact that functions can be represented with dictionaries also makes it possible to optimize computationally expensive functions by storing their computed results in a dictionary instead of recomputing them every time.

For convenience, in the rest of the book, I'll use the term *function* to indicate one of the C# representations of a function, so keep in mind that this doesn't quite match the mathematical definition of the term. You'll learn more about the differences between mathematical and programming functions in chapter 2.

1.4 Higher-order functions

Now that you've got an understanding of what FP is and we've reviewed the functional features of the language, it's time to start exploring some concrete functional techniques. We'll begin with the most important benefit of functions as first-class values: it gives you the ability to define higher-order functions (HOFs).

HOFs are functions that take other functions as inputs or return a function as output, or both. I'll assume that you've already used HOFs to some extent, such as with LINQ. We'll use HOFs *a lot* in this book, so this section should act as a refresher and will possibly introduce some use cases for HOFs that you may be less familiar with. HOFs are fun, and most of the examples in this section can be run in the REPL. Make sure you try a few variations of your own along the way.

1.4.1 Functions that depend on other functions

Some HOFs take other functions as arguments and invoke them in order to do their work, somewhat like a company may subcontract some of its work to another company. You've seen some examples of such HOFs earlier in this chapter: `Sort` (an instance method on `List`) and `Where` (an extension method on `IEnumerable`).

`List.Sort`, when called with a `Comparison` delegate, is a method that says: "OK, I'll sort myself, as long as you tell me how to compare any two elements that I contain." `Sort` does the job of sorting, but the caller can decide what logic to use for comparing.

Similarly, `Where` does the job of filtering, and the caller decides what logic determines whether an element should be included. You can represent the type of `Where` graphically, as shown in figure 1.4.

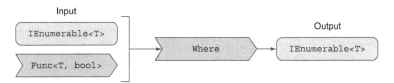

Figure 1.4 `Where` takes a predicate function as input.

Let's look at an idealized implementation of Where.[6]

Listing 1.10 Where: a typical HOF that iteratively applies the given predicate

The task of iterating over the list is an implementation detail of Where.

```csharp
public static IEnumerable<T> Where<T>
    (this IEnumerable<T> ts, Func<T, bool> predicate)
{
    foreach (T t in ts)
        if (predicate(t))
            yield return t;
}
```

The criterion determining which items are included is decided by the caller.

The Where method is responsible for the sorting logic, and the caller provides the *predicate*, which is the criterion based on which the IEnumerable should be filtered.

As you can see, HOFs can help with the separation of concerns in cases where logic can't otherwise be easily separated. Where and Sort are examples of *iterated applications*—the HOF will apply the given function repeatedly for every element in the collection.

One very crude way of looking at this is that you're passing as the argument a function whose code will ultimately be executed inside the body of a loop within the HOF—something you couldn't do by only passing static data. The general scheme is shown in figure 1.5.

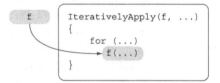

Figure 1.5 A HOF that iteratively applies the function given as an argument

Optional execution is another good candidate for HOFs. This is useful when you want to invoke a given function only in certain conditions, as illustrated in figure 1.6.

For example, imagine a method that looks up an element from the cache. A delegate can be provided and can be invoked in case of a cache miss.

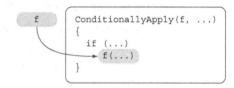

Figure 1.6 A HOF that conditionally applies the function given as an argument

---

Listing 1.11 A HOF that optionally invokes the given function

```csharp
class Cache<T> where T : class
{
    public T Get(Guid id) => //...

    public T Get(Guid id, Func<T> onMiss)
        => Get(id) ?? onMiss();
}
```

---

[6] This implementation is functionally correct, but it lacks the error checking and optimizations in the LINQ implementation.

The logic in `onMiss` could involve an expensive operation such as a database call, so you wouldn't want this to be executed unnecessarily.

The preceding examples illustrate HOFs that take a function as input (often referred to as a *callback* or a *continuation*) and use it to perform a task or to compute a value.[7] This is perhaps the most common pattern for HOFs, and it's sometimes referred to as inversion of control: the caller of the HOF decides what to do by supplying a function, and the callee decides when to do it by invoking the given function.

Let's look at some other scenarios in which HOFs come in handy.

1.4.2 Adapter functions

Some HOFs don't *apply* the given function at all, but rather return a new function, somehow related to the function given as an argument. For example, say you have a function that performs integer division:

```
Func<int, int, int> divide = (x, y) => x / y;
divide(10, 2) // => 5
```

You want to change the order of the arguments so that the divisor comes first. This could be seen as a particular case of a more general problem: changing the order of the arguments.

You can write a generic HOF that modifies any binary function by swapping the order of its arguments:

```
static Func<T2, T1, R> SwapArgs<T1, T2, R>(this Func<T1, T2, R> f)
   => (t2, t1) => f(t1, t2);
```

Technically, it would be more correct to say that `SwapArgs` returns a *new* function that invokes the given function with the arguments in the reverse order. But on an intuitive level, I find it easier to think that I'm getting back a modified version of the original function.

You can now modify the original division function by applying `SwapArgs`:

```
var divideBy = divide.SwapArgs();
divideBy(2, 10) // => 5
```

Playing with this sort of HOF leads to the interesting idea that functions aren't set in stone: if you don't like the interface of a function, you can call it via another function that provides an interface that better suits your needs. That's why I call these *adapter functions*.[8]

---

[7] This is perhaps the most common pattern for HOFs, and it's sometimes referred to as *inversion of control*: the caller of the HOF decides *what* to do by supplying a function, and the function decides *when* to do it by invoking the given function.

[8] The well-known adapter pattern in OOP can be seen as applying the idea of adapter functions to an object's interface.

1.4.3 Functions that create other functions

Sometimes you'll write functions whose primary purpose is to create other functions—you can think of them as *function factories*. The following example uses a lambda to filter a sequence of numbers, keeping only those divisible by 2:

```
var range = Enumerable.Range(1, 20);

range.Where(i => i % 2 == 0)
// => [2, 4, 6, 8, 10, 12, 14, 16, 18, 20]
```

What if you wanted something more general, like being able to filter for numbers divisible by any number, *n*? You could define a function that takes *n* and yields a suitable predicate that will evaluate whether any given number is divisible by *n*:

```
Func<int, bool> isMod(int n) => i => i % n == 0;
```

We haven't looked at a HOF like this before: it takes some static data and returns a function. Let's see how you can use it:

```
using static System.Linq.Enumerable;

Range(1, 20).Where(isMod(2)) // => [2, 4, 6, 8, 10, 12, 14, 16, 18, 20]
Range(1, 20).Where(isMod(3)) // => [3, 6, 9, 12, 15, 18]
```

Notice how you've gained not only in generality, but also in readability! In this example, you're using the isMod HOF to produce a function, and then you're feeding it as input to another HOF, Where, as shown in figure 1.7.

You'll see many more uses of HOFs in the book. Eventually you'll look at them as regular functions, forgetting that they're higher order. Let's now look at how they can be used in a scenario closer to everyday development.

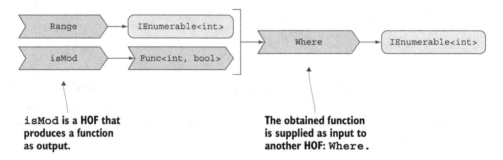

isMod is a **HOF** that produces a function as output.

The obtained function is supplied as input to another HOF: Where.

Figure 1.7   A HOF that produces a function that's given as input to another HOF

1.5 *Using HOFs to avoid duplication*

Another common use case for HOFs is to encapsulate setup and teardown operations. For example, interacting with a database requires some setup to acquire and open a connection, and some cleaning up after the interaction to close the connection and return it to the underlying connection pool. In code, it looks like the following.

Listing 1.12   Connecting to a DB requires some setup and teardown

```
string connString = "myDatabase";

var conn = new SqlConnection(connString));      Setup: acquire and
conn.Open();                                    open a connection.

// interact with the database...

conn.Close();                                   Teardown: close and
conn.Dispose();                                 release the connection.
```

The setup and teardown are always identical, regardless of whether you're reading or writing to the database, or performing one or many actions. The preceding code is usually written with a `using` block, like this:

```
using (var conn = new SqlConnection(connString))
{
    conn.Open();
    // interact with the database...
}
```

This is both shorter and better,[9] but it's still essentially the same. Consider the following example of a simple `DbLogger` class with a couple of methods that interact with the database: `Log` inserts a given log message, and `GetLogs` retrieves all logs since a given date.

Listing 1.13   Duplication of setup/teardown logic

```
using Dapper;                     Exposes Execute and Query as
// ...                            extension methods on the connection

public class DbLogger
{
    string connString;            Assume this is set
                                  in the constructor.
    public void Log(LogMessage msg)
    {
        using (var conn = new SqlConnection(connString))    Setup
```

---

[9] It's shorter because `Dispose` will be called as you exit the `using` block, and it will in turn call `Close`; it's better because the interaction will be wrapped in a `try/finally`, so that the connection will be disposed even if an exception is thrown in the body of the `using` block.

Teardown is performed as part of Dispose.

Persists the LogMessage to the DB

```
        {
            int affectedRows = conn.Execute("sp_create_log"
                , msg, commandType: CommandType.StoredProcedure);
        }
    }

    public IEnumerable<LogMessage> GetLogs(DateTime since)
    {
        var sqlGetLogs = "SELECT * FROM [Logs] WHERE [Timestamp] > @since";
        using (var conn = new SqlConnection(connString))        <— Setup
        {
            return conn.Query<LogMessage>(sqlGetLogs
                , new {since = since});
        }                              <— Teardown
    }
}
```

Queries the DB and deserializes the results

Notice that the two methods have some duplication, namely the setup and teardown logic. Can we get rid of the duplication?

The specifics of the interaction with the database are irrelevant for this discussion, but if you're interested, the code uses the Dapper library (documented on GitHub: https://github.com/StackExchange/dapper-dot-net), which is a thin layer on top of ADO.NET allowing you to interact with the database through a very simple API:

- Query queries the database and returns the deserialized LogMessages.
- Execute runs the stored procedure and returns the number of affected rows (which we're disregarding).

Both methods are defined as extension methods on the connection. More importantly, notice how in both cases, the database interaction depends on the acquired connection and returns some data. This will allow you to represent the database interaction as a function from IDbConnection to "something."

 ASYNCHRONOUS I/O OPERATIONS   In a real-world scenario, I'd recommend you always perform I/O operations asynchronously (so, in this example, GetLogs should really call QueryAsync and return a Task<IEnumerable<LogMessage>>). But asynchrony adds a level of complexity that's not helpful while you're trying to learn the already challenging ideas of FP. For pedagogical purposes, I'll wait until chapter 13 to discuss asynchrony.

As you can see, Dapper exposes a pleasant API, and it will even open the connection if necessary. But you're still required to create the connection, and you should dispose it as soon as possible, once you're done with it. As a result, the meat of your database calls ends up sandwiched between identical pieces of code that perform setup and teardown. Let's look at how you can avoid this duplication by extracting the setup and teardown logic into a HOF.

1.5.1 Encapsulating setup and teardown into a HOF

You're looking to write a function that performs setup and teardown and that's parameterized on what to do in between. This is a perfect scenario for a HOF, because you can represent the logic in between with a function.[10] Graphically, it looks like figure 1.8.

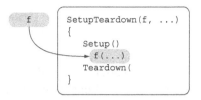

Because connection setup and teardown are much more general than DbLogger, they can be extracted to a new ConnectionHelper class.

Figure 1.8   A HOF that wraps a given function between setup and teardown logic

---

Listing 1.14   Encapsulating setup and teardown of the database connection into a HOF

```
using System;
using System.Data;
using System.Data.SqlClient;

public static class ConnectionHelper
{
    public static R Connect<R>(string connString
      , Func<IDbConnection, R> f)
    {
        using (var conn = new SqlConnection(connString))
        {
            conn.Open();
            return f(conn);
        }
    }
}
```

Setup — `using (var conn = new SqlConnection(connString))` `{`

Teardown ⟶ `}`

What happens in between is now parameterized.

The Connect function performs the setup and teardown, and it's parameterized by what it should do in between. The signature of the body is interesting; it takes an IDb-Connection (through which it will interact with the database), and returns a generic object R. In the use cases we've seen, R will be IEnumerable<LogMessage> in the case of the query and int in the case of the insert. You can now use the Connect function in DbLogger as follows:

```
using Dapper;
using static ConnectionHelper;

public class DbLogger
{
    string connString;

    public void Log(LogMessage message)
        => Connect(connString, c => c.Execute("sp_create_log"
            , message, commandType: CommandType.StoredProcedure));
```

---

[10] For this reason, you may hear this pattern inelegantly called "hole in the middle."

```
public IEnumerable<LogMessage> GetLogs(DateTime since)
   => Connect(connString, c => c.Query<LogMessage>(@"SELECT *
      FROM [Logs] WHERE [Timestamp] > @since", new {since = since}));
}
```

You got rid of the duplication in DbLogger, and DbLogger no longer needs to know the details about creating, opening, or disposing of the connection.

1.5.2 *Turning the using statement into a HOF*

The previous result is satisfactory. But to take the idea of HOFs a bit further, let's be a bit more radical. Isn't the using statement itself an example of setup/teardown? After all, a using block always does the following:

- *Setup*—Acquires an IDisposable resource by evaluating a given declaration or expression
- *Body*—Executes what's inside the block
- *Teardown*—Exits the block, causing Dispose to be called on the object acquired in the setup

So…Yes, it is! At least sort of. The setup isn't always the same, so it too needs to be parameterized. We can then write a more generic setup/teardown HOF that performs the using ceremony.

This is the kind of widely reusable function that belongs in a library. Throughout the book, I'll show you many such reusable constructs that have gone into my LaYumba.Functional library, enabling a better experience when coding functionally.

Listing 1.15   A HOF that can be used instead of the using statement

```
using System;

namespace LaYumba.Functional
{
   public static class F
   {
     public static R Using<TDisp, R>(TDisp disposable
        , Func<TDisp, R> f) where TDisp : IDisposable
     {
        using (disposable) return f(disposable);
     }
   }
}
```

The preceding listing defines a class called F that will contain the core functions of our functional library. The idea is that these functions should be made available without qualification with using static, as shown in the next code sample.

This Using function takes two arguments: the first is the disposable resource, and the second is the function to be executed before the resource is disposed. With this in place, you can rewrite the Connect function more concisely:

```
using static LaYumba.Functional.F;

public static class ConnectionHelper
{
   public static R Connect<R>(string connStr, Func<IDbConnection, R> f)
      => Using(new SqlConnection(connStr)
         , conn => { conn.Open(); return f(conn); });
}
```

The using static on the first line enables you to invoke the Using function as a sort of global replacement for the using statement. Notice that unlike the using *statement,* calling the Using function is an *expression.*[11] This has a couple of benefits:

- It allows you to use the more compact expression-bodied method syntax.
- An expression has a value, so the Using function can be composed with other functions.

We'll dig deeper into the ideas of composition and statements vs. expressions in section 5.5.1.

1.5.3 Tradeoffs of HOFs

Let's look at what you've achieved by comparing the initial and the refactored versions of one of the methods in DbLogger:

```
// initial implementation
public void Log(LogMessage msg)
{
   using (var conn = new SqlConnection(connString))
   {
      int affectedRows = conn.Execute("sp_create_log"
         , msg, commandType: CommandType.StoredProcedure);
   }
}

// refactored implementation
public void Log(LogMessage message)
   => Connect(connString, c => c.Execute("sp_create_log"
      , message, commandType: CommandType.StoredProcedure));
```

This is a good illustration of the benefits you can get from using HOFs that take a function as an argument:

- *Conciseness*—The new version is obviously more concise. Generally speaking, the more intricate the setup/teardown and the more widely it's required, the more benefit you get by abstracting it into a HOF.

---

[11] Here's a quick refresher on the difference: *expressions* return a value; *statements* don't.

- *Avoid duplication*—The whole setup/teardown logic is now performed in a single place.
- *Separation of concerns*—You've managed to isolate connection management into the ConnectionHelper class, so DbLogger need only concern itself with logging-specific logic.

Let's look at how the call stack has changed. Whereas in the original implementation the call to Execute happened on the stack frame of Log, in the new implementation they're four stack frames apart (see figure 1.9).

When Log executes, the code calls Connect, passing it the callback function to invoke when the connection is ready. Connect in turn repackages the callback into a new callback, and passes it to Using.

So, HOFs also have some drawbacks:

- You've increased stack use. There's a performance impact, but it's negligible.
- Debugging the application will be a bit more complex because of the callbacks.

Overall, the improvements made to DbLogger make it a worthy tradeoff.

You probably agree by now that HOFs are very powerful tools, although overuse can make it difficult to understand what the code is doing. Use HOFs when appropriate, but be mindful of readability: use short lambdas, clear naming, and meaningful indentation.

```
class DbLogger
{
    public void Log(LogMessage message)
        => Connect(connString, c => c.Execute("sp_create_log",
            , message, commandType: CommandType.StoredProcedure));
}

public static class ConnectionHelper
{
    public static R Connect<R>(string connStr, Func<IDbConnection, R> f)
        => Using(new SqlConnection(connStr)
            , conn => { conn.Open(); return f(conn); });
}

public static class F
{
    public static R Using<TDisp, R>(TDisp disposable
        , Func<TDisp, R> f) where TDisp : IDisposable
    {
        using (var disp = disposable) return f(disp);
    }
}
```

Figure 1.9   HOFs call back into the calling function.

1.6 Benefits of functional programming

The previous section demonstrated how you can use HOFs to avoid duplication and achieve better separation of concerns. Indeed, one of the advantages of FP is its *conciseness*: you can achieve the same results with fewer lines of code. Multiply that by the tens of thousands of lines of code in a typical application, and conciseness also has a positive effect on the maintainability of the application.

There are many more benefits to be reaped by applying the functional techniques you'll learn in this book, and they roughly fall into three categories:

- *Cleaner code*—Apart from the previously mentioned conciseness, FP leads to more expressive, more readable, and more easily testable code. Clean code is not just a developer's intellectual pleasure, but it also leads to huge economic benefits for the business through reduced maintenance costs.
- *Better support for concurrency*—Several factors, from multi-core CPUs to distributed systems, bring a high degree of concurrency to your applications. Concurrency is traditionally associated with difficult problems such as deadlocks, lost updates, and more; FP offers techniques that prevent these problems from occurring. You'll see an introductory example in chapter 2 and more advanced examples toward the end of the book.
- *A multi-paradigm approach*—They say that if the only tool you have is a hammer, every problem will look like a nail. Conversely, the more angles from which you can view a given problem, the more likely it is that you'll find an optimal solution. If you're already proficient in OOP, learning a different paradigm such as FP will inevitably give you a richer perspective. When faced with a problem, you'll be able to consider several approaches and pick the most effective.

Exercises

I recommend you take the time to do the the exercises and come up with a few of your own along the way. The code samples repository on GitHub (https://github.com/la-yumba/functional-csharp-code) includes placeholders so that you can write, compile, and run your code with minimal setup effort. It also includes solutions that you can check your results against:

1 Browse the methods of `System.Linq.Enumerable` (https://docs.microsoft.com/en-us/dotnet/api/system.linq.enumerable). Which are HOFs? Which do you think imply iterated application of the given function?
2 Write a function that negates a given predicate: whenever the given predicate evaluates to `true`, the resulting function evaluates to `false`, and vice versa.
3 Write a method that uses quicksort to sort a `List<int>` (return a new list, rather than sorting it in place).
4 Generalize the previous implementation to take a `List<T>`, and additionally a `Comparison<T>` delegate.

5   In this chapter, you've seen a `Using` function that takes an `IDisposable` and a
    function of type `Func<TDisp, R>`. Write an overload of `Using` that takes a
    `Func<IDisposable>` as the first parameter, instead of the `IDisposable`. (This
    can be used to avoid warnings raised by some code analysis tools about instanti-
    ating an `IDisposable` and not disposing it.)

Summary

- FP is a powerful paradigm that can help you make your code more concise,
  maintainable, expressive, robust, testable, and concurrency-friendly.
- FP differs from OOP by focusing on functions, rather than objects, and on data
  transformations rather than state mutation.
- FP can be seen as a collection of techniques that are based on two fundamental
  tenets:
    - Functions are first-class values
    - In-place updates should be avoided
- Functions in C# can be represented with methods, delegates, and lambdas.
- FP leverages higher-order functions (functions that take other functions as
  input or output); hence the necessity for the language to have functions as first-
  class values.

Why function
purity matters

2

This chapter covers
- What makes a function pure or impure
- Why purity matters in concurrent scenarios
- How purity relates to testability
- Reducing the impure footprint of your code

The initial name for this chapter was "The irresistible appeal of purity." But if it was so irresistible, we'd have more functional programmers, right? Functional programmers, you see, are suckers for pure functions—functions with no side effects. As you'll see in this chapter, pure functions have some very desirable properties.

Unfortunately, the fascination with pure functions and what you can do with them is partly why FP as a discipline has become disconnected from the industry. As you'll soon realize, there's very little purity in most real-world applications. And yet, purity is still relevant in the real world, as I hope to show in this chapter.

We'll start by looking at what makes a function pure (or impure), and then you'll see how purity affects a program's testability and even correctness, especially in concurrent scenarios. I hope that by the end of the chapter you'll find purity, if not "irresistible," at least "definitely worth keeping in mind."

31

2.1   *What is function purity?*

In chapter 1 you saw that mathematical functions are completely abstract entities. Although some programming functions are close representations of mathematical functions, this is often not the case. You often want a function to write something to the screen, to process a file, or to interact with another system. In short, you often want a function to *do* something—to have a *side effect*. Mathematical functions do nothing of the sort; they only return a value.

There's a second important difference: mathematical functions exist in a vacuum, so that their results are determined strictly by their arguments. The programming constructs we use to represent functions, on the other hand, all have access to a "context": an instance method has access to instance fields, a lambda has access to variables closed over, and many functions access things that are completely outside the scope of the program, such as the system clock, a database, or a remote service.

That this context exists, that its limits aren't necessarily clearly demarcated, and that it may consist of things that change outside of the program's control mean that the behavior of functions in programming is substantially more complex to analyze than functions in mathematics. This has led to a distinction between *pure* and *impure* functions.

2.1.1   *Purity and side effects*

Pure functions closely resemble mathematical functions: they do nothing other than compute an output value based on their input values. Table 2.1 contrasts pure and impure functions.

Table 2.1   Requirements of pure functions

Pure functions	Impure functions
The output depends entirely on the input arguments.	Factors other than input arguments may affect the output.
Cause no side effects.	May cause side effects.

To clarify this definition, we must define exactly what a side effect is. A function is said to have side effects if it does any of the following:

- *Mutates global state*—"Global" here means any state that's visible outside of the function's scope. For example, a private instance field is considered global because it's visible from all methods within the class.
- *Mutates its input arguments*
- *Throws exceptions*[1]
- *Performs any I/O operation*—This includes any interaction between the program and the external world, including reading from or writing to the console, the filesystem, or a database, and interacting with any process outside the application's boundary.

---

[1] Some will argue that a function can be considered pure despite throwing exceptions. However, in throwing exceptions it will cause indeterminism to appear in code that makes some decisions based on exception-handling, or in the absence of exception handling, in the side effect of the program crashing.

In summary, pure functions have no side effects, and their output is solely determined by their inputs.

The deterministic nature of pure functions (that is, the fact that they always return the same output for the same input) has some interesting consequences. Pure functions are easy to test and to reason about.[2] Furthermore, the fact that outputs only depend on inputs means that the order of evaluation isn't important. Whether you evaluate the result of a function now or later, the result will not change. This means that the parts of your program that consist entirely of pure functions can be optimized in a number of ways:

- *Parallelization*—Different threads carry out tasks in parallel
- *Lazy evaluation*—Only evaluate values as needed
- *Memoization*—Cache the result of a function so it's only computed once

On the other hand, using these techniques with impure functions can lead to rather nasty bugs. For these reasons, FP advocates that pure functions should be preferred whenever possible.

2.1.2 Strategies for managing side effects

Ok, let's aim to use pure functions whenever possible. But is it always possible? Is it ever possible? Well, if you look at the list of things considered side effects, it's a pretty mixed bag, so the strategies for managing side effects depend on the types of side effects in question.

ISOLATE I/O EFFECTS

Let's start with I/O, which is always considered a side effect. First, here are a few examples that will clarify why functions that perform I/O can never be pure:

- A function that takes a URL and returns the resource at that URL will yield a different result any time the remote resource changes, or it may throw an error if the connection is unavailable.
- A function that takes a file path and contents to be written to a file may throw an error if the directory doesn't exist, or if the process hosting the program lacks write permissions.
- A function that returns the current time from the system clock will return a different result at any instant.

As you can see, any dependency on the external world gets in the way of function purity because the state of the world affects the function's return value. On the other hand, if your program is to do anything of use, there's no escaping the fact that some I/O is required. Even a purely mathematical program that just performs a computation must perform some I/O to communicate its result. So some of your code will have to be impure.

---

[2] More theoretically inclined authors show how you can reason about pure functions algebraically to prove the correctness of your program; see, for example, *Programming in Haskell*, second edition, by Graham Hutton (Cambridge University Press, 2016).

What you can do is *isolate* the pure, computational parts of your programs from the I/O. In this way, you minimize the footprint of I/O and reap the benefits of purity for the pure part of the program. Consider the following code:

```
WriteLine("Enter your name:");
var name = ReadLine();
WriteLine($"Hello {name}");
```

This trivial program (assume it's wrapped in a Main method) mixes I/O with logic that could be extracted in a pure function:

```
static string GreetingFor(string name) => $"Hello {name}";
```

There are some real-world programs in which separating logic from I/O is relatively simple. For example, take a document-format converter like Pandoc, which can be used to convert a file from, say, Markdown to PDF. When you execute Pandoc, it will perform the steps shown in figure 2.1.

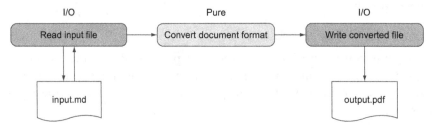

Figure 2.1   A program where I/O can easily be isolated

The computational part of the program, which performs the format conversion, can be made entirely of pure functions. The impure functions that perform I/O can call the pure functions that perform the translation, but the functions that perform the translation can't call any function that performs I/O, or they would also become impure.

LOB applications have a much more complex structure in terms of I/O, so isolating the purely computational parts of the program from I/O is quite a challenge. I'll show you some possible approaches in this chapter and throughout the book.

AVOID MUTATING ARGUMENTS

Another kind of side effect is the mutation of function arguments. Mutating function arguments is a bad idea in *any* programming paradigm, but I've repeatedly stumbled on implementations that do something like this:

```
decimal RecomputeTotal(Order order, List<OrderLine> linesToDelete)
{
    var result = 0m;
    foreach (var line in order.OrderLines)
        if (line.Quantity == 0) linesToDelete.Add(line);
        else result += line.Product.Price * line.Quantity;
    return result;
}
```

This function is meant to be called when the quantity of items in an order is modified. It recomputes the total value of the order and, *as a side effect*, adds to the `linesTo-Delete` list the order lines whose quantity has been changed to zero.

The reason why this is such a terrible idea is that the behavior of the method is now tightly coupled with that of the caller: the caller relies on the method to perform its side effect, and the callee relies on the caller to initialize the list. As such, both methods must be aware of the implementation details of the other, making it impossible to reason about the methods in isolation.[3]

This kind of side effect can easily be avoided by returning all the computed information to the caller instead. For example, the preceding code can be refactored as follows:

```
(decimal, IEnumerable<OrderLine>) RecomputeTotal(Order order)
  => (order.OrderLines.Sum(l => l.Product.Price * l.Quantity)
    , order.OrderLines.Where(l => l.Quantity == 0));
```

Following this principle, you can *always* structure your code in such a way that functions never mutate their input arguments. In fact, it would be ideal to enforce this by always using immutable objects—objects that, once created, cannot be changed. We'll discuss this in detail in chapter 10.

What about the remaining two kinds of side effects: mutating non-local state and throwing exceptions? It turns out that it's always possible to handle errors without relying on exceptions, and it's often possible to avoid state mutation. Indeed, big chunks of this book are devoted to functional error handling and avoiding state mutation to allow you to achieve this.

By learning these techniques, you'll be able to isolate or avoid side effects, and to harness the benefits of pure functions.

2.2 *Purity and concurrency*

That's quite enough theory for now; let's look at some code that demonstrates pure and impure functions in action. Imagine you want to format a list of strings as a numbered list; the casing should be standardized, and each item should be preceded with a counter. To do this, you'll create a `ListFormatter` class that can be used as follows:

```
var shoppingList = new List<string> { "coffee beans", "BANANAS", "Dates" };

new ListFormatter()
    .Format(shoppingList)
    .ForEach(WriteLine);

// prints: 1. Coffee beans
//         2. Bananas
//         3. Dates
```

---

[3] Furthermore, if you were to change the type of the mutated argument from a `class` to a `struct`, you'd get a radically different behavior, because structs are passed by value.

One possible implementation of the `ListFormatter` is shown in the following listing.

Listing 2.1   A list formatter combining pure and impure functions

```
static class StringExt
{                                                          A pure
    public static string ToSentenceCase(this string s)  ◄─┘ function
        => s.ToUpper()[0] + s.ToLower().Substring(1);
}

class ListFormatter
{
    int counter;                                          An impure function
                                                          (it mutates global
    string PrependCounter(string s) => $"{++counter}. {s}";  ◄─┘ state)

    public List<string> Format(List<string> list)
        => list
            .Select(StringExt.ToSentenceCase)    Pure and impure functions
            .Select(PrependCounter)              can be applied similarly.
            .ToList();
}
```

There are a few things to point out with respect to purity:

- `ToSentenceCase` is pure (its output is strictly determined by the input). Because its computation only depends on the input parameter, it can be made static without any problems.[4]
- `PrependCounter` increments the counter, so it's impure. Because it depends on an instance member—the counter—you can't make it static.
- In the `Format` method, you apply both functions to items in the list with `Select`, irrespective of purity. This isn't ideal, as you'll soon learn. In fact, there would ideally be a rule that `Select` should only be used with pure functions.

If the list you're formatting was big enough, would it make sense to perform the string manipulations in parallel? Could the runtime decide to do this as an optimization? We'll tackle these questions next.

2.2.1   *Pure functions parallelize well*

Given a big enough set of data to process, it's usually advantageous to process it in parallel, especially when the processing is CPU-intensive and the pieces of data can be processed independently.

The problem is that pure and impure functions don't parallelize equally well. I'll illustrate this by trying to parallelize our list formatting functions with `ListFormatter`.

---

[4] In many languages, you'd have functions like this as freestanding functions, but methods in C# need to be inside a class, and it's mostly a matter of taste where you put your static functions.

Pure functions parallelize well and are generally immune to the issues that make concurrency difficult. (For a refresher on concurrency and parallelism, see the sidebar on the meaning and types of concurrency.)

Compare these two expressions:

```
list.Select(ToSentenceCase).ToList()
list.AsParallel().Select(ToSentenceCase).ToList()
```

The first expression uses the `Select` method defined on `Enumerable` to apply the pure function `ToSentenceCase` to each element in the list. The second expression is very similar, but it uses methods provided by Parallel LINQ (PLINQ).[5] `AsParallel` turns the list into a `ParallelQuery`. As a result, `Select` resolves to the implementation defined on `ParallelEnumerable`, which will apply `ToSentenceCase` to each item in the list, but now *in parallel.* The list will be split into chunks, and several threads will be fired off to process each chunk. In both cases, `ToList` harvests the results into a list.

As you would expect, the two expressions yield the same results, but one does so sequentially and the other in parallel. This is nice; with just one call to `AsParallel`, you get parallelization *almost* for free.

Why "almost" for free? Why do you have to explicitly instruct the runtime to parallelize the operation? Why can't it just figure out that it's a good idea to parallelize the operation, just like it figures out when it's a good time to run the garbage collector?

The answer is that the runtime doesn't know enough about the function to make an informed decision of whether parallelization might change the program flow. Because of their properties, pure functions can always be applied in parallel, but the runtime doesn't know about the purity of the function being applied.

Meaning and types of concurrency

Concurrency is the general concept of having several things going on at the same time. More formally, concurrency is when a program initiates a task before another one has completed, so that different tasks are executed in overlapping time windows.

There are several scenarios in which concurrency can occur:

- *Asynchrony*—This means that your program performs *non-blocking* operations. For example, it can initiate a request for a remote resource via HTTP and then go on to do some other task while it waits for the response to be received. It's a bit like when you send an email and then go on with your life without waiting for a response.
- *Parallelism*—This means that your program leverages the *hardware* of multi-core machines to execute tasks at the same time by breaking up work into tasks, each of which is executed on a separate core. It's a bit like singing in the shower: you're actually doing two things at exactly the same time.

---

[5] PLINQ is an implementation of LINQ to Objects that works in parallel.

> *(continued)*
> - *Multithreading*—This is a *software* implementation allowing different threads to be executed concurrently. A multithreaded program appears to be doing several things at the same time even when it's running on a single-core machine. This is a bit like chatting with different people through various IM windows; although you're actually switching back and forth, the net result is that you're having multiple conversations at the same time.
>
> Doing several things at the same time can really boost performance. It also means that the order of execution isn't guaranteed, so concurrency can be the source of difficult problems, most notably when multiple tasks concurrently try to update some shared mutable state. (In later chapters, you'll see how FP addresses this by avoiding shared mutable state altogether.)

2.2.2 *Parallelizing impure functions*

Let's see what happens if we naively apply parallelization with the impure `Prepend-Counter` function:

```
list.Select(PrependCounter).ToList()
list.AsParallel().Select(PrependCounter).ToList()
```

Because `PrependCounter` increments the `counter` variable, the parallel version will have multiple threads reading and updating the counter. As is well known, ++ is not an atomic operation, and because there's no locking in place, we'll lose some of the updates and end up with an incorrect result.

   If you test this approach with a large enough input list, you'll get a result like this:

```
Expected string length 20 but was 19. Strings differ at index 0.
Expected: "1000000. Item1000000"
But was:  "956883. Item1000000"
----------^
```

This will look pretty familiar if you have some multithreading experience. Because multiple processes are reading and writing to the counter at the same time, some of the updates are lost. You probably know that this could be fixed by using a lock or the `Interlocked` class when incrementing the counter. But locking is an imperative construct that we'd rather avoid when coding functionally.

   Let's summarize. Unlike pure functions, whose application can be parallelized by default, impure functions don't parallelize out of the box. And because parallel execution is nondeterministic, you may get some cases in which your result is correct and others in which it isn't (this is not the sort of bug I like to face).

   Being aware of whether your functions are pure or not may help you understand those issues. Furthermore, if you develop with purity in mind, it will be easier to parallelize the execution if you decide to do so.

2.2.3   Avoiding state mutation

One possible way to avoid the pitfalls of concurrent updates is to remove the problem at the source: don't use shared state to begin with. How this can be done will vary with each scenario, but I'll show you a solution for the current scenario that will enable us to format the list in parallel.

Let's go back to the drawing board and see if there's a sequential solution that doesn't involve mutation. What if instead of updating a running counter, you generate a list of all the counter values you need, and then pair items from the given list with items from the list of counters?

For the list of integers, you can use `Range`, a convenience method on `Enumerable`.

Listing 2.2   Generating a range of integers

```
Enumerable.Range(1, 3)
// => [1, 2, 3]
```

The operation of pairing two parallel lists is a common operation in FP, and it's called *Zip*. Here's an example.

Listing 2.3   Combining elements from parallel lists with Zip

```
Enumerable.Zip(
   new[] {1, 2, 3},
   new[] {"ichi", "ni", "san"},
   (number, name) => $"In Japanese, {number} is: {name}")

// => ["In Japanese, 1 is: ichi",
//     "In Japanese, 2 is: ni",
//     "In Japanese, 3 is: san"]
```

Using `Range` and `Zip`, you can rewrite the list formatter as follows.

Listing 2.4   List formatter refactored to use pure functions only

```
using static System.Linq.Enumerable;

static class ListFormatter
{
   public static List<string> Format(List<string> list)
   {
      var left = list.Select(StringExt.ToSentenceCase);
      var right = Range(1, list.Count);
      var zipped = Zip(left, right, (s, i) => $"{i}. {s}");
      return zipped.ToList();
   }
}
```

Here you use the list, with `ToSentenceCase` applied to it, as the left side of `Zip`. The right side is constructed with `Range`. The third argument to `Zip` is the pairing function: what to do with each pair of items.

`Zip` can be used as an extension method, so you can write the `Format` method using a more fluent syntax:

```
public static List<string> Format(List<string> list)
    => list
        .Select(StringExt.ToSentenceCase)
        .Zip(Range(1, list.Count), (s, i) => $"{i}. {s}")
        .ToList();
```

After this refactoring, `Format` is pure and can safely be made static. But what about making it parallel? That's a piece of cake, because PLINQ offers an implementation of `Zip` that works with parallel queries. A parallel implementation of the list formatter would then look like this.

Listing 2.5 A pure implementation that executes in parallel

```
                using static System.Linq.ParallelEnumerable;   ◁─┐ Uses Range, exposed by
                                                                  │ Parallel-Enumerable
Turns the      │ static class ListFormatter
original data  │ {
source into a  │     public static List<string> Format(List<string> list)
parallel query └──▷      => list.AsParallel()
                             .Select(StringExt.ToSentenceCase)
                             .Zip(Range(1, list.Count), (s, i) => $"{i}. {s}")
                             .ToList();
                 }
```

This is almost identical to the sequential version; there are only two differences. First, `AsParallel` is used to turn the given list into a `ParallelQuery` so that everything after that is done in parallel. Second, the change in `using static` has the effect that `Range` now refers to the implementation defined on `ParallelEnumerable` (this returns a `ParallelQuery`, which is what the parallel version of `Zip` expects). The rest is the same as the sequential version, and the parallel version of `Format` is still a pure function.

In this case, `ParallelEnumerable` does all the heavy lifting, and you can easily resolve the problem by reducing this specific scenario to the more common scenario of zipping two parallel sequences—a scenario common enough that it's addressed in the framework.

In this scenario it was possible to enable parallel execution by removing state updates altogether, but this isn't always the case, nor is it always this easy. But the ideas you've seen so far already put you in a better position when tackling issues related to parallelism, and more generally concurrency.

The case for static methods

When all variables required within a method are provided as input (or are statically available), the method can be made static. This chapter contains several examples of refactoring instance methods to static methods.

You may feel uneasy about this, especially if—like me—you've seen programs become difficult to test and maintain because of the excessive use of static classes.

Static methods can cause problems if they do either of the following:

- *Act on mutable static fields*—These are effectively the most global variables, and it's well known that maintainability suffers from the presence of global mutable variables.
- *Perform I/O*—In this case, it's testability that's jeopardized. If method A depends on the I/O behavior of static method B, it's not possible to unit test A.

Note that both these cases imply an impure function. On the other hand, when a function is pure, there's no downside to making it static. As a general guideline,

- Make pure functions static.
- Avoid mutable static fields.
- Avoid direct calls to static methods that perform I/O.

As you code more functionally, more of your functions will be pure, so potentially more of your code will be in static classes without causing any problems related to the abuse of static classes.

2.3 *Purity and testability*

In the previous section, you saw the properties of pure functions in a concurrent scenario. Because the side effect had to do with state mutation, you could remove the mutation, and the resulting pure function could be run in parallel without problems.

Now we'll look at the properties of pure functions in relation to unit testing, and in scenarios where the side effect has to do with I/O. Unlike mutation, you can't avoid side effects related to I/O; whereas mutation is an implementation detail, I/O is usually a requirement.

You probably already have some knowledge about unit testing that can help you to understand purity, because the two are strictly linked. Like the previous section, this section should also help to dispel the notion that purity is only of theoretical interest—your manager may not care whether you write pure functions, but he's probably keen on good test coverage.

2.3.1 *In practice: a validation scenario*

I'll start by presenting some code for a hypothetical online banking application for the Bank of Codeland (BOC). A common feature in online banking is allowing users to make money transfers, so we'll start with that. Imagine that a customer can use a

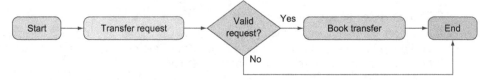

Figure 2.2   Business scenario: validating a transfer request

web or mobile client to request a transfer, as shown in figure 2.2. Before booking the transfer, the server will have to validate this request.

Let's assume that the user's request to make a money transfer is represented by a `MakeTransfer` command. A *command* is a simple data object that encapsulates details about an action to be carried out:

```
public abstract class Command { }

public sealed class MakeTransfer : Command
{
    public Guid DebitedAccountId { get; set; }

    public string Beneficiary { get; set; }
    public string Iban { get; set; }
    public string Bic { get; set; }

    public decimal Amount { get; set; }
    public DateTime Date { get; set; }
}
```

Validation in this scenario can be quite complex, so for the purposes of this explanation we'll only look at the following validation:

- The `Date` field, representing the date on which the transfer should be executed, should not be past.
- The BIC code, a standard identifier for the beneficiary's bank, should be valid.

We'll follow the single-responsibility principle and write one class for each particular validation. Let's draft a simple interface for all these validator classes:

```
public interface IValidator<T>
{
    bool IsValid(T t);
}
```

Now that we have our domain-specific abstractions in place, let's start with a basic implementation:

```
using System.Text.RegularExpressions;

public sealed class BicFormatValidator : IValidator<MakeTransfer>
{
```

```
    static readonly Regex regex = new Regex("^[A-Z]{6}[A-Z1-9]{5}$");

    public bool IsValid(MakeTransfer cmd)
       => regex.IsMatch(cmd.Bic);
}

public class DateNotPastValidator : IValidator<MakeTransfer>
{
    public bool IsValid(MakeTransfer cmd)
       => (DateTime.UtcNow.Date <= cmd.Date.Date);
}
```

That was fairly easy. Is the logic in `BicFormatValidator` pure? Yes, because there are no side effects and the result of `IsValid` is deterministic. What about `DateNotPast-Validator`? In this case, the result of `IsValid` will depend on the current date, so, clearly, the answer is no! What kind of side effect are we facing here? It's I/O: `Date-Time.UtcNow` queries the system clock, which is not in the context of the program.

Functions that perform I/O are difficult to test. For example, the following test passes as I'm writing this, but it will start to fail on the 13th of December, 2016:

```
[Test] public void WhenTransferDateIsFuture_ThenValidationPasses()
{
    var transfer = new MakeTransfer { Date = new DateTime(2016, 12, 12) };
    var validator = new DateNotPastValidator();

    var actual = validator.IsValid(transfer);
    Assert.AreEqual(true, actual);
}
```

Next, we'll look at different ways to address this issue and make your unit tests predictable.

2.3.2 Bringing impure functions under test

The standard object-oriented (OO) technique for ensuring that unit tests behave consistently is to abstract I/O operations in an interface, and to use a deterministic implementation in the tests. I'll call this the *interface-based approach*; it's considered a best practice, but I've come to think of it as an anti-pattern because of the amount of boilerplate it entails. If you're already familiar with this approach, you can skip to the next subsection.

In this approach, instead of calling `DateTime.UtcNow` directly, you abstract access to the system clock like so:

```
public interface IDateTimeService
{
    DateTime UtcNow { get; }
}
```
Encapsulates the impure behavior in an interface

```
public class DefaultDateTimeService : IDateTimeService
{
    public DateTime UtcNow => DateTime.UtcNow;
}
```
Provides a default implementation

You then refactor the date validator to consume this interface, instead of accessing the system clock directly. The validator's behavior now *depends* on the interface, of which an instance should be injected (usually in the constructor), like so:

```
public class DateNotPastValidator : IValidator<MakeTransfer>
{
    private readonly IDateTimeService clock;

    public DateNotPastValidator(IDateTimeService clock)          Interface is injected
    {                                                            in the constructor.
        this.clock = clock;
    }

    public bool IsValid(MakeTransfer request)                    Validation now depends
        => clock.UtcNow.Date <= request.Date.Date;               on the interface.
}
```

 ON TRIVIAL CONSTRUCTORS All that this newly introduced constructor does is store its input arguments in fields. Many languages spare you such ceremony by having "primary constructors"—a feature we'll hopefully see in some future version of C#.

In order to concentrate on meaningful code, I'll usually omit such trivial constructors in the rest of the book. You should assume that class fields are always injected and set in the constructor, unless they're set inline.

Let's look at the refactored IsValid method: is it a pure function? Well, the answer is, it *depends*! It depends, of course, on the implementation of IDateTimeService that's injected:

- When running normally, you'll compose your objects so that you get the "real" *impure* implementation that checks the system clock.
- When running unit tests, you'll inject a "fake" *pure* implementation that does something predictable, such as always returning the same DateTime, enabling you to write tests that are repeatable.

With this approach, tests can be written in this form:

```
public class DateNotPastValidatorTest
{
    static DateTime presentDate = new DateTime(2016, 12, 12);
                                                                 Provides a pure, fake
    private class FakeDateTimeService : IDateTimeService          implementation
    {
        public DateTime UtcNow => presentDate;
    }
                                                                 Injects the fake
    [Test]
    public void WhenTransferDateIsPast_ThenValidationFails()
    {
        var sut = new DateNotPastValidator(new FakeDateTimeService());
```

```
        var cmd = new MakeTransfer { Date = presentDate.AddDays(-1) };
        Assert.AreEqual(false, sut.IsValid(cmd));
    }
}
```

As you can see, there's a strong link between testability and function purity: unit tests need to be isolated (no I/O) and repeatable (always get the same result, given the same inputs). These properties are guaranteed when you use pure functions.

Next, let's look at the code and unit tests with a functional eye and see if there's room for improvement.

2.3.3 Why testing impure functions is hard

When you write unit tests, what are you testing? A unit, of course, but what's a unit exactly? Whatever unit you're testing is a function *or can be viewed as one.*

If what you're testing actually *is* a pure function, testing is easy: you just give it an input and verify that the output is as expected, as illustrated in figure 2.3. If you use the standard Arrange Act Assert (AAA) pattern in your unit tests,[6] and the unit you're testing is a pure function, then the arrange step consists of defining the input values, the act step is the function invocation, and the assert step consists of checking that the output is as expected.

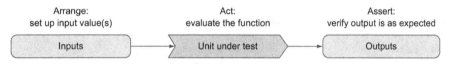

Figure 2.3 Testing a pure function is easy.

If you do this for a representative set of input values, you can have confidence that the function works as intended.

If, on the other hand, the unit you're testing is an *impure* function, its behavior will depend not only on its inputs, but possibly also on the state of the program (that is, any mutable state that's not local to the function under test) and the state of the world (anything outside the context of your program). Furthermore, the function's side effects may lead to a new state of the program and the world. For example,

- The date validator depends on the state of the world, specifically the current time.
- A void-returning method that sends an email has no explicit output to assert against, but it results in a new state of the world.
- A method that sets a non-local variable results in a new state of the program.

---

[6] AAA is a ubiquitous pattern for structuring the code in unit tests. According to this pattern, a test consists of three steps: *arrange* prepares any prerequisites, *act* performs the operation being tested, and *assert* runs assertions against the obtained result.

Figure 2.4   An impure function from the perspective of testability

As a result, you could view an impure function as a pure function that takes as input its arguments, along with the current state of the program and the world, and returns its outputs, along with a new state of the program and the world, as shown in figure 2.4.

Another way to look at this is that an impure function has implicit inputs other than its arguments, or implicit outputs other than its return value, or both.

How does this affect testing? Well, in the case of an impure function, the arrange stage must not only provide the explicit inputs to the function under test but must additionally set up a representation of the state of the program and the world. Similarly, the assert stage must not only check the result, but also that the expected changes have occurred in the state of the program and the world. This is summarized in table 2.2.

Table 2.2   Unit testing from a functional perspective

AAA pattern	Functional thinking
Arrange	Set up the (explicit and implicit) inputs to the function under test
Act	Evaluate the function under test
Assert	Verify the correctness of the (explicit and implicit) outputs

Again we should distinguish between different kinds of side effects with respect to testing:

- The state of the world is managed by using mocks to create an artificial world in which the test runs. It's hard work, but the technique is well understood. This is how you can test code that relies on I/O operations.
- Setting the state of the program and checking that it's updated correctly doesn't require mocks, but it makes for brittle tests and breaks encapsulation.

2.3.4   *Parameterized unit tests*

Unit tests can be parameterized, so that you can show that your tests pass for a variety of input values. Parameterized tests tend to be more functional, because they make you think in terms of inputs and outputs.

For example, you can test that the date-not-past validation works in a variety of cases as follows.

Listing 2.6 Parameterized tests allow you to check your code in a variety of situations

```
public class DateNotPastValidatorTest
{
    static DateTime presentDate = new DateTime(2016, 12, 12);

    private class FakeDateTimeService : IDateTimeService
    {
        public DateTime UtcNow => presentDate;
    }

    [TestCase(+1, ExpectedResult = true)]
    [TestCase( 0, ExpectedResult = true)]
    [TestCase(-1, ExpectedResult = false)]
    public bool WhenTransferDateIsPast_ThenValidatorFails(int offset)
    {
        var sut = new DateNotPastValidator(new FakeDateTimeService());
        var cmd = new MakeTransfer { Date = presentDate.AddDays(offset) };
        return sut.IsValid(cmd);
    }
}
```

The preceding code uses NUnit's `TestCase` attribute to effectively run three tests: a transfer requested to take place today (December 12, 2016), yesterday, and tomorrow.[7]

Parameterized tests have the advantage that you can test a variety of scenarios just by tweaking the parameter values. Should a client be able to request a transfer for a date that's two years away? If so, you can add a test for this with a single line:

```
[TestCase(730, ExpectedResult = true)]
```

Notice that the test method now is itself a function; it maps the given parameter values to an output that NUnit can check. A parameterized test is essentially just an adapter for the function under test. In this example, the test creates an artificial state of the world with hard-coded present data, and it maps the test's input parameter (the offset between the present date and the requested transfer date) to a suitably populated `MakeTransfer` object, which is given as input to the function under test.

I hope you're gradually seeing how functional thinking can breathe a bit of fresh air into day-to-day development tasks, such as writing unit tests.

2.3.5 Avoiding header interfaces

In the preceding sections, you saw the standard, interface-based way of bringing impure functions under test with dependency injection and mocks. I showed this in practice with the date and balance validators, and this approach can be used systematically by following these steps:

1 Define an interface (such as `IDateTimeService`) that abstracts the impure operations consumed in the class under test.

---

[7] XUnit has `Theory` and `InlineData` attributes that allow you to do the same thing. If you're using a testing framework that doesn't support parameterized tests, I recommend you consider changing.

2 Put the impure implementation (such as `DateTime.UtcNow`) in a class that implements that interface (such as `DefaultDateTimeService`).

3 In the class under test, require the interface in the constructor, store it in a field, and consume it as needed.

4 Introduce some bootstrapping logic (manually or with the help of a framework)[8] so that the correct implementation will be injected whenever the class under test is instantiated.

5 Create and inject a fake implementation for the purposes of unit testing.

Unit tests are so valuable that developers gladly put up with all this work, even for something as simple as `DateTime.UtcNow`.

One of the least desirable effects of using this approach systematically is the explosion in the number of interfaces, because you must define an interface for every component that has an I/O element. Most applications are currently developed with an interface for every service, even when only one concrete implementation is envisaged. These are called "header interfaces"—they're not what interfaces were initially designed for (a common contract with several different implementations), but they're used across the board. You end up with more files, more indirection, more assemblies, and code that's difficult to navigate.

In this section I'll show you much simpler alternatives.

PUSHING THE PURE BOUNDARY OUTWARDS

Can we get rid of the whole problem and make everything pure? No. But sometimes we can push the boundaries of pure code. For instance, what if you rewrote the date validator as follows?

Listing 2.7   Injecting a specific value, rather than an interface, makes `IsValid` pure

```
public class DateNotPastValidator : IValidator<MakeTransfer>
{
    private readonly DateTime today;

    public DateNotPastValidator(DateTime today)
    {
        this.today = today;
    }

    public bool IsValid(MakeTransfer cmd)
        => (today <= cmd.Date.Date);
}
```

Instead of injecting an interface, exposing some method you can invoke, inject a *value*. Now the implementation of `IsValid` is pure (because `today` is not mutable).

---

8 Manually composing all classes in a complex application can become quite a chore. To mitigate this, some frameworks allow you to declare what implementations to use for any interface that's required; these are called IoC containers, where IoC stands for *inversion of control*.

You've effectively pushed the side effect of reading the current date outwards, to the code instantiating the validator.

Now whatever code instantiates `DateNotPastValidator` must know how to get the current time. Furthermore, `DateNotPastValidator` must be short-lived. In this case, these constraints seem reasonable: the validator can be instantiated on a per-request basis, and the instantiating code can provide the time.

Requesting a value, rather than having a method or interface supply that value, is an easy win, making more of your code pure and thus easily testable. This approach works well for configuration and environment-specific settings. But things are rarely this easy, so let's move on to an example that's closer to a typical scenario.

INJECTING FUNCTIONS AS DEPENDENCIES

I earlier showed a simple validator that checks that the BIC code is in the correct format. In practice, most online banking applications do better than that: they check that the BIC code actually identifies an existing bank. To do this, you need a validator that can get a list of valid codes and check that the list contains the code in the transfer command:

```
public sealed class BicExistsValidator : IValidator<MakeTransfer>
{
   readonly IEnumerable<string> validCodes;

   public bool IsValid(MakeTransfer cmd)
      => validCodes.Contains(cmd.Bic);
}
```

Naturally, the list of valid codes changes as banks establish new branches or close existing ones, so getting the currently valid codes is an impure operation involving either a query to some external system or reading from mutable state.

Can you require that the list of valid codes be injected in the constructor? I would argue that you can't, because, in that case, who would take the responsibility of retrieving the codes?

- The client code depends on the validator, so it should certainly not do the validator's work.
- The instantiating code doesn't know when or whether the validator will be used. Maybe some prior validation will fail and the valid codes are never required.

In either case, you'd violate the single-responsibility principle. You could, of course, use the interface-based approach and inject some repository from which you can obtain the list of valid code, but, as I've shown, this involves a rather tedious ceremony. What about just requiring a function that you can invoke to query the codes?

```
public sealed class BicExistsValidator : IValidator<MakeTransfer>
{
   readonly Func<IEnumerable<string>> getValidCodes;
```

```
    public BicExistsValidator(Func<IEnumerable<string>> getValidCodes)
    {
        this.getValidCodes = getValidCodes;
    }

    public bool IsValid(MakeTransfer cmd)
        => getValidCodes().Contains(cmd.Bic);
}
```

This solution ticks all the boxes. Now you don't need to define any unnecessary interfaces, and `BicExistsValidator` has no side effects other than the ones caused by invoking `getValidCodes`. This means that you can still easily write unit tests:

```
public class BicExistsValidatorTest
{
    static string[] validCodes = { "ABCDEFGJ123" };        ┐ Injects a function that
                                                           │ deterministically returns
    [TestCase("ABCDEFGJ123", ExpectedResult = true)]       ┘ a hard-coded value
    [TestCase("XXXXXXXXXXX", ExpectedResult = false)]
    public bool WhenBicNotFound_ThenValidationFails(string bic)
        => new BicExistsValidator(() => validCodes)        <───────┘
            .IsValid(new MakeTransfer { Bic = bic });
}
```

Remember, a function signature is an interface; essentially, in this function-based approach to dependency injection, a class declares what functions it depends on. This is equivalent to declaring that it depends on an interface with just one method, but without the noise of header interfaces. We'll pursue this approach further in chapter 7.

2.4   *Purity and the evolution of computing*

I hope that this chapter has made the concept of function purity less mysterious and has shown why extending the footprint of pure code is a worthwhile objective, improving the maintainability and testability of your code.

The evolution of software and hardware also has important consequences for how we think about purity. Our systems are increasingly distributed, so the I/O part of our programs is increasingly important. With microservices architectures becoming mainstream, our programs consist less of doing computation and more of delegating computation to other services, which they communicate with via I/O.

This increase in I/O requirements means purity is harder to achieve. But it also means increased requirements for asynchronous I/O, and as you've seen, purity helps you deal with concurrent scenarios, which includes dealing with asynchronous messages.

Hardware evolution is also important: CPUs aren't getting faster at the same pace as before, so hardware manufacturers are moving toward combining multiple processors. Parallelization is becoming the main road to computing speed, so there's a need to write programs that can be parallelized well. Indeed, the move toward multicore machines is one of the main reasons for the renewed interest we're currently seeing in FP.

Exercises

1 Write a console app that calculates a user's Body Mass Index (BMI):
   a Prompt the user for their height in meters and weight in kilograms.
   b Calculate the BMI as weight / height^2.
   c Output a message: underweight (BMI < 18.5), overweight (BMI >= 25), or healthy.
   d Structure your code so that pure and impure parts are separate.
2 Unit test the pure parts.
3 Unit test the overall workflow using the function-based approach to abstract away the reading from and writing to the console.

Because most of this chapter was devoted to seeing the concept of purity in practice, I encourage you to investigate applying the techniques we discussed to some code you're presently working on: you can learn something new while getting paid for it!

1 Find a place where you're doing some non-trivial operation based on a list (search for `foreach`). See if the operation can be parallelized; if not, see if you can extract a pure part of the operation, and parallelize that part.
2 Search for uses of `DateTime.Now` or `DateTime.UtcNow` in your codebase. If that area isn't under test, bring it under test using both the interface-based approach and the function-based approach described in this chapter.
3 Look for other areas of your code where you're relying on an impure dependency that has no transitive dependencies—the obvious candidates are impure static classes in the framework, such as `ConfigurationManager` or `Environment`. Try to apply the function-based testing pattern.

Summary

- Compared to mathematical functions, programming functions are more difficult to reason about because their output may depend on variables other than their input arguments.
- Side effects include state mutation, throwing exceptions, and I/O.
- Functions without side effects are called *pure*. These functions do nothing other than returning a value that depends solely on their input arguments.
- Pure functions can be more readily optimized and tested than impure ones, and they can be used more reliably in concurrent scenarios, so you should prefer pure functions whenever possible.
- Unlike other side effects, I/O can't be avoided, but you can still isolate the parts of your application that perform I/O in order to reduce the footprint of impure code.

Designing function signatures and types

This chapter covers

- Well-designed function signatures
- Fine-grained control over the inputs to a function
- Using `Option` to represent the possible absence of data

The principles we've covered so far define functional programming in general, regardless of whether you're programming in a statically typed language like C# or a dynamically typed language like JavaScript. In this chapter, you'll learn some functional techniques that are specific to statically typed languages: because both the functions and their arguments are typed, this opens up a whole set of interesting considerations.

Functions are the building blocks of a functional program, so getting the function signature right is paramount. And because a function signature is defined in terms of the types of its inputs and outputs, getting those types right is just as important. Type design and function signature design are really two faces of the same coin.

You may think that, after years of defining classes and interfaces, you know how to design your types and your functions. But it turns out that FP brings a number of interesting concepts to the table that can help you increase the robustness of your programs and the usability of your APIs.

3.1 Function signature design

As you code more functionally, you'll find yourself looking at the function signatures more often. Defining function signatures will be an important step in your development process, often the first thing you do as you approach a problem.

If we're going to talk about function signatures, we'll need some notation, so I'll start by introducing a notation for functions that's standard in the FP community, and we'll use it throughout the book.

3.1.1 Arrow notation

The arrow notation for expressing function signatures is very similar to notation used in languages like Haskell and F#.[1] Let's say we have a function f from `int` to `string`; that is, it takes an `int` as input and yields a `string` as output. We'll notate the signature like this:

```
f : int → string
```

In English, you'd read that as "f *has type* of int to string" or "f takes an `int` and yields a `string`." In C#, a function with this signature is assignable to `Func<int, string>`.

You'll probably agree that the arrow notation is more readable than the C# type, and that's why we'll use it when discussing signatures. When we have no input or no output (`void`), we'll indicate this with `()`.

Let's look at some examples. Table 3.1 shows function types expressed in arrow notation side by side with the corresponding C# delegate type and an example implementation of a function that has the given signature, in lambda notation.

Table 3.1 Expressing function signatures with arrow notation

Function signature	C# type	Example
int → string	Func<int, string>	(int i) => i.ToString()
() → string	Func<string>	() => "hello"
int → ()	Action<int>	(int i) => WriteLine($"gimme {i}")
() → ()	Action	() => WriteLine("Hello World!")
(int, int) → int	Func<int, int, int>	(int a, int b) => a + b

---

[1] These languages have a Hindley-Milner type system (significantly different from C#'s type system), and signatures in arrow notation are called Hindley-Milner type signatures. I'm not interested in following it rigorously; instead I'll try to make it approachable to the C# programmer.

The last example in table 3.1 shows multiple input arguments: we'll just group them with parentheses (parentheses are used to indicate tuples; that is, we're notating a binary function as a unary function whose input argument is a binary tuple).

Now let's move on to more complex signatures, namely those of HOFs. Let's start with the following method (from chapter 1) that takes a string and a function from IDbConnection to R and returns an R:

```
public static R Connect<R>(string connStr, Func<IDbConnection, R> func)
   => Using(new SqlConnection(connStr)
      , conn => { conn.Open(); return func(conn); });
```

How would you notate this signature? The second argument is itself a function, so it can be notated as IDbConnection → R. The HOF's signature will be notated as follows:

```
(string, (IDbConnection → R)) → R
```

And this is the corresponding C# type:

```
Func<string, Func<IDbConnection, R>, R>
```

The arrow syntax is slightly more lightweight, and is more readable, especially as the complexity of the signature increases. There's great benefit to learning it, because you'll find it in books, articles, and blogs on FP: it's the *lingua franca* used by functional programmers from different languages.

3.1.2 How informative is a signature?

Some function signatures are more expressive than others, by which I mean that they give us more information about what the function is doing, what inputs are permissible, and what outputs we can expect. The signature `()` → `()`, for example, gives us no information at all: it may print some text, increment a counter, launch a spaceship... who knows! On the other hand, consider this signature:

```
(IEnumerable<T>, (T → bool)) → IEnumerable<T>
```

Take a minute and see if you can guess what a function with this signature does. Of course, you can't really know for sure without seeing the actual implementation, but you can make an educated guess. The function returns a list of T's as input; it also takes a list of T's, as well as a second argument, which is a function from T to bool: a *predicate* on T.

It's reasonable to assume that the function will use the predicate on T to somehow filter the elements in the list. In short, it's a filtering function. Indeed, this is exactly the signature of `Enumerable.Where`.

Let's look at another example:

```
(IEnumerable<A>, IEnumerable<B>, ((A, B) → C)) → IEnumerable<C>
```

Can you guess what the function does? It returns a sequence of C's and takes a sequence of A's, a sequence of B's, and a function that computes a C from an A and a B. It's reasonable to assume that this function applies the computation to elements from the two input sequences, returning a third sequence with the computed results. This function could be the `Enumerable.Zip` function, which we discussed in chapter 2.

These last two signatures are so expressive that you can make a good guess at the implementation, which is, of course, a desirable trait. When you write an API, you want it to be clear, and if the signature goes hand in hand with good naming in expressing the intent of the function, all the better.

Of course, there are limits on how much a function signature can express. For instance, `Enumerable.TakeWhile`, a function that traverses a given sequence, yielding all elements, as long as a given predicate evaluates to true, has the same signature as `Enumerable.Where`. This makes sense, because `TakeWhile` can also be viewed as a filtering function, but one that works differently than `Where`.

In summary, some signatures are more expressive than others. As you develop your APIs, make your signatures as expressive as possible—this will facilitate the consumption of your API and add robustness to your programs. We'll look at a few examples showing why as we proceed through the chapter.

3.2 Capturing data with data objects

Much of this chapter will focus on ways to represent the absence, or the possible absence, of data. These can seem somewhat abstract concepts, so let's start with what happens when we actually *do* have some data to represent.

To represent data, we use *data objects*: objects that contain data, but no logic. These are also called "anemic" objects, but there's no negative connotation in the name. In FP (unlike OOP) it's natural to draw a separation between logic and data:

- Logic is encoded in functions.
- Data is captured with data objects, which are used as inputs and outputs to these functions.

Imagine that, in the context of a life or health insurance application, you need to write a function that calculates a customer's risk profile, based on their age. The risk profile will be captured with an `enum`:

```
enum Risk { Low, Medium, High }
```

You're pairing with a colleague who comes from a dynamically typed language, and he has a stab at implementing the function. He runs it in the REPL with a few inputs to see that it works as expected:

```
Risk CalculateRiskProfile(dynamic age)
   => (age < 60) ? Risk.Low : Risk.Medium;

CalculateRiskProfile(30) // => Low
CalculateRiskProfile(70) // => Medium
```

Although the implementation does seem to work when given reasonable inputs, you're surprised by his choice of dynamic as the argument type, so you show him that his implementation allows client code to invoke the function with a string, causing a runtime error:

```
CalculateRiskProfile("Hello")
// => runtime error: Operator '<' cannot be applied to operands of type
    'string' and 'int'
```

You explain to your colleague that "you can tell the compiler what type of input your function expects, so that invalid inputs can be ruled out," and you rewrite the function, taking an int as the type of the input argument:

```
Risk CalculateRiskProfile(int age)
   => (age < 60) ? Risk.Low : Risk.Medium;

CalculateRiskProfile("Hello")
// => compiler error: cannot convert from 'string' to 'int'
```

Is there still room for improvement?

3.2.1 *Primitive types are often not specific enough*

As you keep testing your function, you find that the implementation still allows for invalid inputs:

```
CalculateRiskProfile(-1000) // => Low
CalculateRiskProfile(10000) // => Medium
```

Clearly, these are not valid values for a customer's age. What's a valid age, anyway? You have a word with the business to clarify this, and they indicate that a reasonable value for an age must be positive and less than 120. Your first instinct is to add some validation to your function—if the given age is outside of the valid range, throw an exception:

```
Risk CalculateRiskProfile(int age)
{
   if (age < 0 || 120 <= age)
      throw new ArgumentException($"{age} is not a valid age");

   return (age < 60) ? Risk.Low : Risk.Medium;
}

CalculateRiskProfile(10000)
// => runtime error: 10000 is not a valid age
```

As you type this, you're thinking that this is rather annoying:

- You'll have to write additional unit tests for the cases in which validation fails.
- There are a few other areas of the application where an age is expected, so you're probably going to need the same validation in those places. This will cause some duplication.

Duplication is usually a sign that separation of concerns has been broken: the `CalculateRiskProfile` function, which should only concern itself with the calculation, now also concerns itself with validation. Is there a better way?

3.2.2 *Constraining inputs with custom types*

In the meantime, another colleague, who comes from a statically typed functional language, joins the session. She looks at your code so far and finds that the problem lies in your use of `int` to represent age. She comments: "You can tell the compiler what type of input your function expects, so that invalid inputs can be ruled out."

Your dynamically typed colleague listens in amazement, because those were the very words you patronized him with a few moments earlier. You're not sure what she means exactly, so she starts to implement `Age` as a custom type that can only represent a valid value for an age.

Listing 3.1 A custom type that can only be instantiated with a valid value

```
public class Age
{
    public int Value { get; }

    public Age(int value)
    {
        if (!IsValid(value))
            throw new ArgumentException($"{value} is not a valid age");

        Value = value;
    }

    private static bool IsValid(int age)
        => 0 <= age && age < 120;
}
```

In this implementation, `Age` still uses an `int` in its underlying representation, but the constructor ensures that `Age` can only be instantiated with a valid value.

This is functional thinking in action, because the `Age` type is being created precisely to represent the domain of the `CalculateRiskProfile` function, which can now be rewritten as follows:

```
Risk CalculateRiskProfile(Age age)
    => (age.Value < 60) ? Risk.Low : Risk.Medium;
```

This new implementation has several advantages. You're guaranteeing that only valid values can be given; `CalculateRiskProfile` no longer causes runtime errors; and the concern of validating the age value is captured in the constructor of the `Age` type, removing the need for duplicating validation wherever an age is processed. You're still throwing an exception in the `Age` constructor, but we'll remedy that before the end of the chapter.

You can still improve things somewhat. In the preceding implementation, you're using Value to extract the underlying value of the age, so you're still comparing two integers. There are a couple of problems with that:

- Reading the Value property not only creates a bit of noise, it also means that you're relying on the internal representation of Age, which you might want to change in the future.
- Because you're performing integer comparison, you're also not protected if, say, someone accidentally changes the hardcoded value of 60 to 600.

You can address these issues by modifying the definition of Age as follows.

Listing 3.2   Encapsulating the internal representation of Age and the logic for comparison

```
public class Age
{
    private int Value { get; }          ◁──┐ The internal representation
                                            │ is kept private.

    public static bool operator <(Age l, Age r)      ◁──┐ Logic for comparing an
        => l.Value < r.Value;                            │ Age with another Age
    public static bool operator >(Age l, Age r)
        => l.Value > r.Value;

    public static bool operator <(Age l, int r)      ◁──┐ For readability, makes it possible
        => l < new Age(r);                               │ to compare an Age with an int;
    public static bool operator >(Age l, int r)          │ the int will first be converted
        => l > new Age(r);                               │ into an Age
}
```

Now the internal representation of an age is encapsulated, and the logic for comparison is within the Age class. You can now rewrite your function as follows:

```
Risk CalculateRiskProfile(Age age)
    => (age < 60) ? Risk.Low : Risk.Medium;
```

What happens now is that a new Age will be constructed from the value 60, so that the usual validation will be applied. (If this throws a runtime error, that's fine, because it indicates a developer error; more about this in chapter 6.) When the input age is then compared, this comparison happens in the Age class, using the comparison operators you've defined. Overall, the code is just as readable as before, but more robust.

In summary, primitive types are often used too liberally. If you need to constrain the inputs of your functions, it's usually better to define a custom type. This follows the idea of making invalid state unrepresentable—in the preceding example, you can't represent an age outside of the valid bounds.

The new implementation of CalculateRiskProfile is identical to its original implementation, except for the input type, which is now Age, and this ensures the validity of the data, as well as making the function signature more explicit. A functional programmer might say that now the function is "honest." What does that mean?

3.2.3 *Writing "honest" functions*

You might hear functional programmers talk about *honest* or *dishonest* functions. An honest function is simply one that does what it says on the tin; it honors its signature— *always*. For instance, consider the function you ended up with:

```
Risk CalculateRiskProfile(Age age)
    => (age < 60) → Risk.Low : Risk.Medium;
```

Its signature is `Age` → `Risk`, which declares "Give me an `Age` and I will give you back a `Risk`." Indeed, there's no other possible outcome.[2] This function behaves as a mathematical function, mapping each element from the domain to an element of the codomain, as shown in figure 3.1.

Compare this to the previous implementation, which looked like this:

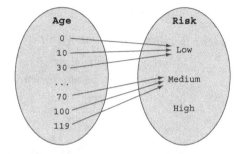

Figure 3.1 An honest function does exactly what the signature says.

```
Risk CalculateRiskProfile(int age)
{
    if (age < 0 || 120 <= age)
        throw new ArgumentException($"{age} is not a valid age");

    return (age < 60) ? Risk.Low : Risk.Medium;
}
```

Remember, a signature is a contract. The signature `int` → `Risk` says "Give me an `int` (*any* of the 2^{32} possible values for `int`) and I'll return a `Risk`." But the implementation doesn't abide by its signature, throwing an `ArgumentException` for what it considers invalid input. (See figure 3.2.)

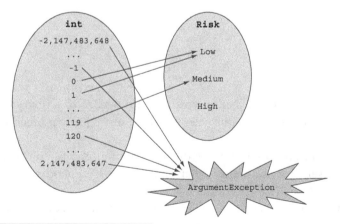

Figure 3.2 A dishonest function can have an outcome that isn't accounted for in the signature.

---

[2] There is, of course, the possibility of hardware failure, of the program running out of memory, and so on, but these are not intrinsic to the function implementation.

That means this function is "dishonest"—what it *really* should say is "Give me an int, and I *may* return a Risk, or I may throw an exception instead." Sometimes there are legitimate reasons why a computation can fail, but in this example, constraining the function input so that the function always returns a valid value, is a much cleaner solution.

In summary, a function is honest if its behavior can be predicted by its signature: it returns a value of the declared type; no throwing exceptions, and no null return values. Note that these requirements are less stringent than function purity—"honesty" is an informal term, less technical and less rigorously defined than purity, but still useful.

3.2.4 *Composing values with tuples and objects*

You might require more data to fine-tune the implementation of your calculation of health risk. For instance, women statistically live longer than men, so you may want to account for this:

```
enum Gender { Female, Male }

Risk CalculateRiskProfile(Age age, Gender gender)
{
    var threshold = (gender == Gender.Female) ? 62 : 60;
    return (age < threshold) ? Risk.Low : Risk.Medium;
}
```

The signature of the function thus defined is as follows:

```
(Age, Gender) → Risk
```

How many possible input values are there? Well, there are two possible values for Gender and 120 for Age, so in total there are 2 * 120 = 240 possible inputs. Notice that if you define a tuple of Age and Gender, 240 tuples are possible. The same is true if you define a custom object to hold that same data, like this:

```
class HealthData
{
    public Age Age;
    public Gender Gender;
}
```

Whether you call a binary function that accepts Age and Gender or a unary function that takes HealthData, 240 distinct inputs are possible; they're just packaged up a bit differently.

Earlier I said that types represent sets, so the Age type represents a set of 120 elements and Gender a set of 2 elements. What about more complex types, such as HealthData, which is defined in terms of the former two?

Essentially, creating an instance of HealthData is equivalent to taking all the possible combinations of the two sets Age and Gender (a Cartesian product), and picking one element. More generally, every time you add a field to an object (or a tuple),

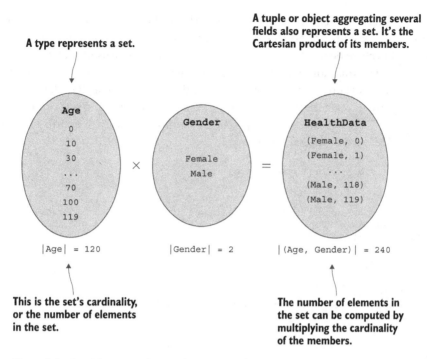

A type represents a set.

A tuple or object aggregating several fields also represents a set. It's the Cartesian product of its members.

This is the set's cardinality, or the number of elements in the set.

The number of elements in the set can be computed by multiplying the cardinality of the members.

Figure 3.3   An object or tuple as a Cartesian product

you're creating a Cartesian product and adding a dimension to the space of the possible values of the object, as illustrated in figure 3.3.

This concludes our brief foray into data object design. The main takeaway is that you should model objects in a way that gives you fine control over the range of inputs that your functions will need to handle. Counting the number of possible instances can bring clarity. Once you have control over these simple values, it's easy to aggregate them into more complex data objects.

Now let's move on to the simplest value of all: the empty tuple, or `Unit`.

3.3   *Modeling the absence of data with Unit*

We've discussed how to represent data; what about when there is no data to represent? Many functions are called for their side effects and return `void`. But this doesn't play well with many functional techniques, so in this section I'll introduce `Unit`: a type that can be used to represent the absence of data, without the problems of `void`.

3.3.1   *Why void isn't ideal*

Let me start by illustrating why `void` is less than ideal. In chapter 1 we covered the all-purpose `Func` and `Action` delegate families. But if they're so all-purpose, why do we need two of them? Why can't we just use `Func<Void>` to represent a function that returns nothing, just as we use `Func<string>` to represent a function that returns a `string`?

The problem is that although the framework has the System.Void type and the void keyword to represent "no return value," Void receives special treatment by the compiler and can't therefore be used as a return type (in fact, it can't be used at all from C# code).

Let's see why this can be a problem in practice. Say you need to gain some insight as to how long certain operations take, and to do so you write a HOF that starts a stopwatch, runs the given function, and stops the stopwatch, printing out some diagnostic information. This is a typical example of the setup/teardown scenario illustrated in chapter 1. Here's the implementation:

```
public static class Instrumentation
{
    public static T Time<T>(string op, Func<T> f)
    {
        var sw = new Stopwatch();
        sw.Start();

        T t = f();

        sw.Stop();
        Console.WriteLine($"{op} took {sw.ElapsedMilliseconds}ms");
        return t;
    }
}
```

If you wanted to read the contents of a file and log how long the operation took, you could use this function like this:

```
var contents = Instrumentation.Time("reading from file.txt"
    , () => File.ReadAllText("file.txt"));
```

It would be quite natural to want to use this with a void-returning function. For example, you might want to time how long it takes to *write* to a file, so you'd like to write this:

```
Instrumentation.Time("writing to file.txt"
    , () => File.AppendAllText("file.txt", "New content!", Encoding.UTF8));
```

The problem is that AppendAllText returns void, so it can't be represented as a Func. To make the preceding code work, you'd need to add an overload of Instrumentation.Time that takes an Action, like this:

```
public static void Time(string op, Action act)
{
    var sw = new Stopwatch();
    sw.Start();

    act();

    sw.Stop();
    Console.WriteLine($"{op} took {sw.ElapsedMilliseconds}ms");
}
```

This is terrible! You have to duplicate the entire implementation just because of the incompatibility between the Func and Action delegates. (The same dichotomy exists in the world of asynchronous operations, between Task and Task<T>.) How can you avoid this?

3.3.2 Bridging the gap between Action and Func with Unit

If you're going to use functional programming, it's useful to have a different representation for "no return value." Instead of using void, which is a special language construct, we'll use a special *value*: the empty tuple. The empty tuple has no members, so it can only have one possible value; since it contains no information whatsoever, that's as good as no value.

The empty tuple is available in the System namespace;[3] uninspiringly, it's called ValueTuple, but I'll follow the FP convention of calling it Unit (so called because only one value exists for this type):[4]

```
using Unit = System.ValueTuple;
```

If you have a HOF that takes a Func, but you wish to use it with an Action, how can you go about it? In chapter 1, I introduced the idea that you can write "adapter" functions to modify existing functions to suit your needs. In this case, you want a way to easily convert an Action into a Func<Unit>, and in my functional library I've defined ToFunc, an extension method on Action that does just that.

Listing 3.3 Converting Action into Func<Unit>

```
using Unit = System.ValueTuple;    ⟵── Aliases the empty tuple as Unit

 namespace LaYumba.Functional
{
   using static F;

   public static partial class F
   {
      public static Unit Unit() => default(Unit);    ⟵
   }

   public static class ActionExt
   {
```

Convenience method that allows you to simply write `return Unit()` in functions that return Unit

---

[3] Depending on what version of .NET you're using, you may need to import the System.ValueTuple package via NuGet to make tuples available. Newer versions of each framework have (or will have) ValueTuple included in their core libraries.

[4] Until recently, functional libraries have tended to define their own Unit type as a struct with no members. The obvious downside is that these custom implementations aren't compatible, so I would call for library developers to adopt the nullary ValueTuple as the standard representation for Unit.

```
    public static Func<Unit> ToFunc(this Action action)
        => () => { action(); return Unit(); };

    public static Func<T, Unit> ToFunc<T>(this Action<T> action)
        => (t) => { action(t); return Unit(); };

    // more overloads to cater for Action's with more arguments...
    }
}
```

Adapter functions that convert an Action into a Unit-returning Func

When you call `ToFunc` with a given `Action`, you get back a `Func<Unit>`: a function that, when invoked, will run the `Action` and return `Unit`.

With this in place, you can expand the `Instrumentation` class with a method that accepts an `Action`, converts it into a `Func<Unit>`, and calls the existing overload that works with any `Func<T>`.

Listing 3.4   Writing HOFs that take a Func or an Action, without duplication

```
using LaYumba.Functional;
using Unit = System.ValueTuple;

public static class Instrumentation
{
    public static void Time(string op, Action act)
        => Time<Unit>(op, act.ToFunc());

    public static T Time<T>(string op, Func<T> f) // same as before...
}
```

Includes an overload that takes an Action

Converts the Action to a Func<Unit> and passes it to the overload taking a Func<T>

As you can see, this enables you to avoid duplicating any logic in the implementation of `Time`. You must still expose the overload taking an `Action`, so that callers need not manually provide a function that returns `Unit`. Given the constraints of the language, this is the best compromise for handling both `Action` and `Func`.

While you may not be fully sold on `Unit` based on this example alone, you'll see more examples in this book where `Unit` and `ToFunc` are needed to take advantage of functional techniques. In summary,

- Use `void` to indicate the absence of data, meaning that your function is only called for side effects and returns no information.
- Use `Unit` as an alternative, more flexible representation when there's a need for consistency in the handling of `Func` and `Action`.

In this section we've looked at the sort of issues caused by the wide use of `void`, and you've seen how you can represent the absence of data with `Unit`. Next, you'll see how to represent data that *could* be absent, and the much greater problems of `null`.

3.4 *Modeling the possible absence of data with Option*

The Option type is used to represent the possibility of the absence of data, something that in C# and many other programming languages (as well as databases) is normally represented with null. I hope to show you that Option gives a more robust and expressive representation of the possible absence of data.

3.4.1 *The bad APIs you use every day*

The problem of representing the possible absence of data isn't handled very gracefully in the framework libraries. Imagine you go for a job interview and are given the following quiz:

Question: What does this program print?

```
using System;
using System.Collections.Generic;
using System.Collections.Specialized;
using static System.Console;

class IndexerIdiosyncracy
{
    public static void Main()
    {
        try
        {
            var empty = new NameValueCollection();
            var green = empty["green"];                     ❶
            WriteLine("green!");

            var alsoEmpty = new Dictionary<string, string>();
            var blue = alsoEmpty["blue"];                   ❷
            WriteLine("blue!");
        }
        catch (Exception ex)
        {
            WriteLine(ex.GetType().Name);
        }
    }
}
```

> **TIP** NameValueCollection is a map from string to string. For example, when you call ConfigurationManager.AppSettings to get the settings of a .config file, you get a NameValueCollection.

Take a moment to read through the code. Then, write down what you think the program prints (making sure nobody's looking). And once you've answered that question, how much would you be willing to bet that you got the right answer? If you're like me, and have a nagging feeling that as a programmer you should really be concerned with other things than these annoying details, the rest of this section will help you see why the problem lies with the APIs themselves, and not with your lack of knowledge.

The code uses indexers to retrieve items from two empty collections, so both operations will fail. Indexers are, of course, just normal functions—the [] syntax is just sugar—so both indexers are functions of type string → string, and both are dishonest.

The NameValueCollection indexer ❶ returns null if a key isn't present. It's somewhat open to debate whether null is actually a string, but I'd tend to say no.[5] You give the indexer a perfectly valid input string, and it returns the useless null value—not what the signature claims.

The Dictionary indexer ❷ throws a KeyNotFoundException, so it's a function that says "Give me a string and I'll return you a string," when it should actually say "give me a string and I *may* return you a string, or I may throw an exception instead."

To add insult to injury, the two indexers are dishonest in inconsistent ways. Knowing this, it's easy to see that the program prints the following:

```
green!
KeyNotFoundException
```

That is, the interface exposed by two different associative collections in .NET is inconsistent. Who'd have thought? And the only way to find out is by looking at the documentation (boring) or stumbling on a bug (worse).

Let's look at the functional approach to representing the possible absence of data.

3.4.2 *An introduction to the Option type*

Option is essentially a container that wraps a value…or no value. It's like a box that *may* contain a thing, or it could be empty. The symbolic definition for Option is as follows:

```
Option<T> = None | Some(T)
```

Let's see what that means. T is a type parameter—the type of the inner value—so an Option<int> may contain an int, or not. The | sign means *or*, so the definition says that an Option<T> can be one of two things—or, equivalently, it can be in one of two "states":

- None—A special value indicating the absence of a value. If the Option has no inner value, we say that "the Option is None."
- Some(T)—A container that wraps a value of type T. If the Option has an inner value, we say that "the Option is Some."

 Option IS ALSO CALLED Maybe Different functional frameworks use varying terminology to express similar concepts. A common synonym for Option is Maybe, with the Some and None states called Just and Nothing respectively.

---

[5] In fact, the language specification itself says so: if you assign null to a variable, as in string s = null;, then s is string evaluates to false.

Such naming inconsistencies are unfortunately quite common in FP, and this doesn't help in the learning process. In this book, I'll try to present the most common synonyms for each pattern or technique, and then stick with one name.

So from now on, I'll stick to Option; just know that if you run across Maybe— say, in a JavaScript or Haskell library—it's the same concept.

We'll look at implementing Option in the next subsection, but first let's take a look at its basic usage so you're familiar with the API. I recommend you follow along in the REPL; you'll need a bit of setup, and that's described in the "Using the LaYumba.Functional library in the REPL" sidebar.

Using the LaYumba.Functional library in the REPL

Playing with the constructs in the LaYumba.Functional library in the REPL requires a bit of setup:

1 If you haven't done so already, download and compile the code samples from https://github.com/la-yumba/functional-csharp-code.
2 Reference the LaYumba.Functional library in your REPL. Just how this works depends on your setup. On my system (using the REPL in Visual Studio, with the code samples solution open), I can do so by typing the following:

```
#r "functional-csharp-code\LaYumba.Functional\bin\Debug\
 netstandard1.6\LaYumba.Functional.dll"
```

3 Type the following imports into the REPL:

```
using LaYumba.Functional;
using static LaYumba.Functional.F;
```

Once you're set up, you can create some Options:

**Creates an Option
in the None state**

```
Option<string> _ = None;              ←──┐
Option<string> john = Some("John");   ←──┘
```

**Creates an Option
in the Some state**

That was easy! Now that you know how to create Options, how can you interact with them? At the most basic level, you can do so with Match, a method that performs pattern matching. Simply put, it allows you to run different code depending on whether the Option is None or Some.

For example, if you have an optional name, you can write a function that returns a greeting for that name, or a general-purpose message if no name is given. Type the following into the REPL:

```
string greet(Option<string> greetee)             If greetee is None, Match
    => greetee.Match(                            will evaluate this function.
        None: () => "Sorry, who?",        ◄──┘
        Some: (name) => $"Hello, {name}");      ◄──┐
                                                   If greetee is Some, Match will
greet(None) // => "Sorry, who?"                    evaluate this function, passing it
                                                   greetee's inner value.
greet(Some("John")) // => "Hello, John"
```

As you can see, Match takes two functions: the first one says what to do in the None case, the second what to do in the Some case. In the Some case, the function will be given the inner value of the Option (in this case, the string "John", the value given when the Option was created).

In the preceding call to Match, the named arguments None: and Some: are used for extra clarity. It's possible to omit those:

```
string greet(Option<string> greetee)
    => greetee.Match(
        () => "Sorry, who?",
        (name) => $"Hello, {name}");
```

In general, I will omit them because the empty parens () in the first lambda already suggest an empty container (that is, an Option in the None state), whereas the parens with an argument inside, (name), suggest a container with a value inside.

If this is all a bit confusing right now, don't worry; things will fall into place as we go along. For now, these are the things to remember:

- Use Some(value) to wrap a value into an Option.
- Use None to create an empty Option.
- Use Match to run some code depending on the state of the Option.

For now, you can think of None as a replacement for null, and Match as a replacement for a null-check. Conceptually, the preceding code is not so different from this:

```
string greet(string name)
    => (name == null)
        ? "Sorry, who?"
        : $"Hello, {name}";
```

You'll see in subsequent sections why using Option is actually preferable to null, and why, eventually, you won't need to use Match very often. First, though, let's have a look under the hood.

3.4.3   *Implementing Option*

You can skip this section on first reading, or if you're only interested in understanding enough to be able to *use* Option. Here I'll show you the techniques I used in the implementation of Option I included in LaYumba.Functional. This is both to show you that there's very little magic involved, and to show possible ways to work around some limitations of the C# type system.

In many typed functional languages, `Option` can be defined with a one-liner along these lines:

```
type Option t = None | Some t
```

In C#, more work is required. First, you need `None` and `Some<T>` to represent each possible state for an `Option`.

Listing 3.5 Implementing the `Some` and `None` types

```
namespace LaYumba.Functional
{
   public static partial class F
   {
      public static Option.None None          ◄──── The None value
         => Option.None.Default;

      public static Option.Some<T> Some<T>(T value)  ◄─┐ The Some function wraps the
         => new Option.Some<T>(value);                 │ given value into a Some.
   }

   namespace Option
   {                                    ┌── None has no members
      public struct None               │   because it contains no data.
      {                         ◄───────┘
         internal static readonly None Default = new None();
      }

      public struct Some<T>
      {                              ┌── Some simply
         internal T Value { get; }   │   wraps a value.
                               ◄──────┘
         internal Some(T value)
         {
            if (value == null)
               throw new ArgumentNullException();  ◄─┐ Some represents the
            Value = value;                           │ presence of data, so don't
         }                                           │ allow the null value.
      }
   }
}
```

The `F` class is meant as the entry point for client code; it exposes the value `None`, which is the empty option, and the function `Some`, which will wrap a given `T` into a `Some<T>`.

`None` represents the absence of a value, so it's a type with no instance fields. Just like `Unit`, there's only one possible value for `None`. `Some` has a single field that holds the inner value; this can't be `null`.

The preceding code allows you to explicitly create values in the None or Some state:

```
using static LaYumba.Functional.F;

var firstName = Some("Enrico");
var middleName = None;
```

The next step is to define the more general Option<T> type, which could be either None or Some<T>. In terms of sets, Option<T> is the *union* of the set Some<T> with the singleton set None (see figure 3.4).

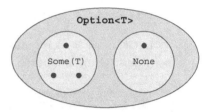

Figure 3.4   Option<T> **is the union of the set** Some (T) **with the singleton set** None.

This turns out not to be so easy, because C# doesn't have language support for defining such "union types." Ideally I'd like to be able to write something like this.

Listing 3.6   Idealized relation of Option **to its cases** None **and** Some

```
namespace LaYumba.Functional
{
    interface Option<out T> { }

    namespace Option
    {
        public struct None : Option<T> { /* ... */ }

        public struct Some<T> : Option<T> { /* ... */ }
    }
}
```

That is, I'd like to say that None is an Option<T>, and so is Some<T>. Unfortunately, there are several problems with the preceding code (which, as a consequence, doesn't compile):

- None doesn't have (and doesn't need) a type parameter T; it can't therefore implement the generic interface Option<T>. It would be nice if None could be treated as an Option<T> *regardless* of what type the type parameter T is eventually assigned, but this isn't supported by C#'s type system.
- An Option<T> can only be one of two things: None or Some<T>. It shouldn't be possible for any client assembly to define any other implementations of Option<T>, but there's no language feature to enforce this.

Given these issues, using an interface or abstract class for Option doesn't work very well. Instead, I defined Option<T> as a separate class and defined methods so that both None and Some<T> can be implicitly converted into Option<T> (inheritance by implicit conversion, if you like).

Listing 3.7 `Option<T>` can capture both the `Some` and `None` states

```
public struct Option<T>
{
    readonly bool isSome;          ◄─── Captures the state of the Option: true
    readonly T value;              ◄─── if the Option is Some

                                        The inner value of the Option
    private Option(T value)
    {
        this.isSome = true;
        this.value = value;
    }
                                                                    Converts
                                                                    None into
    public static implicit operator Option<T>(Option.None _)   ◄─── an Option
        => new Option<T>();

    public static implicit operator Option<T>(Option.Some<T> some)   ◄───┐
        => new Option<T>(some.Value);                                    │
                                        Converts Some into an Option  ───┘
    public static implicit operator Option<T>(T value)    ◄───┐
        => value == null ? None : Some(value);                │ "Lifts" a regular value
                                                              │ into an Option
    public R Match<R>(Func<R> None, Func<T, R> Some)   ◄───┐
        => isSome ? Some(value) : None();                  │ Match takes two functions
}                                                          │ and evaluates one or the
                                                           │ other depending on the
                                                           │ state of the Option.
```

This implementation of `Option` can represent both `None` and `Some`; it has a Boolean value to discriminate between these two states, as well as a field of type `T` to store the inner value of a `Some`.

You can now treat `None` as an `Option<T>` for *any* type `T`. When `None` is converted to an `Option<T>`, the `isSome` flag will be `false`; the inner value will be the default value for `T` and will be disregarded. When `Some<T>` is converted into an `Option<T>`, the `isSome` flag is true and the inner value is stored.

I also added a method to implicitly lift a value of type `T` into an `Option<T>`, which will prove convenient in some scenarios. It yields an `Option` in the `None` state if the value is `null`, and it wraps the value into a `Some` otherwise.

The most important part is `Match`, which allows you to run code depending on the state of the `Option`. `Match` is a method that says "Tell me what you want done when there's no value, and what you want done when there is a value, and I'll do whatever's appropriate."

With this in place, you can consume an `Option`. Take another look at the use of `Match` I showed earlier. It should be clearer now:

```
string greet(Option<string> greetee)
    => greetee.Match(
        None: () => "Sorry, who?",
        Some: (name) => $"Hello, {name}");
```

```
greet(None) // => "Sorry, who?"

greet(Some("John")) // => "Hello, John"
```

Note that there are many other possible ways to define an Option in C#. I've chosen this particular implementation because it allows the cleanest API from the perspective of client code. But Option is a concept, not a particular implementation, so don't be alarmed if you see a different implementation in another library or tutorial.[6] It will still have the defining features of an Option:

- A value None that indicates the absence of a value
- A function Some that wraps a value, indicating the presence of a value
- A way to execute code conditionally on whether a value is present (in our case, Match)

Next, let's see why it's better to use Option than null to represent the possible absence of a value.

3.4.4 *Gaining robustness by using Option instead of null*

I mentioned earlier that None should be used instead of null, and Match instead of a null-check. Let's see what we gain by doing so with a practical example.

Imagine you have a form on your website that allows people to subscribe to a newsletter. A subscriber enters their name and email, and this causes the creation of a Subscriber instance, defined as follows, which is persisted to the database:

```
public class Subscriber
{
    public string Name { get; set; }
    public string Email { get; set; }
}
```

When it's time to send out the newsletter, a custom greeting is computed for the subscriber, which will be prepended to the body of the newsletter:

```
public string GreetingFor(Subscriber subscriber)
    => $"Dear {subscriber.Name.ToUpper()},";
```

This all works fine. Name can't be null because it's a required field in the signup form, and it's not nullable in the database.

Some months later, the rate at which new subscribers sign up drops, so the business decides to lower the barrier to entry by no longer requiring new subscribers to enter their name. The name field is removed from the form, and the database is modified accordingly.

This should be considered a *breaking change*, because it's not possible to make the same assumptions about the data any more. If you allow Name to be null, the code will

---

[6] For example, the popular mocking framework NSubstitute includes an implementation of Option.

happily compile, and `GreetingFor` will throw an exception when it receives a `Subscriber` without a `Name`.

By this time, the person responsible for making the name optional in the database may be on a different team than the person maintaining the code that sends out the newsletter. The code may be in different repositories. In short, it may not be simple to look up all the uses of `Name`.

Instead, it's better to explicitly indicate that `Name` is now optional. The `Subscriber` class should be modified to look like this:

```
public class Subscriber
{
    public Option<string> Name { get; set; }      Name is now explicitly
    public string Email { get; set; }             marked as optional.
}
```

This not only clearly conveys the fact that a value for `Name` may not be available; it causes `GreetingFor` to no longer compile. `GreetingFor`, and any other code that was accessing the `Name` property, will have to be modified to take into account the possibility of the value being absent. For example, you might modify it like so:

```
public string GreetingFor(Subscriber subscriber)
    => subscriber.Name.Match(
        () => "Dear Subscriber,",
        (name) => $"Dear {name.ToUpper()},");
```

By using `Option`, you're forcing the users of your API to handle the case in which no data is available. This places greater demands on the client code, but it effectively removes the possibility of a `NullReferenceException` occurring. Changing a `string` to an `Option<string>` is a breaking change: in this way, you're trading runtime errors for compile-time errors, thus making a compiling application more robust.

3.4.5 *Option as the natural result type of partial functions*

We've discussed how functions map elements from one set to another, and how types in typed programming languages describe such sets. There's an important distinction to make between *total* and *partial* functions:

- *Total functions* are mappings that are defined for *every* element of the domain.
- *Partial functions* are mappings that are defined for *some*, but not all, elements of the domain.

Partial functions are problematic because it's not clear what the function should do when given an input for which it can't compute a result? The `Option` type offers a perfect solution to model such cases: if the function is defined for the given input, it returns a `Some` wrapping the result; otherwise, it returns `None`.

Let's look at some common use cases in which we can use this approach.

PARSING STRINGS

Imagine a function that parses a string representation of an integer. You could model this as a function of type string → int. This is clearly a partial function because not all strings are valid representations of integers. In fact, there are infinitely many strings that can't be mapped to an int.

You can provide a safer representation of parsing with Option, by having the parser function return an Option<int>. This will be None if the given string couldn't be parsed, as illustrated in figure 3.5.

A parser function with the signature string → int is partial, and it's not clear from the signature what will happen if you supply a string that can't be converted to an int. On the other hand, a parser function with signature string → Option<int> is total, because for any given string it will return a valid Option<int>.

Here's an implementation that uses the framework methods to do the grunt work but exposes an Option-based API:

```
public static class Int
{
    public static Option<int> Parse(string s)
    {
        int result;
        return int.TryParse(s, out result)
            ? Some(result) : None;
    }
}
```

The helper functions in this subsection are included in LaYumba.Functional, so you can try them out in the REPL:

```
Int.Parse("10")    // => Some(10)
Int.Parse("hello") // => None
```

Similar methods are defined to parse strings into other commonly used types, like doubles and dates, and, more generally, to convert data in one form to another more restrictive form.

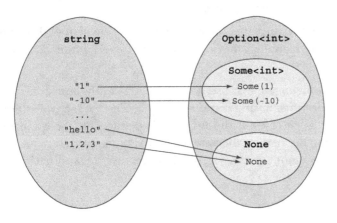

Figure 3.5   Parsing a string as an int is a partial function

LOOKING UP DATA IN A COLLECTION

In the opening part of this section, I showed you that the framework collections expose an API that's neither honest nor consistent in representing the absence of data. The gist was as follows:

```
new NameValueCollection()["green"]
// => null

new Dictionary<string, string>()["blue"]
// => runtime error: KeyNotFoundException
```

The fundamental problem is the following. An associative collection maps keys to values, and can therefore be seen as a function of type TKey → TValue. But there's no guarantee that the collection contains a value for every possible key of type TKey, so looking up a value can always be a partial function.

A better, more explicit way to model the retrieval of a value is by returning an Option. It's possible to write adapter functions that expose an Option-based API, and I generally name these Option-returning functions Lookup:

```
Lookup : (NameValueCollection, string) → Option<string>
```

Lookup takes a NameValueCollection and a string (the key), and will return Some with the value if the key exists, and None otherwise. Here's the implementation:

```
public static Option<string> Lookup
   (this NameValueCollection @this, string key)
   => @this[key];
```

That's it! The expression @this[key] is of type string, whereas the return value is Option<string>, so the string value will be implicitly converted into an Option<string>. (Remember, in the implementation of Option shown earlier, implicit conversion from a value T to an Option<T> was defined to return None if the value was null, and to lift the value into a Some otherwise.) We've gone from a null-based API to an Option-based API.

Here's an overload of Lookup that takes an IDictionary. The signature is similar:

```
Lookup : (IDictionary<K, T>, K) → Option<T>
```

The Lookup function can be implemented as follows:

```
public static Option<T> Lookup<K, T>
   (this IDictionary<K, T> dict, K key)
{
   T value;
   return dict.TryGetValue(key, out value)
      ? Some(value) : None;
}
```

We now have an honest, clear, and consistent API to query both collections. When you access these collections with `Lookup`, the compiler forces you to handle the `None` case and you know exactly what to expect:

```
new NameValueCollection().Lookup("green")
// => None

new Dictionary<string, string>().Lookup("blue")
// => None
```

No more `KeyNotFoundException` or `NullReferenceException` because you asked for a key that wasn't present in the collection. The same approach can be applied when querying other data structures.

THE SMART CONSTRUCTOR PATTERN

Earlier in this chapter, we defined the `Age` type, a type more restrictive than `int`, that only allows the representation of a valid value for a person's age. When creating an `Age` from an `int`, we needed to account for the possibility that the given `int` didn't represent a valid age. You can again model this with `Option`, as shown in figure 3.6.

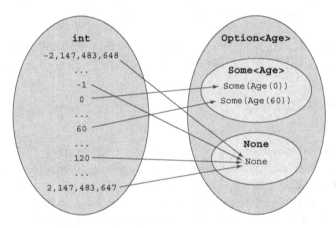

Figure 3.6   Converting from `int` to `Age` can also be modeled with `Option`.

If you need to create an `Age` from an `int`, instead of calling the constructor (which has to throw an exception if it's unable to create a valid instance), you can define a function that returns `Some` or `None` to indicate the successful creation of an `Age`. This is known as a *smart constructor*: it's "smart" in the sense that it's aware of some rules and can prevent the construction of an invalid object.

Listing 3.8   Implementing a smart constructor for `Age`

```
public struct Age
{
    private int Value { get; }

    public static Option<Age> Of(int age)          A smart constructor
                                                    returning an Option
```

```
      => IsValid(age) ? Some(new Age(age)) : None;

   private Age(int value)
   {
      if (!IsValid(value))
         throw new ArgumentException($"{value} is not a valid age");

      Value = value;
   }

   private static bool IsValid(int age)
      => 0 <= age && age < 120;
}
```

The constructor can be marked as `private`.

If you now need to obtain an `Age` from an `int`, you'll get an `Option<Age>` instead, which forces you to account for the failure case. If your `Option<Age>` is `None`, what do you do with it? Well, that depends on the context and requirements. In upcoming chapters we'll look at how you can work effectively with `Options`. Although `Match` is the basic way of interacting with an `Option`, we'll build a rich, high-level API starting in the next chapter.

In summary, `Option` should be your default choice when representing a value that's, well, optional! Use it in your data objects to model the fact that a property may not be set, and in your functions to indicate the possibility that a suitable value may not be returned. Apart from reducing the chance of a `NullReferenceException`, this will enrich your model and make your code more self-documenting.

 GUARDING AGAINST `NullReferenceException` To further bulletproof your code against lurking `NullReferenceExceptions`, *never* write a function that explicitly returns `null`, and always check that the inputs to public methods in your APIs aren't `null`.[7] The only reasonable exception for this is optional arguments, which need their default value to be a compile-time constant.

Using `Option` in your function signature is one way you can attain the overarching recommendation of this chapter: designing function signatures that are honest and highly descriptive of what can be expected from the function. I've tried to show how this makes your application more robust by reducing the chances of runtime errors, but nothing beats proof by experiment, so try these ideas out in your own code.

In the next chapter, we'll enrich the `Option` API. `Option` will be your friend, not only when you use it in your programs, but also as a simple structure through which I'll illustrate many FP concepts.

---

[7] This tedious task can be automated using PostSharp. If you're inclined to go this way, check out NullGuard (https://github.com/haacked/NullGuard), which allows you to disallow `null` arguments on a per-assembly basis, giving you the best protection with the least amount of boilerplate.

Exercises

1 Write a generic function that takes a string and parses it as a value of an enum. It should be usable as follows:

```
Enum.Parse<DayOfWeek>("Friday")  // => Some(DayOfWeek.Friday)
Enum.Parse<DayOfWeek>("Freeday") // => None
```

2 Write a `Lookup` function that will take an `IEnumerable` and a predicate, and return the first element in the `IEnumerable` that matches the predicate, or `None` if no matching element is found. Write its signature in arrow notation:

```
bool isOdd(int i) => i % 2 == 1;

new List<int>().Lookup(isOdd)      // => None
new List<int> { 1 }.Lookup(isOdd) // => Some(1)
```

3 Write a type `Email` that wraps an underlying string, enforcing that it's in a valid format. Ensure that you include the following:
   - A smart constructor
   - Implicit conversion to string, so that it can easily be used with the typical API for sending emails

4 Take a look at the extension methods defined on `IEnumerable` in `System.LINQ.Enumerable`.[8] Which ones could potentially return nothing, or throw some kind of not-found exception, and would therefore be good candidates for returning an `Option<T>` instead?

5 Write implementations for the methods in the following `AppConfig` class. (For both methods, a reasonable one-line method body is possible. Assume the settings are of type string, numeric, or date.) Can this implementation help you to test code that relies on settings in a `.config` file?

```
using System.Collections.Specialized;
using System.Configuration;
using LaYumba.Functional;

public class AppConfig
{
    NameValueCollection source;

    public AppConfig() : this(ConfigurationManager.AppSettings) { }

    public AppConfig(NameValueCollection source)
    {
        this.source = source;
    }
}
```

---

[8] See the Microsoft documentation of Enumerable Methods: https://docs.microsoft.com/en-us/dotnet/api/system.linq.enumerable

```
public Option<T> Get<T>(string name)
{
    // your implementation here...
}

public T Get<T>(string name, T defaultValue)
{
    // your implementation here...
}
}
```

Summary

- Make your function signatures as specific as possible. This will make them easier to consume and less error-prone.
- Make your functions honest. An honest function always does what its signature says, and given an input of the expected type, it yields an output of the expected type—no Exceptions, no nulls.
- Use custom types rather than ad hoc validation code to constrain the input values of a function, and use smart constructors to instantiate these types.
- Use the Option type to express the possible absence of a value. An Option can be in one of two states:
  - None, indicating the absence of a value
  - Some, a simple container wrapping a a non-null value
- To execute code conditionally, depending on the state of an Option, use Match with the functions you'd like to evaluate in the None and Some cases.

Patterns in
functional programming

A pattern is a solution that can be applied to solve a variety of problems. The patterns we'll discuss in this chapter are simply functions; functions that are so ubiquitous when coding functionally that they can be seen as the *core functions* of FP.

You're probably familiar with some of these functions, like `Where` and `Select`, having used them with `IEnumerable`. But you'll see that the same operations can be applied to other structures, hence establishing a pattern. I'll illustrate this with `Option` in this chapter; other structures will follow in coming chapters.

As usual, I suggest you type along in the REPL and see how these core functions can be used (you'll need to import the `LaYumba.Functional` library as previously shown).

4.1 Applying a function to a structure's inner values

The first core function is Map. It takes a structure and a function, and applies the function to the inner value(s) of the structure. Let's start with the familiar case, in which the structure in question is an IEnumerable.

4.1.1 Mapping a function onto a sequence

An implementation of Map for IEnumerable can be written as follows.

> **Listing 4.1 Map applies a function to each element of the given IEnumerable**

```
public static IEnumerable<R> Map<T, R>
   (this IEnumerable<T> ts, Func<T, R> f)
{
   foreach (var t in ts)
      yield return f(t);
}
```

Map maps a list of T's to a list of R's by applying a function T → R to each element in the source list. Notice that in this implementation the results are packaged into an IEnumerable as a result of using the yield return statement.

 A NOTE ABOUT NAMING In FP it's normal to use variable names like t for a value of type T, ts for a collection of T's, and f (g, h, and so on) for a function. You can use more descriptive names when coding for more specific scenarios, but when a function is as general as Map, where you really know nothing about the value t or the function f, variables have correspondingly general names.

Graphically, Map can be illustrated as in figure 4.1.

Let's look at a simple usage:

```
Func<int, int> times3 = x => x * 3;

Range(1, 3).Map(times3);
// => [3, 6, 9]
```

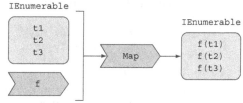

Figure 4.1 Mapping a function over an IEnumerable

Maybe you recognized that this is exactly the behavior you get when you call LINQ's Select method. Indeed, Map can be defined in terms of Select:

```
public static IEnumerable<R> Map<T, R>
   (this IEnumerable<T> ts, Func<T, R> f)
   => ts.Select(f);
```

This is potentially more efficient, because LINQ's implementation of Select is optimized for some specific implementations of IEnumerable. The point is that I'm going to use the name Map, rather than Select, because Map is the standard terminology in FP, but you should consider Map and Select synonyms.

4.1.2 *Mapping a function onto an Option*

Now let's see how Map can be defined for a different structure: Option. The signature of Map for IEnumerable is

```
(IEnumerable<T>, (T → R)) → IEnumerable<R>
```

Let's follow the pattern and just replace IEnumerable with Option:

```
(Option<T>, (T → R)) → Option<R>
```

This signature says you have an Option that *may* contain a T, and a function from T to R; you must return an Option that *may* contain an R. Can you think of an implementation?

Let's see. If the Option is None, there is no T available, and all you can do is return None. An implementation that only handles the None case would look like this:

```
public static Option<R> Map<T, R>
   (this Option.None _, Func<T, R> f)
   => None;
```

The implementation doesn't do anything: you start with None and end up with None, and the given function f is disregarded.

On the other hand, if the Option is Some, then its inner value is a T, so you can apply the given function to it, obtaining an R, which you can then wrap in a Some. Hence, the implementation for the Some case would look like this:

```
public static Option<R> Map<T, R>
   (this Option.Some<T> some, Func<T, R> f)
   => Some(f(some.Value));
```

The actual implementation caters to both possible states of the given Option, as you can see in the following listing.

> ### Listing 4.2 Definition of Map for Option

```
public static Option<R> Map<T, R>
   (this Option<T> optT, Func<T, R> f)
   => optT.Match(
      () => None,
      (t) => Some(f(t)));
```

If the given option is None, Map will just return an Option of the expected return type in the None state. If it's Some(t), where t is the wrapped value, it will feed t to the given function (T → R) and then lift the resulting value into a new Option. You can see this in figure 4.2.

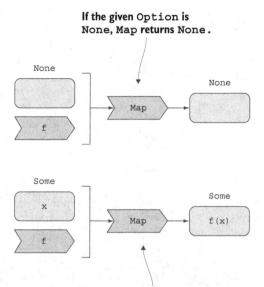

If the given `Option` **is**
`None`, **Map returns** `None`.

If the given `Option` **is** `Some`,
Map applies `f` **to its inner value**
and wraps the result in a `Some`.

Figure 4.2 Mapping a function over an `Option`

Intuitively, it can be useful to think of `Option` as a special kind of list that can either be empty (`None`) or contain exactly one value (`Some`). If you look at it in this light, it becomes very clear that the implementations of `Map` for `Option` and `IEnumerable` are consistent: the given function gets applied to *all* available inner values of the structure.

Let's look at a simple example:

```
Func<string, string> greet = name => $"hello, {name}";

Option<string> _        = None;
Option<string> optJohn = Some("John");

_.Map(greet);        // => None
optJohn.Map(greet); // => Some("hello, John")
```

Here's a real-life analogy: you have a lovely, old aunt whose specialty is making apple pies. She hates to go shopping, but boy, does she love baking pies (single responsibility principle).

You often drop a basket of apples outside her door on your way to work, and in the evening you'll find a basket of freshly made pies! Your aunt also has a sense of humor, so if you get smart and leave an empty basket by her door, you'll find an empty basket in return.

In this analogy, the basket represents the `Option`. The apples are the inner value of the input option, and your aunt's cooking skills are the function that gets applied to this inner value. `Map` is the process of unboxing the apples, giving them to your aunt for processing, and reboxing the baked pie.

```
class Apple { }
class ApplePie { public ApplePie(Apple apple) { } }

Func<Apple, ApplePie> makePie = apple => new ApplePie(apple);

Option<Apple> full  = Some(new Apple());
Option<Apple> empty = None;

full.Map(makePie)   // => Some(ApplePie)
empty.Map(makePie)  // => None
```

4.1.3   *How Option raises the level of abstraction*

A really important thing to realize is that `Option` abstracts away the question of whether a value is present or not. If you directly apply a function to a value, you have to somehow ensure that the value is available. Instead, if you `Map` that function onto an `Option`, you don't really care whether the value is there or not—`Map` will apply the function or not, as appropriate.

This may not be fully clear at this point, but it will become so as you proceed through the book. For now, let's see if I can illustrate this idea. In chapter 3, we defined a function that would calculate `Risk` based on `Age`, as follows:

```
Risk CalculateRiskProfile(Age age)
   => (age.Value < 60) ? Risk.Low : Risk.Medium;
```

Now, assume you're doing a survey where people volunteer some personal information and receive some statistics. Survey takers are modeled with a `Subject` class, defined as follows:

```
class Subject
{
    public Option<Age> Age { get; set; }
    public Option<Gender> Gender { get; set; }
    // many more fields...
}
```

Some fields, like `Age`, are modeled as optional, because survey takers can choose whether or not to disclose this information.

This is how you'd compute the `Risk` of a particular `Subject`:

```
Option<Risk> RiskOf(Subject subject)
    => subject.Age.Map(CalculateRiskProfile);
```

Because `Risk` is based on the subject's age, which is optional, the computed `Risk` is also optional. You don't have to worry about whether the `Age` is there or not; instead, you can map the function that computes risk regardless, and allow the optionality to "spread" by returning the result wrapped in an `Option`.

Next, let's look at the `Map` pattern in a more general light.

4.1.4 Introducing functors

You've seen that `Map` is a function that follows a precise pattern, and that it's used to apply a function to the inner value(s) of a structure such as an `IEnumerable` or an `Option`, as well as many others, like sets, dictionaries, trees, and more.

Let's generalize the pattern. Let `C<T>` indicate a generic "container" that wraps some inner value(s) of type `T`. Then the signature of `Map` can be generally written as follows:

```
Map : (C<T>, (T → R)) → C<R>
```

That is, `Map` can be defined as a function that takes a container `C<T>` and a function *f* of type `(T → R)`, and returns a container `C<R>` wrapping the value(s) resulting from applying *f* to the container's inner value(s).

In FP, a type for which such a `Map` function is defined is called a *functor*.[1] `IEnumerable` and `Option` are functors, as you've just seen, and you'll meet many more in the book. For practical purposes, we can say that anything that has a reasonable implementation of `Map` is a functor. But what's a reasonable implementation? Essentially, `Map` should apply a function to the container's inner value(s) and, equally importantly, it should do *nothing else*; that is, `Map` should have no side effects.[2]

---

[1] Unfortunately, the term *functor* has different connotations depending on the context. In mathematics, it identifies the function that is being mapped; in programming, it's the container over which you can map the function.

[2] This is not the official definition, but it's essentially equivalent.

Why is functor not an interface?

If both `Option` and `IEnumerable` support the `Map` operation, why are we not capturing this with an interface? Indeed, it would be nice to do so, but unfortunately it's not possible in C#. To illustrate why, let's try to define such an interface:

```
interface Functor<F<>, T>
{
   F<R> Map<R>(Func<T, R> f);
}

public struct Option<T> : Functor<Option, T>
{
   public Option<R> Map<R>(Func<T, R> f) => // ...
}
```

This doesn't compile: we can't use `F<>` as a type variable because unlike `T`, it doesn't indicate a type, but rather a *kind*; that is, a type that's in turn parameterized with a generic type. And it's not enough for `Map` to return a `Functor`; it must return a functor of the very same kind as the current instance.

Other languages (including Haskell and Scala) support so-called "higher-kinded types," so it's possible to represent these more general interfaces with *typeclasses*, but in C# (and F#) we must content ourselves with a lesser level of abstraction and follow a pattern-based approach.[3]

4.2 *Performing side effects with ForEach*

In chapter 3, we discussed the dichotomy between `Func` and `Action`. We have this problem again with `Map`: `Map` takes a `Func`, so what do we do if we want to perform an `Action` for each value in a given structure?

You may know that `List<T>` has a `ForEach` method that takes an `Action<T>`, which it invokes for each item in the list:

```
using static System.Console;

new List<int> { 1, 2, 3 }.ForEach(Write);
// prints: 123
```

This is essentially what we want. Let's generalize this so we can call `ForEach` on any `IEnumerable`:

```
public static IEnumerable<Unit> ForEach<T>
   (this IEnumerable<T> ts, Action<T> action)
   => ts.Map(action.ToFunc()).ToImmutableList();
```

The code changes the `Action` to a `Unit`-returning function, and then relies on the implementation of `Map`. This will only create a lazily evaluated sequence of `Unit`s. Here we

---

[3] It's possible to use the C# type system creatively and find a representation analogous to typeclasses, but the resulting code is rather intricate and therefore not suitable for the intent of this book.

actually want the side effects to be performed; hence the call to `ToImmutableList`. The usage is, unsurprisingly,

```
Enumerable.Range(1, 5).ForEach(Write);
// prints: 12345
```

Now let's see the definition of `ForEach` for `Option`. This is defined trivially in terms of `Map`, using the `ToFunc` function that converts an `Action` into a `Func`:[4]

```
public static Option<Unit> ForEach<T>
    (this Option<T> opt, Action<T> action)
    => Map(opt, action.ToFunc());
```

The `ForEach` name can be slightly counterintuitive—remember, an `Option` has at most one inner value, so the given action will be invoked exactly once (if the `Option` is `Some`) or never (if it's `None`).

Here's an example of using `ForEach` to apply an `Action` to an `Option`:

```
var opt = Some("John");

opt.ForEach(name => WriteLine($"Hello {name}"));
// prints: Hello John
```

However, remember from chapter 2 that we should aim to separate pure logic from side effects. We should use `Map` for logic and `ForEach` for side effects, so it would be preferable to rewrite the preceding code as follows:

```
opt.Map(name => $"Hello {name}")
   .ForEach(WriteLine);
```

 ISOLATE SIDE EFFECTS Make the scope of the `Action` that you apply with `ForEach` as small as possible: use `Map` for data transformations and `ForEach` for side effects. This follows the general FP idea of avoiding side effects if possible, and isolating them otherwise.

Take a moment to experiment in the REPL, and see that `Map` and `ForEach` can be used with both `IEnumerable` and `Option`. Here's an example:

```
using static System.Console;
using String = LaYumba.Functional.String;

Option<string> name = Some("Enrico");
```

---

[4] You may ask yourself, Why not just add an overload for `Map` that takes an `Action`? The problem is that in this case, the compiler fails to resolve to the right overload when we call `Map` without specifying its generic arguments. The reason for this is fairly technical: overload resolution doesn't take into account output parameters, so it can't distinguish between `Func<T, R>` and `Action<T>` when it comes to overload resolution. The price to pay for such an overload would be to always specify generic arguments when calling `Map`, again causing noise. In short, the best solution is to introduce a dedicated `ForEach` method.

```
name
    .Map(String.ToUpper)
    .ForEach(WriteLine);

// prints: ENRICO

IEnumerable<string> names = new[] { "Constance", "Albert" };

names
    .Map(String.ToUpper)
    .ForEach(WriteLine);

// prints: CONSTANCE
//         ALBERT
```

Notice that you can use the same patterns, whether you're working with `Option` or `IEnumerable`. Isn't that nice? You can now view both `Option` and `IEnumerable` as *specialized containers*, and you have a set of core functions that allow you to interact with them. If you're presented with a new kind of container, and `Map` or `ForEach` are defined, you'll probably have a very good idea of what they do because you recognize the pattern.

 NOTE In the preceding code, I used `LaYumba.Functional.String`, a class that exposes some commonly used functionality of `System.String` through static methods. This allows me to refer to `String.ToUpper` as a function, without the need to specify the instance on which the `ToUpper` instance method acts, as in: `s => s.ToUpper()`.

In summary, `ForEach` is similar to `Map`, but it takes an `Action` rather than a function, so it's used to perform side effects. Let's move on to the next core function.

4.3   *Chaining functions with Bind*

`Bind` is another very important function, similar to `Map` but slightly more complex. I'll introduce the need for `Bind` with a simple example. Suppose you want a simple program that reads the user's age from the console and prints out some related message. You also want error handling: the age should be valid!

Remember, in the last chapter we defined `Int.Parse` to parse a string as an `int`. We also defined `Age.Of`, a smart constructor that creates an `Age` instance from the given `int`. Both functions return an `Option`:

```
Int.Parse : string → Option<int>
Age.Of    : int → Option<Age>
```

Let's see what happens if we combine them with `Map`:

```
string input;
Option<int> optI = Int.Parse(input);
Option<Option<Age>> ageOpt = optI.Map(i => Age.Of(i));
```

As you can see, we have a problem—we end up with a nested value: `Option` of `Option` of `Age`...How are we going to work with that?

4.3.1 Combining Option-returning functions

It's in such scenarios that `Bind` is handy. For `Option`, this is the signature of `Bind`:

```
Option.Bind : (Option<T>, (T → Option<R>)) → Option<R>
```

That is, `Bind` takes an `Option` and an `Option`-returning function, and applies the function to the inner value of the `Option`. Here's the implementation.

Listing 4.3 Implementation of `Bind` and `Map` for `Option`

```
public static Option<R> Bind<T, R>
   (this Option<T> optT, Func<T, Option<R>> f)       ◁──┐ Bind takes an Option-
   => optT.Match(                                        │ returning function.
      () => None,
      (t) => f(t));

public static Option<R> Map<T, R>
   (this Option<T> optT, Func<T, R> f)
   => optT.Match(                                     ◁──┐ Map takes a regular
      () => None,                                        │ function.
      (t) => Some(f(t)));
```

The preceding listing replicates the definition of `Map` so that you can see how similar these are. Simply put, the `None` case always returns `None`, so that the given function won't be applied. The `Some` case does apply the function; unlike `Map`, there's no need to package the result into an `Option` because `f` already returns an `Option`.

Now let's see how we can put `Bind` to work in the example of parsing a string representing a person's age.

Listing 4.4 Using `Bind` to compose two functions that return an `Option`

```
Func<string, Option<Age>> parseAge = s
   => Int.Parse(s).Bind(Age.Of);

parseAge("26");          // => Some(26)
parseAge("notAnAge");    // => None
parseAge("180");         // => None
```

The function `parseAge` uses `Bind` to combine `Int.Bind` (which returns an `Option<int>`) and `Age.Of` (which returns an `Option<Age>`). As a result, `parseAge` combines the check that the string represents a valid integer and the check that the integer is a valid age value.

Let's now see this in the context of a simple program that reads an age from the console and prints out a related message:

```
public static class AskForValidAgeAndPrintFlatteringMessage
{
    public static void Main()
        => WriteLine($"Only {ReadAge()}! That's young!");
```

Recursively calls itself as long as parsing the age fails

```
static Age ReadAge()
    => ParseAge(Prompt("Please enter your age"))
    .Match(
        () => ReadAge(),
        (age) => age);

    static Option<Age> ParseAge(string s)
        => Int.Parse(s).Bind(Age.Of);
```

Combines parsing a string as an int and creating an age from the int

```
    static string Prompt(string prompt)
    {
        WriteLine(prompt);
        return ReadLine();
    }
}
```

Here's a sample interaction with this program (user inputs are shown in bold):

```
Please enter your age
hello
Please enter your age
500
Please enter your age
45
Only 45! That's young!
```

Now let's see how Bind works with IEnumerable.

4.3.2 *Flattening nested lists with Bind*

You've just seen how you can use Bind to avoid having nested Options. The same idea applies to lists. But what are nested lists? Two-dimensional lists! We need a function that will apply a list-returning function to a list. But rather than returning a two-dimensional list, it should flatten the result into a one-dimensional list.

Remember that Map loops over a given IEnumerable and applies a function to each element. Bind is similar, but with a nested loop, because applying the "bound" function also yields an IEnumerable. The resulting list is flattened to a one-dimensional list. It's probably easier to see this in code:

```
public static IEnumerable<R> Bind<T, R>
    (this IEnumerable<T> ts, Func<T, IEnumerable<R>> f)
{
    foreach (T t in ts)
        foreach (R r in f(t))
            yield return r;
}
```

If you're intimately familiar with LINQ, you'll recognize that this implementation is virtually identical to SelectMany. So for IEnumerable, Bind and SelectMany are identical. Again, in this book I'll use the name Bind because it's standard in FP-speak.

Let's see it in action with an example. Suppose you have a list of neighbors, and each neighbor has a list of pets. You want a list of all pets in the neighborhood:

```
var neighbors = new[]
{
    new { Name = "John", Pets = new Pet[] {"Fluffy", "Thor"} },
    new { Name = "Tim", Pets = new Pet[] {} },
    new { Name = "Carl", Pets = new Pet[] {"Sybil"} },
};

IEnumerable<IEnumerable<Pet>> nested = neighbors.Map(n => n.Pets);
// => [["Fluffy", "Thor"], [], ["Sybil"]]

IEnumerable<Pet> flat = neighbors.Bind(n => n.Pets);
// => ["Fluffy", "Thor", "Sybil"]
```

Notice how using Map yields a nested IEnumerable, whereas Bind yields a flat IEnumerable. (Also notice that whichever way you look at the results of the preceding example, Bind doesn't necessarily yield more items than Map does, which does make the choice of the name SelectMany seem rather odd.)

Figure 4.3 shows a graphical representation of Bind for IEnumerable, particularized to the types and data in the neighborhood example.

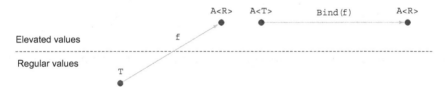

Figure 4.3 Bind on IEnumerable returns a flat list.

As you can see, each function application yields an IEnumerable, and then the results for all applications are flattened into a single IEnumerable.

4.3.3 Actually, it's called a monad

Let's now generalize the pattern for Bind. If we use C<T> to indicate some structure that contains value(s) of type T, then Bind takes an instance of the container and a function with signature (T → C<R>) and returns a C<R>. So the signature of Bind is always in this form:

```
Bind : (C<T>, (T → C<R>)) → C<R>
```

You saw that, for all practical purposes, functors are types for which a suitable Map function is defined. Similarly, *monads* are types for which a Bind function is defined.

You'll sometimes hear people talk of *monadic bind* to clarify that they're not just talking about some function called Bind, but about *the* Bind function that allows the type to be treated as a monad.

4.3.4   *The Return function*

In addition to the Bind function, monads must also have a Return function that "lifts" a normal value T into a monadic value C<T>. For Option, this is the Some function we defined in chapter 3.

What's the Return function for IEnumerable? Well, since there are many implementations of IEnumerable, there are many possible ways to create an IEnumerable. In my functional library, I have a suitable Return function for IEnumerable called List.

To stick with functional design principles, it uses an immutable implementation:

```
using System.Collections.Immutable;

public static IEnumerable<T> List<T>(params T[] items)
   => items.ToImmutableList();
```

The List function doesn't only satisfy the requirement of the Return function—allowing us to raise a simple T into an IEnumerable<T>—but also, thanks to the params arguments, gives us a nice shorthand syntax for initializing lists:

```
using static F;

var empty     = List<string>();             // => []
var singleton = List("Andrej");             // => ["Andrej"]
var many      = List("Karina", "Natasha");  // => ["Karina", "Natasha"]
```

To summarize, a monad is a type M<T> for which the following functions are defined:

```
Return : T → M<T>
Bind   : (M<T>, (T → C<R>)) → C<R>
```

There are certain properties that Bind and Return must observe for the type to be considered a "proper" monad; these are called the *monad laws*. To avoid overloading this chapter with theory, I'll postpone a discussion of the monad laws until chapter 8.

Suffice it to say, Return should only do the *minimal* amount of work required to lift a T into a M<T>, and nothing else. It should be as dumb as possible.

4.3.5   *Relation between functors and monads*

I said that functors are types for which Map is defined, whereas monads are types for which Return and Bind are defined. You've also seen that both Option and IEnumerable are functors *and* monads, because all these functions are defined.

So the question naturally arises, is every monad also a functor? Is every functor also a monad? To answer that, let's take another look at the signatures of the core functions:

```
Map    : (C<T>, (T → R)) → C<R>
Bind   : (C<T>, (T → C<R>)) → C<R>
Return : T → C<T>
```

If you have an implementation of `Bind` and `Return`, you can implement `Map` in terms of these: the function T → R that `Map` takes as input can be turned into a function of type T → C<R> by composing it with `Return`, and this function can be used as input to `Bind`. To convince yourself of this, I propose in the exercises that you implement `Map` in terms of `Bind` and `Return`. Although the implementation will be correct, it may be suboptimal, so normally `Map` will be given its own implementation that doesn't rely on `Bind`.

As for the second question, it turns out that the answer is *no*: not every functor is a monad. `Bind` can't be defined in terms of `Map`, so having an implementation of `Map` gives you no guarantee that a `Bind` function can be defined. For example, some kinds of trees support `Map` but not `Bind`. On the other hand, for most of the types we'll discuss in this book, both `Map` and `Bind` can be defined.

4.4 Filtering values with Where

In chapter 1, you saw several uses of `Where` to filter the values of an `IEnumerable`. It turns out that `Where` can also be defined for `Option`.

Listing 4.5 Filtering the inner value of an `Option`

```
public static Option<T> Where<T>
    (this Option<T> optT, Func<T, bool> pred)
    => optT.Match(
        () => None,
        (t) => pred(t) ? optT : None);
```

Given an `Option` and a predicate, you get back `Some` if the given `Option` was `Some` to begin with *and* its inner value satisfies the predicate; otherwise, you get `None`. Again, if you think of `Option` as a list with at most one item, this makes sense.

Here's a simple usage:

```
bool IsNatural(int i) => i >= 0;
Option<int> ToNatural(string s) => Int.Parse(s).Where(IsNatural);

ToNatural("2")     // => Some(2)
ToNatural("-2")    // => None
ToNatural("hello") // => None
```

Here we build upon `Int.Parse`, which already returns an `Option` signaling whether the string has been correctly parsed as an `int`, and we then use `Where` to additionally enforce that the value be positive.

This concludes our initial exploration of the core functions. You'll see a couple more as you progress through the book, but the four functions described up to this point can take you a surprisingly long way—as you'll see in the next chapter.

The many names of the core functions

One of the hurdles of learning FP is that the same construct is given different names in different languages or libraries. This is true of the core functions, so I've included the following table to help you make sense of these synonyms when you encounter them elsewhere.

LaYumba.Functional	LINQ	Common synonyms
Map	Select	fMap, Project, Lift
Bind	SelectMany	FlatMap, Chain, Collect, Then
Where	Where	Filter
ForEach	n/a	Iter

When writing this book and the LaYumba.Functional library, I had do decide which names to choose for these functions, and these choices are necessarily somewhat arbitrary. ForEach and Where are good names and standard in .NET, but Select and SelectMany would be poor names if used for functors/monads other than IEnumerable, so I chose to use Map and Bind, which are more general, shorter, and very standard in the FP literature.

4.5   *Combining Option and IEnumerable with Bind*

I've mentioned that one way to look at Option is as a special case of a list that can either be empty (None) or contain exactly one value (Some). You can even express this in code by making it possible to convert an Option into an IEnumerable as follows:

```
public struct Option<T>
{
    public IEnumerable<T> AsEnumerable()
    {
        if (IsSome) yield return Value;
    }
}
```

If the Option is Some, the resulting IEnumerable will yield one item; if it's None, it will yield no items. You now have access to all the extension methods defined on IEnumerable, as in the following example:

```
Some("thing").AsEnumerable().Count() // => 1
```

Is this actually useful? In practice, IEnumerable is often used to store data and Option to skip a computation when a value isn't present, so their intent is usually different.

Still, there are some cases in which it's useful to combine them. There are scenarios in which you may end up with an IEnumerable<Option<T>>, or vice versa, an Option<IEnumerable<T>>, and you may want to flatten it into an IEnumerable<T>.

For example, let's go back to the example of a survey, where each participant is modeled as a Subject, and because it's optional for participants to disclose their age, Subject.Age is modeled as an Option<Age>:

```
class Subject
{
    public Option<Age> Age { get; set; }
}

IEnumerable<Subject> Population => new[]
{
    new Subject { Age = Age.Of(33) },
    new Subject { },                        This person did not
    new Subject { Age = Age.Of(37) },       disclose their age.
};
```

You have the details of your participants stored in an IEnumerable<Subject>. Now suppose you need to compute the average age of the participants, for those who chose to disclose their age. How can you go about it? You can start by selecting all the values for Age:

```
var optionalAges = Population.Map(p => p.Age);
// => [Some(Age(33)), None, Some(Age(37))]
```

If you use Map to select the age of the survey takers, you get a list of options. And because an Option can be viewed as a list, optionalAges can be viewed as a list of lists.

To translate this intuition into code, let's add some overloads to Bind that convert the Option into an IEnumerable, so that Bind can be applied as though we were flattening a nested IEnumerable:

```
public static IEnumerable<R> Bind<T, R>
    (this IEnumerable<T> list, Func<T, Option<R>> func)
    => list.Bind(t => func(t).AsEnumerable());

public static IEnumerable<R> Bind<T, R>
    (this Option<T> opt, Func<T, IEnumerable<R>> func)
    => opt.AsEnumerable().Bind(func);
```

Even though according to FP theory Bind should only work on one type of container, the fact that an Option can always be "promoted" to the more general IEnumerable makes these overloads valid, and quite useful in practice:

- The first overload can be used to get an IEnumerable<T> where Map would give you an IEnumerable<Option<T>>, as in the current survey example.
- The second overload can be used to get an IEnumerable<T> where Map would give you an Option<IEnumerable<T>>.

In the survey scenario, we can now use `Bind` to filter out all `None`s and get a list of all the ages that were actually given:

```
var optionalAges = Population.Map(p => p.Age);
// => [Some(Age(33)), None, Some(Age(37))]

var statedAges = Population.Bind(p => p.Age);
// => [Age(33), Age(37)]

var averageAge = statedAges.Map(age => age.Value).Average();
// => 35
```

This allows us to take advantage of the "flattening" nature of `Bind` to filter out all the `None` cases. The preceding output shows the results of calling both `Map` and `Bind` so that you can compare the results.

4.6   *Coding at different levels of abstraction*

Abstraction (in English, not in OOP) means that specific features of different concrete things are removed in order for a general, common feature to emerge: a concept. For example, when you say "You'll see a row of houses," or "Put your ducks in a row," the *row* concept removes anything that makes ducks differ from houses, and only captures their spatial disposition.

Types like `IEnumerable` and `Option` have such a conceptual abstraction at their core: all specific features of their inner value(s) are abstracted away; these types only capture the ability to enumerate the values, or the possible absence of a value, respectively. The same can be said for most generic types.

Let's try to generalize this, so that what you've learned for `Option` can help you understand other constructs that you'll see later in the book (and in other libraries).

4.6.1   *Regular vs. elevated values*

When you're dealing with a type like, say, `IEnumerable<int>` or `Option<Employee>`, you're coding at a higher level of abstraction than when dealing with a non-generic type, like `int` or `Employee`. Let's divide the world of values we deal with into two categories:

- *Regular* values, such as `T`
- *Elevated* values, such as `A<T>`

Here, "elevated" values imply an abstraction of the corresponding regular types.[5] These abstractions are constructs that enable us to better work with and represent operations on the underlying types. More technically put, an abstraction is a way to add an "effect" to the underlying type.[6]

---

[5] Other authors refer to elevated values as wrapped, amplified values, and so on.

[6] In this context, *effect* has a completely different meaning and shouldn't be confused with *side effect*. This is unfortunate, but standard, terminology.

Let's look at some examples:

- Option adds the effect of *optionality effect*—not a T, but the *possibility* of a T.
- IEnumerable adds the effect of *aggregation effect*—not a T or two, but a *sequence* of T's.
- Func adds the effect of *laziness effect*—not a T, but a *computation* that can be evaluated to obtain a T.
- Task adds the effect of *asynchrony*—not a T, but a *promise* that at some point you'll get a T.

As you can see from the preceding examples, things that are very different in nature can be considered abstractions, so there's little point in trying to fit the concept in a box. It's more interesting to see how these abstractions can be put to work.

Coming back to regular versus elevated values, you can visualize these different kinds of values as in figure 4.4. This diagram shows an example of a regular type, int, with some sample values, and the corresponding abstraction A<int>, where A could be an arbitrary abstraction. The arrows that take a regular value and wrap it in a corresponding A represent the Return function.

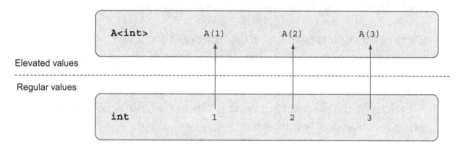

Figure 4.4   Regular values and elevated values

4.6.2   *Crossing levels of abstraction*

Now that we have this classification of types, we can classify functions accordingly. We have functions that remain within the same level of abstraction and functions that cross between levels of abstraction, as illustrated in figure 4.5.[7]

Let's look at a few examples. The function (int i) => i.ToString() has signature int → string, so it maps one regular type to another and is clearly of the first kind.

The Int.Parse function we've been using all along has type string → Option<int>, so it's an upward-crossing function—the third kind. Scott Wlaschin calls these *world-crossing* functions, since they go from the *world* of normal values T to the world of *elevated* values E<T> (extraterrestrial?).[8]

---

[7] This classification isn't exhaustive because you can envisage more categories where the application of a function would cause you to jump by several levels of abstraction or would take you from one type of abstraction to another. But these are probably the most usual kinds of functions you'll encounter, so the classification is still useful.

[8] See Scott's "Understanding map and apply" article here: http://fsharpforfunandprofit.com/posts/elevated-world/.

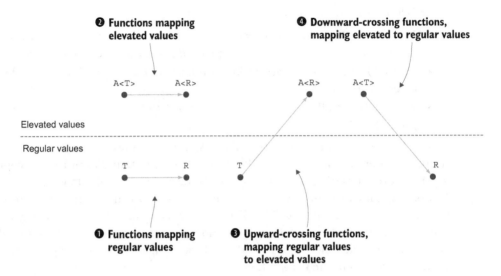

Figure 4.5   Functions classified in relation to levels of abstractions

The Return function (which for any abstraction A has type T → A<T>), is a special case of an upward-crossing function that does nothing other than upward-crossing; that's why I show Return as a vertical upward arrow, and any other upward-crossing function as a diagonal arrow.

Functions of the second kind remain within the abstraction. So, for instance, the following function is a clear match:

```
(IEnumerable<int> ints) => ints.OrderBy(i => i)
```

Its signature is in the form A<T> → A<R>. But we should also include in this category any function in which we start with an A<T>, have some additional arguments, and ultimately end up with an A<R>. That is, any function whose application keeps us within the abstraction; its signature will be in the form (A<T>, ...) → A<R>. This includes many HOFs we've looked at, such as Map, Bind, Where, OrderBy, and others.

Finally, downward-crossing functions—in which we start with an elevated value and end up with a regular value—include, for IEnumerable, Average, Sum, Count; and for Option, Match.

Notice that, given an abstraction A, it's not always possible to define a downward counterpart to Return; that is, there is often no vertical downward arrow. You can always lift an int into an Option<int>, but you can't reduce an Option<int> to an int—what if it's None? Similarly, you can wrap a single Employee into an IEnumerable<Employee>, but there's no obvious way to reduce an IEnumerable<Employee> to a single Employee.

4.6.3   *Map vs. Bind, revisited*

Let's see how we can use this new classification to better understand the difference between Map and Bind.

Figure 4.6 **Map in terms of regular vs. elevated values**

Map takes an elevated value a of type A<T> and a *regular* function f of type T → R and returns an elevated value of type A<R> (computed by applying f to the content of a and lifting the result into an A). This is illustrated in figure 4.6.

Bind also takes an elevated value a of type A<T> but an *upward-crossing* function f of type T → A<R> and returns an elevated value of type A<R> (computed by applying f to the content of a). See figure 4.7.[9]

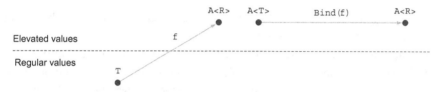

Figure 4.7 **Bind in terms of regular vs. elevated values**

If you use Map with an upward-crossing function of type T → A<R>, you'll end up with a nested value of type A<A<R>>. This is usually not the desired effect, and you should probably use Bind instead.

4.6.4 *Working at the right level of abstraction*

This idea of working at different levels of abstraction is important. If you always deal with regular values, you'll probably be stuck with low-level operations such as for loops, null checks, and so on. Working at such a low level of abstraction is inefficient and error-prone.

There's a definite sweet spot when working within one abstraction, as in the following snippet (from chapter 1):

```
Enumerable.Range(1, 100).
   Where(i => i % 20 == 0).
   OrderBy(i => -i).
   Select(i => $"{i}%")
 // => ["100%", "80%", "60%", "40%", "20%"]
```

Once you've used Range to go from regular values to an IEnumerable<int>, all following computations stay within the IEnumerable abstraction. That is, staying within one

---

9 How exactly the value is calculated depends on the abstraction, but this is a good approximation for now.

abstraction gives you the ability to nicely compose several operations—something we'll delve into in the next chapter.

There's also the danger of going too deep, where you're dealing with values in the form A<B<C<D<T>>>>, where each level adds an abstraction and it's difficult to deal with the deeply buried T. This is something I'll address in chapter 13.

In this chapter, you've seen the implementation of some core functions for working with Option and IEnumerable. Although the implementations are simple, you've seen how this has given us a rich API for working with Option, just as you're used to with IEnumerable. Several common operations can be defined for both Option and IEnumerable—patterns that apply to different kinds of structures. With this API in place, and a better understanding of the core functions of FP, you're ready to tackle more complex scenarios.

Exercises

1 Implement Map for ISet<T> and IDictionary<K, T>. (Tip: start by writing down the signature in arrow notation.)

2 Implement Map for Option and IEnumerable in terms of Bind and Return.

3 Use Bind and an Option-returning Lookup function (such as the one we defined in chapter 3) to implement GetWorkPermit, shown below. Then enrich the implementation so that GetWorkPermit returns None if the work permit has expired.

4 Use Bind to implement AverageYearsWorkedAtTheCompany, shown below (only employees who have left should be included).

```
Option<WorkPermit> GetWorkPermit(Dictionary<string, Employee> people
   , string employeeId) => // your implementation here...

double AverageYearsWorkedAtTheCompany(List<Employee> employees)
   => // your implementation here...

public class Employee
{
   public string Id { get; set; }
   public Option<WorkPermit> WorkPermit { get; set; }

   public DateTime JoinedOn { get; }
   public Option<DateTime> LeftOn { get; }
}

public struct WorkPermit
{
   public string Number { get; set; }
   public DateTime Expiry { get; set; }
}
```

Summary

- Structures like `Option<T>` and `IEnumerable<T>` can be seen as containers or abstractions, allowing you to work more effectively with the underlying values of type `T`.

- You can distinguish between *regular* values, say, `T`, and *elevated* values, like `Option<T>` or `IEnumerable<T>`.

- Some of the core functions of FP allow you to work effectively with elevated values:

  - `Return` is a function that takes a regular value and lifts it into an elevated value.

  - `Map` applies a function to the inner value(s) of a structure, and returns a new structure wrapping the result.

  - `ForEach` is a side-effecting variant of `Map` that takes an action, which it performs for each of the container's inner values.

  - `Bind` maps an `Option`-returning function onto an `Option` and flattens the result to avoid producing a nested `Option`—and similarly for `IEnumerable` and other structures.

  - `Where` filters the inner value(s) of a structure according to a given predicate.

- Types for which `Map` is defined are called *functors*. Types for which `Return` and `Bind` are defined are called *monads*.

Designing programs
with function composition

This chapter covers

- Defining workflows with function composition and method chaining
- Writing functions that compose well
- An end-to-end example of handling server requests with workflows

Function composition is not only powerful and expressive but also pleasant to work with. It's used to some extent in any programming style, but in FP it's used extensively. For example, have you noticed that when you use LINQ to work with lists, you can get a lot done with only a few lines of code? That's because LINQ is a functional API, designed with composition in mind.

In this chapter we'll cover the basic concept and techniques of function composition and illustrate its use with LINQ. We'll also implement an end-to-end server-side workflow, in which we'll use the Option API introduced in chapter 4. This example will illustrate many of the ideas and benefits of the functional approach, so we'll end the chapter with a discussion of those.

5.1 Function composition

Let's start by reviewing function composition and how it relates to method chaining. Function composition is part of any programmer's implicit knowledge. It's a mathematical concept you learn in school and then use every day without thinking about it too much, so let's quickly brush up on the definition.

5.1.1 Brushing up on function composition

Given two functions f and g, you can define a function h to be the composition of those two functions, notated as follows:

$$h = f \bullet g$$

Applying h to a value x is the same as applying g to that same value x to obtain an intermediate result, and then applying f to that intermediate result. That is,

$$h(x) = (f \bullet g)(x) = f(g(x))$$

For example, say you want to get an email address for someone working at Manning. You can have a function calculate the local part (identifying the person) and another append the domain:

```
static string AbbreviateName(Person p)
   => Abbreviate(p.FirstName) + Abbreviate(p.LastName);

static string AppendDomain(string localPart)
   => $"{localPart}@manning.com";

static string Abbreviate(string s)
   => s.Substring(0, 2).ToLower();
```

AbbreviateName and AppendDomain are two functions that you can compose to get a new function that will yield the Manning email for my hypothetical collaborator.

> **Listing 5.1 Defining a function as the composition of two existing functions**

```
Func<Person, string> emailFor =
   p => AppendDomain(AbbreviateName(p));          ◁────┐  emailFor is the composition
                                                       │  of AppendDomain with
var joe = new Person("Joe", "Bloggs");                 │  AbbreviateName.
var email = emailFor(joe);
// => jobl@manning.com
```

There are a couple of things worth noting. First, you can only compose functions with matching types: if you're composing $(f \bullet g)$, the output of g must be assignable to the input type of f.

Second, in function composition, functions appear in the reverse order in which they're performed. For example, in AppendDomain(AbbreviateName(p)), you *first* execute the rightmost function, and then the one to its left. This is, of course, not ideal for readability, especially if you want to compose several functions.

Unlike other languages, C# doesn't have any special syntactic support for function composition, and although you could define a HOF `Compose` to compose two or more functions, this doesn't improve readability. This is why in C# it's usual to resort to method chaining instead.

5.1.2 Method chaining

The method chaining syntax (that is, chaining the invocation of several methods with the `.` operator) provides a more readable way of achieving function composition in C#. Given an expression, you can chain to it any method that's defined as an instance or extension method on the type of the expression.

For instance, the previous example would need to be modified as follows:

```
static string AbbreviateName(this Person p)
    => Abbreviate(p.FirstName) + Abbreviate(p.LastName);

static string AppendDomain(this string localPart)
    => $"{localPart}@manning.com";
```

> Add the `this` keyword to make it an extension method.

You can now chain these methods to obtain the email for the person.

Listing 5.2 Using method chaining syntax to compose functions

```
var joe = new Person("Joe", "Bloggs");
var email = joe.AbbreviateName().AppendDomain();
// => jobl@manning.com
```

Notice that now the extension methods appear in the order in which they will be executed. This significantly improves readability, especially as the complexity of the workflow increases (longer method names, additional parameters, more methods to be chained), and it's why method chaining is the preferable way of achieving function composition in C#.

5.1.3 Composition in the elevated world

Function composition is so important that it should also hold in the world of elevated values. Let's stay with the current example of determining a person's email address, but now we'll have an `Option<Person>` as a starting value. You would assume that the following holds:

```
Func<Person, string> emailFor =
    p => AppendDomain(AbbreviateName(p));

var opt = Some(new Person("Joe", "Bloggs"));

var a = opt.Map(emailFor);
```

> `emailFor` is the composition of `AppendDomain` with `AbbreviateName`.

> ⟵——— **Maps the composed functions**

```
var b = opt.Map(AbbreviateName)           Maps AbbreviateName and
             .Map(AppendDomain);            AppendDomain in separate steps

Assert.AreEqual(a, b);
```

That is, whether you map `AbbreviateName` and `AppendDomain` in separate steps, or map their composition `emailFor` in a single step, the result shouldn't change, and you should be able to safely refactor between these two forms.

More generally, if $h = f \bullet g$, then mapping h onto a functor should be equivalent to mapping g over that functor and then mapping f over the result. This should hold for any functor, and for any pair of functions—it's one of the *functor laws*, so any implementation of `Map` should observe it.

If this sounds complicated, that's probably because it describes something that you intuitively feel should always, obviously hold. Indeed, it's not easy to break this law, but you could come up with a mischievous functor that, say, keeps an inner counter of how many times `Map` is applied (or otherwise changes its state with every call to `Map`), and then the preceding wouldn't hold, because b would have a greater inner count than a.[1]

Simply put, `Map` should apply a function to the functor's inner value(s), and do nothing else, so that function composition holds when working with functors just as it does with normal values. The beauty of this is that you can use any functional library in any programming language, and use any functor with confidence that a refactoring such as changing between a and b in the preceding snippet will be safe.

5.2 Thinking in terms of data flow

You can write entire programs with function composition. Each function somehow processes its input, and the output becomes the input to the following function. When you do this, you start to look at your program in terms of data flow: the program is just a set of functions, and data flows through the program, through one function and into the next. Figure 5.1 illustrates a linear flow—the simplest and most useful kind.

Figure 5.1   Data flowing through a sequence of functions

5.2.1 Using LINQ's composable API

In the previous example, we made the `AbbreviateName` and `AppendDomain` methods chainable by making them extension methods. This is also the approach taken in the design of LINQ, and if you look at the `System.Linq.Enumerable` class, you'll see that it

---

[1] There's another, even simpler functor law: that if you `Map` the identity function ($x \Rightarrow x$) over a functor f, the resulting functor is identical to f. Simply put, the identity function should hold in the elevated world of functors.

contains dozens of extension methods for working with IEnumerable. Let's look at an example of composing functions with LINQ.

Imagine that, given a population, you want to find the average earnings of the richest quartile (that is, the richest 25% of people in the target population). You could write something like this.

Listing 5.3 Defining a query by chaining methods in `Linq.Enumerable`

```
static decimal AverageEarningsOfRichestQuartile(List<Person> population)
  => population
      .OrderByDescending(p => p.Earnings)
      .Take(population.Count / 4)
      .Select(p => p.Earnings)
      .Average();
```

Notice how cleanly you can write this query using LINQ (compared to, say, writing the same query imperatively, with control flow statements). You may have some sense that internally the code will iterate over the list, and that Take will have an if check to only yield the requested number of items, but you don't really care.

Instead, you can lay out your function calls in the form of a "flat" workflow; that is, a linear sequence of instructions:

- First, sort the population (richest at the top).
- Then, only take the top 25%.
- Then, take each person's earnings and average them.

Notice how similar the code is to the workflow description. Let's look at it in terms of data flow: you can see the AverageEarningsOfRichestQuartile function as a very simple program. Its input is a List<Person>, and the output is a decimal.

Furthermore, AverageEarningsOfRichestQuartile is effectively the composition of four functions, so that the input data "flows" through four transformative steps and is thus stepwise transformed into the output value, as shown in figure 5.2.

The first function, OrderByDescending, preserves the type of the data and yields a population sorted by earnings. The second step also preserves the type of the data,

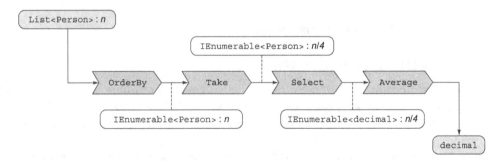

Figure 5.2   Data flow through the `AverageEarningsOfRichestQuartile` function

but changes the cardinality: if the input population is composed of *n* people, `Take` only yields *n/4* people. `Select` preserves the cardinality but changes the type to a list of `decimal`s, and `Average` again changes the type to return a single `decimal` value.[2]

Let's try to generalize this idea of data flow so that it applies not only to queries on `IEnumerable`, but to data in general. Whenever something of interest happens in your program (a request, a mouse click, or simply your program being started) you can think of that something as *input*. That input, which is data, will then go through a series of transformations, as the data flows through a sequence of functions in you program.

5.2.2 Writing functions that compose well

The simple `AverageEarningsOfRichestQuartile` function, shown in listing 5.3, demonstrates how the design of the LINQ library allows you to compose general-purpose functions into specific queries.

There are some properties that make some functions more composable than others:[3]

- *Pure*—If your function has side effects, it's less reusable.
- *Chainable*—A `this` argument (implicit on instance methods and explicit on extension methods) makes it possible to compose through chaining.
- *General*—The more specific the function, the fewer cases there will be where it's useful to compose it.
- *Shape-preserving*—The function preserves the "shape" of the structure; so, if it takes an `IEnumerable`, it returns an `IEnumerable`, and so on.

And, naturally, functions are more composable than actions. Because an `Action` has no output value, it's a dead end, so it can only come at the end of a pipeline.

Notice that the LINQ functions we've used all score 100% based on these criteria, with the exception of `Average`, which is not shape-preserving. Also note that the core functions we defined in the `Option` API do very well.

How composable is `AverageEarningsOfRichestQuartile`? Well, about 40%: It's pure, and it has an output value, but it's not an extension method, and it's extremely specific. Let's see how that would affect some client code, and test it while we're at it:

```
[TestCase(ExpectedResult = 75000)]
public decimal AverageEarningsOfRichestQuartile()
{
    var population = Range(1, 8)
        .Select(i => new Person { Earnings = i * 10000 })
        .ToList();

    return PopulationStatistics
        .AverageEarningsOfRichestQuartile(population);
}
```

---

[2] `Average` also causes the whole chain of methods to be evaluated, because it's the only "greedy" method in the chain.

[3] These are general guidelines: it will always be possible to compose functions that don't have these properties, but, in practice, these properties are good indicators of how easy and useful it will be to compose those functions.

The test passes, but it shows that `AverageEarningsOfRichestQuartile` doesn't share the qualities of the LINQ methods it's composed of: it's not chainable, and it's so specific that you'd hardly hope to reuse it. Let's change that:

1 Split it into two more general functions: `AverageEarnings` (so that you can query the average earnings for any segment of the population) and `Richest-Quartile` (after all, there are many other properties of the richest quartile you may be interested in).

2 Make them extension methods so that they can be chained:

```
public static decimal AverageEarnings
    (this IEnumerable<Person> population)
    => population.Average(p => p.Earnings);

public static IEnumerable<Person> RichestQuartile
    (this List<Person> pop)
    => pop.OrderByDescending(p => p.Earnings)
        .Take(pop.Count / 4);
```

Notice how easy it was to do this refactoring! This is because of the compositional nature of the function we refactored: the new functions just compose fewer of the original building blocks. (If you had an implementation of the same logic with `for` and `if` statements, the refactoring would probably not have been as easy.)

You can now rewrite the test as follows:

```
[TestCase(ExpectedResult = 75000)]
public decimal AverageEarningsOfRichestQuartile()
    => SamplePopulation
        .RichestQuartile()
        .AverageEarnings();

List<Person> SamplePopulation
    => Range(1, 8)
        .Select(i => new Person { Earnings = i * 10000 })
        .ToList();
```

You can see how much more readable the test is now. By refactoring to smaller functions, and to the extension method syntax, you've created more composable functions and a more readable interface.

In this section, you've seen how LINQ provides (among many other things) a set of readily composable functions that work effectively with `IEnumerable`. Next, we'll see how we can use declarative, flat *workflows* when working with `Option`. Let's start by clarifying what we mean by workflows and why they matter.

5.3 *Programming workflows*

Workflows are a powerful way of understanding and expressing application requirements. A workflow is a meaningful sequence of operations leading to a desired result. For example, a cooking recipe describes the workflow for preparing a dish.

Workflows can be effectively modeled through function composition. Each operation in the workflow can be performed by a function, and these functions can be composed into *function pipelines* that perform the workflow—just as you saw in the previous example involving data flowing through different transformations in a LINQ query.

We're now going to look at a more complex workflow of a server processing a command. The scenario is that of a user requesting to make a money transfer through the Bank of Codeland (BOC) online banking application. We're only concentrating on the server side, so the workflow is kicked off when the server receives a request to make a transfer. We can write down a specification for the workflow as follows:

1 Validate the requested transfer.
2 Load the account.
3 If the account has sufficient funds, debit the amount from the account.
4 Persist the changes to the account.
5 Wire the funds via the SWIFT network.[4]

5.3.1 A simple workflow for validation

The entire money transfer workflow is fairly complex, so to get us started, let's simplify it as follows:

1 Validate the requested transfer.
2 Book the transfer (all subsequent steps).

That is, let's say that all steps following validation are part of the subworkflow of actually booking the transfer—which, of course, should only be triggered if validation passes (see figure 5.3).

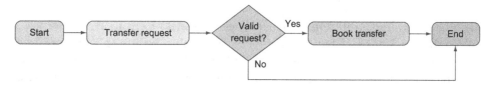

Figure 5.3   Example workflow: validating a request before processing it

Let's take a stab at implementing this very high-level workflow. Assume that the server uses ASP.NET Core to expose an HTTP API and that it's set up so that requests are authenticated and routed to the appropriate MVC controller, making it the entry point for implementing the workflow:

```
using Microsoft.AspNetCore.Mvc;

public class MakeTransferController : Controller
{
```

---

[4]   SWIFT is an interbank network; as far as we're concerned, it's just a third-party application with which we need to communicate.

```
IVvalidator<MakeTransfer> validator;

[HttpPost, Route("api/MakeTransfer")]
public void MakeTransfer
   ([FromBody] MakeTransfer transfer)
{
   if (validator.IsValid(transfer))
      Book(transfer);
}

void Book(MakeTransfer transfer)
   => // actually book the transfer...
}
```

POST requests to this route are routed to this method.

The request body will be deserialized into a `MakeTransfer`.

The details about the requested transfer are captured in a `MakeTransfer` type, which is sent in the body of the user's request. Validation is delegated to a service on which the controller depends, which implements this interface:

```
public interface IValidator<T>
{
   bool IsValid(T t);
}
```

Now to the interesting part, the workflow itself:

```
public void MakeTransfer([FromBody] MakeTransfer transfer)
{
   if (validator.IsValid(transfer))
      Book(transfer);
}

void Book(MakeTransfer transfer)
   => // actually book the transfer...
```

That's the imperative approach of explicit control flow. I'm always very wary of using ifs: a single if may look harmless, but if you start allowing one if, nothing is keeping you from having dozens of nested ifs as additional requirements come in, and the complexity that ensues is what makes applications error-prone and difficult to reason about.

Next, we'll look at how to use function composition instead.

5.3.2   *Refactoring with data flow in mind*

Remember that idea we had about data flowing through various functions? Let's try to think of the transfer request as data flowing through validation and into the Book method that will perform the transfer. Figure 5.4 shows how this would look.

MakeTransfer   Validate   Book   ()

Figure 5.4   Viewing validation as a step in the data flow

There's a bit of a problem with types: IsValid returns a Boolean, whereas Book requires a MakeTransfer object, so these two functions don't compose, as illustrated in figure 5.5.

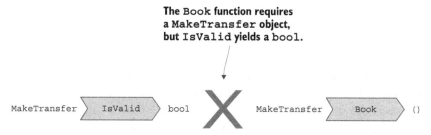

Figure 5.5 A type mismatch preventing function composition

Furthermore, we need to ensure that the request data flows through the validation and into Book *only* if it passes validation. This is where Option can help us: we can use None to represent an invalid transfer request, and Some<MakeTransfer> for a valid one.

Notice that, in doing so, we're expanding the meaning we give to Option: we interpret Some not just to indicate the presence of data, but also the presence of *valid* data, just like we do in the smart constructor pattern.

We can now rewrite the controller method like so.

Listing 5.4 Using Option to represent passing/failing validation

```
public void MakeTransfer([FromBody] MakeTransfer transfer)
   => Some(transfer)
      .Where(validator.IsValid)
      .ForEach(Book);

void Book(MakeTransfer transfer)
   => // actually book the transfer...
```

We lift the transfer data into an Option and apply the IsValid predicate with Where; this will yield a None if validation fails, in which case Book won't be called. In this example, Where is the highly composable function that allows us to glue everything together. This style may be unfamiliar, but it's actually very readable: "Keep the transfer if it's valid, then book it."

5.3.3 *Composition leads to greater flexibility*

Once you have a workflow in place, it becomes easy to make changes such as adding a step to the workflow. Suppose you wanted to normalize the request before validating it, so that things like whitespace and casing don't cause validation to fail.

How would you go about it? You just need to define a function that performs the new step, and then integrate it into your workflow.

Listing 5.5 Adding a new step to an existing workflow

```
public void MakeTransfer([FromBody] MakeTransfer transfer)
   => Some(transfer)
      .Map(Normalize)          ◁——— Plug a new step into the workflow.
```

```
.Where(validator.IsValid)
.ForEach(Book);
```

```
MakeTransfer Normalize(MakeTransfer request) => // ...
```

More generally, if you have a business workflow, you should aim to express it by composing a set of functions, where *each function represents a step in the workflow*, and their composition represents the workflow itself. Figure 5.6 shows this one-to-one translation from steps in the workflow to functions in a pipeline.

Figure 5.6   Modeling a linear workflow with function composition

To be precise, in this case we're not composing these functions directly— as you've seen, the signatures don't allow this—but rather as arguments to the HOFs defined on `Option`, as shown in figure 5.7.

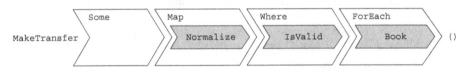

Figure 5.7   The `Option` API helps us compose existing functions.

Next, let's see how we can implement the rest of the workflow.

5.4 *An introduction to functional domain modeling*

Domain modeling means creating a representation for the entities and behaviors specific to the business domain in question. In this case, we need a representation for the bank account from which the transferred funds will be debited. We'll look at domain modeling in more detail in chapter 9, but it's good to see the fundamentals in the current scenario.

Let's start with a ridiculously simplistic representation of a bank account that just captures the account balance. This is enough to illustrate the fundamental differences between the OO and functional approaches. An OO implementation could look like this.

Listing 5.6   In OOP, objects capture both data and behavior

```
public class Account
{
    public decimal Balance { get; private set; }

    public Account(decimal balance) { Balance = balance; }
```

```
public void Debit(decimal amount)
{
    if (Balance < amount)
        throw new InvalidOperationException("Insufficient funds");

    Balance -= amount;
}
}
```

In OOP, data and behavior live in the same object, and methods in the object can typically modify the object's state. By contrast, in FP data is captured with "dumb" data objects while behavior is encoded in functions, so we'll separate the two. We'll use an AccountState object that only contains state, and a static Account class that will contain functions for interacting with an account.

More importantly, notice how the preceding implementation of Debit is full of side effects: exceptions if business validation fails, and state mutation. Instead, we're going to make Debit into a pure function. Instead of modifying the existing instance, we'll return a new AccountState with the new balance. What about avoiding the debit if the funds on the account are insufficient? Well, by now you should have learned the trick! Use None to signal an invalid state, and skip the following computations!

Here's a functional counterpart to the code in listing 5.6.

Listing 5.7 FP separates data and behavior

No setters, so AccountState is immutable.

```
public class AccountState          ⟵──── Only contains data
{
    public decimal Balance { get; }

    public AccountState(decimal balance) { Balance = balance; }
}

public static class Account        ⟵──── Only contains pure logic
{
    public static Option<AccountState> Debit
        (this AccountState acc, decimal amount)
        => (acc.Balance < amount)
            ? None
            : Some(new AccountState(acc.Balance - amount));   ⟵──┐
}
```

None here signals that the debit operation failed.

Some wraps the new state of the account as a result of the operation.

Notice how the OO implementation of Debit in listing 5.6 isn't composable: it has side effects and returns void. The functional counterpart in listing 5.7 is completely different: it's a pure function, and it returns a value, which can be used as input to the next function in the chain. Next we'll integrate this into the end-to-end workflow.

5.5   *An end-to-end server-side workflow*

Now that we have the main workflow skeleton and our simple domain model in place, we're ready to complete the end-to-end workflow. We still need to implement the Book function, which should do the following:

- Load the account.
- If the account has sufficient funds, debit the amount from the account.
- Persist the changes to the account.
- Wire the funds via the SWIFT network.

Let's define two services that capture DB access and SWIFT access:

```
public interface IRepository<T>
{
   Option<T> Get(Guid id);
   void Save(Guid id, T t);
}

interface ISwiftService
{
   void Wire(MakeTransfer transfer, AccountState account);
}
```

Using these interfaces is still an OO pattern, but let's stick to it for now (you'll see how to use *just* functions in chapter 7). Note that IRepository.Get returns an Option to acknowledge the fact that there's no guarantee that an item will be found for any given Guid.

Here's the fully implemented controller, including the Book method that was missing until now.

Listing 5.8   **Implementation of the end-to-end workflow in the controller**

```
public class MakeTransferController : Controller
{
   IValidator<MakeTransfer> validator;
   IRepository<AccountState> accounts;
   ISwiftService swift;

   public void MakeTransfer([FromBody] MakeTransfer transfer)
      => Some(transfer)
         .Map(Normalize)
         .Where(validator.IsValid)
         .ForEach(Book);

   void Book(MakeTransfer transfer)
      => accounts.Get(transfer.DebitedAccountId)
         .Bind(account => account.Debit(transfer.Amount))
         .ForEach(account =>
            {
               accounts.Save(transfer.DebitedAccountId, account);
               swift.Wire(transfer, account);
            });
}
```

Let's look at the newly added `Book` method. Notice that `accounts.Get` returns an `Option` (in case no account was found with the given ID), and `Debit` also returns an `Option` (in case there were insufficient funds). Therefore, we compose these two operations with `Bind`. Finally, we use `ForEach` to perform the side effects we need: saving the account with the new, lower balance, and wiring the funds to SWIFT.

There are a couple of obvious shortcomings in the overall solution. First, we're effectively using `Option` to stop the computation if something goes wrong along the way, but we're not giving any feedback to the user as to whether the request was successful or why. In chapter 6, you'll see how to remedy this with `Either` and related structures; this allows you to capture error details without fundamentally altering the approach shown here.

Another problem is that saving the account and wiring the funds should be done atomically: if the process fails in the middle, we could have debited the funds without sending them to SWIFT. Solutions to this issue tend to be infrastructure-specific and aren't specific to FP.[5] Now that I've come clean about what's missing, let's discuss the good bits.

5.5.1 Expressions vs. statements

Something that should stand out when you look at the controller in listing 5.8 is that there are no `if` statements, no `for` statements... In fact, there are practically no *statements* at all!

One fundamental difference between the functional and imperative style is that imperative code relies on statements; functional code relies on expressions. For a refresher on how these differ, see the "Expressions, statements, declarations" sidebar. In essence, expressions have a value; statements don't. While expressions such as function calls *can* have side effects, statements *only* have side effects, so they don't compose.

If you create workflows by composing functions as we have, side effects naturally gravitate towards the end of the workflow: functions like `ForEach` don't have a useful return value, so that's where the pipeline ends. This helps to isolate side effects, even visually.

The idea of programming without using statements can seem quite foreign at first, but as the code in this and previous chapters demonstrates, it's perfectly feasible in C#. Notice that the only statements are the two within the last `ForEach`; this is fine, because we want to have two side effects—there's no point hiding that.

---

[5] This problem is difficult and fairly common in distributed architectures. If you're storing the accounts in a database, you could be tempted to open a DB transaction, save the account within the transaction, wire the funds, and only commit once that's done. This still leaves you unprotected if the process dies after wiring the funds but before committing the transaction. A thorough solution is to atomically create a single "task" representing both operations, and have a process that performs both and removes the task only when both have successfully been carried out. This means that any of the operations is potentially performed more than once, so provisions need to be made for the operations to be idempotent. A reference text on these sorts of problems and solutions is *Enterprise Integration Patterns* by Gregor Hohpe and Bobby Woolf (Addison-Wesley, 2004).

I recommend you try coding using just expressions. It doesn't guarantee good design, but it certainly promotes better design. (Tip: since C# 6 there's a giveaway—if you have braces, it's a statement.)

Expressions, statements, declarations

Expressions include anything that produces a value, such as these:

- literals, such as `123` or `"something"`
- variables, such as `x`
- invocations, such as `"hello".ToUpper()` or `Math.Sqrt(Math.Abs(n) + m)`
- operators and operands, such as `a || b, b ? x : y` or `new object()`

Expressions can be used wherever a value is expected: for example, as arguments in function invocations or as return values of a function.

Statements are instructions to the program, such as assignments, conditionals (`if/else`), loops, and so on.

Declarations (of classes, methods, fields, and so on) are often considered statements, but for the purpose of this discussion are best thought of as a category in their own right. Whether you prefer statements or expressions, declarations are equally necessary, so they're best left out of the "statements vs. expressions" argument.

5.5.2   *Declarative vs. imperative*

When we prefer expressions to statements, our code becomes more declarative. It "declares" what's being computed, rather than instructing the computer on what specific operations to carry out in the computation. In other words, it's higher-level, and closer to the way in which we communicate with other human beings.

For example, the top-level workflow in our controller reads as follows:

```
=> Some(transfer)
   .Map(Normalize)
   .Where(validator.IsValid)
   .ForEach(Book);
```

Discounting things like `Map` and `Where`, which essentially act as glue between the operations, this reads very much like the verbal, bullet-point definition of the workflow. This means the code is closer to language, and hence easier to understand and to maintain. Let's contrast the imperative and declarative styles in table 5.1.

Table 5.1   Comparing the imperative and declarative styles

Imperative	Declarative
Tells the computer what to do; for example, "Add this item to this list."	Tells the computer what you want; for example, "Give me all the items that match a condition."
Relies mainly on statements.	Relies mainly on expressions.

Table 5.1   Comparing the imperative and declarative styles *(continued)*

Imperative	Declarative
Side effects are ubiquitous.	Side effects naturally gravitate toward the end of the expression evaluation.[a]
Statements can be readily translated into machine instructions.	There is more indirection (hence, potentially more optimizations) in the process of translating expressions to machine instructions.

a This is because side-effecting functions don't normally return a useful value that can be used in further evaluation.

Another thing worth pointing out is that, because declarative code is higher-level, it's hard to look at the implementation and see that it works without the confidence of unit tests. This is actually a good thing: it's much better to convince yourself through unit tests than to rely on the false confidence of looking at the code and seeing that it looks like it's doing the right thing.

5.5.3   *The functional take on layering*

The implementation we've looked at sheds some light on a natural way to structure applications with function composition. In any reasonably complex application, we tend to introduce some form of *layering*, distinguishing a hierarchy of high- to low-level components, where the highest level components are entry points into the application (in our example, the controller), and the lowest are exit points (in our example, the repository and SWIFT service).

Unfortunately, I've worked on many projects where layering is more of a curse than a blessing, as you need to traverse several layers for any operation. This is because there's a tendency to structure invocations between layers as in figure 5.8.

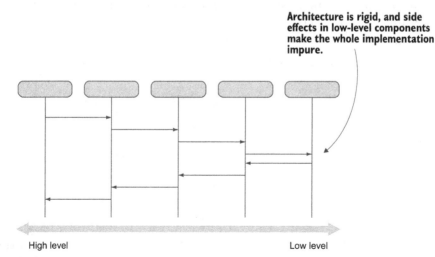

Architecture is rigid, and side effects in low-level components make the whole implementation impure.

High level   Low level

Figure 5.8   An unhelpful way to structure interaction between layers

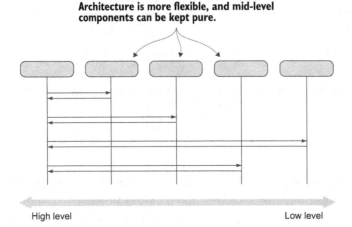

Architecture is more flexible, and mid-level components can be kept pure.

High level   Low level

Figure 5.9 A top-level workflow composing functions exposed by lower-level components

In this approach, there's an implicit assumption that a layer should only call into an immediately adjacent layer. This makes the architecture rigid. Furthermore, it means that the whole implementation will be impure: because the lowest-level components have side effects (they typically access the DB or external APIs), everything above is also impure—a function that calls an impure function is itself impure.

In the approach demonstrated in this chapter, the interaction between layers looks more like figure 5.9.

That is, a higher-level component can depend on any lower-level component, but not vice versa—this is a more flexible and effective approach to layering. In our example, there's a top-level workflow that composes functions exposed by lower-level components.

There are a couple of advantages here:

- You get a clear, synthetic overview of the workflow within the top-level component (but note that this doesn't preclude you from defining subworkflows within a lower-level component).
- Mid-level components can be pure.

In our example, the interaction between components looks like figure 5.10.

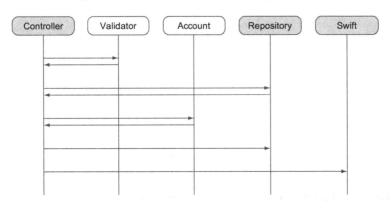

Controller   Validator   Account   Repository   Swift

Figure 5.10 Mid-level components can be pure.

As you can see, the domain representation can (and should!) consist of pure functions only, because there's no interaction with lower-level components; there's only computation of a result based on inputs. The same could be true of other functionality, such as validation (depending on what the validation consists of). Therefore, this approach helps you to isolate side effects and facilitates testing. Because the domain model and other mid-level components are pure functions, they can easily be tested without the need for mocks.

Exercises

1 Without looking at any code or documentation, write the type of the functions OrderBy, Take, and Average, which were used to implement AverageEarnings-OfRichestQuartile.

2 Check your answer with the MSDN documentation: https://docs.microsoft.com/en-us/dotnet/api/system.linq.enumerable. How is Average different?

3 Implement a general purpose Compose function that takes two unary functions and returns the composition of the two.

Summary

- Function composition means combining two or more functions into a new function, and it's widely used in FP.
- In C#, the extension method syntax allows you to use function composition by chaining methods.
- Functions lend themselves to being composed if they are pure, chainable, and shape-preserving.
- Workflows are sequences of operations that can be effectively expressed in your programs through function pipelines: one function for each step of the workflow, with the output of each function fed into the next.
- The LINQ library has a rich set of easily composable functions to work with IEnumerables, and you can use it as inspiration to write your own APIs.
- Functional code prefers expressions over statements, unlike imperative code.
- Relying on expressions leads to your code becoming more declarative, and hence more readable.

Part 2

Becoming functional

In this part we'll build on the foundations laid so far, and you'll see how some techniques introduced in part 1 for limited scenarios can be generalized, enabling you to write entire applications in a functional style.

Chapter 6 discusses the functional take on validation and error handling.

Chapter 7 shows how you can modularize and compose an application with functions only, using techniques like partial application and the powerful Aggregate function (fold).

Another core function, Apply, is discussed in chapter 8, which also teaches you about implementing the LINQ query pattern and compares some functional patterns like *applicatives* and *monads*. Chapter 8 also introduces a technique called *property-based testing*, which verifies that your code observes certain properties by throwing random data at it.

Chapter 9 discusses the functional approach to representing state, identity, and change through immutable data objects and data structures. These principles can be applied not only to in-memory data, but also at the database level, and this is shown in chapter 10.

By the end of part 2, you'll have acquired a set of tools enabling you to effectively tackle many programming tasks using an end-to-end functional approach.

Functional
error handling

This chapter covers

- Representing alternative outcomes with `Either`
- Chaining operations that may fail
- Distinguishing business validation from technical errors

Error handling is an important part of our applications, and one aspect in which the functional and imperative programming styles differ starkly:

- Imperative programming uses special statements like `throw` and `try/catch`, which disrupt the normal program flow, thus introducing side effects, as discussed in chapter 2.
- Functional programming strives to minimize side effects, so throwing exceptions is generally avoided. Instead, if an operation can fail, it should return a representation of its outcome including an indication of success or failure, as well as its result (if successful), or some error data otherwise. In other words, errors in FP are just *payload*.

There are lots of problems with the imperative, exception-based approach. It has been said that throw has similar semantics to goto, and this begs the question of why imperative programmers have banished goto but not throw.[1] There's also a lot of confusion around when to use exceptions and when to use other error-handling techniques. I feel that the functional approach brings a lot more clarity to the complex area of error handling, and I hope to convince you of this through the examples in this chapter.

We'll look at how the functional approach can be put into practice, and how you can make explicit that a function can fail through its signature, by using types that include error information in their payload. Errors can then be consumed in the calling function just like any other value.

6.1   *A safer way to represent outcomes*

In chapter 3, you saw that you could use Option not just to represent the absence of a value, but also the absence of a *valid* value. That is, you can use Some to signal that everything went OK, and None to signal that something went wrong. In other words, functional error handling can sometimes be satisfactorily achieved by using the Option type. Here are a couple of examples:

- *Parsing a number*—A function parsing a string representation of a number can return None to indicate that the given string wasn't a valid representation for a number.
- *Retrieving an item from a collection*—You can return None to indicate that no suitable item was found, and use Some to wrap a correctly retrieved value.

In scenarios like these, there's really only one way for the function to not return a valid result, and that's represented with None. Functions that return Option<T>, rather than just T, are acknowledging in their signature that the operation may fail, and you could take the isSome flag that indicates the state of the Option (see listing 3.7) as the additional payload that signals success or failure.

What if there are several ways in which an operation could fail? What if, for instance, the BOC application receives a complex request, such as a request to make a money transfer? Surely the user would need to know not only *whether* the transfer was successfully booked, but also, in case of failure, the *reason(s)* for failure.

In such scenarios, Option is too limited, because it doesn't convey any details about why an operation has failed. Accordingly, we'll need a richer way to represent outcomes—one that includes information about what exactly has gone wrong.

6.1.1   *Capturing error details with Either*

A classic functional approach to this problem is to use the Either type, which, in the context of an operation with two possible outcomes, captures details about the outcome that

---

[1] In fact, I think throw is much worse than goto. The latter at least jumps to a well-defined location; with throw, you don't really know what code will execute next, unless you explore all possible paths into the code where throw occurs.

has taken place. By convention, the two possible outcomes are indicated with `Left` and `Right` (as shown in
figure 6.1), likening the `Either`-producing operation
to a *fork*: things can go one way or another.

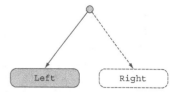

Although `Left` and `Right` can be seen in a neutral
light, by far the most common use of `Either` is to represent the outcome of an operation that may fail, in
which case `Left` is used to indicate failure and `Right`
to indicate success. So, remember this:

Figure 6.1 `Either` represents
one of two possible outcomes.

- `Right` = "all right"
- `Left` = "something wrong"

In this biased acceptation, `Either` is just like an `Option` that has been enriched with
some data about the error. An `Option` can be in the `None` or `Some` state, and `Either`
can similarly be in the `Left` or `Right` state, as summarized in table 6.1.

Table 6.1 `Option` and `Either` can both represent possible failure

	Failure	**Success**
`Option<T>`	`None`	`Some(T)`
`Either<L, R>`	`Left(L)`	`Right(R)`

If `Option` can be symbolically defined as

```
Option<T> = None | Some(T)
```

then `Either` can similarly be defined like this:

```
Either<L, R> = Left(L) | Right(R)
```

Notice that `Either` has two generic parameters and can be in one of two states:

- `Left(L)` wraps a value of type L, capturing details about the error.
- `Right(R)` wraps a value of type R, representing a successful result.

Let's see how an `Option`-based interface may differ from an `Either`-based one. Imagine you're doing some DIY and go to the store to get a tool you need. If the item isn't
available, an `Option`-based shopkeeper would just say, "Sorry, it's not available," and
that's it. An `Either`-based shopkeeper would give you more information, such as,
"We're out of stock until next week," or "This product has been discontinued"; you
can base your further decisions on this information.

What about a deceiving shopkeeper who, having run out of stock, will sell you a
product that looks just like the one you're after, but which will explode in your face
when you put it to use? Well, that's the imperative, exception-throwing interface.

"Sorry."

"we'll get new stock tomorrow."

Because the definition of `Either` is so similar to `Option`, it can be implemented using the same techniques. In my `LaYumba.Functional` library, I have two generic types, `Left<L>` and `Right<R>`, that wrap a single value, and both are implicitly convertible to `Either<L, R>`. For convenience, values of type `L` and `R` are also implicitly convertible to `Either<L, R>`.

You can see the full implementation in the code samples, but I won't include it here because there's nothing new compared to what was discussed in section 3.4.3 about the implementation of `Option`. Instead, let's play around with `Either` in the REPL. As usual, you need to start by referencing `LaYumba.Functional`:

```
#r "functional-csharp-code\src\LaYumba.Functional\bin\Debug\netstandard1.6\
  LaYumba.Functional.dll"
using LaYumba.Functional;
using static LaYumba.Functional.F;
```

Now create some Ethers:

```
Right(12)
// => Right(12)
```
⟵ **Creates an `Either`
in the `Right` state**

```
Left("oops")
// => Left("oops")
```
⟵ **Creates an `Either`
in the `Left` state**

That was easy! Now let's write a function that uses `Match` to compute a different value depending on the state of an `Either`:

```
string Render(Either<string, double> val) =>
    val.Match(
        Left: l => $"Invalid value: {l}",
        Right: r => $"The result is: {r}");

Render(Right(12d))
// => "The result is: 12"

Render(Left("oops"))
// => "Invalid value: oops"
```

Now that you know how to create and consume an Either, let's look at a slightly more interesting example. Imagine a function that performs a simple calculation:

$$f(x, y) \rightarrow sqrt(x / y)$$

For the calculation to be performed correctly, we need to ensure that y is non-zero and that the ratio x/y is non-negative. If one of these conditions isn't met, we'd like to know which one. So the calculation returns, let's say, a double in the happy path, and a string with an error message otherwise. That means the return of this function should be Either<string, double>—remember, the successful type is the one on the right. Here's the implementation.

Listing 6.1   Capturing error details with Either

```
using static System.Math;

Either<string, double> Calc(double x, double y)
{
    if (y == 0) return "y cannot be 0";

    if (x != 0 && Sign(x) != Sign(y))
        return "x / y cannot be negative";

    return Sqrt(x / y);
}
```

The signature of Calc clearly declares that it will return a structure wrapping "either a string, or a double," and indeed the implementation returns either a string (an error message) or a double (the result of the computation). In either case, the returned value will be implicitly lifted into an Either.

Let's test it out in the REPL:

```
Calc(3, 0)   // => Left("y cannot be 0")
Calc(-3, 3)  // => Left("x / y cannot be negative")
Calc(-3, -3) // => Right(1)
```

Because Either is so similar to Option, you might guess that the core functions you've seen in relation to Option will have counterparts for Either. Let's find out.

6.1.2   Core functions for working with Either

Like with `Option`, we can define `Map`, `ForEach`, and `Bind` in terms of `Match`. The `Left` case is used to signal failure, so the computation is skipped in the `Left` case:

```
public static Either<L, RR> Map<L, R, RR>
    (this Either<L, R> either, Func<R, RR> f)
    => either.Match<Either<L, RR>>(
        l => Left(l),
        r => Right(f(r)));

public static Either<L, Unit> ForEach<L, R>
    (this Either<L, R> either, Action<R> act)
    => Map(either, act.ToFunc());

public static Either<L, RR> Bind<L, R, RR>
    (this Either<L, R> either, Func<R, Either<L, RR>> f)
    => either.Match(
        l => Left(l),
        r => f(r));
```

In the `Left` case, the computation is skipped and the `Left` value is passed along.

There are a couple of things to point out here. In all cases, the function is applied *only* if the `Either` is `Right`.[2] This means that if we think of `Either` as a fork, then whenever we take the left path, we go to a dead end.

Also notice that when you use `Map` and `Bind`, the R type changes. Just as `Option<T>` is a functor on T, `Either<L, R>` is a functor on R, meaning that you can use `Map` to apply functions to R. The L type, on the other hand, remains the same.

What about `Where`? Remember, you can call `Where` with a predicate and "filter out" the inner value of an `Option` if it fails to satisfy the predicate:

```
Option<int> three = Some(3);

three.Where(i => i % 2 == 0) // => None
three.Where(i => i % 2 != 0) // => Some(3)
```

With `Either`, you can't do that: failure to meet a condition should yield a `Left`, but because `Where` takes a predicate, and a predicate only returns a Boolean, there's no reasonable value type L with which you can populate the `Left` value. It's probably easier to see if you try to implement `Where` for `Either`:

```
public static Either<L, R> Where<L, R>
    (this Either<L, R> either, Func<R, bool> predicate)
    => either.Match(
        l => either,
        r => predicate(r)
            : either
            ? /* now what? I don't have an L */ );
```

---

[2] This is what's called a *biased* implementation of `Either`. There are also different, *unbiased* implementations of `Either` that aren't used to represent error/success disjunctions, but two equally valid paths. In practice, the biased implementations are much more widely used.

As you can see, if the Either is Right, but its inner value doesn't satisfy the predicate, you should return a Left, but there's no available value of type L with which you could populate a Left.

You've just learned that Where is less general than Map and Bind: it can only be defined for structures for which a *zero* value exists (such as an empty sequence for IEnumerable, or None for Option). There's no *zero* value for Either<L, R> because L is an arbitrary type. You can only cause an Either to fail by explicitly creating a Left, or by calling Bind with a function that may return a suitable L value.

You'll see this in practice in the next example, where I'll show you an Option-based implementation and an Either-based one side by side.

6.1.3 Comparing Option and Either

Imagine we're modeling a recruitment process. We'll start with an Option-based implementation, in which Some(Candidate) represents a candidate that has passed the interview process so far, whereas None represents rejection.

Listing 6.2 An Option-based implementation modeling the recruitment process

```
Func<Candidate, bool> IsEligible;
Func<Candidate, Option<Candidate>> TechTest;
Func<Candidate, Option<Candidate>> Interview;

Option<Candidate> Recruit(Candidate c)
   => Some(c)
      .Where(IsEligible)
      .Bind(TechTest)
      .Bind(Interview);
```

The recruitment process consists of a technical test first, and then an interview. Fail the test, and the interview won't take place. But even prior to the test, we'll check that the candidate is eligible to work. With Option, we can apply the IsEligible predicate with Where so that if the candidate isn't eligible, the subsequent steps won't take place.

Now, imagine that HR isn't happy to just know whether a candidate has passed or not; they also want to know details about the reasons for failure because this information allows them to refine the recruitment process. We can refactor to an Either-based implementation, capturing the reasons for rejection with a Rejection object. The Right type will be Candidate as before, and the Left type will be Rejection.

Listing 6.3 An equivalent Either-based implementation

```
Func<Candidate, bool> IsEligible;
Func<Candidate, Either<Rejection, Candidate>> TechTest;
Func<Candidate, Either<Rejection, Candidate>> Interview;

Either<Rejection, Candidate> CheckEligibility(Candidate c)
{
```

<── Turn the predicate into an Either-returning function.

```
    if (IsEligible(c)) return c;
    else return new Rejection("Not eligible");
}


Either<Rejection, Candidate> Recruit(Candidate c)
   => Right(c)
      .Bind(CheckEligibility)          <—— Apply using Bind.
      .Bind(TechTest)
      .Bind(Interview);
```

We now need to be more explicit about failing the IsEligible test, so we turn this predicate into an Either-returning function, CheckEligibility, providing a suitable Left value (the Rejection) for when the predicate isn't passed. We can now compose CheckEligibility into the workflow using Bind.

Notice that the Either-based implementation is more verbose, and this makes sense, since we choose Either when we need to be explicit about failure conditions.

6.2   *Chaining operations that may fail*

Either lends itself particularly well to representing a chain of operations where any operation may cause a deviation from the happy path. For example, once every so often, you prepare your boy- or girl-friend's favorite dish. The workflow may look like this:

```
    o WakeUpEarly
   / \
  L   R ShopForIngredients
     / \
    L   R CookRecipe
       / \
      L   R EnjoyTogether
```

At each step of the way, something may go wrong: you could oversleep, you could wake up to stormy weather that prevents you from getting to the shops, you could get distracted and let everything burn… In short, only if *everything* goes well do you get to a happy meal together.

Using `Either`, we can model the preceding workflow like so.

Listing 6.4 Using `Bind` to chain several `Either`-returning functions

```
Func<Either<Reason, Unit>> WakeUpEarly;
Func<Unit, Either<Reason, Ingredients>> ShopForIngredients;
Func<Ingredients, Either<Reason, Food>> CookRecipe;

Action<Food> EnjoyTogether;
Action<Reason> ComplainAbout;
Action OrderPizza;

void Start()
{
   WakeUpEarly()
      .Bind(ShopForIngredients)
      .Bind(CookRecipe)
      .Match(
         Right: dish => EnjoyTogether(dish),
         Left: reason =>
         {
            ComplainAbout(reason);
            OrderPizza();
         });
}
```

Remember from the definition of `Bind` that if the state is `Left`, the `Left` value just gets passed along. So in the preceding listing, when we say `ComplainAbout(reason)`, the reason is whatever failed in *any* of the previous steps: if we failed to wake up, `ComplainAbout` will receive the reason for that; likewise if we failed to shop, and so on.

The previous tree-like diagram is a correct logical representation of the workflow; another way to look at it, closer to the implementation details, is shown in figure 6.2.

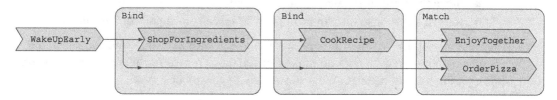

Figure 6.2 Chaining `Either`-returning functions

Each function returns a two-part structure, the `Either`, and is chained with the next function via `Bind`. A workflow obtained by chaining several `Either`-returning functions can be seen as a two-track system:[3]

---

[3] In a tutorial on this style of error handling, F# evangelist Scott Wlaschin builds a "railway" analogy. I encourage you to look at his "Railway Oriented Programming" article and video conference, available on his site at http://fsharpforfunandprofit.com/rop/.

- There's a *main track* (the happy path), going from R1 to Rn.
- There's an auxiliary, *parallel track*, on the Left side.
- Once you're on the Left track, you stay on it until the end of the road.
- If you're on the Right track, with each function application, you will either proceed along the Right track, or be diverted to the Left track.
- Match is the end of the road, where the disjunction of the parallel tracks takes place.

Although the "favorite dish" example is rather frivolous, it's representative of many programming scenarios. For example, imagine a stateless server that, upon receiving a request, must perform the following steps:

1 Validate the request.
2 Load the model from the DB.
3 Make changes to the model.
4 Persist changes.

Any of these operations could potentially fail, and failure at any step should prevent the workflow from continuing, and the response should include details about the success or failure of the requested operation.

Next, we'll look at using Either in such a scenario.

6.3   *Validation: a perfect use case for Either*

Let's revisit the scenario of requesting a money transfer, but in this case we'll address the simpler scenario in which a client explicitly requests a transfer to be carried out on some future date.

The application should do the following:

1 Validate the request.
2 Store the transfer details for future execution.
3 Return a response with an indication of success, or details of any failure.

We can model the fact that the operation may fail with Either. If the transfer request is successfully stored, there's no meaningful data to return to the client, so the Right type parameter will be Unit. What should the Left type be?

6.3.1   *Choosing a suitable representation for errors*

Let's look at a few types you could use to capture error details. You saw that when applying functions to Either via Map or Bind, the Right type changes, while the Left type remains the same. So once you choose a type for Left, this type will remain the same throughout the workflow.

I've used string in some of the previous examples, but this seems limiting; you might want to add more structured details about the errors. What about Exception? It's a base class that can be extended with arbitrarily rich subtypes. Here, however, the semantics are wrong: Exception denotes that something exceptional has occurred. Instead, here we're coding for errors that are "business as usual."

Instead, I've included a very simple base Error class, exposing just a Message property. We can subclass this for specific errors.

Listing 6.5   A base class for representing failure

```
namespace LaYumba.Functional
{
    public class Error
    {
        public virtual string Message { get; }
    }
}
```

Although, strictly speaking, the representation of Error is part of the domain, this is a general enough requirement that I've added the type to the functional library. My recommended approach is to *create one subclass for each error type*.

For example, here are some error types we'll need in order to represent some cases of failed validation.

Listing 6.6   Distinct types capture details about specific errors

```
namespace Boc.Domain
{
    public sealed class InvalidBic : Error
    {
        public override string Message { get; }
            = "The beneficiary's BIC/SWIFT code is invalid";
    }

    public sealed class TransferDateIsPast : Error
    {
        public override string Message { get; }
            = "Transfer date cannot be in the past";
    }
}
```

And, for convenience, we'll add a static class, Errors, that contains factory functions for creating specific subclasses of Error:

```
public static class Errors
{
    public static InvalidBic InvalidBic
        => new InvalidBic();

    public static TransferDateIsPast TransferDateIsPast
        => new TransferDateIsPast();
}
```

This is a trick that will help us keep the code where the business decisions are made cleaner, as you'll see below. It also provides good documentation, because it gives us an overview of all the specific errors defined for the domain.

6.3.2 *Defining an Either-based API*

Let's assume that the details about the transfer request are captured in a data-transfer object of type `BookTransfer`: this is what we receive from the client, and it's the input data for our workflow. We've also established that the workflow should return an `Either<Error, Unit>`; that is, nothing of note in case of success, or an `Error` with details of failure.

That means the main function we need to implement to represent this workflow has type

```
BookTransfer → Either<Error, Unit>
```

We're now ready to introduce a skeleton of the implementation. Notice the preceding signature is captured in `Handle`:

```
public class BookTransferController : Controller
{
    Either<Error, Unit> Handle(BookTransfer cmd)
       => Validate(cmd)
           .Bind(Save);

    Either<Error, BookTransfer> Validate(BookTransfer cmd)
       => // TODO: add validation...

    Either<Error, Unit> Save(BookTransfer cmd)
       => // TODO: save the request...
}
```

Uses `Bind` to chain two operations that may fail

Uses `Either` to acknowledge that validation may fail

Uses `Either` to acknowledge that persisting the request may fail

The `Handle` method defines the high-level workflow: first validate, then persist. Both `Validate` and `Save` return an `Either` to acknowledge that the operation may fail. Also note that the signature of `Validate` is `Either<Error, BookTransfer>`. That is, we need the `BookTransfer` command on the right side, so that the transfer data is available and can be piped to `Save`.

Next, let's add some validation.

6.3.3 *Adding validation logic*

Let's start by validating a couple of simple conditions about the request:

- That the date for the transfer is indeed in the future
- That the provided BIC code is in the right format[4]

We can have a function perform each validation. The typical scheme will be as follows:

---

[4] The BIC code is a standard identifier for a bank branch, also known as SWIFT code.

```
Regex bicRegex = new Regex("[A-Z]{11}");

Either<Error, BookTransfer> ValidateBic(BookTransfer cmd)
{
    if (!bicRegex.IsMatch(cmd.Bic))
        return Errors.InvalidBic;

    else return cmd;
}
```

Failure: the error will be wrapped in an `Either` in the `Left` state.

Success: the original request will be wrapped in an `Either` in the `Right` state.

That is, each validator function takes a request as input and returns *either* the (validated) request *or* the appropriate error. (I would normally use the ternary `if` operator here, but it doesn't work well with implicit conversion.)

Each validation function is a world-crossing function (going from a "normal" value, `BookTransfer`, to an "elevated" value, `Either<Error, BookTransfer>`), so we can combine several of these functions using `Bind`.

Listing 6.7   Chaining several validation functions with `Bind`

```
public class BookTransferController : Controller
{
    DateTime now;
    Regex bicRegex = new Regex("[A-Z]{11}");

    Either<Error, Unit> Handle(BookTransfer cmd)
        => Right(cmd)
            .Bind(ValidateBic)
            .Bind(ValidateDate)
            .Bind(Save);

    Either<Error, BookTransfer> ValidateBic(BookTransfer cmd)
    {
        if (!bicRegex.IsMatch(cmd.Bic))
            return Errors.InvalidBic;
        else return cmd;
    }

    Either<Error, BookTransfer> ValidateDate(BookTransfer cmd)
    {
        if (cmd.Date.Date <= now.Date)
            return Errors.TransferDateIsPast;
        else return cmd;
    }

    Either<Error, Unit> Save(BookTransfer cmd) => //...
}
```

Lifts the command into an `Either`

Applies all subsequent operations that can fail with `Bind`

In summary, use `Either` to acknowledge that an operation may fail and `Bind` to chain several operations that may fail. But if the application internally uses `Either` to represent outcomes, how should it represent outcomes to client applications that communicate with it over some protocol such as HTTP? This is a question that also applies to `Option`. Whenever you use these elevated types, you'll need to define a translation when communicating with other applications. We'll look at this next.

6.4   *Representing outcomes to client applications*

You've now seen quite a few use cases for using `Option` and `Either`. Both types can be seen as representing outcomes: in the case of `Option`, `None` can signify failure; in the case of `Either`, it's `Left`. We've defined `Option` and `Either` as C# types, but in this section you'll see how you can translate them to the outside world.

Although we've defined `Match` for both types, we've used it quite rarely, relying instead on `Map`, `Bind`, and `Where` to define workflows. Remember, the key difference here is that the latter work *within the abstraction* (you start with, say, Option<T>, and end up with an Option<R>). `Match`, on the other hand, allows you to *leave the abstraction* (you start with Option<T> and end up with an R). See figure 6.3.

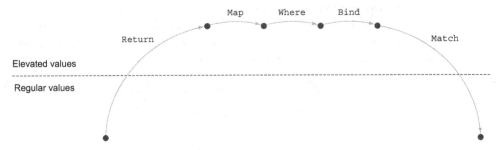

Figure 6.3   With `Option` and `Either`, `Match` is used to leave the abstraction.

As a general rule, once you've introduced an abstraction like `Option`, it's best to stick with it as long as possible. What does "as long as possible" mean? Ideally, it means that you'll leave the abstract world when you cross application boundaries.

It's good practice to design applications with some separation between the application *core*, which contains services and domain logic, and an outer layer containing a set of adapters, through which your application interacts with the outside world. You can see your application as an orange, where the skin is composed of a layer of adapters, as shown in figure 6.4.

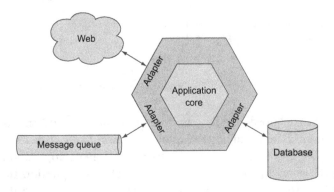

Figure 6.4   The outer layer of an application consists of adapters.

Abstractions such as `Option` and `Either` are useful within the application core, but they may not translate well to the message contract expected by the interacting applications. Thus, the outer layer is where you need to leave the abstraction and translate to the representation expected by your client applications.

6.4.1 Exposing an Option-like interface

Imagine that within our banking scenario we have an API that, given a "ticker" (an identifier for a stock or other financial instrument, such as AAPL, GOOG, or MSFT), returns details about the requested financial instrument. These details could include the market on which the instrument is traded, the current price level, and so on.

Within the application core, we could have a service that exposes this functionality:

```
public interface IInstrumentService
{
    Option<InstrumentDetails> GetInstrumentDetails(string ticker);
}
```

We can't know whether the string given as `ticker` actually identifies a valid instrument, so this is modeled within the application core with `Option`.

Next, let's see how we can expose this data to the outer world. We'll create an API endpoint by mapping it to a method on a class extending `Controller`. The controller effectively acts as an adapter between the application core and the clients consuming the API.

The API returns, let's say, JSON over HTTP—a format and protocol that doesn't deal in `Options`—so the controller is the last point where we can "translate" our `Option` into something that's supported by that protocol. This is where we'll use `Match`. We could implement the controller as in the following listing.

Listing 6.8 Translating None to status code 404

```
using Microsoft.AspNet.Mvc;

public class InstrumentsController : Controller
{
    Func<string, Option<InstrumentDetails>> getInstrumentDetails;

    [HttpGet, Route("api/instruments/{ticker}/details")]
    public IActionResult GetInstrumentDetails(string ticker)
        => getInstrumentDetails(ticker)
            .Match<IActionResult>(
                () => NotFound(),
                (result) => Ok(result));
}
```

None is mapped to a 404.

Some is mapped to a 200.

In fact, the preceding method body can be written more tersely:

```
=> getInstrumentDetails(ticker)
    .Match<IActionResult>(
        None: NotFound,
        Some: Ok);
```

(It could be written even more tersely, without the parameter names.)

 POINT-FREE STYLE   This style of omitting the explicit parameter (in our case, `result`) is sometimes called "point-free" because the "data points" are omitted. It's a bit daunting at first, but it's cleaner once you get used to it.

Let's pause and see why we can write this so concisely. Remember, `Match` expects the following:

- A nullary function to invoke if the `Option` is `None`
- A function accepting the type of the `Option`'s inner value, to invoke if the `Option` is `Some`

Particularized for the current case, where `T` is `InstrumentDetails` and the desired result type is `IActionResult`, we need functions of these types:

```
None : () → IActionResult
Some : InstrumentDetails → IActionResult
```

Here we use two methods defined on the base `Controller` class:

- `HttpNotFound`—To translate `None` as a 404 response
- `Ok`—To translate the `Option`'s inner value to a response with a status code of 200

Let's look at the types of these methods:

```
HttpNotFound : () → HttpNotFoundResult
Ok : object → HttpOkObjectResult
```

The types line up because both `HttpOkObjectResult` and `HttpNotFoundResult` implement `IActionResult`, and naturally `InstrumentDetails` is an `object`.

You've now seen how you can take a workflow modeled with an `Option`-based interface and expose it through an HTTP API. Next, let's see about an `Either`-based interface.

6.4.2   *Exposing an Either-like interface*

Just like with `Option`, once you've lifted your value to the elevated world of `Either`, it's best to stay there until the end of the workflow. But all good things must come to an end, so at some point you'll need to leave your application domain and expose a representation of your `Either` to the external world.

Let's go back to the banking scenario we looked at in this chapter—that of a request from a client to book a transfer on a future date. Our service layer returns an `Either<Error, Unit>` and we must translate that to, say, JSON over HTTP.

One approach is similar to what we just looked at for `Option`: we can use HTTP status code 400 to signal that we received a bad request.

Listing 6.9 Translating `Left` to status code 400

```
public class BookTransferController : Controller
{
    private IHandler<BookTransfer> transfers;

    [HttpPost, Route("api/transfers/future")]
    public IActionResult BookTransfer([FromBody] BookTransfer request)
        => transfers.Handle(request).Match<IActionResult>(
            Left: BadRequest,
            Right: _ => Ok());
}
```

This works. The only downside is that the convention of how business validation relates to HTTP error codes is very shaky. Some people will argue that 400 signals a *syntactically* incorrect request—not a *semantically* incorrect request, as is the case here.

In situations of concurrency, a request that's valid when the request is made may no longer be valid when the server receives it (for example, the account balance may have gone down). Does a 400 convey this?

Instead of trying to figure out which HTTP status code best suits a particular error scenario (after all, HTTP wasn't designed with RESTful APIs in mind), another approach is to return a representation of the outcome in the response. We'll explore this option next.

6.4.3 *Returning a result DTO*

This approach involves always returning a successful status code (because, at a low level, the response was correctly received and processed), along with an arbitrarily rich representation of the outcome in the response body.

This representation is just a simple data transfer object (DTO) that represents the full result, with its left and right components.

Listing 6.10 A DTO representing the outcome, to be serialized in the response

```
public class ResultDto<T>
{
    public bool Succeeded { get; }
    public bool Failed => !Succeeded;

    public T Data { get; }
    public Error Error { get; }

    public ResultDto(T data) { Succeeded = true; Data = data; }
    public ResultDto(Error error) { Error = error; }
}
```

This `ResultDto` is very similar to `Either`. But unlike `Either`, whose internal values are only accessible via higher-order functions, the DTO exposes them for easy serialization and access on the client side.

We can then define a utility function that translates an `Either` to a `ResultDto`:

```
public static ResultDto<T> ToResult<T>(this Either<Error, T> either)
   => either.Match(
      Left: error => new ResultDto<T>(error),
      Right: data => new ResultDto<T>(data));
```

Now we can just expose the `Result` in our API method, as follows.

Listing 6.11   Returning error details as part of a successful response payload

```
public class BookTransferController : Controller
{
   [HttpPost, Route("api/transfers/book")]
   public ResultDto<Unit> BookTransfer([FromBody] BookTransfer cmd)
      => Handle(cmd).ToResult();

   Either<Error, Unit> Handle(BookTransfer cmd) //...
}
```

This approach means, overall, less code in your controllers. More importantly, it means you're not relying on the idiosyncrasies of the HTTP protocol in your representation of results, but can instead create the structure that best suits you to represent whatever conditions you choose to see as `Left`.

In the end, both approaches are viable and both are used in APIs in the wild. Which approach you choose has more to do with API design than with functional programming. The point is that you'll generally have to make some choices when exposing to client applications outcomes that you can model with `Either` in your application.

I've illustrated "lowering" values from abstractions through the example of an HTTP API, since this is such a common requirement, but the concepts don't change if you expose another kind of endpoint. In summary, use `Match` if you're in the skin of the orange; stay with the juicy abstractions within the core of the orange.

6.5   *Variations on the Either theme*

`Either` takes us a long way toward functional error handling. In contrast to exceptions, which cause the program to "jump" out of its normal execution flow and into an exception handling block in some arbitrary function up the stack, `Either` maintains the normal program execution flow and instead *returns* a representation of the outcome.

So there's a lot to be liked about `Either`. There are also some possible objections:

- The Left type always stays the same, so how can you compose functions that return an Either with a different Left type?
- Always having to specify two generic arguments makes the code too verbose.
- The names Either, Left, and Right are too cryptic. Can't we have something more user-friendly?

In this section, I'll address these concerns and see how they can be mitigated with some variations on the Either pattern.

6.5.1 *Changing between different error representations*

As you saw, Map and Bind allow you to change the R type, but not the L type. Although having a homogeneous representation for errors is preferable, it may not always be possible. What if you write a library where the L type is always Error, and someone else writes a library where it's always string? How can you to integrate the two?

It turns out this can be resolved simply with an overload of Map that allows you to apply a function to the left value *as well as* the right one. This overload takes an Either<L, R>, and then not one but *two* functions: one of type $(L \to LL)$, which will be applied to the left value (if present), and another one of type $(R \to RR)$ to be applied to the right value:

```
public static Either<LL, RR> Map<L, LL, R, RR>
   (this Either<L, R> either, Func<L, LL> left, Func<R, RR> right)
   => either.Match<Either<LL, RR>>(
      l => Left(left(l)),
      r => Right(right(r)));
```

This variation of Map allows you to arbitrarily change both types, so that you can interoperate between functions where the L types are different.[5] Here's an example:

```
Either<Error, int> Run(double x, double y)
   => Calc(x, y)
      .Map(
         left: msg => Error(msg),
         right: d => d)
      .Bind(ToIntIfWhole);

Either<string, double> Calc(double x, double y) //...
Either<Error, int> ToIntIfWhole(double d) //...
```

It's best to avoid the noise and stick to a consistent representation for errors, but different representations aren't a stumbling block.

---

[5] Because there's no shortage of terminology in FP, functors for which a Map in this form is defined are called *bifunctors*, and in languages without method overloading, the function is called BiMap.

6.5.2 *Specialized versions of Either*

Let's look at the other shortcomings of using `Either` in C#.

First, having two generic arguments adds noise to the code.[6] For example, imagine you want to capture multiple validation errors, and for this you choose `IEnumerable<Error>` as your `Left` type. You'd end up with signatures that look like this:

```
public Either<IEnumerable<Error>, Rates> RefreshRates(string id) //...
```

You now have to read through three things (`Either`, `IEnumerable`, and `Error`) before you get to the most meaningful part, the desired return type `Rates`. Compared to signatures that say nothing about failure, as we discussed in chapter 3, it seems we've fallen into the opposite extreme.

Second, the very names `Either`, `Left`, and `Right` are too abstract. Software development is complex enough, so we should opt for the most intuitive names possible.

Both issues can be addressed by using more specialized versions of `Either` that have a fixed type to represent failure (hence, a single generic parameter), and more user-friendly names. Note that such variations on `Either` are common, but not standardized. You'll find a multitude of different libraries and tutorials that each have their own minor variations in terminology and behavior.

For this reason, I thought it best to first give you a thorough understanding of `Either`, which is ubiquitous and well established in the literature and will allow you to grasp any variations you may encounter. (You can then choose the representation that serves you best, or even implement your own type for representing outcomes if you're so inclined.)

`LaYumba.Functional` includes the following two variations for representing outcomes:

- `Validation<T>`—You can think of this as an `Either` that has been *particularized* to `IEnumerable<Error>`:

  ```
  Validation<T> = Invalid(IEnumerable<Error>) | Valid(T)
  ```

  `Validation` is just like an `Either` where the failure case is fixed to `IEnumerable<Error>`, making it possible to capture multiple validation errors.

- `Exceptional<T>`—Here, failure is fixed to `System.Exception`:

  ```
  Exceptional<T> = Exception | Success(T)
  ```

  `Exceptional` can be used as a bridge between an exception-based API and functional error handling, as you'll see in the next example.

---

[6] You can look at this as a shortcoming of `Either`, or of C#'s type system. `Either` is successfully used in the ML-languages, where types can (nearly) always be inferred, so even complex generic types don't add any noise to the code. This is a classic example showing that although the principles of FP are language-independent, they need to be adapted based on the strengths and weaknesses of each particular language.

Table 6.2 shows these variations side by side.

Table 6.2 Some particularized versions of `Either` and their state names

Type	Success case	Failure case	Failure type
Either<L, R>	Right	Left	L
Validation<T>	Valid	Invalid	IEnumerable<Error>
Exceptional<T>	Success	Exception	Exception

These new types have friendlier, more intuitive names than `Either`, and you'll see an example of using them next.

6.5.3 *Refactoring to Validation and Exceptional*

Let's go back to the scenario of a user booking a money transfer for future execution. Previously we modeled the simple workflow that included validation and persistence—both of which could fail—with `Either`. Let's now see how the implementation would change by using the more specific `Validation` and `Exceptional` instead.

A function that performs validation should, naturally, yield a `Validation`. In our scenario, its type would be

```
Validate : BookTransfer → Validation<BookTransfer>
```

Because `Validation` is just like `Either`, particularized to the `Error` type, the implementation of the validation functions would be the same as in the previous `Either`-based implementation, except for the change in signature. Here's an example:

```
DateTime now;

Validation<BookTransfer> ValidateDate(BookTransfer cmd)
{
    if (cmd.Date.Date <= now.Date)
        return Invalid(Errors.TransferDateIsPast);    ⟵  Wraps an Error in
                                                           a Validation in
                                                           the Invalid state
    else return Valid(cmd);    ⟵  Wraps the command in a
}                                 Validation in the Valid state
```

As usual, implicit conversion is defined, so in this example you could omit the calls to `Valid` and `Invalid`.

BRIDGING BETWEEN AN EXCEPTION-BASED API AND FUNCTIONAL ERROR HANDLING

Next, let's look at persistence. Unlike validation, failure here would indicate a fault in the infrastructure or configuration, or another technical error. We consider such errors exceptional,[7] so we can model this with `Exceptional`:

```
Save : BookTransfer → Exceptional<Unit>
```

---

[7] In this context, *exceptional* doesn't necessarily mean "occurring very rarely"; it denotes a technical error, as opposed to an error from the point of view of the business logic.

The implementation of Save could look something like the following.

Listing 6.12   Translating an Exception-based API to an Exceptional value

```
string connString;
                              The return type acknowledges
                              the possibility of an exception.

Exceptional<Unit> Save(BookTransfer transfer)    ◁
{
    try                                                  The call to a third-
    {                                                    party API that
        ConnectionHelper.Connect(connString             throws an exception
            , c => c.Execute("INSERT ...", transfer));  is wrapped in a try.
    }
    catch (Exception ex) { return ex; }     ◁───  The exception is wrapped
    return Unit();        ◁──────────            in an Exceptional in the
}                                                Exception state.
        The resulting Unit is wrapped in an
        Exceptional in the Success state.
```

Notice that the scope of the try/catch is *as small as possible*: we want to catch any exceptions that may be raised when connecting to the database, and immediately translate to the functional style, wrapping the result in an Exceptional. As usual, implicit conversion will create an appropriately initialized Exceptional.

Notice how this pattern allows us to go from a third-party exception-throwing API to a functional API, where errors are handled as payload and the possibility of errors is reflected in the return type.

FAILED VALIDATION AND TECHNICAL ERRORS SHOULD BE HANDLED DIFFERENTLY

The nice thing about using Validation and Exceptional is that they have distinct semantic connotations:

- Validation indicates that some business rule has been violated.
- Exception denotes an unexpected technical error.

We'll now look at how using these different representations allows us to handle each case appropriately. We still need to combine validation and persistence; this is done in Handle here:

```
            public class BookTransferController : Controller
            {
                Validation<Exceptional<Unit>> Handle(BookTransfer cmd)
                    => Validate(cmd)
Combines            .Map(Save);
validation and
persistence     Validation<BookTransfer> Validate(BookTransfer cmd)
                    => ValidateBic(cmd)
Top-level validation    .Bind(ValidateDate);
function combining
various validations  Validation<BookTransfer> ValidateBic(BookTransfer cmd) // ...
                Validation<BookTransfer> ValidateDate(BookTransfer cmd) // ...

                Exceptional<Unit> Save(BookTransfer cmd) // ...
            }
```

Because Validate returns a Validation, whereas Save returns an Exceptional, we can't compose these types with Bind. But that's OK: we can use Map instead, and end up with the return type Validation<Exceptional<Unit>>. This is a nested type expressing the fact that we're combining the *effect* of validation (that is, we may get validation errors instead of the desired return value) with the *effect* of exception handling (that is, even after validation passes, we may get an exception instead of the return value).[8]

As a result, Handle is acknowledging that the operation may fail for business reasons *as well as* technical reasons by "stacking" the two monadic effects. Figure 6.5 illustrates how in both cases we express errors by including them as part of the payload.

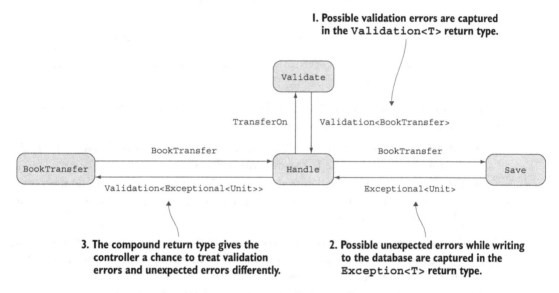

Figure 6.5   Errors are treated as part of the returned payload.

To complete the end-to-end scenario, we need only add the entry point. This is where the controller receives a BookTransfer command from the client, invokes Handle as defined previously, and translates the resulting Validation<Exceptional<Unit>> into a result to send back to the client (see listing 6.13).

---

[8] Remember, these are "monadic effects," *not* "side effects," but in FP-speak they're simply called "effects."

Listing 6.13 Different treatment for validation errors and exceptional errors

```
public class BookTransferController : Controller
{
    ILogger<BookTransferController> logger;

    [HttpPost, Route("api/transfers/book")]
    public IActionResult BookTransfer([FromBody] BookTransfer cmd)
        => Handle(cmd).Match(
            Invalid: BadRequest,
            Valid: result => result.Match(
                Exception: OnFaulted,
                Success: _ => Ok()));

    IActionResult OnFaulted(Exception ex)
    {
        logger.LogError(ex.Message);
        return StatusCode(500, Errors.UnexpectedError);
    }
    Validation<Exceptional<Unit>> Handle(BookTransfer cmd) //...
}
```

Unwraps the value inside the Validation → (points to `=> Handle(cmd).Match(`)

If validation failed, sends a 400 ← (points to `Invalid: BadRequest,`)

Unwraps the value inside the Exceptional → (points to `Valid: result => result.Match(`)

If persistence failed, sends a 500 ← (points to `Success: _ => Ok()));`)

Here we use two nested calls to Match to first unwrap the value inside the Validation, and then the value inside the Exceptional:

- If validation failed, we send a 400, which will include the full details of the validation errors, so that the user can address them.
- If persistence failed, on the other hand, we don't want to send the details to the user. Instead we return a 500 with a more generic error type; this is also a good place to log the exception.

As you can see, an explicit return type from each of the functions involved allows you to clearly distinguish and customize how you treat failures related to business rules versus those related to technical issues.

In summary, Either gives you an explicit, functional way to handle errors without introducing side effects (unlike throwing/catching exceptions). But as our relatively simple banking scenario illustrates, using specialized versions of Either, such as Validation and Exceptional, leads to an even more expressive and readable implementation.

6.5.4 *Leaving exceptions behind?*

In this chapter you've gained a solid understanding of the ideas behind functional error handling.[9] You may feel this is a radical departure from the exception-based approach, and indeed it is.

I mentioned that throwing exceptions disrupts the normal program flow, introducing side effects. More pragmatically, it makes your code more difficult to maintain and reason about: if a function throws an exception, the only way to analyze the implications

---

[9] We'll revisit error handling in part 3, in the context of laziness and asynchrony, but the fundamental aspects have all been covered in this chapter.

of this for the application is to follow all possible code paths into the function, and then look for the first exception handler up the stack. With functional error handling, errors are just part of the return type of the function, so you can still reason about the function in isolation.

Having realized the detrimental effects of using exceptions, several younger programming languages such as Go, Elixir, and Elm have embraced the idea that errors should simply be treated as values, so that equivalents to the throw and try/catch statements are used only very rarely (Elixir), or are absent from the language altogether (Go, Elm). The fact that C# includes exceptions doesn't mean you need to use them for error handling; instead, you can use functional error handling within your application, and use adapter functions to convert the outcomes of calls to exception-based APIs to something like Exceptional, as shown previously.

Are there any cases in which exceptions are still useful? I believe so:

- *Developer errors*—For example, if you're trying to remove an item from an empty list, or if you're passing a null value to a function that requires that value, it's OK for that function or for the list implementation to throw an exception. Such exceptions are never meant to be caught and handled in the calling code; they indicate that the application logic is wrong.
- *Configuration errors*—For example, if an application relies on a message bus to connect to other systems and can't effectively perform anything useful unless connected, failure to connect to the bus upon startup should result in an exception. The same applies if a critical piece of configuration, like a database connection, is missing. These exceptions should only be thrown upon initialization and aren't meant to be caught (other than possibly in an outermost, application-wide handler), but should rightly cause the application to crash.

Exercises

1 Write a ToOption extension method to convert an Either into an Option; the left value is thrown away if present. Then write a ToEither method to convert an Option into an Either, with a suitable parameter that can be invoked to obtain the appropriate Left value if the Option is None. (Tip: start by writing the function signatures in arrow notation.)

2 Take a workflow where two or more functions that return an Option are chained using Bind. Then change the first of the functions to return an Either. This should cause compilation to fail. Either can be converted into an Option, as you saw in the previous exercise, so write extension overloads for Bind so that functions returning Either and Option can be chained with Bind, yielding an Option.

3 Write a function with signature

```
TryRun : (() → T) → Exceptional<T>
```

that runs the given function in a try/catch, returning an appropriately populated Exceptional.

4 Write a function with signature

```
Safely : ((() → R), (Exception → L)) → Either<L, R>
```

that runs the given function in a try/catch, returning an appropriately populated Either.

Summary

- Use Either to represent the result of an operation with two different possible outcomes, typically success or failure. An Either can be in one of two states:
  - Left indicates failure and contains error information for an unsuccessful operation.
  - Right indicates success and contains the result of a successful operation.
- Interact with Either using the equivalents of the core functions already seen with Option:
  - Map and Bind apply the mapped/bound function *if* the Either is in the Right state; otherwise they just pass along the Left value.
  - Match works similarly to how it does with Option, allowing you to handle the Right and Left cases differently.
  - Where is not readily applicable, so Bind should be used in its stead for filtering, while providing a suitable Left value.
- Either is particularly useful for combining several validation functions with Bind, or, more generally, for combining several operations, each of which can fail.
- Because Either is rather abstract, and because of the syntactic overhead of its two generic arguments, in practice it's better to use a particularized version of Either, such as Validation and Exceptional.
- When working with functors and monads, prefer using functions that stay within the abstraction, like Map and Bind. Use the downward-crossing Match function as little or as late as possible.

Structuring an application with functions

7

Structuring a complex, real-world application is no easy task. There are entire books written on the subject, so this chapter by no means aims to provide a comprehensive view. We'll focus on the techniques that you can use to modularize and compose an application consisting entirely of functions, and how the result compares to how this is usually done in OOP.

We'll get there gradually. First, you'll need to learn about a classic but fairly low-level functional technique called *partial application*. This allows you to write highly general functions whose behavior is parameterized, and then supply those parameters, obtaining more specialized functions that have the parameters given so far "baked in."

We'll then look at how partial application can be used in practice to first specify configuration arguments that are available at startup, and purely runtime arguments later, as they're received.

Finally, we'll look at how you can take the approach one step further and use partial application for dependency injection, to the point of composing an entire application out of functions, without losing any of the granularity or decoupling you'd expect when composing it with objects.

7.1   *Partial application: supplying arguments piecemeal*

Imagine that you're having your house redecorated. Your interior designer, Ada, calls Fred, her trusted paint supplier:

Clearly, the shop needs to know both *what* the customer wants to buy and *how much* in order to fulfill the order, and in this case the information was given at different points in time. Why? Well, it's Ada's responsibility to choose the color and brand (she wouldn't trust Bruno to remember the exact color and brand she wants). Bruno, on the other hand, has the task of measuring the surface and calculating the amount of paint required, and of picking it up from the supplier.

What I've just described is a real-life analogy of partial application. In programming, this means giving a function its input arguments piecemeal. Just as in my real-life example, this has to do with *separation of concerns*: it may be best to provide the various arguments that a function needs at different points in the application lifecycle, and from different components.

Let's see this in code. The idea here is that you have a function that needs several pieces of information to do its work (analogous to Fred, the paint supplier). For instance, in the following listing we have the function `greet`, which takes a general greeting and a name and produces a greeting personalized for the given name.

Listing 7.1   A binary function mapped over a list

```
using Name = System.String;
using Greeting = System.String;
using PersonalizedGreeting = System.String;

Func<Greeting, Name, PersonalizedGreeting> greet
   = (gr, name) => $"{gr}, {name}";

Name[] names = { "Tristan", "Ivan" };

names.Map(g => greet("Hello", g)).ForEach(WriteLine);
// prints: Hello, Tristan
//         Hello, Ivan
```

 TRY IT IN THE REPL   If you've never used partial application before, it's really important that you type the examples in this section into the REPL to get a hands-on feel for how it works.

The `using` statements at the top of listing 7.1 just allow us to attach some semantic meaning to specific uses of the `string` type, thus making the function signatures more meaningful. You could go the extra mile and define specific types (as discussed in chapter 3), thus ensuring that, say, a `PersonalizedGreeting` can't accidentally be given as input to the `greet` function. But for the present discussion, I'm not too worried about enforcing business rules—just about having meaningful, unequivocal signatures, because we'll be looking at the signatures a lot. So this is the signature of `greet`:

(Greeting, Name) → PersonalizedGreeting

We then have a list of names and map `greet` over the list to obtain a greeting for each name in the list. Notice that the `greet` function is always called with `"Hello"` as its first argument, whereas the second argument varies with each name in the list.

This feels slightly odd. We have a single greeting and *n* names, but we're repeating that one greeting *n* times. Somehow it seems we're repeating ourselves. Wouldn't it be better to "fix" the greeting to be "Hello" outside the scope of `Map`? How can we express the fact that deciding on "Hello" as the general greeting that we'll use for all names in the list is a more general decision that can be taken first, and that the function passed to `Map` should only consume the name?

In listing 7.1 we can't do this because `greet` expects two arguments, and we're using *normal* function application. That is, we call `greet` with the two arguments it expects. (It's called "application" because we're *applying* the function `greet` to its arguments.)

We can solve this with *partial* application. The idea is to allow some code to decide on the general greeting, giving that greeting to greet as its first argument (like how Ada decides on the color). This will generate a new function with "Hello" already baked in as the greeting to use. Some other code can then invoke this function with the name of the person to greet.

There are a couple of ways to make this possible. You'll first see how to write a specific function in a way that supports partial application, and then how to define a general Apply function that will enable partial application for any given function.

7.1.1 *Manually enabling partial application*

One way to supply the arguments independently would be to rewrite the function like so:

```
Func<Greeting, Func<Name, PersonalizedGreeting>> greetWith
   = gr => name => $"{gr}, {name}";
```

This new function, greetWith, takes a single argument, the general greeting, and returns a new function of type Name → Greeting. Notice that when the function is called with its first argument, gr, this is captured in a closure and is therefore "remembered" until the returned function is called with the second argument, name. You'd use it like this:

```
var greetFormally = greetWith("Good evening");
names.Map(greetFormally).ForEach(WriteLine);
// prints: Good evening, Tristan
//         Good evening, Ivan
```

We've achieved our goal of fixing the greeting outside of the scope of Map.

Notice that greet and greetWith rely on the same implementation, but their signatures are different. Let's compare them:

```
greet      : (Greeting, Name) → PersonalizedGreeting
greetWith : Greeting → (Name → PersonalizedGreeting)
```

greetWith is a function that takes a Greeting and returns a function, and this should be clear from the preceding signature. In fact, arrow notation is right-associative, so the parentheses in the second case are redundant, and the type of greetWith would normally be written as follows:

```
greetWith : Greeting → Name → PersonalizedGreeting
```

greetWith is said to be in *curried* form; that is, all arguments are supplied one by one via function invocation (notice there's no comma-separated list of parameters in the signature).

Again, greet and greetWith rely on the same implementation. What changes is the signature and the fact that arguments are provided independently and are captured in closures. This is a good indicator that we should be able to do partial application mechanically, without the need to rewrite the function, so let's look at how to do this next.

7.1.2 Generalizing partial application

In the following example you can see the implementation of a general `Apply` function that provides a given value as the first argument to a binary and ternary function, respectively:

```
public static Func<T2, R> Apply<T1, T2, R>
   (this Func<T1, T2, R> f, T1 t1)
   => t2 => f(t1, t2);

public static Func<T2, T3, R> Apply<T1, T2, T3, R>
   (this Func<T1, T2, T3, R> f, T1 t1)
   => (t2, t3) => func(t1, t2, t3);
```

In the first overload, `Apply` takes a binary function, partially applies it to the given argument, and returns a unary function accepting the second argument. As you can see, it's quite simple: the supplied input argument, `t1`, is captured in a closure, yielding a new function that will call the original function, `f`, whenever the second parameter is provided.

Notice how expression-bodied methods and the lambda notation give us good syntactic support to define this sort of function transformation. The second overload does the same with a ternary function, and similar overloads can be defined for functions of greater arity.

You've now learned that you need not manually create a function like `greetWith`, but could instead just use `Apply` to give the original `greet` function its first argument:

```
var greetInformally = greet.Apply("Hey");
names.Map(greetInformally).ForEach(WriteLine);
// prints: Hey, Tristan
//         Hey, Ivan
```

So what's the pattern here? We're essentially starting with a *general* function (like `greet`) and using partial application to create a *specialized* version of this function (like `greetInformally`). This is now a unary function that can be passed around, and the code that uses it doesn't even need to be aware that this new function was partially applied.

Figure 7.1 graphically summarizes the steps we've covered so far.

In summary, partial application is always about going from general to specific. It allows you to define very general functions and then fine tune their behavior by giving them arguments. Ultimately, writing such general functions ups the level of abstraction and potentially allows greater code reuse.

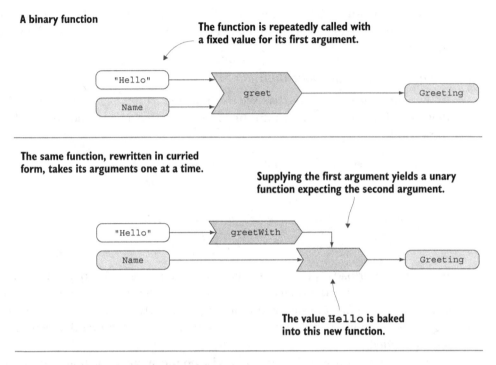

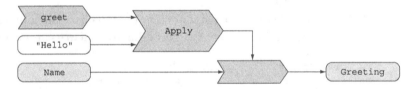

Figure 7.1   Partial application summary

7.1.3   *Order of arguments matters*

The greet function shows what is generally a good order of arguments: the more general parameters, which are likely to be applied early in the life of the application, should come first, followed by the more specific parameters. We learn to say "Hello" early in life, but we keep meeting and greeting new people until we're old.

As a rule of thumb, if you think of a function as an operation, its arguments typically include the following:

- The object(s) that the operation will affect. These are likely to be received late and should be left to last.
- Some options that determine *how* the function will operate, or dependencies that the function requires to do its work, These are likely to be determined early and should come first.

Of course, it's not always easy to establish the best order for parameters. You'll shortly see how you can use partial application even if the order of parameters is wrong for your intended use.

In summary, whenever you have a multi-argument function, and it's desirable to separate the responsibilities of supplying the different arguments it takes, you have a good case for using partial application.

There is, however, one catch that we should iron out before proceeding to more practical uses of partial application. The catch has to do with type inference, and we'll tackle this next.

7.2   Overcoming the quirks of method resolution

So far, we've freely used methods, lambdas, and delegates to *represent* functions. To the compiler, however, these are all different things, and type inference for methods is not as good as we'd like it to be.

Let's first see what happens when things go well, like when we use `Option.Map`:

```
Some(9.0).Map(Math.Sqrt) // => 3.0
```

Here, the name `Math.Sqrt` identifies a *method*, and `Map` expects a delegate of type `Func<T, R>`. More precisely, `Math.Sqrt` identifies a "method group"; because of method overloading, there may be several methods with the same name. The compiler is smart enough to not only pick the right overload (in this case, there's only one), but also to infer the generic types of the `Func`, so that we don't have to specify the type arguments to `Map`:

```
Some(9.0).Map<double, double>(Math.Sqrt)
```

This is all very well and good. It keeps us from having to convert between methods (or, alternatively, lambdas) and delegates, and from specifying the generic types, given that these can be inferred from the method signature. Unfortunately, for methods taking two or more arguments, all this goodness goes away.

Let's see what happens if we try to rewrite the `greet` function as a method—here it's called `GreeterMethod`. What we *would like* to write is this.

Listing 7.2   Type inference fails with multi-argument methods

```
PersonalizedGreeting GreeterMethod(Greeting gr, Name name)
   => $"{gr}, {name}";

Func<Name, PersonalizedGreeting> GreetWith(Greeting greeting)
   => GreeterMethod.Apply(greeting);
```

⊲— If we write our greeting function as a *method*...

⊲— ... then this expression does not compile.

Here we've written the greeter function as a method, and we now want a `GreetWith` method to partially apply it to a given greeting. Unfortunately this code doesn't compile because the name `GreeterMethod` identifies a `MethodGroup`, whereas `Apply` expects a `Func`, and the compiler doesn't make the inference for us.

 TYPE INFERENCE IN LOCAL FUNCTIONS   C# 7 introduces "local functions"—functions that are declared within the scope of a method—but they should actually be called "local methods." Internally they're implemented as methods (even though this gives no benefit—you can't overload them), so in terms of type inference, they have the same characteristics as normal methods.

If you want to use the generic `Apply` to supply arguments to a method, you have to use one of the following forms.

Listing 7.3   Using multi-argument methods as arguments to HOFs requires messy syntax

```
PersonalizedGreeting GreeterMethod(Greeting gr, Name name)
   => $"{gr}, {name}";

Func<Name, PersonalizedGreeting> GreetWith_1(Greeting greeting)
   => FuncExt.Apply<Greeting, Name, PersonalizedGreeting>
         (GreeterMethod, greeting);

Func<Name, PersonalizedGreeting> GreetWith_2(Greeting greeting)
   => new Func<Greeting, Name, PersonalizedGreeting>(GreeterMethod)
      .Apply(greeting);
```

> **Foregoes extension method syntax and provides all generic arguments explicitly**

> **Explicitly converts the method to a delegate before calling `Apply`**

I personally find the syntactic noise in both cases unacceptable. Fortunately, these issues are specific to *method* resolution. They go away if you use delegates (think `Func`) instead. There are different ways to create a delegate.

Listing 7.4   Different ways of obtaining a delegate instance

```
public class TypeInference_Delegate
{
   string separator = "! ";

   // 1. field
   Func<Greeting, Name, PersonalizedGreeting> GreeterField
      = (gr, name) => $"{gr}, {name}";

   // 2. property
   Func<Greeting, Name, PersonalizedGreeting> GreeterProperty
      => (gr, name) => $"{gr}{separator}{name}";

   // 3. factory
   Func<Greeting, T, PersonalizedGreeting> GreeterFactory<T>()
      => (gr, t) => $"{gr}{separator}{t}";
}
```

> **Declaration and initialization of a delegate field; note that you couldn't reference `separator` here.**

> **A getter-only property has its body introduced by `=>`.**

> **A method that acts as a factory of functions can have generic parameters.**

Let's briefly discuss these options. Declaring a delegate field would seem the most natural option. Unfortunately it's not very powerful. For example, if you combine declaration and initialization, as shown in listing 7.4, you can't reference any instance variables, like separator, in the delegate body.

This problem can be overcome by using a property instead. In the class exposing the delegate, this amounts to just replacing = with => to declare a getter-only property, and this is completely transparent to client code. But the most powerful way is to have a *factory* method: a method that's there just to create the delegate you want. The big difference here is that you can also have generic parameters, which isn't possible with fields or properties.

Whichever way you obtain a delegate instance, type resolution will work fine, so that in all cases you can supply the first argument like so:

```
GreeterField.Apply("Hi");
GreeterProperty.Apply("Hi");
GreeterFactory<Name>().Apply("Hi");
```

The takeaway from this section is that if you want to use HOFs that take multi-argument functions as arguments, it's sometimes best to move away from using methods and write Funcs instead—or methods that return Funcs. While less idiomatic than methods, Funcs save you the syntactic overhead of explicitly specifying type arguments, making the code much more readable.

Now that you know about partial application, let's move on to a related concept: currying. It's a technique that assumes and arguably simplifies partial application.

7.3 *Curried functions: optimized for partial application*

Named after mathematician Haskell Curry, *currying* is the process of transforming an *n*-ary function *f* that takes arguments *t1*, *t2*, …, *tn* into a unary function that takes *t1* and yields a new function that takes *t2*, and so on, ultimately returning the same result as *f* once the arguments have all been given.

In other words, an *n*-ary function with signature

```
(T1, T2, ..., Tn) → R
```

when curried, has signature

```
T1 → T2 → ... → Tn → R
```

You've seen an example of this in the first section of this chapter:

```
Func<Greeting, Name, PersonalizedGreeting> greet
   = (gr, name) => $"{gr}, {name}";

Func<Greeting, Func<Name, PersonalizedGreeting>> greetWith
   = gr => name => $"{gr}, {name}";
```

I mentioned that greetWith is like greet, but in curried form. Indeed, compare the signatures:

```
greet      : (Greeting, Name) → PersonalizedGreeting
greetWith : Greeting → Name → PersonalizedGreeting
```

This means that you could call the curried greetWith function like so:

```
greetWith("hello")("world") // => "hello, world"
```

This is two function invocations, and it's effectively the same as calling greet with two arguments. Of course, if you're going to pass in all the parameters at the same time, this is fairly pointless. But it becomes useful when you're interested in partial application.

If a function is curried, partial application is achieved simply by invoking the function:

```
var greetFormally = greetWith("Good evening");
names.Map(greetFormally).ForEach(WriteLine);
// prints: Good evening, Tristan
//         Good evening, Ivan
```

A function can be written in curried form, like greetWith here, and this is called *manual* currying. Alternatively, it's possible to define generic functions that will take an *n*-ary function and curry it. For binary and ternary functions, Curry looks like this:

```
public static Func<T1, Func<T2, R>> Curry<T1, T2, R>
    (this Func<T1, T2, R> func)
    => t1 => t2 => func(t1, t2);

public static Func<T1, Func<T2, Func<T3, R>>> Curry<T1, T2, T3, R>
    (this Func<T1, T2, T3, R> func)
    => t1 => t2 => t3 => func(t1, t2, t3);
```

Similar overloads can be defined for functions of other arities. As an exercise, write the signatures of the preceding functions in arrow notation.

Let's look at how we could use such a generic Curry function to curry the greet function:

```
var greetWith = greet.Curry();
var greetNostalgically = greetWith("Arrivederci");

names.Map(greetNostalgically).ForEach(WriteLine);
// prints: Arrivederci, Tristan
//         Arrivederci, Ivan
```

Of course, if you want to use the generic Curry function, the same caveats about method resolution apply as with Apply.

Partial application and currying are closely related yet distinct concepts, and this is often confusing when you're introduced to them. Let's spell out the differences:

- *Partial application*—You give a function fewer arguments than the function expects, obtaining a function that's particularized with the values of the arguments given so far.
- *Currying*—You don't give any arguments; you just transform an *n*-ary function into a unary function, to which arguments can be successively given to eventually get the same result as the original function.

As you can see, currying doesn't really *do* anything; rather, it "optimizes" a function for partial application. You can do partial application without currying, as we've done previously in this chapter, with the use of the generic `Apply` functions. On the other hand, currying *by itself* is pointless: you curry a function (or write a function in curried form) so that you can more easily use partial application.

Partial application is so commonly used in FP that in many functional languages all functions are curried by default. For this reason, function signatures in arrow notation are given in curried form in the FP literature, like this:

```
T1 → T2 → ... → Tn → R
```

In the rest of the book, I'll always use the curried notation, even for functions that aren't in fact curried.

Even though functions aren't curried by default in C#, you can still take advantage of partial application, allowing you to write highly general—and hence widely reusable—functions by parameterizing their behavior, and then use partial application to create the more specific functions that you'll require from time to time.

As you've seen so far, you can achieve this in different ways:

- By writing functions in curried form
- By currying functions with `Curry`, and then invoking the curried function with subsequent arguments
- By supplying arguments one by one with `Apply`

Which technique you use is a matter of taste, although I personally find that using `Apply` is the most intuitive.

7.4   *Creating a partial-application-friendly API*

Now that you've seen the basic mechanism of partial application, and how to work around poor type inference by using `Func`s instead of methods, we can move on to a more complex scenario, in which we'll use a third party library and realistic real-world requirements.

One good scenario for partial application is when a function requires some configuration that's available at startup and doesn't change, along with more transient arguments that could vary with every invocation. In such cases, a bootstrapping component can supply the configuration arguments, obtaining a specialized function that only expects invocation-specific arguments. This can then be given to the final consumer of the functionality, which is thus freed from having to know anything about configuration.

In this section, we'll look at such an example: that of accessing a SQL database. Imagine an application that, like most, needs to perform a number of queries using different parameters to retrieve different kinds of data from a database.

Let's think about this in terms of partial application:

- Imagine a very general function for retrieving data.
- It can be particularized to query a specific database.
- It can be further particularized to retrieve objects of a given type.
- It can be further particularized with a given query and parameters.

Let's explore this through a simple example: imagine we want to be able to load an `Employee` by ID, or to search for `Employees` by last name. We'd need to implement functions of these types:

```
lookupEmployee : Guid → Option<Employee>
findEmployeesByLastName : string → IEnumerable<Employee>
```

Implementing these functions is our high-level goal. At a low level, we're going to use the Dapper library to query a SQL Server database.[1] For retrieving data, Dapper exposes the `Query` method with the following signature:

```
public static IEnumerable<T> Query<T>
   ( this IDbConnection conn
   , string sqlQuery
   , object param = null
   , SqlTransaction tran = null
   , bool buffered = true)
```

Table 7.1 lists the arguments we need to provide when calling `Query`, including the generic parameter T. We won't worry about the remaining parameters, as the default values are fine for our purposes.

Table 7.1 Arguments to Dapper's `Query` method

T	The type that should be populated from the data returned by the query. In our case, this will be `Employee`—Dapper automatically maps columns to fields.
conn	The connection to the database. (Notice that `Query` is an extension method on the connection, but that doesn't matter as far as partial application is concerned.)
sqlQuery	This is a template for the SQL query you want to execute, such as `"SELECT * FROM EMPLOYEES WHERE ID = @Id"`—notice the `@Id` placeholder.
param	An object whose properties will be used to populate the placeholders in the `sqlQuery`. For instance, the preceding query will need the corresponding `param` object to include a field called `Id`, whose value will be evaluated and rendered in the `sqlQuery` instead of `@Id`.

---

[1] Dapper is a lightweight ORM that has gained a lot of popularity for being fast and simple to use (we used it first in chapter 1). It's available on GitHub at https://github.com/StackExchange/dapper-dot-net and you can find more documentation there.

This is a great example of order of parameters, because the connection and the SQL query can be applied as part of the application setup, whereas the param object will be specific to each call to Query. Right?

Err… well, actually, wrong! SQL connections are lightweight objects and should be obtained and disposed of whenever a query is performed. In fact, as you may remember from chapter 1, the standard use of Dapper's API follows this pattern:

```
using (var conn = new SqlConnection(connString))
{
    conn.Open();
    var result = conn.Query("SELECT 1");
}
```

This means our first parameter, the connection, is less general than the second parameter, the SQL template. But all is not lost. Remember, if you don't like the API you have, you can change it! That's what adapter functions are for.[2] Next, we'll write an API that better supports partial application in order to create specialized functions that retrieve the data we're interested in.

7.4.1 *Types as documentation*

The most general parameter for reading data is the connection string. Many applications connect to a single database, so that the connection string never changes throughout the life of the application, and it can be read from configuration once and for all when the application starts up.

Let's apply an idea introduced in chapter 3—namely, that we can use types to make our code more expressive—and create a dedicated type for connection strings.

Listing 7.5 A custom type for connection strings

```
public class ConnectionString
{
    string Value { get; }
    public ConnectionString(string value) { Value = value; }

    public static implicit operator string(ConnectionString c)
        => c.Value;
    public static implicit operator ConnectionString(string s)
        => new ConnectionString(s);

    public override string ToString() => Value;
}
```

Implicit conversion to and from string

Whenever a string is not just a string, but a DB connection string, we'll wrap it in a ConnectionString. This can be done trivially through implicit conversion.

---

[2] We discussed adapter functions in chapter 1: if you don't like the signature of a function, you can change it by defining a function that calls another and exposes an interface better suited to your needs.

For example, on startup we can populate it from configuration like so:

```
ConnectionString connString = configuration
   .GetSection("ConnectionString").Value;
```

The same thinking applies to the SQL template, so I've also defined a `SqlTemplate` type along the same lines. Most strongly typed functional languages let you define custom types in terms of built-in types with a one-liner like this:

```
type ConnectionString = string
```

In C#, it's a bit more laborious but still worth the effort. First, it makes your function signatures more intention-revealing: you're using types to document what your function does. For example, a function can declare that it depends on a connection string as follows.

Listing 7.6   Function signatures are more explicit when using custom types

```
public Option<Employee> lookupEmployee
   (ConnectionString conn, Guid id) => //...
```

This is much more explicit than depending on a `string`.

The second benefit is that you can now define extension methods on `Connection-String`, which wouldn't make sense on `string`. You'll see this next.

7.4.2   *Particularizing the data access function*

Now that we've looked at representing and acquiring a connection string, let's look at what's next, from general to specific:

- The type of data we want to retrieve, such as `Employee`
- The SQL query template, such as `"SELECT * FROM EMPLOYEES WHERE ID = @Id"`
- The `param` object that will be used to render the SQL template, such as `new { Id = "123" }`

Now comes the crux of the solution. We can define an extension method on `ConnectionString` that takes the parameters we need.

Listing 7.7   An adapter function that's better suited for partial application

```
using static ConnectionHelper;

public static class ConnectionStringExt
{
   public static Func<SqlTemplate, object, IEnumerable<T>>
   Query<T>(this ConnectionString connString)
      => (sql, param)
      => Connect(connString, conn => conn.Query<T>(sql, param));
}
```

Notice that we're relying on `ConnectionHelper.Connect`, which we implemented in chapter 1, and which internally takes care of opening and disposing the connection. It doesn't matter if you don't remember the implementation details; just notice that here the general, non-changing connection string is the first parameter, whereas the connection object itself is short-lived and will be created with every query.

This is the signature of the preceding method:

```
ConnectionString → (SqlTemplate, object) → IEnumerable<T>
```

That is, once we provide a connection string, we get a function that's still waiting for two more parameters before returning a list of retrieved entities. Also notice that defining `Query` as an extension method is a bit of a trick that allows us to specify the connection string *before* the type we're querying. It's not otherwise possible to "defer" the resolution of a method's type arguments.

This definition of `Query` is a thin shim on top of Dapper's `Query` function. It provides a partial-application friendly API, for two reasons:

- Arguments this time truly go from general to specific.
- Supplying the first argument yields a `Func`, which resolves the issues of type inference when applying subsequent arguments.

We can now supply arguments piecemeal to get the functions we set out to define.

Listing 7.8 Supplying arguments to get a function of the desired signature

```csharp
ConnectionString connString = configuration
   .GetSection("ConnectionString").Value;

SqlTemplate sel = "SELECT * FROM EMPLOYEES"
   , sqlById = $"{sel} WHERE ID = @Id"
   , sqlByName = $"{sel} WHERE LASTNAME = @LastName";

// (SqlTemplate, object) → IEnumerable<Employee>
var queryEmployees = conn.Query<Employee>();          ◁────  The connection
                                                             string and retrieved
                                                             type are fixed.

// object → IEnumerable<Employee>
var queryById = queryEmployees.Apply(sqlById);        ◁──┐
                                                         │  The SQL query to
// object → IEnumerable<Employee>                        │  be used is fixed.
var queryByLastName = queryEmployees.Apply(sqlByName); ◁──┘

// Guid → Option<Employee>
Option<Employee> lookupEmployee(Guid id)              ◁──┐
   => queryById(new { Id = id }).FirstOrDefault();       │  The functions
                                                         │  we set out to
// string → IEnumerable<Employee>                        │  implement
IEnumerable<Employee> findEmployeesByLastName(string lastName) ◁──┘
   => queryByLastName(new { LastName = lastName });
```

Here we define `queryEmployees` by parameterizing the previously discussed `Query` method to use a specific connection string and to retrieve `Employees`. It's still open to further parameterization, so we supply two different `SqlTemplates` to obtain `query-ById` and `queryByLastName`.

We now have two unary functions that expect a `param` object (which wraps values that will be used to replace the placeholder in the `SqlTemplate`). All that's left to do is to define `lookupEmployee` and `findEmployeesByLastName` with the signature we set out to expose at the beginning of the section. These just act as adapter functions that translate their input argument to a suitably populated `param` object.

Notice how we started with an extremely general function for running any query against any SQL database (which was simply an adapter on top of Dapper's `Query` method, to give us a better-suited API), and we ended up with highly specialized functions.

7.5 *Modularizing and composing an application*

As applications grow, we need to modularize them and break them down into components. For example, in chapter 6 you saw an end-to-end example of handling a request to book a transfer. We put all the code in the controller, and by the end the list of members in the controller looked like this.

Listing 7.9 A controller with too many responsibilities?

```
public class BookTransferController : Controller
{
    DateTime now;
    static readonly Regex regex = new Regex("^[A-Z]{6}[A-Z1-9]{5}$");
    string connString;
    ILogger<BookTransferController> logger;

    public IActionResult BookTransfer([FromBody] BookTransfer request)

    IActionResult OnFaulted(Exception ex)

    Validation<Exceptional<Unit>> Handle(BookTransfer request)

    Validation<BookTransfer> Validate(BookTransfer cmd)
    Validation<BookTransfer> ValidateBic(BookTransfer cmd)
    Validation<BookTransfer> ValidateDate(BookTransfer cmd)

    Exceptional<Unit> Save(BookTransfer transfer)
}
```

If this were a real-world banking application, you'd have not two, but dozens of rules for checking the validity of the transfer request. You'd also have functionality to do with identity and session management, instrumentation, and so on. In short, the controller would quickly become too big, and you'd need to break it down into separate components with more discrete responsibilities. This makes your code more modular and more manageable.

The other big drive for modularity is code reuse: logic for, say, session management or authorization could be required by several controllers and should therefore be placed in a separate component. Once you've broken up an application into components, you need to compose it back together, so that all required components can collaborate at runtime.

In this section, we'll look at how to deal with modularity, and how the OO and functional approaches differ in this respect. We'll illustrate this by refactoring Book-TransferController.

7.5.1 Modularity in OOP

Modularity in OOP is usually obtained by assigning responsibilities to different objects, and capturing these responsibilities with interfaces. For instance, we might define an IValidator interface for validation and an IRepository for persistence.

> **Listing 7.10 Interfaces in OOP capture the components' responsibilities**

```
public interface IValidator<T>
{
    Validation<T> Validate(T request);
}

public interface IRepository<T>
{
    Option<T> Lookup(Guid id);
    Exceptional<Unit> Save(T entity);
}
```

The controller would then depend on these interfaces in order to do its work, as shown in figure 7.2.

This follows a pattern called *dependency inversion*, according to which a higher-level component (such as the controller) doesn't consume lower-level components directly, but rather through *abstractions*, which is usually understood to mean interfaces that the lower-level components (such as the validators and repository) implement.[3] There are a couple of benefits to this approach:

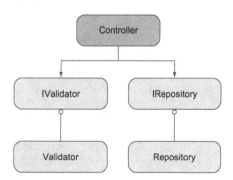

Figure 7.2 A higher-level component consumes lower-level components via interfaces.

---

[3] Note that there's a difference between dependency injection and dependency inversion. *Dependency injection* is far more general: it just means you're injecting something that a class, method, or function requires. For example, if you inject a concrete implementation, a primitive value, or a configuration object, you're using dependency injection, but not dependency inversion. *Dependency inversion* relies on dependency injection, but the opposite is not true.

- *Decoupling*—You could swap out the repository implementation (changing it from writing to a database to writing to a queue) and this wouldn't impact the controller. You'd only need to change how the two are wired up. (This is usually defined in some bootstrapping logic.)
- *Testability*—You can unit-test the handler without hitting the database, by injecting a fake `IRepository`.

There's also a rather high cost associated with dependency inversion:

- There's an explosion in the number of interfaces, adding boilerplate and making the code difficult to navigate.
- The bootstrapping logic to compose the application is often not trivial.
- Building fake implementations for testability can be complex.

To manage this extra complexity, third-party frameworks are often used; namely IoC containers and mocking frameworks. If we follow this approach, the implementation of the controller ends up looking like this.

Listing 7.11   An implementation that's functional in the small and OO in the large

```
public class BookTransferController : Controller
{
    IValidator<BookTransfer> validator;          Dependencies
    IRepository<BookTransfer> repository;         are objects.

    public BookTransferController(IValidator<BookTransfer> validator
        , IRepository<BookTransfer> repository)
    {
        this.validator = validator;              Dependencies are injected
        this.repository = repository;            in the constructor.
    }

    [HttpPost, Route("api/transfers/book")]
    public IActionResult TransferOn([FromBody] BookTransfer cmd)
        => validator.Validate(cmd)
            .Map(repository.Save)                 Consumes dependencies
            .Match(
                Invalid: BadRequest,
                Valid: result => result.Match<IActionResult>(
                    Exception: _ => StatusCode(500, Errors.UnexpectedError),
                    Success: _ => Ok())));
}
```

You could say that the preceding implementation is "functional in the small and OO in the large." The main components (controller, validator, repository) are indeed objects, and the program behavior is encoded in methods on these objects. On the other hand, many functional concepts are then used in the implementation of the methods and in defining their signatures.

This approach of using functional techniques within an overall OO software architecture is a perfectly valid way to integrate FP with OOP. It's also possible to push the functional approach, so that all behavior is captured in functions. You'll see this next.

7.5.2 Modularity in FP

If the fundamental units of OOP are objects, in FP they're functions. Modularity in FP is achieved by assigning responsibilities to functions, and composition by combining functions. In a functional approach, we don't define interfaces, because function signatures already provide all the interface we need.

For instance, in chapter 2 you saw that a validator class that needs to know the current time doesn't need to depend on a "service" object, but can just depend on a function that returns the current time.

Listing 7.12 Injecting functions as dependencies

```
public class DateNotPast : IValidator<BookTransfer>
{
   Func<DateTime> clock;
   public DateNotPastValidator(Func<DateTime> clock) { this.clock = clock; }

   public Validation<BookTransfer> Validate(BookTransfer cmd)
      => cmd.Date.Date < clock().Date
         ? Errors.TransferDateIsPast
         : Valid(cmd);
}
```

After all, what is a clock if not a function that you can invoke to get the current time? But let's take this one step further: why would you even need the `IValidator` interface in the first place? After all, what is a validator, if not a function that you can call to find out if a given object is valid? Let's instead use a delegate to represent validation:

```
// T → Validation<T>
public delegate Validation<T> Validator<T>(T t);
```

If we follow this approach, `BookTransferController` depends not on an `IValidator` object, but on a `Validator` function. And to implement a `Validator`, you don't even need to have an object and to store dependencies as fields; instead, dependencies can be passed as function arguments.

Listing 7.13 Dependencies can be passed as arguments to a function

```
public static Validator<BookTransfer> DateNotPast(Func<DateTime> clock)
   => cmd
   => cmd.Date.Date < clock().Date
      ? Errors.TransferDateIsPast
      : Valid(cmd);
```

Here, `DateNotPast` is a HOF that takes a function `clock` (the dependency it needs in order to know the current date) and returns a function of type `Validator`. Notice how this approach spares you the whole ceremony of creating interfaces, injecting them in the constructor, and storing them in fields.

Let's see how you would create a `Validator`. When bootstrapping the application, you'd give `DateNotPast` a function that reads from the system clock:

```
Validator<BookTransfer> val = DateNotPast(() => DateTime.UtcNow());
```

For testing purposes, however, you can provide a `clock` that returns a constant date:

```
var uut = DateNotPast(() => new DateTime(2020, 20, 10));
```

Notice that this is in fact partial application: `DateNotPast` is a binary function (in curried form) that needs a clock and a command to compute its result. You supply the first argument when composing the application (or in the *arrange* phase of a unit test), and the second argument when actually processing the received request (or in the *act* phase of a unit test).

Apart from the validator, `BookTransferController` also needs a dependency to persist the `BookTransfer` request data. If we're going to use functions, we can represent this with the following signature:

```
BookTransfer → Exceptional<Unit>
```

Again, we can create such a function by starting with a very general function that writes to the DB, with this signature:

```
TryExecute : ConnectionString → SqlTemplate → object → Exceptional<Unit>
```

We can then parameterize it with a connection string from configuration and a SQL template with the command we want to execute. This is very similar to the code you saw in section 7.3, so I'll omit the full details here. Our controller implementation will now look like this:

```
public class BookTransferController : Controller
{
    Validator<BookTransfer> validate;
    Func<BookTransfer, Exceptional<Unit>> save;

    [HttpPut, Route("api/transfers/book")]
    public IActionResult BookTransfer([FromBody] BookTransfer cmd)
        => validate(cmd).Map(save).Match( //...
}
```

Of course, if we take this approach to its logical conclusion, we should question why we need a controller class at all, when all the logic we're using could be captured in a function of this type:

```
BookTransfer → IActionResult
```

Indeed, we could define such a function outside the scope of a controller and configure the ASP.NET request pipeline to run it when requests are received that match the associated route.[4] I'm not going to show this refactoring here, both in the interest of space, and also because ASP.NET doesn't currently offer very good support for this style of handling HTTP requests,[5] so using a controller method as an entry point is preferable in most cases.

7.5.3 Comparing the two approaches

In the implementation just shown, all the controller's dependencies are functions. Notice that with this approach, you still have the benefits associated with dependency inversion:

- *Decoupling*—The controller knows nothing about the implementation details of the functions it consumes.
- *Testability*—When testing a controller method, you can just pass it functions that return a predictable result.

You also mitigate some of the problems associated with dependency inversion in its OOP version:

- You don't need to define any interfaces.
- This makes testing easier, because you don't need to set up fakes.

For example, a test for the use case we developed in this section could look like this.

> **Listing 7.14 When dependencies are functions, unit tests can be written without fakes**

```
[Test]
public void WhenCmdIsValid_AndSaveSucceeds_ThenResponseIsOk()
{
    var controller = new BookTransferController(
        validate: cmd => Valid(cmd),                    Injects functions that
        save: _ => Exceptional(Unit()));                return a predictable result

    var result = controller.BookTransfer(new BookTransfer());

    Assert.AreEqual(typeof(OkResult), result.GetType());
}
```

So far, the functional approach seems preferable. There's also another difference to point out. In the OO implementation (listing 7.10), the controller depended on an `IRepository` interface defined as follows:

---

[4] For a better understanding of ASP.NET Core, the application pipeline, and how this can be configured, see https://docs.asp.net/en/latest/fundamentals/startup.html.

[5] Namely, you have to handle low-level details, like serializing the request and response body and setting the status code of the response. When using MVC controllers, these low-level details are taken care of.

```
public interface IRepository<T>
{
    Option<T> Lookup(Guid id);
    Exceptional<Unit> Save(T entity);
}
```

But notice that the controller only uses the Save method. This violates the *interface segregation* principle (ISP), which states that clients shouldn't depend on methods they don't use. The idea is that just because you're trusting your 13-year-old son with your house keys, that doesn't mean he should have your car keys as well. The IRepository interface should actually be broken up into two single-method interfaces, and the controller should depend on a smaller interface, like this:

```
public interface ISaveToRepository<T>
{
    Exceptional<Unit> Save(T entity);
}
```

This further increases the number of interfaces in the application. If you push the ISP hard enough, you'll end up with a prevalence of single-method interfaces that convey the same information as a function signature, ultimately making it simpler to just inject functions, as you've seen in the functional approach.

Of course, if the controller did require both a function to read and write, then in the functional style we'd have to inject two functions, increasing the number of dependencies. As usual, the functional style is more explicit.

7.5.4   Composing the application

Finally, let's see how all the pieces are wired up. This is an ASP.NET application, so the bootstrapping logic should be defined in an IControllerActivator, which the framework calls whenever a request is received that should be routed to the controller.

> **Listing 7.15   Composing the services required to fulfill the BookTransfer request**

```
public class ControllerActivator : IControllerActivator
{
    IConfigurationRoot configuration;

    public object Create(ControllerContext context)
    {
        var type = context.ActionDescriptor.ControllerTypeInfo;
        if (type.AsType().Equals(typeof(BookTransferController)))
            return ConfigureBookTransferController();

        //...
    }

    BookTransferController ConfigureBookTransferController()
    {
        ConnectionString connString = configuration
```

```
                .GetSection("ConnectionString").Value;

        var save = Sql.TryExecute
            .Apply(connString)
            .Apply(Sql.Queries.InsertTransferOn);

        var validate = Validation.DateNotPast(() => DateTime.UtcNow);
        return new BookTransferController(validate, save);
    }
}
```

Sets up persistence

◁— **Sets up validation**

Some of this code is ASP.NET-specific, and configuring another type of application, like a console application or a Windows service may be easier. The interesting bit is the `ConfigureBookTransferController` method, where you compose the dependencies required by the controller with partial application.

There's one last thing left. Notice that you're passing it a single validator that validates that the date is OK. But what you really need is a validator that will ensure that *many* validation rules (each represented by a specific function) are satisfied.

In OOP, you could use a *composite validator* that implements `IValidator` and internally uses a list of specific `IValidators`. But we want to do this in a functional style and have a `Validator` function that will internally combine the rules of many `Validators`. We'll look at this next, but in order to do so, we must first take a step back and look at a general pattern for reducing a list of values to a single value.

7.6 Reducing a list to a single value

Reducing a list of values into a single value is a common operation, but one we haven't discussed so far. In FP-speak, this operation is called *fold* or *reduce*, and these are the names you'll encounter in most languages or libraries and in the FP literature. Characteristically, LINQ uses a different name: `Aggregate`. If you're already familiar with `Aggregate`, you can skip the next subsection.

7.6.1 LINQ's Aggregate method

Note that most of the functions we've used so far with `IEnumerable` also return an `IEnumerable`. For example, `Map` takes a list of n things and returns another list of n things, possibly of a different type. `Where` and `Bind` also stay within the abstraction; that is, they take an `IEnumerable` and return an `IEnumerable`, although the size of the list or the type of the elements may vary.

`Aggregate` is different from these functions in that it takes a list of n things and returns *exactly one* thing (just like the SQL aggregate functions COUNT, SUM, and AVERAGE, which you may be familiar with).

Given an `IEnumerable<T>`, `Aggregate` takes an initial value, called *accumulator*, and a *reducer* function—a binary function accepting the accumulator and an element in the list, and returning the new value for the accumulator. `Aggregate` then traverses the list, applying the function to the current value of the accumulator and each element in the list.

For example, you could have a list of lemons and aggregate it into a glass of lemon juice. The accumulator would be an empty glass, and this is what you get back if the list of lemons is empty. The reducer function takes a glass and a single lemon, and returns a glass with the lemon squeezed into it. Given these arguments, `Aggregate` traverses the list, squeezing each lemon into the glass, finally returning the glass with juice from all the lemons.

The signature for `Aggregate` is

```
(IEnumerable<T>, Acc, ((Acc, T) → Acc)) → Acc
```

Figure 7.3 shows it graphically. If the list is empty, `Aggregate` just returns the given accumulator, *acc*. If it contains one item, *t0*, it will return the result of applying *f* to *acc* and *t0*; let's call this value *acc1*. If it contains more items, it will compute *acc1* and then apply *f* to *acc1* and *t1* to obtain *acc2*, and so on, finally returning *accN* as a result. *Acc* can be seen as an initial value, on top of which all values in the list are applied, using the given function.

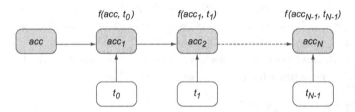

Figure 7.3 Reducing a list to a single value with `Aggregate`

The `Sum` function (available in its own right in LINQ) is a special case of `Aggregate`. What's the sum of all the numbers in an empty list? Naturally, 0! So that's our accumulator value. The binary function is just addition, so we can express `Sum` as follows.

Listing 7.16 `Sum` as a special case of `Aggregate`

```
Range(1, 5).Aggregate(0, (acc, i) => acc + i) // => 15
```

Notice that this expands to the following:

```
((((0 + 1) + 2) + 3) + 4) + 5
```

More generally, `ts.Aggregate(acc, f)` expands to

```
f(f(f(f(acc, t0), t1), t2), ... tn)
```

`Count` can also be seen as a special case of `Aggregate`:

```
Range(1, 5).Aggregate(0, (count, _) => count + 1) // => 5
```

Notice that the type of the accumulator isn't necessarily the type of the list items. For example, let's say we have a list of things, and we want to add them to a tree. The type in our list would be, say, T, and the type of the accumulator would be Tree<T>. We could start with an empty tree as accumulator and add each item as we traverse the list.

> **Listing 7.17   Using Aggregate to create a tree of all items in a list**

```
Range(1, 5).Aggregate(Tree<int>.Empty, (tree, i) => tree.Insert(i))
```

In this example, I'm assuming that tree.Insert(i) returns a tree with the newly inserted value.

Aggregate is such a powerful method that it's possible to implement Map, Where, and Bind in terms of Aggregate—something I suggest as an exercise.

There's also a less general overload that doesn't take an accumulator argument, but uses the first element of the list as accumulator. The signature for this overload is

```
(IEnumerable<T>, ((T, T) → T)) → T
```

When using this overload, the result type is the same as the type of the elements in the list, and the list can't be empty.

7.6.2   *Aggregating validation results*

Now that you know how to reduce a list of values to a single value, let's apply this knowledge and see how we can "reduce" a list of validators to a single validator. To do this, we'll need to implement a function with type

```
IEnumerable<Validator<T>> → Validator<T>
```

Notice that, because Validator is itself a function type, the preceding type expands to this:

```
IEnumerable<T → Validation<T>> → T → Validation<T>
```

First of all, we need to decide how we want the combined validation to work:

- *Fail fast*—If validation should be optimized for efficiency, the combined validation should fail as soon as one validator fails, thus minimizing the use of resources. This is a good approach if you're validating a request made programmatically from an application.
- *Harvest errors*—You may want to identify all the rules that have been violated, so that they can be fixed prior to making another request. This is a better approach when validating a request made by a user through a form.

The fail-fast strategy is easier to implement: every validator returns a Validation, and Validation exposes a Bind function that only applies the bound function if the state is Valid (just like Option and Either), so we can use Aggregate to traverse the list of validators, and Bind each validator to the running result.

Listing 7.18   Using Aggregate and Bind to apply all validation in a sequence

```
public static Validator<T> FailFast<T>
   (IEnumerable<Validator<T>> validators)
   => t
   => validators.Aggregate(Valid(t)
      , (acc, validator) => acc.Bind(_ => validator(t)));
```

Notice that the FailFast function takes a list of Validators and returns a Validator: a function that expects an object of type T to validate. Upon receiving the validand, t, it traverses the list of validators using Valid(t) as accumulator (that is, if the list of validators is empty, then t is valid), and applies each validator in the list to the accumulator with Bind.

Conceptually, the call to Aggregate expands as follows:

```
Valid(t)
   .Bind(validators[0]))
   .Bind(validators[1]))
   . . .
   .Bind(validators[n - 1]));
```

Because of how Bind is defined for Validation, whenever a validator fails, the subsequent validators will be skipped, and the whole validation fails.

Not all validation is equally expensive. For instance, validating that the BIC code is well formed with a regular expression (as shown in listing 6.7) is very cheap. Suppose that you also need to ensure that the given BIC code identifies an existing bank branch. This might involve a DB lookup or a remote call to a service with a list of valid codes, which is clearly more expensive.

To ensure that overall validation is efficient, you need to order the list of validators accordingly. In this case, you'd need to apply the (cheap) regular expression validation first, and only then the (expensive) remote lookup.

7.6.3   *Harvesting validation errors*

The opposite approach is to prioritize *completeness*; that is, to include the details of *all* failing validations. In this case, you don't want failure to prevent further computation; on the contrary, you want to ensure that all the validators run, and that all errors, if any, are harvested.

This is useful if, say, you're validating a form with lots of fields, and you want the user to see everything they need to fix in order to make a valid submission.

Let's see how we could rewrite the method that combines the different validators.

Listing 7.19 Collecting errors from all validators that fail

```
public static Validator<T> HarvestErrors<T>
   (IEnumerable<Validator<T>> validators)
   => t =>
   {
       var errors = validators
          .Map(validate => validate(t))
          .Bind(v => v.Match(
              Invalid: errs => Some(errs),
              Valid: _ => None))
          .ToList();

       return errors.Count == 0
          ? Valid(t)
          : Invalid(errors.Flatten());
   };
```

Runs all validators independently

Collects validation errors

Disregards passed validation

If there were no errors, the overall validation passes.

Here, instead of using Aggregate, we use Map to map the list of validators to the results of running the validators on the object to be validated. This ensures that all validators are called independently, and we end up with an IEnumerable of Validations.

We're then interested in harvesting all the errors. To do this, we use Option: we map Invalids to a Some wrapping the errors, and Valids to None. Remember from chapter 4 that Bind can be used to filter out Nones from a list of Options, and that's what we're doing here to obtain a list of all errors. Because each Invalid contains a list of errors, errors is actually a list of lists. In case of failure, we need to flatten it into a one-dimensional list and use it to populate an Invalid. If there were no errors, we return the validand in a Valid.[6]

Exercises

1 Partial application with a binary arithmetic function:

   a Write a function, Remainder, that calculates the remainder of integer division (and works for negative input values!). Notice how the expected order of parameters isn't the one that's most likely to be required by partial application (you're more likely to partially apply the divisor).

   b Write an ApplyR function that gives the rightmost parameter to a given binary function. (Try to do so without looking at the implementation for Apply.) Write the signature of ApplyR in arrow notation, both in curried and non-curried forms.

   c Use ApplyR to create a function that returns the remainder of dividing any number by 5.

   d Write an overload of ApplyR that gives the rightmost argument to a ternary function.

---

[6] There's actually a simpler way to accomplish this using applicatives and traverse—tools we haven't covered yet. You'll see this in chapter 13.

2   Ternary functions:

    a   Define a `PhoneNumber` class with three fields: number type (home, mobile, ...), country code ('it', 'uk', ...), and number. `CountryCode` should be a custom type with implicit conversion to and from `string`.

    b   Define a ternary function that creates a new number, given values for these fields. What's the signature of your factory function?

    c   Use partial application to create a binary function that creates a UK number, and then again to create a unary function that creates a UK mobile.

3   Functions everywhere. You may still have a feeling that objects are ultimately more powerful than functions. Surely a logger object should expose methods for related operations such as `Debug`, `Info`, and `Error`? To see that this is not necessarily so, challenge yourself to write a very simple logging mechanism (logging to the console is fine) that doesn't require any classes or structs. You should still be able to inject a `Log` value into a consumer class or function, exposing the operations `Debug`, `Info`, and `Error`, like so:

```
void ConsumeLog(Log log)
   => log.Info("look! no classes!");
```

4   Open exercise: in your day-to-day coding, start paying more attention to the signatures of the functions you write and consume. Does the order of arguments make sense; that is, do they go from general to specific? Is there some argument that you always invoke with the same value, so that you could partially apply it? Do you sometimes write similar variations of the same code, and could these be generalized into a parameterized function?

5   Implement `Map`, `Where`, and `Bind` for `IEnumerable` in terms of `Aggregate`.

Summary

- Partial application means giving a function its arguments piecemeal, effectively creating a more specialized function with each argument given.

- Currying means changing the signature of a function so that it will take its arguments one at a time.

- Partial application enables you to write highly general functions by parameterizing their behavior, and then supplying arguments to obtain increasingly specialized functions.

- The order of arguments matters: you give the leftmost argument first, so that a function should declare its arguments from general to specific.

- When working with multi-argument functions in C#, method resolution can be problematic and lead to syntactic overhead. This can be overcome by relying on `Func`s rather than on methods.

- You can inject the dependencies required by your functions by declaring them as arguments. This allows you to compose your application entirely of functions, without compromising on the separation of concerns, decoupling, and testability.

Working effectively with
multi-argument functions

This chapter covers

- Using multi-argument functions with elevated types
- Using LINQ syntax with any monadic type
- The fundamentals of property-based testing

The main goal of this chapter is to teach you to use multi-argument functions in the world of *effectful* types, so the "effectively" in the title is also a pun! Remember, effectful types are types such as Option (which adds the effect of optionality), Exceptional (exception handling), IEnumerable (aggregation), and others. In part 3, you'll see several more effects related to state, laziness, and asynchrony.

As you code more functionally, you'll come to rely heavily on these effects. You probably already use IEnumerable a lot. If you embrace the fact that types like Option and some variation of Either add robustness to your programs, you'll soon be dealing in elevated types in much of your code.

Although you've seen the power of core functions like Map and Bind, there's an important technique you haven't seen yet: how to integrate multi-argument functions in your workflows, given that Map and Bind both take unary functions.

It turns out that there are two possible approaches: the applicative and monadic approaches. We'll first look at the applicative approach, which uses the `Apply` function—a pattern you haven't seen yet. We'll then revisit monads, and you'll see how you can use `Bind` with multi-argument functions, and how LINQ syntax can be very helpful in this area. We'll then compare the two approaches and see why both can be useful in different cases.

Along the way, I'll also present some of the theory related to monads and applicatives, and I'll introduce a technique for unit testing called *property-based testing*.

8.1 *Function application in the elevated world*

In this section I'll introduce the applicative approach, which relies on the definition of a new function, `Apply`, that performs function application in the elevated world. `Apply`, like `Map` and `Bind`, is one of the core functions in FP.

To warm up, start the REPL, import the `LaYumba.Functional` library as usual, and type the following:

```
Func<int, int> @double = i => i * 2;

Some(3).Map(@double) // => Some(6)
```

So far, nothing new: you have a number wrapped in an `Option`, and you can apply the *unary* function @double to it with `Map`. Now, say you have a *binary* function like multiplication, and you have two numbers each wrapped in an `Option`. How can you apply the function to its arguments?

Here's the key concept: currying (which was covered in chapter 7) allows you to turn any *n*-ary function into a unary function that, when given its argument, will return a *(n-1)*-ary function. This means you can use `Map` with any function, as long as it's curried! Let's see this in practice.

Listing 8.1 Mapping a curried function onto an `Option`

```
Func<int, Func<int, int>> multiply = x => y => x * y;

var multBy3 = Some(3).Map(multiply);
// => Some(y => 3 * y))
```

Remember, when you `Map` a function onto an `Option`, `Map` "extracts" the value in the `Option` and applies the given function to it. In the preceding listing, `Map` will extract the value 3 from the `Option` and feed it to the `multiply` function: 3 will replace the variable x, yielding the function y => 3 * y.

Let's look at the types:

```
multiply              : int → int → int
Some(3)               : Option<int>
Some(3).Map(multiply) : Option<int → int>
```

So when you map a multi-argument function, the function is partially applied to the argument wrapped in the `Option`. Let's look at this from a more general point of view. Here's the signature of `Map` for a functor F:

```
Map : F<T> → (T → R) → F<R>
```

Now imagine that the type of R happens to be T1 → T2, so R is actually a function. In that case, the signature expands to

```
F<T> → (T → T1 → T2) → F<T1 → T2>
```

But look at the second argument: T → T1 → T2—that's a binary function in curried form. This means that you can really use `Map` with functions of any arity! In order to free the caller from having to curry functions, my functional library includes overloads of `Map` that accept functions of various arities and take care of currying; for example:

```
public static Option<Func<T2, R>> Map<T1, T2, R>
   (this Option<T1> opt, Func<T1, T2, R> func)
   => opt.Map(func.Curry());
```

As a result, the following code also works.

Listing 8.2 Mapping a binary function onto an `Option`

```
Func<int, int, int> multiply = (x, y) => x * y;

var multBy3 = Some(3).Map(multiply);
// => Some(y => 3 * y))
```

Now that you know you can effectively use `Map` with multi-argument functions, let's look at the resulting value. This is something you've not seen before: an elevated function—a function wrapped in an elevated type, as illustrated in figure 8.1.

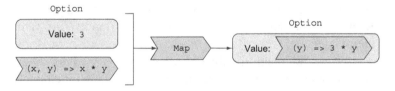

Figure 8.1 Mapping a binary function onto an `Option` yields a unary function wrapped in an `Option`.

There's nothing special about an elevated function. Functions are just values, so it's just another value wrapped in one of the usual containers.

And yet, how do you deal with an elevated value that's a function? Now that you have a unary function wrapped in an `Option`, how do you supply it its second argument? And what if the second argument is also wrapped in an `Option`? A crude approach would be to explicitly unwrap both values and then apply the function to the argument, like this:

```
Func<int, int, int> multiply = (x, y) => x * y;

Option<int> optX = Some(3)
           , optY = Some(4);

var result = optX.Map(multiply).Match(
    () => None,
    (f) => optY.Match(
        () => None,
        (y) => Some(f(y))
    )
);

result // => Some(12)
```

This code isn't nice: it leaves the elevated world of `Option` to apply the function, only to lift the result back up into an `Option`. Is it possible to abstract this, and integrate multi-argument functions in a workflow without leaving the elevated world? This is indeed what the `Apply` function does, and we'll look at it next.

8.1.1 *Understanding applicatives*

Before we look at defining `Apply` for elevated values, let's briefly review the `Apply` function we defined in chapter 7, which performs partial application in the world of *regular* values. We defined various overloads for `Apply` that take an *n*-ary function and an argument, and return the result of applying the function to the argument. The signatures are in the form

```
Apply : (T → R) → T → R
Apply : (T1 → T2 → R) → T1 v (T2 → R)
Apply : (T1 → T2 → T3 → R) → T1 → (T2 → T3 → R)
```

These signatures say, "Give me a function and a value, and I'll give you the result of applying the function to the value," whether that's the function's return value, or the partially applied function.

In the elevated world, we need to define overloads of `Apply` where the input and output values are wrapped in elevated types. In general, for any functor `A` for which `Apply` can be defined, the signatures of `Apply` will be in the form

```
Apply : A<T → R> → A<T> → A<R>
Apply : A<T1 → T2 → R> → A<T1> → A<T2 → R>
Apply : A<T1 → T2 → T3 → R> → A<T1> → A<T2 → T3 → R>
```

It's just like the regular `Apply`, but in the elevated world: "Give me a function wrapped in an `A`, and a value wrapped in an `A`, and I'll give you the result of applying the function to the value, also wrapped in an `A`, of course." This is illustrated in figure 8.2.

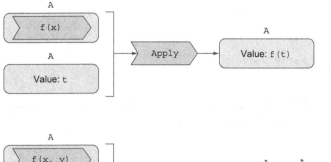

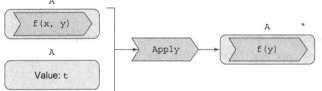

Figure 8.2 Apply performs function application in the elevated world.

An implementation of `Apply` must unwrap the function, unwrap the value, apply the function to the value, and wrap the result back up. When a suitable implementation of `Apply` is defined for a functor A, this is called an *applicative functor*, or simply an *applicative*.

Let's look at how `Apply` is defined for `Option`, making it an applicative.

Listing 8.3 Implementation of `Apply` for `Option`

```
public static Option<R> Apply<T, R>
   (this Option<Func<T, R>> optF, Option<T> optT)
   => optF.Match(
       () => None,
       (f) => optT.Match(
           () => None,
           (t) => Some(f(t))));
```
Only applies the wrapped function to the wrapped value if both `Options` are `Some`

```
public static Option<Func<T2, R>> Apply<T1, T2, R>
   (this Option<Func<T1, T2, R>> optF, Option<T1> optT)
   => Apply(optF.Map(F.Curry), optT);
```
Curries the wrapped function and uses the overload that takes an `Option` wrapping a unary function

---

The first overload is the important one. It takes a unary function wrapped in an `Option`, and an argument to that function, also wrapped in an `Option`. The implementation returns `Some` only if both inputs are `Some`, and `None` in all other cases.

As usual, overloads are required for the various arities of the wrapped functions, but those can be defined in terms of the unary version, as the second overload demonstrates.

Now that the low-level details of wrapping and unwrapping are taken care of, let's see how you can use `Apply` with a binary function:

```
Func<int, int, int> multiply = (x, y) => x * y;

Some(3).Map(multiply).Apply(Some(4));
 // => Some(12)
Some(3).Map(multiply).Apply(None);
// => None
```

In short, if you have a function wrapped in a container, `Apply` allows you to supply arguments to it. Let's take this idea one step further.

8.1.2 Lifting functions

In the examples so far, you've seen functions "lifted" into a container by mapping a multi-argument function onto an elevated value, like this:

```
Some(3).Map(multiply)
```

Alternatively, you could lift a function into a container by simply using the container's `Return` function, just like with any other value. After all, the wrapped function doesn't care *how* it gets there. So you can write this:

```
                          ┌─  Lifts the function
                          │   into an Option
Some(multiply)      <─────┘
    .Apply(Some(3))      ┌─  Supplies arguments
    .Apply(Some(4))      │   with Apply
// => Some(12)
```

This can be generalized to functions of any arity. And, as usual, you get the safety of `Option`, so that if any value along the way is `None`, the final result will also be `None`:

```
Some(multiply)
    .Apply(None)
    .Apply(Some(4))
// => None
```

As you can see, there are two distinct but equivalent ways of evaluating a binary function in the elevated world. You can see these side-by-side in the following listing.

> ### Listing 8.4 Two equivalent ways to achieve function application in the elevated world

Map the function, then `Apply`.	Lift the function, then `Apply`.
```Some(3) .Map(multiply) .Apply(Some(4))```	```Some(multiply) .Apply(Some(3)) .Apply(Some(4))```

The second way, of first lifting the function with `Return` and then applying arguments, is more readable and more intuitive because it's similar to partial application in the world of regular values, as shown in listing 8.5.

Listing 8.5 Partial application in the worlds of regular and elevated values

Partial application with regular values	Partial application with elevated values

```
multiply
   .Apply(3)
   .Apply(4)
// => 12
```

```
Some(multiply)
   .Apply(Some(3))
   .Apply(Some(4))
// => Some(12)
```

Whether you obtain the function by using `Map` or lifting it with `Return` doesn't matter in terms of the resulting functor. This is a requirement, and it will hold if the applicative is correctly implemented, so that it's sometimes called the *applicative law*.[1]

8.1.3 An introduction to property-based testing

Can we write some unit tests to prove that the functions we've been using to work with `Option` satisfy the applicative law? There's a specific technique for this sort of testing— that is, testing that an implementation satisfies certain laws or properties. It's called *property-based testing*, and a supporting framework called FsCheck is available for doing property-based testing in .NET.[2]

Property-based tests are parameterized unit tests whose assertions should hold for *any* possible value of the parameters. That is, you write a parameterized test and then let a framework such as FsCheck repeatedly run the test with a large set of randomly generated parameter values.

It's easiest to understand this by example. The following listing shows what a property test for the applicative law could look like.

Listing 8.6 A property-based test illustrating the applicative law

```
using FsCheck.Xunit;
using Xunit;
// ...

Func<int, int, int> multiply = (i, j) => i * j;

[Property]
void ApplicativeLawHolds(int a, int b)
{
   var first = Some(multiply)
      .Apply(Some(a))
      .Apply(Some(b));
```

Marks a property-based test → (points to `[Property]`)

FsCheck will randomly generate a large set of input values to run the test with. ← (points to `void ApplicativeLawHolds(int a, int b)`)

---

[1] In reality, there are four laws that correct implementations of `Apply` and `Return` must satisfy; these essentially hold that the identity function, function composition, and function application work in the applicative world as they do in the normal world. The applicative law I refer to in the text holds as a consequence of these, and it's more important than the underlying four laws in terms of refactoring and practical use. I won't discuss the four laws in detail here, but if you want to learn more, you can see the documentation for the applicative module in Haskell at https://hackage.haskell.org/package/base-4.9.0.0/docs/Control-Applicative.html. In addition, you can view property-based tests illustrating the applicative laws in the code samples, LaYumba.Functional.Tests/Option/ApplicativeLaws.cs.

[2] FsCheck is written in F# and is available freely (https://github.com/fscheck/FsCheck). Like many similar frameworks written for other languages, it's a port from Haskell's QuickCheck.

```
        var second = Some(a)
            .Map(multiply)
            .Apply(Some(b));

        Assert.Equal(first, second);
    }
```

If you look at the signature of the test method, you'll see that it's parameterized with two int values. But unlike the parameterized tests you saw in chapter 2, here we're not providing any values for the parameters. Instead, we're just decorating the test method with the `Property` attribute defined in `FsCheck.Xunit`.[3] When you run your tests, FsCheck will randomly generate a large number of input values and run the test with these values.[4] This frees you from having to come up with sample inputs and gives you much better confidence that edge cases are covered.

This test passes, but we're taking ints as parameters and lifting them into Options, so it only illustrates the behavior with Options in the Some state. We should also test what happens with None. The signature of our test method should really be

```
void ApplicativeLawHolds(Option<int> a, Option<int> b)
```

That is, we'd also ideally like FsCheck to randomly generate Options in the Some or None state and feed them to the test.

If we try to run this, FsCheck will complain that it doesn't know how to randomly generate an Option<int>. Fortunately, we can teach FsCheck how to do this.

Listing 8.7   Teaching FsCheck to create an arbitrary `Option`

```
static class ArbitraryOption
{
    public static Arbitrary<Option<T>> Option<T>()
    {
        var gen = from isSome in Arb.Generate<bool>()
                  from val in Arb.Generate<T>()
                  select isSome && val != null ? Some(val) : None;
        return gen.ToArbitrary();
    }
}
```

FsCheck knows how to generate primitive types such as bool and int, so generating an Option<int> should be easy: generate a random bool and then a random int; if

---

[3]   This also has the effect of integrating the property-based tests with your testing framework: when you run your tests with dotnet test, all property-based tests will be run as well as the regular unit tests. Although an FsCheck.NUnit package exists, exposing the Property attribute for NUnit, integration with NUnit at the time of this writing is poor.

[4]   By default, FsCheck generates 100 values, but the number and range of input values can be customized. If you start using property-based testing seriously, being able to fine-tune the parameters with which the values are generated becomes quite important.

the bool is false, return None, and otherwise wrap the generated int into a Some. This is the essential meaning of the preceding code above—don't worry about the exact details at this point.

Now we just need to instruct FsCheck to look into the ArbitraryOption class when a random Option<T> is required.

> **Listing 8.8 The property-based test, parameterized with arbitrary Options**

```
[Property(Arbitrary = new[] { typeof(ArbitraryOption) })]
void ApplicativeLawHolds(Option<int> a, Option<int> b)
   => Assert.Equal(
        Some(multiply).Apply(a).Apply(b),
        a.Map(multiply).Apply(b)
      );
```

Sure enough, FsCheck is now able to randomly generate the inputs to this test, which passes and beautifully illustrates the applicative law. Does it *prove* that our implementation always satisfies the applicative law? Not entirely, because it only tests that the property holds for the multiply function, whereas the law should hold for *any* function. Unfortunately, unlike with numbers and other values, it's impossible to randomly generate a meaningful set of functions. But this sort of property-based test still gives us good confidence—certainly better than a unit test, even a parameterized one.

 REAL-WORLD PROPERTY-BASED TESTING Property-based testing is not just for theoretical stuff but can be effectively applied to LOB applications. Whenever you have an invariant, you can write property tests to capture it. Here's a really simple example: if you have a randomly populated shopping cart, and you remove a random number of items from it, the total of the modified cart must always be less than or equal to the total of the original cart. You can start with such simple properties and then add other properties until they capture the essence of your model.[5]

Now that we've covered the mechanics of the Apply function, let's compare applicatives with the other patterns we've previously discussed. Once that's done, we'll look at applicatives in action with a more concrete example and at how they compare, especially to monads.

8.2   Functors, applicatives, monads

Let's recap three important patterns you've seen so far: functors, applicatives, and monads.[6] Remember that functors are defined by an implementation of Map, monads

---

[5] For more inspiration on how you can capture business rules through properties, see Scott Wlaschin's "Choosing properties for property-based testing" article at https://fsharpforfunandprofit.com/posts/property-based-testing-2/.

[6] As pointed out in chapter 4, in some languages, like Haskell, these patterns can be captured explicitly with "type classes," which are akin to interfaces but more powerful. The C# type system doesn't support these generic abstractions, so you can't idiomatically capture Map or Bind in an interface.

by an implementation of `Bind` and `Return`, and applicatives by an implementation of `Apply` and `Return`, as summarized in table 8.1.

Table 8.1 Summary of the core functions and how they define patterns

Pattern	Required functions	Signature
Functor	Map	F<T> → (T → R) → F<R>
Applicative	Return Apply	T → A<T> A<(T → R)> → A<T> → A<R>
Monad	Return Bind	T → M<T> M<T> → (T → M<R>) → M<R>

First, why is `Return` a requirement for monads and applicatives, but not for functors? You need a way to somehow put a value `T` into a functor `F<T>`; otherwise you couldn't create anything on which to `Map` a function. The point, really, is that the functor laws—the properties that `Map` should observe—don't rely on a definition of `Return`, whereas the monad and applicative laws do. So, this is mostly a technicality.

More interestingly, you may be wondering what the relation is between these three patterns. In chapter 5 you saw that monads are more powerful than functors. Applicatives are also more powerful than functors, because you can define `Map` in terms of `Return` and `Apply`. `Map` takes an elevated value and a regular function, so you can just lift the function using `Return`, and then apply it to the elevated value using `Apply`. For `Option`, that looks like this:

```
public static Option<R> Map<T, R>
   (this Option<T> opt, Func<T, R> f)
   => Some(f).Apply(opt);
```

The implementation for any other applicative would be the same, using the relevant `Return` function instead of `Some`.

Finally, monads are more powerful than applicatives, because you can define `Apply` in terms of `Bind` like so:

```
public static Option<R> Apply<T, R>
   (this Option<Func<T, R>> optF, Option<T> optT)
   => optT.Bind(t => optF.Bind<Func<T, R>, R>(f => f(t)));
```

This enables us to establish a hierarchy, in which functor is the most general pattern, and applicative sits between functor and monad, as represented in figure 8.3.

You can read this as a class diagram: if functor were an interface, applicative would extend it. Furthermore, in chapter 7 I discussed the *fold* function, or `Aggregate` as it's called in LINQ, which is the most powerful of them all because you can define `Bind` in terms of it.

Applicatives aren't as commonly used as functors and monads, so why even bother? It turns out that although `Apply` can be defined in terms of `Bind`, it generally receives its own implementation, both for efficiency and because `Apply` can have interesting behavior that's lost when you define `Apply` in terms of `Bind`. In this book I'll show two monads for which the implementation of `Apply` has such interesting behavior: `Validation`, later in this chapter, and `Task`, in chapter 13.

Next, let's go back to the topic of monads to see how you can use `Bind` with multi-argument functions.

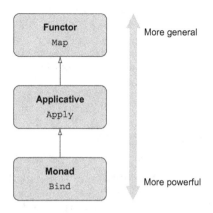

Figure 8.3   Relation of functor, applicative, and monad

8.3   *The monad laws*

I'll now discuss the monad laws, as promised in chapter 4, where I first introduced the term *monad*. If you're not interested in the theory, skip to section 8.3.4.

Remember, a monad is a type, `M`, for which the following functions are defined:

- `Return`, which takes a regular value of type `T` and *lifts* it into a monadic value of type `M<T>`
- `Bind`, which takes a monadic value, `m`, and a world-crossing function, `f`, and "extracts" from `m` its inner value `t` and applies `f` to it

`Return` and `Bind` should have the following three properties:

1. Right identity
2. Left identity
3. Associativity

For the present discussion, we're mostly interested in the third law, associativity, but the first two are simple enough that we can cover them too.

8.3.1   *Right identity*

The property of *right identity* states that if you `Bind` the `Return` function onto a monadic value, `m`, you end up with `m`. In other words, the following should hold:

```
m == m.Bind(Return)
```

If you look at the preceding equation, on the right side `Bind` unwraps the value inside `m` and applies `Return`, which lifts it back up, so it's not surprising that the net effect should be nought.

Listing 8.9   A property-based test proving that right identity holds for the `Option` type

```
[Property(Arbitrary = new[] { typeof(ArbitraryOption) })]
void RightIdentityHolds(Option<object> m)
    => Assert.Equal(
        m,
        m.Bind(Some)
    );
```

8.3.2   Left identity

The property of *left identity* states that if you first use `Return` to lift a t and then `Bind` a function, `f`, over the result, that should be equivalent to applying f to t:

```
Return(t).Bind(f)  ==  f(t)
```

If you look at this equation, on the left side you're lifting t with `Return`, and then `Bind` extracts it before feeding it to `f`. So this law states that this lifting and extracting should have no side effects, and it should also not affect t in any way.

Listing 8.10   A property-based test illustrating left identity for `IEnumerable`

```
Func<int, IEnumerable<int>> f = i => Range(0, i);

[Property] void LeftIdentityHolds(int t) => Assert.Equal(
    f(t),
    List(t).Bind(f)
);
```

Taken together, left and right identity ensure that the lifting operation performed in `Return` and the unwrapping that occurs as part of `Bind` are neutral operations that have no side effects and don't distort the value of t or the behavior of f, regardless of whether this wrapping and unwrapping happens before (left) or after (right) a value is lifted into the monad. We could write a monad that internally keeps a count of how many times `Bind` is called, or otherwise creates some random noise, and that would break this property.

In simpler words, `Return` should be *as dumb as possible*: no side effects, no conditional logic, no acting upon the given t. Only the minimal work required to satisfy the signature T → C<T>.

Let's see a counterexample. Look at the following property-based test that supposedly illustrates left identity for `Option`:

```
Func<string, Option<string>> f = s => Some($"Hello {s}");

[Property] void LeftIdentityHolds(string t) => Assert.Equal(
    f(t),
    Some(t).Bind(f)
);
```

It turns out that the preceding property fails when the value of t is null. This is because our implementation of Some is "too smart" and throws an exception if given null, whereas this particular function, f, is null-tolerant and yields Some("Hello ").

If you wanted left identity to hold for any value, including null, you'd need to change the implementation of Some to lift null into a Some. This would be a very bad idea, because then Some would indicate the presence of data when in fact there is none.

8.3.3 Associativity

Let's now move on to the third law, which is the most meaningful for our present discussion. I'll start with a reminder of what associativity means for addition: if you need to add more than two numbers, it doesn't matter how you group them. That is, for any numbers a, b, and c, the following is true:

```
(a + b) + c  ==  a + (b + c)
```

Bind can also be thought of as a binary operator and can be indicated with the symbol >>=, so that instead of m.Bind(f) you can symbolically write m >>= f, where m indicates a monadic value and f a world-crossing function. The symbol >>= is a fairly standard notation for Bind, and it's supposed to graphically reflect what Bind does: extract the inner value of the left operand and feed it to the function that's the right operand.

It turns out that Bind is also associative in some sense, so you should be able to write the following equation:

```
(m >>= f) >>= g  ==  m >>= (f >>= g)
```

Let's look at the left side: here you compute the first Bind operation, and then you use the resulting monadic value as input to the next Bind operation. This would expand to m.Bind(f).Bind(g), which is how we normally use Bind.

Let's now look at the right side. As it's written, it's syntactically wrong: (f >>= g) doesn't work because >>= expects the left operand to be a monadic value, whereas f is a function. But note that f can be expanded to its lambda form, x => f(x), so you can rewrite the right side as follows:

```
m >>= (x => f(x) >>= g)
```

The associativity of Bind can be then summarized with this equation:

```
(m >>= f) >>= g  ==  m >>= (x => f(x) >>= g)
```

Or, if you prefer, the following:

```
m.Bind(f).Bind(g)  ==  m.Bind(x => f(x).Bind(g))
```

Let's see this translated into code with a property-based test that illustrates how the associative property holds for Option.

Listing 8.11   A property-based test illustrating `Bind` associativity for `Option`

```
using Double = LaYumba.Functional.Double;                    ◁—┐  Exposes an Option-
                                                                 returning Parse function
Func<double, Option<double>> safeSqrt = d
   => d < 0 ? None : Some(Math.Sqrt(d));

[Property(Arbitrary = new[] { typeof(ArbitraryOption) })]
void AssociativityHolds(Option<string> m)
   => Assert.Equal(
         m.Bind(Double.Parse).Bind(safeSqrt),
         m.Bind(x => Double.Parse(x).Bind(safeSqrt))
      );
```

When we associate to the left, as in `m.Bind(f).Bind(g)`, that gives the more readable syntax, and the one we've been using so far. But if we associate to the right and expand g to its lambda form, we get this:

```
m.Bind(x => f(x).Bind(y => g(y)))
```

The interesting thing is that here g has visibility not only of y, but also of x. This is what enables you to integrate multi-argument functions in a monadic flow (by which I mean a workflow chaining several operations with `Bind`). We'll look at this next.

8.3.4   *Using Bind with multi-argument functions*

Let's look at how calling `Bind` inside a previous call to `Bind` allows you to integrate multi-argument functions. For instance, imagine multiplication where both arguments are optional, because they must be parsed from strings. In this example, `Int.Parse` takes a string and returns an `Option<int>`:

```
static Option<int> MultiplicationWithBind(string strX, string strY)
   => Int.Parse(strX).Bind(x => Int.Parse(strY)
        .Bind<int, int>(y => multiply(x, y)));
```

That works, but it's not at all readable. Imagine if you had a function taking three or more arguments! The nested calls to `Bind` make the code very difficult to read, so you certainly wouldn't want to write or maintain code like this. The applicative syntax was much clearer.

It turns out that there's a much better syntax for writing nested applications of `Bind`, and that syntax is called LINQ.

8.4   *Improving readability by using LINQ with any monad*

Depending on context, the name *LINQ* is used to indicate different things:

- It can simply refer to the `System.Linq` library
- It can indicate a special SQL-like syntax that can be used to express queries on various kinds of data. In fact, LINQ stands for *Language-Integrated Query.*

Naturally, the two are linked, and they were both introduced in tandem in C# 3. So far, all usages of the LINQ library you've seen in this book have used normal method invocation, but sometimes using the LINQ syntax can result in more readable queries.

For example, type the following two expressions into the REPL to see that they're equivalent.

Listing 8.12   LINQ is a dedicated syntax for expressing queries

Normal method invocation

```
Enumerable.Range(1, 100).
    Where(i => i % 20 == 0).
    OrderBy(i => -i).
    Select(i => $"{i}%")
```

LINQ expression

```
from i in Enumerable.Range(1, 100)
where i % 20 == 0 orderby -i
select $"{i}%"
```

These two expressions aren't just equivalent in the sense that they produce the same result; they actually compile to the same code. When the C# compiler finds a LINQ expression, it translates its clauses to method calls in a pattern-based way—you'll see what this means in more detail in a moment.

This means that it's possible for you to implement the query pattern for your own types and work with them using LINQ syntax, which can significantly improve readability.

Next, we'll look at implementing the query pattern for `Option`.

8.4.1   Using LINQ with arbitrary functors

The simplest LINQ queries have single `from` and `select` clauses, and they resolve to the `Select` method. For example, here's a simple query using a range as a data source:

```
using System.Linq;
using static System.Linq.Enumerable;

from x in Range(1, 4)
select x * 2;
// => [2, 4, 6, 8]
```

`Range(1, 4)` yields a sequence with the values `[1, 2, 3, 4]`, and this is the data source for the LINQ expression. We then create a "projection," by mapping each item x in the data source to x * 2, to produce the result. What happens under the hood?

Given a LINQ expression like the preceding one, the compiler will look at the type of the data source (in this case, `Range(1, 4)` has type `RangeIterator`), and will look for an instance or extension method called `Select`. The compiler uses its normal strategy for method resolution, prioritizing the most specific match in scope, which in this case is `Enumerable.Select`, defined as an extension method on `IEnumerable`.

Below you can see the LINQ expression and its translation side by side. Notice how the lambda given to `Select` combines the identifier x in the `from` clause and the selector expression x * 2 in the `select` clause.

Listing 8.13   A LINQ expression with a single `from` clause and its interpretation

```
from x in Range(1, 4)              Range(1, 4).
select x * 2                           Select(x => x * 2)
```

Remember from chapter 4 that `Select` is the LINQ equivalent for the operation more commonly known in FP as `Map`. LINQ's pattern-based approach means that you can define `Select` for any type you please, and the compiler will use it whenever it finds that type as the data source of a LINQ query. Let's do that for `Option`:

```
public static Option<R> Select<T, R>
    (this Option<T> opt, Func<T, R> f)
    => opt.Map(f);
```

The preceding code effectively just "aliases" `Map` with `Select`, which is the name that the compiler looks for. That's all you need to be able to use an `Option` inside a simple LINQ expression! Here are some examples:

```
from x in Some(12)
select x * 2
// => Some(24)

from x in (Option<int>)None
select x * 2
// => None

(from x in Some(1) select x * 2) == Some(1).Map(x => x * 2)
// => true
```

In summary, you can use LINQ queries with a single `from` clause with any functor by providing a suitable `Select` method. Of course, for such simple queries, the LINQ notation isn't really beneficial; standard method invocation even saves you a couple of keystrokes. Let's see what happens with more complex queries.

8.4.2   Using LINQ with arbitrary monads

Let's look at queries with multiple `from` clauses—queries that combine data from multiple data sources. Here's an example:

```
var chars = new[] { 'a', 'b', 'c' };
var ints = new [] { 2, 3 };

from c in chars
from i in ints
select (c, i)
// => [(a, 2), (a, 3), (b, 2), (b, 3), (c, 2), (c, 3)]
```

As you can see, this is somewhat analogous to a nested loop over the two data sources, and you probably are thinking you could have achieved the same with `Bind`.

Indeed, you could write an equivalent expression using `Map` and `Bind` as follows:

```
chars
    .Bind(c => ints
        .Map(i => (c, i)));
```

Or, equivalently, using the standard LINQ method names (`Select` instead of `Map` and `SelectMany` instead of `Bind`):

```
chars
    .SelectMany(c => ints
        .Select(i => (c, i)));
```

Notice that you can construct a result that includes data from both sources because you "close over" the variable c.

You might guess that when multiple `from` clauses are present in a query, they're interpreted with the corresponding calls to `SelectMany`. Your guess would be correct, but there's a twist. For performance reasons, the compiler doesn't perform the preceding translation, translating instead to an overload of `SelectMany` with a different signature:

```
public static IEnumerable<RR> SelectMany<T, R, RR>
   ( this IEnumerable<T> source
   , Func<T, IEnumerable<R>> bind
   , Func<T, R, RR> project)
{
   foreach (T t in source)
      foreach (R r in bind(t))
         yield return project(t, r);
}
```

That means this LINQ query

```
from c in chars
from i in ints
select (c, i)
```

will actually be translated as follows:

```
chars.SelectMany(c => ints, (c, i) => (c, i))
```

Let's compare the plain vanilla implementation of `SelectMany`, which has the same signature as `Bind`, and this extended overload (see listing 8.14).

Listing 8.14 Two overloads of `SelectMany` are required to implement the query pattern

```
// plain vanilla SelectMany
public static IEnumerable<R> SelectMany<T, R>
   ( this IEnumerable<T> source
   , Func<T, IEnumerable<R>> func)
```

← Plain vanilla `SelectMany`, equivalent to `Bind`

```
{
    foreach (T t in source)
        foreach (R r in func(t))
            yield return r;
}

// SelectMany that actually gets called
public static IEnumerable<RR> SelectMany<T, R, RR>
    ( this IEnumerable<T> source
    , Func<T, IEnumerable<R>> bind
    , Func<T, R, RR> project)
{
    foreach (T t in source)
        foreach (R r in bind(t))
            yield return project(t, r);
}
```

Extended overload of `SelectMany`, **which is used when translating a query with multiple** `from` **clauses**

Compare the signatures and you'll see that the second overload is obtained by "squashing" the plain vanilla `SelectMany` with a call to a selector function; not the usual selector in the form $T \rightarrow R$, but a selector that takes two input arguments (one for each data source).

The advantage is that with this more elaborate overload of `SelectMany`, there's no longer any need to nest one lambda inside another, improving performance.[7]

The extended `SelectMany` is more complex than the plain vanilla version we identified with monadic `Bind`, but it's still functionally equivalent to a combination of `Bind` and `Select`. This means we can define a reasonable implementation of the LINQ-flavored `SelectMany` for any monad. Let's see it for `Option`:

```
public static Option<RR> SelectMany<T, R, RR>
    (this Option<T> opt, Func<T, Option<R>> bind, Func<T, R, RR> project)
    => opt.Match(
        () => None,
        (t) => bind(t).Match(
            () => None,
            (r) => Some(project(t, r)))));
```

If you want an expression with three or more `from` clauses, the compiler will also require the plain vanilla version of `SelectMany`, which you can provide trivially by aliasing `Bind` with `SelectMany`.

You can now write LINQ queries on `Option`s with multiple `from` clauses. For example, here's a simple program that prompts the user for two integers and computes their sum, using the `Option`-returning function `Int.Parse` to validate that the inputs are valid integers:

```
WriteLine("Enter first addend:");
var s1 = ReadLine();

WriteLine("Enter second addend:");
```

---

[7] The designers of LINQ noticed that performance deteriorated rapidly as several `from` clauses were used in a query.

```
var s2 = ReadLine();

var result = from a in Int.Parse(s1)
             from b in Int.Parse(s2)
             select a + b;

WriteLine(result.Match(
   Some: r => $"{s1} + {s2} = {r}",
   None: () => "Please enter 2 valid integers"));
```

Let's take the query from the preceding example and see how the LINQ syntax compares with alternative ways to write the same expression.

```
// 1. using LINQ query
from a in Int.Parse(s1)
from b in Int.Parse(s2)
select a + b

// 2. normal method invocation
Int.Parse(s1)
   .Bind(a => Int.Parse(s2)
     .Map(b => a + b))

// 3. the method invocation that the LINQ query will be converted to
Int.Parse(s1)
   .SelectMany(a => Int.Parse(s2)
     , (a, b) => a + b)

// 4. using Apply
Some(new Func<int, int, int>((a, b) => a + b))
   .Apply(Int.Parse(s1)
   .Apply(Int.Parse(s2))
```

There's little doubt that LINQ provides the most readable syntax in this scenario. `Apply` compares particularly poorly because you must specify that you want your projection function to be used as a `Func`.[8] You may find it unfamiliar to use the SQL-ish LINQ syntax to do something that has nothing to do with querying a data source, but this use is perfectly legitimate. LINQ expressions simply provide a convenient syntax for working with monads, and they were modeled after equivalent constructs in functional languages.[9]

8.4.3   *let, where, and other LINQ clauses*

In addition to the `from` and `select` clauses you've seen so far, LINQ provides a few other clauses. The `let` clause is useful for storing the results of intermediate computations. For example, let's look at a program that calculates the hypotenuse of a right triangle, having prompted the user for the lengths of the legs.

---

[8] This is because lambda expressions can be used to represent `Expressions` as well as `Funcs`.
[9] For instance, `do` blocks in Haskell, or `for` comprehensions in Scala.

Listing 8.16   Using the `let` clause with `Option`

Exposes an `Option`-returning `Parse` function

```
using Double = LaYumba.Functional.Double;

string s1 = Prompt("First leg:")
      , s2 = Prompt("Second leg:");

var result = from a in Double.Parse(s1)
             let aa = a * a
             from b in Double.Parse(s2)
             let bb = b * b
             select Math.Sqrt(aa + bb);

WriteLine(result.Match(
    () => "Please enter two valid numbers",
    (h) => $"The hypotenuse is {h}"));
```

Assumes `Prompt` is a convenience function that reads user input from the console

A `let` clause allows you to store intermediate results.

The `let` clause allows you to put a new variable, like aa in this example, within the scope of the LINQ expression. To do so, it relies on `Select`, so no extra work is needed to enable the use of `let`.

One more clause you can use with `Option` is the `where` clause. This resolves to the `Where` method we've already defined, so no extra work is necessary in this case. For example, for the calculation of the hypotenuse, you should check not only that the user's inputs are valid numbers, but also that they are positive.

Listing 8.17   Using the `where` clause with `Option`

```
string s1 = Prompt("First leg:")
      , s2 = Prompt("Second leg:");

var result = from a in Double.Parse(s1)
             where a >= 0
             let aa = a * a

             from b in Double.Parse(s2)
             where b >= 0
             let bb = b * b

             select Math.Sqrt(aa + bb);

WriteLine(result.Match(
    () => "Please enter two valid, positive numbers",
    (h) => $"The hypotenuse is {h}"));
```

As these examples show, the LINQ syntax allows you to concisely write queries that would be very cumbersome to write as combinations of calls to the corresponding `Map`, `Bind`, and `Where` functions.

LINQ also contains various other clauses, such as `orderby`, which you've seen in a previous example. These clauses make sense for collections but have no counterpart in structures like `Option` and `Either`.

In summary, for any monad you can implement the LINQ query pattern by providing implementations for `Select` (Map), `SelectMany` (Bind), and the ternary overload to `SelectMany` you've seen. Some structures may have other operations that can be included in the query pattern, such as `Where` in the case of `Option`.

Now that you've seen how LINQ provides a lightweight syntax for using `Bind` with multi-argument functions, let's go back to comparing `Bind` and `Apply`, not just based on readability, but on actual functionality.

8.5 *When to use Bind vs. Apply*

LINQ provides a very good syntax for using `Bind`, even with multi-argument functions—even better than using `Apply` with normal method invocation. Should we still care about `Apply`? It turns out that in some cases `Apply` can have interesting behavior. One such case is validation—you'll see why next.

8.5.1 *Validation with smart constructors*

Consider the following implementation of a `PhoneNumber` class. Can you see anything wrong with it?

```
public class PhoneNumber
{
   public string Type { get; }
   public string Country { get; }
   public long Nr { get; }
}
```

The answer should be staring you in the face: the types are wrong! This class allows you to create a `PhoneNumber` with, say `Type` = "green", `Country` = "fantasyland", and `Nr` = -10.

You saw in chapter 3 how defining custom types enables you to ensure that invalid data can't creep into your system. Here's a definition of a `PhoneNumber` class that follows this philosophy:

```
public class PhoneNumber
{
   public NumberType Type { get; }
   public CountryCode Country { get; }
   public Number Nr { get; }

   public enum NumberType { Mobile, Home, Office }
   public struct Number { /* ... */ }
}

public class CountryCode { /* ... */ }
```

Now the three fields of a `PhoneNumber` all have specific types, which should ensure that only valid values can be represented. `CountryCode` may be used elsewhere in the application, but the remaining two types are specific to phone numbers, so they're defined inside the `PhoneNumber` class.

We still need to provide a way to construct a `PhoneNumber`. For that, we can define a private constructor, and a public factory function, `Create`:

```
public class PhoneNumber
{
    public static Func<NumberType, CountryCode, Number, PhoneNumber>
    Create = (type, country, number)
        => new PhoneNumber(type, country, number);

    PhoneNumber(NumberType type, CountryCode country, Number number)
    {
        Type = type;
        Country = country;
        Nr = number;
    }
}
```

Now imagine we're given three strings as raw input, and based on them we need to create a `PhoneNumber`. Each property can be validated independently, so we can define three smart constructors with the following signatures:

```
validCountryCode : string → Validation<CountryCode>
validNnumberType : string → Validation<PhoneNumber.NumberType>
validNumber      : string → Validation<PhoneNumber.Number>
```

The implementation details of these functions aren't important (see the code samples if you want to know more). The gist is that `validCountryCode` will take a `string` and return a `Validation` in the `Valid` state only if the given string represents a valid `CountryCode`. The other two functions are similar.

8.5.2 Harvesting errors with the applicative flow

Given the three input strings, we can combine these three functions in the process of creating a `PhoneNumber`. With the applicative flow, we can lift the `PhoneNumbers` factory function into a `Valid`, and apply its three arguments.

> **Listing 8.18 Validation using an applicative flow**

```
          Validation<PhoneNumber> CreatePhoneNumber
              (string type, string countryCode, string number)
          => Valid(PhoneNumber.Create)
              .Apply(validNumberType(type))
              .Apply(validCountryCode(countryCode))
              .Apply(validNumber(number));
```

Lifts the factory function into a `Validation` ⟶

Supplies arguments, each of which is also wrapped in a `Validation`

This function yields `Invalid` if any of the functions we're using to validate the individual fields yields `Invalid`.

Let's see its behavior, given a variety of different inputs:

```
CreatePhoneNumber("Mobile", "ch", "123456")
// => Valid(Mobile: (ch) 123456)

CreatePhoneNumber("Mobile", "xx", "123456")
// => Invalid([xx is not a valid country code])

CreatePhoneNumber("Mobile", "xx", "1")
// => Invalid([xx is not a valid country code, 1 is not a valid number])
```

The first expression shows the successful creation of a PhoneNumber. In the second case, we're passing an invalid country code and get a failure as expected. In the third case, both the country and number are invalid, and we get a validation with two errors—remember, the Invalid case of a Validation holds an IEnumerable<Error> precisely to capture multiple errors.

But how are the two errors, which are returned by different functions, harvested in the final result? This is due to the implementation of Apply for Validation.

Listing 8.19 Implementation of Apply for Validation

```
public static Validation<R> Apply<T, R>
    (this Validation<Func<T, R>> valF, Validation<T> valT)
    => valF.Match(
        Valid: (f) => valT.Match(
            Valid: (t) => Valid(f(t)),          <──  If both inputs are valid, the
            Invalid: (err) => Invalid(err)),         wrapped function is applied to the
        Invalid: (errF) => valT.Match(               wrapped argument, and the result
            Valid: (_) => Invalid(errF),             is lifted into a Validation in the
            Invalid: (errT) => Invalid(errF.Concat(errT))));   Valid state.
```

If both inputs have errors, a Validation in
the Invalid state is returned that collects
the errors from both valF and valT.

As we'd expect, Apply will apply the wrapped function to the wrapped argument only if both are valid. But, interestingly, if both are invalid, it will return an Invalid that combines errors from both arguments.

8.5.3 *Failing fast with the monadic flow*

Let's now create a PhoneNumber using LINQ.

Listing 8.20 Validation using a monadic flow

```
Validation<PhoneNumber> CreatePhoneNumberM
    (string typeStr, string countryStr, string numberStr)
    => from type    in validNumberType(typeStr)
       from country in validCountryCode(countryStr)
       from number  in validNumber(numberStr)
       select PhoneNumber.Create(type, country, number);
```

Let's run this new version with the same test values as before:

```
CreatePhoneNumberM("Mobile", "ch", "123456")
// => Valid(Mobile: (ch) 123456)

CreatePhoneNumberM("Mobile", "xx", "123456")
// => Invalid([xx is not a valid country code])

CreatePhoneNumberM("Mobile", "xx", "1")
// => Invalid([xx is not a valid country code])
```

The first two cases work as before, but the third case is different: only the first validation error appears. To see why, let's look at how `Bind` is defined (the LINQ query actually calls `SelectMany`, but this is implemented in terms of `Bind`).

Listing 8.21   Implementation of `Bind` for `Validation`

```
public static Validation<R> Bind<T, R>
  (this Validation<T> val, Func<T, Validation<R>> f)
  => val.Match(
     Invalid: (err) => Invalid(err),
     Valid: (r) => f(r));
```

If the given monadic value is `Invalid`, the given function isn't evaluated. In this listing, validCountryCode returns `Invalid`, so validNumber is never called. Therefore, in the monadic version we never get a chance to accumulate errors, because any error along the way causes the subsequent functions to be bypassed.

You can probably grasp the difference more clearly if we compare the signatures of `Apply` and `Bind`:

```
Apply : Validation<(T → R)> → Validation<T> → Validation<R>
Bind  : Validation<T> → (T → Validation<R>) → Validation<R>
```

With `Apply`, both arguments are of type `Validation`; that is, the `Validation`s and any possible errors they contain have already been evaluated independently, prior to the call to `Apply`. Because errors from both arguments are present, it makes sense to collect them in the result value.

With `Bind`, only the first argument has type `Validation`. The second argument is a function that yields a `Validation`, but this hasn't been evaluated yet, so the implementation of `Bind` can avoid calling the function altogether if the first argument is `Invalid`.[10]

Hence, `Apply` is about combining two elevated values that are computed independently; `Bind` is about sequencing computations that yield an elevated value. For this reason, the monadic flow allows short-circuiting: if an operation fails along the way, the following operations will be skipped.

---

[10] Of course, you *could* provide an implementation of `Bind` that doesn't perform any such short-circuiting but always executes the bound function and collects any errors. This is possible, but it's counterintuitive, because it breaks the behavior that we've come to expect from similar types, like `Option` and `Either`.

I think what the case of Validation shows is that despite the apparent rigor of functional patterns and their laws, there's still room for designing elevated types in a way that suits the particular needs of a particular application. Given my implementation of Validation and the current scenario of creating a valid PhoneNumber, you'd use the monadic flow to fail fast, but the applicative flow to harvest errors.

In summary, you've seen three ways to use multi-argument functions in the elevated world: the good, the bad, and the ugly. Nested calls to Bind is certainly the ugly, and it's best avoided. Which of the other two is good or bad depends on your requirements: if you have an implementation of Apply with some desirable behavior, as you've seen with Validation, use the applicative flow; otherwise, use the monadic flow with LINQ.

Exercises

1 Implement Apply for Either and Exceptional.
2 Implement the query pattern for Either and Exceptional. Try to write down the signatures for Select and SelectMany without looking at any examples. For the implementation, just follow the types—if it type checks, it's probably right!
3 Come up with a scenario in which various Either-returning operations are chained with Bind. (If you're short of ideas, you can use the favorite-dish example from chapter 6.) Rewrite the code using a LINQ expression.

Summary

- The Apply function can be used to perform function application in an elevated world, such as the world of Option.
- Multi-argument functions can be lifted into an elevated world with Return, and then arguments can be supplied with Apply.
- Types for which Apply can be defined are called *applicatives*. Applicatives are more powerful than functors, but less powerful than monads.
- Because monads are more powerful, you can also use nested calls to Bind to perform function application in an elevated world.
- LINQ provides a lightweight syntax for working with monads that reads better than nesting calls to Bind.
- To use LINQ with a custom type, you must implement the LINQ query pattern, particularly providing implementations of Select and SelectMany with appropriate signatures.
- For several monads, Bind has short-circuiting behavior (the given function won't be applied in some cases), but Apply doesn't (it's not given a function, but rather an elevated value). For this reason, you can sometimes embed desirable behavior into applicatives, such as collecting validation errors in the case of Validation.
- FsCheck is a framework for property-based testing. It allows you to run a test with a large number of randomly generated inputs, giving high confidence that the test's assertions hold for any input.

Thinking
about data functionally

9

This chapter covers

- The pitfalls of state mutation
- Representing change without mutation
- Enforcing immutability
- Functional data structures

Greek philosopher Heraclitus said that we cannot step into the same river twice; the river constantly changes, so the river that was there a moment ago is no longer. Many programmers would disagree, objecting that it's the same river but its *state* has now changed. Functional programmers try to stay true to Heraclitus's thinking and would create a new river with every observation.

Most programs are built to represent things and processes in the real world, and because the world constantly changes, programs must somehow represent that change. The question is *how* we represent change. Commercial applications written in the imperative style have state mutation at their very core: objects represent entities in the business domain, and change in the world is modeled by mutating the state of these objects.

We'll start by looking at the weaknesses we introduce in our programs whenever we use mutation. We'll then see how we can avoid these problems at the source, by representing change *without* using mutation and, more pragmatically, how to enforce immutability in C#. Finally, because much of our programs' data is stored in data structures, we'll introduce the concepts and techniques behind functional data structures, which are also immutable.

9.1 The pitfalls of state mutation

State mutation is when memory is updated in-place, and an important problem with it is that concurrent access to shared mutable state is unsafe. You've already seen examples demonstrating loss of information due to concurrent updates in chapters 1 and 2; let's now look at a more object-oriented scenario.

Imagine a `Product` class with an `Inventory` field, representing the number of units in stock:

```
public class Product
{
    public int Inventory { get; private set; }
    public void ReplenishInventory(int units) => Inventory += units;
    public void ProcessSale(int units) => Inventory -= units;
}
```

If `Inventory` is mutable, as in this example, and you have concurrent threads updating its value, this is known as a *race condition*, and the results can be unpredictable. Imagine that you have a thread replenishing the inventory, while another thread concurrently processes a sale, diminishing the inventory accordingly, as in figure 9.1. If both threads read the value at the same time, and the thread with the sale has the last update, you'll end up with an overall decrease in inventory.

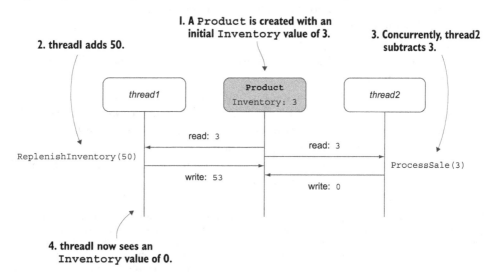

Figure 9.1 Loss of data as a result of concurrent updates

Not only has the update to replenish the inventory been lost, but the first thread now potentially faces a completely invalid state: a product that's just been replenished has zero inventory.[1]

If things can fail when a single variable is set, imagine when an update to an entity involves updating several fields. For example, imagine that when you update the inventory, you also set a flag indicating whether the product is low on inventory.

Listing 9.1   Temporary inconsistency as a result of non-atomic updates

```
class Product
{
    int inventory;

    public bool IsLowOnInventory { get; private set; }
    public int Inventory
    {
        get { return inventory; }
        private set
        {
            inventory = value;

            IsLowOnInventory = inventory <= 5;
        }
    }
}
```

At this point the object can be in an invalid state, from the perspective of any thread reading its properties.

In a single-threaded setting, there aren't any problems with the preceding code. But in a multi-threaded setting, another thread could be reading the state of this object just as the update is taking place, in the small window during which `Inventory` has been updated but `IsLowOnInventory` hasn't. To that other thread, the object would appear to be in an invalid state. This will, of course, happen very rarely, and it will be very difficult to reproduce. This is part of the reason why bugs caused by race conditions are so hard to diagnose.

Indeed, race conditions are known to have caused some of the most spectacular failures in the software industry. If you have a system with concurrency and state mutation, it's impossible to prove that the system is free of race conditions.[2] In other words, if you want concurrency (and, given today's tendency toward multicore processors and distributed computing, you hardly have a choice) *and* strong guarantees of correctness, you simply must give up mutation.

Lack of safe concurrent access may be the biggest pitfall of shared mutable state, but it's not the only one. Another problem is the risk of introducing *coupling*—a high

---

[1] If you've done some basic multithreading, you're probably thinking, "Easy! You just need to wrap the updates to `Inventory` in a critical section using the `lock` statement." It turns out that this solution, which works for this simple case, can become the source of some very difficult bugs as the complexity of the system increases. (A sale will affect not only the inventory, but the sales order, the company balance sheet, and so on.)

[2] The preceding examples refer to multithreading, but the same problems can arise if the source of concurrency is asynchrony or parallelism.

degree of interdependence between different parts of your system. In listing 9.1, `Inventory` is *encapsulated*, meaning it can only be set from within the class, and—according to OOP theory—that's supposed to give you a sense of comfort. But how many methods in the `Product` class can set the inventory value? How many code paths lead into these methods, so that they ultimately affect the value of `Inventory`? How many parts of the application can get the same instance of the `Product` and rely on the value of `Inventory`, and how many will be affected if you introduce a new component that causes `Inventory` to change?

For a non-trivial application, it's very difficult to answer these questions completely. As a result, mutable state couples the behavior of the various components that read or update that state, making it difficult to reason about the behavior of the system as a whole.

Finally, shared mutable state implies *loss of purity*. As explained in chapter 2, mutating global state (remember, that's all state that's not local to a function, including private variables) constitutes a side effect. So if you represent change in the world by mutating objects in your system, you lose the benefits of function purity.

For these reasons, when coding functionally, it's best to avoid state mutation altogether. In this chapter, you'll learn how to work with immutable data. That's an important technique, but keep in mind that it's not sufficient to represent entities that change with time. For that, you'll need other techniques, which we'll cover in chapters 10, 12, and 14.

Local mutation is OK

Not all state mutation is equally evil. Mutating local state (state that's only visible within the scope of a function) is inelegant but benign. For example, imagine the following function:

```
int Sum(int[] ints)
{
    var result = 0;
    foreach (int i in ints) result += i;
    return result;
}
```

Although we're updating `result`, this isn't visible from outside the scope of the function. As a result, this implementation of `Sum` is actually a *pure* function: it has no *observable* side effects from the point of view of a calling function.

Naturally, this code is also very low-level. You can normally achieve what you want with built-in functions like `Sum`, `Aggregate`, and so on. In practice, it's rare that you'll find a legitimate case for mutating local variables.

9.2   *Understanding state, identity, and change*

Let's look more closely at change and mutation. By "change," I mean change in the real world, such as when 50 units of stock become available for sale. "Mutation" means data is updated in place; as you saw in the `Product` class, when the `Inventory` value is updated, the previous value for `Inventory` is lost.

In FP we represent change without mutation: values aren't updated in place. Instead, we create new instances that represent the data with the desired changes. The fact that the current level of inventory is 53 doesn't obliterate the fact that it was previously 3, as shown in figure 9.2.

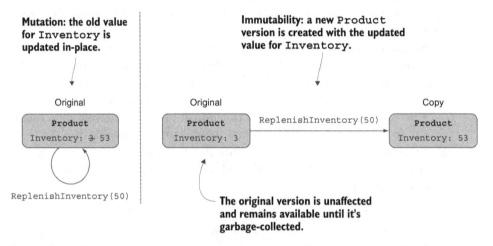

Figure 9.2   In FP, change can be represented by creating new versions of the data.

So, in FP, we work with *immutable* values: once a value is defined, it's never updated. To refine our intuition about this, it's useful to distinguish between things that change and things that don't.

9.2.1   *Some things never change*

There are some things that we think of as inherently immutable. For example, your age may change from 30 to 31, but the number 30 is still the number 30, and 31 is still 31.

This is modeled in the framework, in that *all primitive types are immutable*. What about more complex types? Dates are a good example. The third of March is still the third of March, even though you may change an appointment in your calendar from the third of March to the fourth. This is also reflected in the framework, in that `Date-Time` is immutable.

See this for yourself by typing the following in the REPL:

```
var momsBirthday = new DateTime(1966, 12, 13);
var johnsBirthday = momsBirthday;                    ◁──┐ John has the same
                                                        │ birthday as Mom.
// some time goes by...
```

```
johnsBirthday = johnsBirthday.AddDays(1);        You then realize that John's birthday
                                                 is actually one day later.
johnsBirthday // => 14/12/1966
momsBirthday  // => 13/12/1966        Mom's birthday
                                      was not affected.
```

In the preceding example, we start by saying that Mom and John have the same birthday, so we assign the same value to `momsBirthday` and `johnsBirthday`. When we then use `AddDays` to create a later date and assign it to `johnsBirthday`, this leaves `momsBirthday` unaffected. In this example, we are doubly protected from mutating the date:

- Because `System.DateTime` is a struct, it's copied upon assignment, so `momsBirthday` and `johnsBirthday` are different instances.
- Even if `DateTime` were a class, so that `momsBirthday` and `johnsBirthday` pointed to the same instance, the behavior would still be the same, because `AddDays` creates a new instance, leaving the underlying instance unaffected.

If, on the other hand, `DateTime` were a mutable class, and `AddDays` mutated the days of its instance, the value of `momsBirthday` would be updated as a result—or, rather, as a side-effect—of updating `johnsBirthday`. (Imagine explaining to Mom that that's the reason for your belated birthday wishes.)

> **Immutable types in the .NET framework**
> A few reference types in the framework are immutable. These are the most commonly used:
>
> - `DateTime, TimeSpan, DateTimeOffset`
> - `Delegate`
> - `Guid`
> - `Nullable<T>`
> - `String`
> - `Tuple<T1>, Tuple<T1, T2>, ...`
> - `Uri`
> - `Version`
>
> Furthermore, all primitive types in the framework are immutable.

Now let's define a custom immutable type. Say we represent a `Circle` like so:

```
struct Circle
{
   public Point Center { get; }
   public double Radius { get; }

   public Circle(Point center, double radius)
   {
```

```
        Center = center;
        Radius = radius;
    }
}
```

You would probably agree that it makes no sense that a circle should ever grow or shrink, since it's a completely abstract geometric entity. This is reflected in the preceding implementation, where `Radius` and `Center` are getter-only auto-properties whose values can only be set in the constructor. That is, once created, the state of the circle can never change.[3]

 STRUCTS SHOULD BE IMMUTABLE Notice that I've defined `Circle` as a value type. Because value types are copied when passed between functions, it makes sense that structs should be immutable. This isn't enforced by the compiler, so you *could* create a mutable struct. If you do, any changes you make to the struct will propagate down, but not up, the call stack.

If you have a circle, and you'd like a circle double the size, you can define functions to create a new circle based on an existing one. Here's an example:

```
static Circle Scale(this Circle circle, double factor)
   => new Circle(circle.Center, circle.Radius * factor);
```

OK, so far we haven't used mutation, and these examples are pretty intuitive. What do numbers, dates, and geometric entities have in common? The fact that their value captures their identity: they are *value objects*. If you change the *value* of a date...well, it *identifies* a different date!

The problems begin when we consider objects whose value and identity are different things. We'll look at this next.

9.2.2 *Representing change without mutation*

Many real-world entities change with time: your bank account, your calendar, your contacts list—all these things have a state that changes with time. (See figure 9.3.)

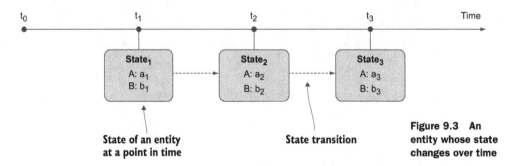

Figure 9.3 An entity whose state changes over time

---

[3] In reality, you can still mutate read-only variables by using reflection. But making a field read-only is a clear signal to any clients of your code that the field isn't meant to be mutated.

For such entities, their identity isn't captured by their value, because their identity remains constant, whereas their value changes with time. Instead, their identity is associated with different *states* at different points in time. Your age may change, or your salary, but your identity doesn't.

To represent such entities, programs must model not only an entity's state (that's the easy part) but the transitions from one state to another, and often the association of an identity with the entity's current state.

We've discussed some reasons why mutation provides an imperfect mechanism for managing state transitions. In FP, states are not mutated; they're snapshots that, like the frames of a film, represent an evolving reality but are in themselves static.

To illustrate this idea, let's start working on `AccountState`, which we'll use to represent the state of a bank account in the BOC application. We'll start simply, with just a few fields.

> **Listing 9.2   A simple model for the state of a bank account**

```
public enum AccountStatus
{ Requested, Active, Frozen, Dormant, Closed }

public class AccountState
{
   public AccountStatus Status { get; set; }
   public CurrencyCode Currency { get; set; }
   public decimal AllowedOverdraft { get; set; }
   public List<Transaction> TransactionHistory { get; set; }

   public AccountState()
      => TransactionHistory = new List<Transaction>();
}
```

In this approach, we're using an empty constructor and public setters. This allows us to create new instances elegantly with the object initializer syntax, as in the following listing.

> **Listing 9.3   Using the convenient object initializer syntax**

```
var account = new AccountState
{
   Status = AccountStatus.Active
};
```

This creates a new account with the `Status` property set explicitly; other properties are initialized to sensible default values. Note that the object initializer syntax calls the parameterless constructor and the public setters defined in `AccountState`.

If we want to represent a change in state, such as if the account is frozen, we'd create a new `AccountState` with the new `Status`. We can do this by adding a convenience method on `AccountState`.

> **Listing 9.4 Defining a copy method**

```
public class AccountState
{
    public AccountState WithStatus(AccountStatus newStatus)
       => new AccountState
       {
           Status = newStatus,
           Currency = this.Currency,
           AllowedOverdraft = this.AllowedOverdraft,
           TransactionHistory = this.TransactionHistory
       };
}
```

The updated field → `Status = newStatus,`

All other fields are copied from the current state.

`WithStatus` is a method that returns a copy of the instance, identical to the original in everything except the `Status`, which is as given. This is similar to how we previously obtained a new date by calling `AddDays` on a `DateTime` instance.

Methods like `WithStatus` are called *copy methods*, or *with-ers* because the convention is to name them "`With[Property]`." You would then represent a change in the state of the account as follows.

> **Listing 9.5 Obtaining a modified version of the object**

```
var newState = account.WithStatus(AccountStatus.Frozen);
```

Every time you want to change a property, you should create a new instance. "But isn't that terribly inefficient?" you may be thinking. In fact, this isn't as inefficient as you might think, as the "Performance implications" sidebar explains in more detail.

Performance implications of using immutable objects

Working with immutable objects means that you create modified copies rather than mutating the object in-place. This implies a small performance penalty for creating the modified copy, as well as creating a greater number of objects that will eventually need to be garbage-collected. This is also why FP isn't practical in languages that lack automatic memory management.

The performance impact is smaller than one might think because a typical copy method like `WithStatus` creates a *shallow copy*. That is, objects referenced by the original object aren't copied; only the reference is copied. In other words, with the exception of the field being updated, the new object is a bitwise replica of the original.

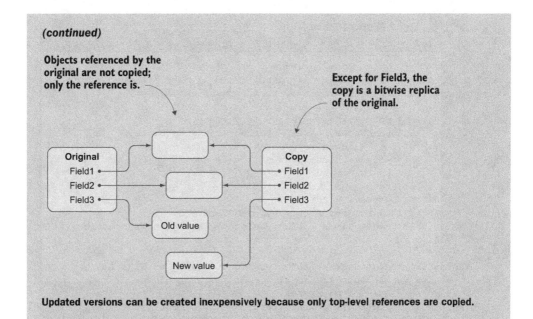

(continued)

Objects referenced by the original are not copied; only the reference is.

Except for Field3, the copy is a bitwise replica of the original.

Original	Copy
Field1	Field1
Field2	Field2
Field3	Field3

Old value

New value

Updated versions can be created inexpensively because only top-level references are copied.

For example, when you create a new `AccountState` by calling `WithStatus`, the list of transactions won't be copied. Instead, the new object will reference the original list of transactions. (As you'll see shortly, this too must be immutable, so it's OK for two different instances to share it.)

If you apply this principle, copy methods are fast. Of course, in-place updates are even faster, so there's a tradeoff between performance and safety. The performance penalty of creating shallow copies is likely to be negligible in the wide majority of cases, so my advice is to put safety first, and optimize later as needed.

9.3 *Enforcing immutability*

The implementation shown in the previous section uses property setters to initially populate an object, and copy methods to obtain updated versions. This approach is called *immutability by convention*: you use convention and discipline to avoid mutation. The setters are exposed, but they should never be called after the object has been initialized.

But this doesn't prevent a mischievous colleague who's not sold on immutability from setting the fields directly:

```
account.Status = AccountStatus.Frozen;
```

If you want to prevent this, you'll have to make your object immutable by removing property setters altogether. New instances must then be populated by passing all values as arguments to the constructor.

Listing 9.6   Refactoring towards immutability: removing all setters

```
public class AccountState
{
    public AccountStatus Status { get; }
    public CurrencyCode Currency { get; }
    public decimal AllowedOverdraft { get; }
    public List<Transaction> Transactions { get; }

    public AccountState(CurrencyCode Currency
        , AccountStatus Status = AccountStatus.Requested
        , decimal AllowedOverdraft = 0
        , List<Transaction> Transactions = null)
    {
        this.Status = Status;
        this.Currency = Currency;
        this.AllowedOverdraft = AllowedOverdraft;
        this.Transactions = Transactions ?? new List<Transaction>();
    }

    public AccountState WithStatus(AccountStatus newStatus)
        => new AccountState(
            Status: newStatus,
            Currency: this.Currency,
            AllowedOverdraft: this.AllowedOverdraft,
            Transactions: this.TransactionHistory
        );
}
```

In the constructor, I've used named parameters and default values in such a way that I can create a new instance with a syntax very similar to the object initializer syntax we were using before. We can now create a new account with sensible values like this:

```
var account = new AccountState
(
    Currency: "EUR",
    Status: AccountStatus.Active
);
```

The WithStatus copy method can be called just like before.

Notice that we've now enforced that a value must be provided for Currency, which isn't possible when you use the object initializer syntax. So we've kept readability while making the implementation more robust.

 USE CONSTRUCTORS TO ENFORCE BUSINESS RULES   Forcing the clients of your code to use a constructor or a factory function to instantiate an object improves the robustness of your code, because you can enforce business rules at this point, making it impossible to create an object in an invalid state, such as an account with no currency.

9.3.1   *Immutable all the way down*

We're still not done, because for an object to be immutable, all its constituents must be immutable too. Here we're using a mutable `List`, so your mischievous colleague could still effectively mutate the account state by writing this:

```
account.Transactions.Clear();
```

The most effective way to prevent this is to create a copy of the list given to the constructor, and store its contents in an immutable list, for which we can use the `ImmutableList` type in the `System.Collections.Immutable` library:[4]

Listing 9.7   Preventing mutation by using immutable collection

```
using System.Collections.Immutable;
// ...                                        Mark the class as
                                              sealed to prevent
                                       ┌───── mutable subclasses.
public sealed class AccountState    ◄─┘
{
    public IEnumerable<Transaction> TransactionHistory { get; }

    public AccountState(CurrencyCode Currency
        , AccountStatus Status = AccountStatus.Requested
        , decimal AllowedOverdraft = 0
        , IEnumerable<Transaction> Transactions = null)
    {                                                       Create and store
        // ...                                              a defensive copy
        TransactionHistory = ImmutableList.CreateRange      of the given list.
            (Transactions ?? Enumerable.Empty<Transaction>());
    }
}
```

When a new `AccountState` is created, the given list of transactions is copied and stored in an `ImmutableList`. This is called a *defensive copy*. Now the list of transactions of an `AccountState` can't be altered by any consumers, and it remains unaffected even if the list given in the constructor is altered at a later point. Fortunately, `CreateRange` is smart enough that if it's given an `ImmutableList`, it just returns it, so that copy methods won't incur any additional overhead.

Furthermore, `Transaction` and `Currency` must also be immutable types. I've also marked `AccountState` as sealed to prevent the creation of mutable subclasses. Now `AccountState` is truly immutable. In theory, that is—in practice, one could still mutate an instance using reflection,[5] so that your mischievous colleague can still have the upper hand. But at least now there's no room for mutating the object by mistake.

---

[4]   The `System.Collections.Immutable` library was developed by Microsoft to complement the mutable collections in the framework, so its feel should be familiar. It's not part of the framework, so you must get it from NuGet.

[5]   The utilities in `System.Reflection` allow you to view and modify the value of any field at runtime, including `private` and `readonly` fields, and the backing fields of auto-properties.

How can you add a new transaction to the list? You don't. You create a new list that has the new transaction as well as all existing ones, and that will be part of a new `AccountState`.

Listing 9.8   Adding a child to an immutable object requires creation of a new parent object

```
using LaYumba.Functional;                        Prepend as an extension
                                                 method on IEnumerable
public sealed class AccountState
{                                                     A new IEnumerable,
    public AccountState Add(Transaction t)            including existing values
        => new AccountState(                          and the one being added
            Transactions: TransactionHistory.Prepend(t),
            Currency: this.Currency,
            Status: this.Status,                 All other fields are
            AllowedOverdraft: this.AllowedOverdraft   copied as usual.
        );
}
```

Notice that in this particular case we're *prepending* the transaction to the list. This is domain-specific; in most cases you're interested in the *latest* transactions, so it's most efficient to keep the latest ones at the front of the list.

Copying a list every time a single element is added or removed may sound terribly inefficient, but this isn't necessarily the case. We'll discuss why in section 9.4.

9.3.2   Copy methods without boilerplate?

Now that we've managed to properly implement `AccountState` as an immutable type, let's face one of the pain points: *writing copy methods is no fun!* Imagine an object with 10 properties, all of which need copy methods. If there are any collections, you'll need to copy them into immutable collections and add copy methods that add items to or remove them from those collections. That's a lot of boilerplate!

A way to mitigate this is to write a single `With` method, with named optional arguments, much like how we used them in defining the constructor for `AccountState`.

Listing 9.9   A single `With` method that can set any property

```
public AccountState With
    ( AccountStatus? Status = null           null indicates that the
    , decimal? AllowedOverdraft = null)      field wasn't specified.
    => new AccountState(
        Status: Status ?? this.Status,
        AllowedOverdraft: AllowedOverdraft ?? this.AllowedOverdraft,
        Currency: this.Currency,
        Transactions: this.TransactionHistory     If no value was specified,
    );                                             use the current
                                                   instance's value.
    You can prevent
    arbitrary changes.
```

The default value of null indicates that the value hasn't been specified, in which case the current instance's value is used to populate the copy. For value-type fields, you can use the corresponding nullable type for the argument type to allow a default of null. Because the default value null indicates that the field hasn't been specified, and hence the current value will be used, it's not possible to use this method to set a field to null, but given the discussion on null vs. Option in chapter 3, you can probably see that this isn't a good idea anyway.

Notice that in listing 9.9 we're only allowing changes to two fields, because we're assuming that we can never change the currency of a bank account or make arbitrary changes to the transaction history. This approach allows us to reduce boilerplate while still retaining fine-grained control over what operations we want to allow. The usage is as follows:

```
public static AccountState Freeze(this AccountState account)
   => account.With(Status: AccountStatus.Frozen);

public static AccountState RedFlag(this AccountState account)
   => account.With
   (
      Status: AccountStatus.Frozen,
      AllowedOverdraft: 0m
   );
```

This not only reads very clearly but gives us better performance compared to using the classic With[Property] methods: if we need to update multiple fields, a single new instance is created. I definitely recommend using this single With method over defining a copy method for every field.

Another approach is to define a generic helper that will do the copying and updating, without the need for any boilerplate. I've implemented such a general-purpose With method in the LaYumba.Functional.Immutable class, and it can be used as follows.

> **Listing 9.10 Using a general-purpose copy method**

```
using LaYumba.Functional;

var oldState = new AccountState("EUR", AccountStatus.Active);
var newState = oldState.With(a => a.Status, AccountStatus.Frozen);

oldState.Status    // => AccountStatus.Active
newState.Status    // => AccountStatus.Frozen
newState.Currency  // => "EUR"
```

Here, With is an extension method on object that takes an Expression identifying the property to be updated, and the new value. Using reflection, it then creates a bitwise copy of the original object, identifies the backing field of the specified property, and sets it to the given value.

In short, it does what we want, but for any field and any type. On the up side, this saves us from having to write tedious copy methods. On the down side, reflection is relatively slow, and we lose the fine-grained control available when we explicitly choose what fields can be updated in With.

As you can see, enforcing immutability is a thorny business, and it's one of the biggest hurdles when programming functionally in C#.

9.3.3   *Leveraging F# for data types*

There is a third option, which is to use F# to model your data objects. When coding functionally, it's natural to separate data from behavior: data is encoded in data types that have little or no behavior (they typically represent the events, view models, data-transfer objects, entities, and value objects of your domain), whereas behavior is encoded in functions that transform that data or perform side effects.

This demarcation makes it easy to write your program behavior in C# while taking advantage of F#'s type system to define your data objects. Learning F# can seem a daunting prospect (and migrating an existing C# codebase to F# even more so), but I'm not suggesting you do that: I'm suggesting writing *just* the data types in F#. This is really easy, and you can get started literally in minutes.

The F# syntax for declaring types is very clear and concise, and most importantly, *all types are immutable* without the need for any extra work.[6] For example, the Account-State type, with all its subtypes, can be defined in F# as follows.

Listing 9.11   Writing the domain model in F#

Use a "discriminated union" instead of enum.

```
namespace Boc.Domain
open System                    ← Equivalent to a using
                                 statement in C#

type AccountStatus =
    Requested | Active | Frozen | Dormant | Closed

type CurrencyCode = string    ← A "type alias"

type Transaction = {          ← Use "record types"
    Amount: decimal             instead of classes.
    Description: string
    Date: DateTime
}

type AccountState = {
    Status: AccountStatus
    Currency: CurrencyCode
    AllowedOverdraft: decimal
    TransactionHistory: Transaction list
}
```

---

[6]   All types in F# are immutable unless you explicitly specify otherwise using the CLIMutable attribute. This is particularly useful if you're working with a deserializer that relies on property setters.

This model is equivalent to the C# implementation shown previously, so it should be easy to see what's what.

F# has copy methods built in, in the form of copy and update expressions. This allows you to easily enrich `AccountState` with copy methods that can be called from C# code, as follows.

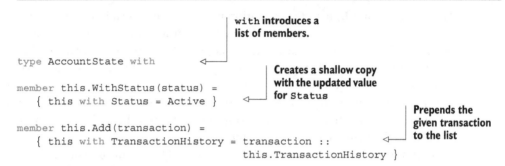

Listing 9.12 Using F# copy and update expressions

`with` introduces a list of members.

```
type AccountState with

member this.WithStatus(status) =
    { this with Status = Active }

member this.Add(transaction) =
    { this with TransactionHistory = transaction ::
                            this.TransactionHistory }
```

Creates a shallow copy with the updated value for `Status`

Prepends the given transaction to the list

The first line of the code introduces a list of members, which are functions that will be "attached" to the `AccountState` type—you can think of these as extension methods. Thus, `WithStatus` and `Add` will be visible as methods on `AccountState` from C# code. Their implementation just relies on copy and update expressions (using the `with` keyword).

As you can see, you don't need to become a proficient F# programmer to take advantage of F#'s powerful type system: the syntactic elements in the previous couple of listings are pretty much all you need to know to write your domain model in F#. Because this book is specifically about C#, I won't pursue this approach, but in a real-world project, mixing the two languages is an option worth considering.

9.3.4 *Comparing strategies for immutability: an ugly contest*

To summarize, avoiding mutation and enforcing immutability are different things, and although I urge you to systematically avoid mutation, enforcing immutability isn't easily done—and if you factor in the use of reflection, it can't be done at all. We've discussed a few different approaches, each with their pros and cons:

- *Immutability by convention*—In this approach, you don't do any extra work to *prevent* mutation; you just *avoid* it, like you probably avoid the use of goto, unsafe pointer access, and bitwise operations, just to mention a few things that the language allows but that have proven problematic. This can be a viable choice if you're working independently, or with a team that's sold on this approach from day one. The downside is, of course, that mutation can creep in.
- *Define immutable objects in C#*—This approach will give you a more robust model that *communicates* to other developers that the object shouldn't be mutated. This approach is much better suited if you're working on a project where

immutability isn't used across the board. Compared to immutability by convention, it requires at least some extra work in defining constructors.

- *Write data objects in F#*—Given the little amount of F# knowledge required to do this, and the advantages that come with using F#'s type system, this is a very attractive option, and perhaps the best option as of today. The main caveat is that this may influence your assembly structure, because F# objects need to go into their own assembly.

The main reason why avoiding mutation in C# can be painstaking—whether enforced or by convention—is because of the need to define copy methods. If you write your objects in F#, you can take advantage of copy-and-update expressions. In C#, you can avoid the boilerplate of copy methods by using the generic, reflection-based With method illustrated in listing 9.10. For specific cases where the performance impact is noticeable, or you want to have more fine-grained control over which fields can be affected and how (for example, to permit transactions to be added to an account, but not removed), manually define copy methods.

If you feel frustrated by the lack of a hard-and-fast solution, you're in good company. In fact, to make things even more complicated, third-party libraries may have limitations that dictate your choices. Traditionally, deserializers and ORMs for .NET have used the empty constructor and settable properties to create and populate objects. If you're relying on libraries with such requirements, immutability by convention may be your only option.

On the up side, this is an area in constant evolution. Improving support for immutability is strong on the list of features being considered for future versions of the language (remember how getter-only auto-properties in C# 6 already provided an improvement in this direction).[7] Deserializer libraries are also evolving and improving support for creating objects via the constructor, in the absence of property setters.

Now that you know about immutable objects, let's look at some of the principles behind the design of immutable data structures. You'll see that the principles are the same—after all, objects are just ad hoc data structures.

9.4   *A short introduction to functional data structures*

The pitfalls of mutation are particularly evident when dealing with data structures: because it takes longer to process a large collection than to update a single object, there are greater chances of a race condition occurring between different threads accessing the same collection concurrently. You saw an example of this in chapter 1.

If you commit to only working with immutable data, all data structures should also be immutable. For example, you should never add an element to a list or one by changing its structure, but rather create a new list with the desired changes.

---

[7] Most importantly, one proposal for C# 7 was the introduction of record types. Like record types in F#, these would be immutable and feature a new syntax for copy-and-update expressions. Although this feature didn't make it into C# 7, we may yet see it in future versions.

This may initially cause you to raise your eyebrows: "To add an item to a list, I need to copy all existing elements into a new list along with the extra item? How inefficient is that?"

To give you an idea of why this isn't necessarily inefficient, let's look at some simple functional data structures. You'll see that adding a new element to a collection does yield a new collection, but this doesn't involve copying every item in the original collection.

 NOTE The implementations shown in this section are very naive. They're helpful in understanding the basic concepts, but they're not for use in production. For real-world applications, use a proven library, such as `System.Collections.Immutable`.

9.4.1 *The classic functional linked list*

We'll start with the classic functional linked list. While deceptively simple, this is the basic list you'll find in the core library of most functional languages. Symbolically, we can describe it as follows:

```
List<T> = Empty | Cons(T, List<T>)
```

In other words, a `List` of `T`'s can be one of two things:

- `Empty`—A special value representing the empty list
- `Cons`—A non-empty list "*cons*-tructed" from two values:
  - A single `T`, called the *head* and representing the first element in the list
  - Another `List` of `T`'s, called the *tail*, representing all the other elements

The tail can, in turn, be `Empty` or a `Cons`, and so on. Thus, `List` is an example of a *recursive type*: a type that's defined in terms of itself. This is how with just two cases we can cater for lists of any length.

For example, the structure of a list containing `["a", "b", "c"]` is as follows:

```
Cons("a", Cons("b", Cons("c", Empty)
```

It can be represented graphically as in figure 9.4, where each `Cons` is represented as a box with a value (the head) and a pointer to the rest of the list (the tail).

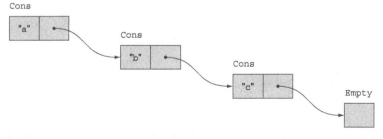

Figure 9.4 A linked list containing the values `["a", "b", "c"]`

Let's look at how we can implement this in C#. I'll simply use a `bool` to indicate whether we're in the `Empty` case.

Listing 9.13   Implementation of a functional singly linked list

```
public sealed class List<T>
{
    readonly bool isEmpty;
    readonly T head;
    readonly List<T> tail;                    Creates an
                                              empty list
    internal List() { isEmpty = true; }

    internal List(T head, List<T> tail)       Creates a non-
    {                                         empty list
        this.head = head;
        this.tail = tail;
    }

    public R Match<R>(Func<R> Empty, Func<T, List<T>, R> Cons)
        => isEmpty ? Empty() : Cons(head, tail);
}
```

This looks almost too simple. The only way to interact with a list is with `Match`, which will execute different paths depending on whether the list is empty or not. If the list isn't empty, the function given to `Match` is given the head and tail of the list.

In fact, we can implement all the common operations you'd expect on a list in terms of `Match`, and they always rely on the type's recursive definition. For example, if you want to know the length of the list, you `Match`—the empty list obviously has length 0, whereas the non-empty list has the length of its tail plus 1:

```
public static int Length<T>(this List<T> list)
    => list.Match(
        Empty: () => 0,
        Cons: (head, tail) => 1 + tail.Length());
```

You may have noticed that both constructors are marked as internal. As usual, I'll expose factory functions through a static class.

In many cases, creating the whole structure explicitly with `new List("a", new List("b", ...` would be tedious, so let's add a list initializer to which we can pass a few hard-coded items:

```
public static class LinkedList
{
    public static List<T> List<T>(T h, List<T> t)
        => new List<T>(h, t);

    public static List<T> List<T>(params T[] items)
        => items.Reverse().Aggregate(new List<T>()
            , (acc, t) => List(t, acc));
}
```

The first factory function just calls the `List` constructor, which takes a head and a tail. The following function is a convenience list initializer. The `params` keyword already collects all the arguments into an array, so we just need to "translate" the array into a suitable combination of Empty and Cons. That's done with Aggregate, using Empty as the accumulator, and creating a Cons in the reducer function. Because List prepends the item to the list, we must reverse the list first.

Now that you've seen the main building blocks, let's play with List in the REPL. The data structures discussed in this section are defined in the LaYumba.Functional .Data assembly, so you'll need to import it and the relevant namespaces first:

```
#r "functional-csharp-code\LaYumba.Functional.Data\bin\Debug\netstandard1.6\
➥ LaYumba.Functional.Data.dll"
using LaYumba.Functional.Data.LinkedList;
using static LaYumba.Functional.Data.LinkedList.LinkedList;

var empty = List<string>();
// => []

var letters = List("a", "b");
// => [a, b]

var taxi = List("c", letters);
// => [c, a, b]
```

This code demonstrates how you can create a list, empty or prepopulated, and how you can create a Cons by adding a single item to an existing list.

COMMON LIST OPERATIONS

Let's now look at how we can perform some common operations with this list, like those we've become accustomed to with IEnumerable. For example, here's Map:

```
public static List<R> Map<T, R>(this List<T> list, Func<T, R> f)
   => list.Match(
       () => List<R>(),
       (head, tail) => List(f(head), tail.Map(f)));
```

Map takes a list and a function to be mapped onto the list. It then uses pattern matching: if the list is empty, it returns an empty list; otherwise, it applies the function to the head and recursively maps the function onto the tail, and returns the Cons of these two.

If we had a list of integers and wanted the sum, we could implement this along the same lines:

```
public static int Sum(this List<int> list)
   => list.Match(
       () => 0,
       (head, tail) => head + tail.Sum());
```

As you know, Sum is a special case of Aggregate, so let's see how we could implement the more generic Aggregate for List:

```
public static Acc Aggregate<T, Acc>
      (this List<T> list, Acc acc, Func<Acc, T, Acc> f)
   => list.Match(
       () => acc,
       (head, tail) => Aggregate(tail, f(acc, head), f));
```

Again, we pattern match, and in the Cons case we apply the reducer function f to the accumulator and the head. Then we recursively call Aggregate with the new accumulator and the tail of the list.

(!) **WARNING**   The implementations shown here aren't stack-safe. That is, if the list is long enough, they'll cause a StackOverflowException.

Now that we've looked at how we can work with the linked list, let's see about operations that "modify" the list.

MODIFYING AN IMMUTABLE LIST

Let's say we want to "add" an item to an existing list (by which I naturally mean we'll obtain a new list with an additional item). With a singly linked list, the natural approach is to add items at the front:

```
public static List<T> Add<T>(this List<T> list, T value)
    => List(value, list);
```

Given an existing list and a new value, we just construct a new list with a new head. The head of the new list will be a list node holding the new value and a pointer to the head of the original list. That's all! There's no need to copy all the elements, so we can add an element in constant time, creating just one new object.

Here's an example of adding to our immutable linked list:

```
var fruit = List("pineapple", "banana");
// => ["pineapple", "banana"]

var tropicalMix = fruit.Add("kiwi");
// => ["kiwi", "pineapple", "banana"]

var yellowFruit = fruit.Add("lemon");
// => ["lemon", "pineapple", "banana"]
```

The fruit list is initialized with two items. We then "add" a third fruit to obtain a new list, tropicalMix. Because the list is immutable, our original fruit list hasn't changed and still contains two items. This is apparent because we can reuse it to create a new, modified version of the list containing yellow fruit.[8]

Figure 9.5 offers a graphical representation of the objects that are created in the code above, and shows that the original fruit list is not altered, nor do its elements need to be copied, when creating new lists with an added item.

---

[8] Immutable data structures are often referred to as *persistent* data structures. The term "persistence" in this context doesn't indicate persistence onto some media, but simply persistence in memory: the original data structure is unaffected by any operation that creates a new version, such as adding or removing elements. Furthermore, the term "persistent" applied to a data structure implies that it offers certain guarantees in terms of the running time of certain operations. Namely, operations should be just as efficient in a persistent data structure as in the corresponding mutable structure, or at least be within the same order of magnitude. This goes deeper into data structure and algorithm design, so here I'll just stick with the terms *immutable/functional* data structures/collections.

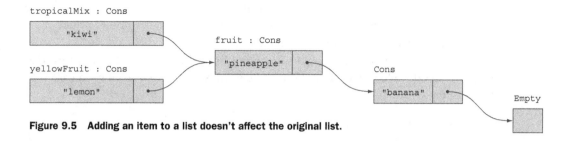

Figure 9.5 Adding an item to a list doesn't affect the original list.

Think what this means in terms of decoupling: when you have an immutable list—and more generally, an immutable object—you can expose it without ever having to worry about what some other component will do to the data. There's nothing they can do to the data at all!

What about removing an item? The singly linked list is biased to work well with the first item, so we'll remove the first item (the head) and return the rest of the list (the tail):

```
public static List<T> Tail<T>(this List<T> list)
    => list.Match(
        () => { throw new IndexOutOfRangeException(); },
        (_, tail) => tail);
```

Again, we can remove the first element from the list in constant time, and without altering the original list. (Notice that this is one of very few places where throwing an exception is justified, because calling `Tail` on an empty list is a developer error. If there's a chance of the list being empty, a correct implementation should use `Match` rather than calling `Tail`.)

You may find these examples rather limited because we've only interacted with the first element of the list. But in practice, this can be used to cover quite a number of use cases. For example, it's a perfect starting point if you need a stack. Common operations like `Map` and `Where` would be $O(n)$ for a list of length n, just as with any other list.

You can define functions to insert or remove an element at index m, and these operations are $O(m)$, because they would require traversing m elements and creating m new `Cons` objects. If you need to append or remove from the end of a long list often (for example, if you need to implement a queue), you'd use a different data structure.

9.4.2 Binary trees

Trees are also very common data structures. Most list implementations other than linked lists use trees as their underlying representation, because this allows certain operations to be performed more efficiently. We'll just look at a very basic binary tree,[9] defined as follows:

```
Tree<T> = Leaf(T) | Branch(Tree<T>, Tree<T>)
```

---

[9] "Binary" here means that every branch has two subtrees.

That is, a tree can be a `Leaf`, which is a terminal node and contains a `T`, or it can be a `Branch`, a non-terminal node that contains two children or "subtrees," which can in turn be leaves or branches, and so on recursively.

With `List`, I used a single class to represent both the `Empty` and `Cons` cases. Here, the possible values for a tree are a bit more complex, so I'll represent each case with a different type:

```
public abstract class Tree<T> { }
internal class Leaf<T> : Tree<T>
{
    public T Value { get; }
}
internal class Branch<T> : Tree<T>
{
    public Tree<T> Left { get; }
    public Tree<T> Right { get; }
}
```

In other words, rather than using a Boolean, I'm using the type system to tell me whether a particular tree is a `Branch` or a `Leaf`. We still need an implementation of `Match` to execute different code in each case and to access the tree's inner value. This can be implemented as follows:

```
public abstract class Tree<T>
{
    public abstract R Match<R>
        (Func<T, R> Leaf, Func<Tree<T>, Tree<T>, R> Branch);
}
public class Leaf<T> : Tree<T>
{
    public override R Match<R>
        (Func<T, R> Leaf, Func<Tree<T>, Tree<T>, R> Branch)
        => Leaf(Value);
}
public class Branch<T> : Tree<T>
{
    public override R Match<R>
        (Func<T, R> Leaf, Func<Tree<T>, Tree<T>, R> Branch)
        => Branch(Left, Right);
}
```

Here, I've declared a `Match` method with the desired signature in the abstract `Tree` class; each subclass provides an implementation that calls the appropriate function. The runtime will then decide which overload to execute.[10]

---

[10] You may dislike the fact that the base class "knows" about the subclasses. If you think about this code in terms of inheritance, this would indeed be a violation of the Open-Closed principle: if you added a new subclass, you'd have to modify the base class. But in this case, inheritance is an implementation detail, and `Tree` isn't meant to be open for extension. There should never be any subclasses of `Tree` other than `Leaf` and `Branch` (unfortunately, the language doesn't let us express this). The `Match` methods are just surrogates for the lack of a good syntax for pattern matching in C#. Again, there are good indications that this will improve in future versions.

From the caller's point of view, it's `Match` as usual:

```
myTree.Match(
    Leaf: t => $"It's a leaf containing '{t}'",
    Branch: (left, right) => "It's a branch");
```

I've omitted the usual creational boilerplate: constructors and factory functions `Leaf` and `Branch`. These are included in the code samples, and they allow you to create a tree in the REPL like this:

```
using static LaYumba.Functional.Data.BinaryTree.Tree;

Branch(
    Branch(Leaf(1), Leaf(2)),
    Leaf(3)
)
```

That would represent a tree like this:

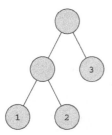

Now let's look at some common operations. What about `Map`? Try to avoid looking at the following solution and write down how you think `Map` might work. Naturally, `Map` should create a new tree. You can pattern-match, and if you have a leaf, then you extract its value, apply the function to the leaf, and wrap it in a new leaf. Otherwise, you create a new branch whose left and right subtrees are the result of mapping the function onto the original subtrees:

```
public static Tree<R> Map<T, R>(this Tree<T> tree, Func<T, R> f)
    => tree.Match(
        Leaf: t => Leaf(f(t)),
        Branch: (left, right) => Branch
            (
                Left: left.Map(f),
                Right: right.Map(f)
            )
    );
```

Map yields a new tree, isomorphic to the original one, with the mapped function applied to each value in the original tree, as shown in figure 9.6.

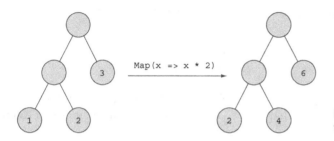

Figure 9.6 The `Map` function for a binary tree

It's also reasonable to define an `Aggregate` function that reduces all the values in the tree to a single value:

```
public static Acc Aggregate<T, Acc>
   (this Tree<T> tree, Acc acc, Func<Acc, T, Acc> f)
   => tree.Match(
      Leaf: t => f(acc, t),
      Branch: (l, r) =>
      {
         var leftAcc = l.Aggregate(acc, f);
         return r.Aggregate(leftAcc, f);
      });
```

More interestingly, let's look at operations that change the structure of a tree, such as inserting an element. Here's a very simple implementation.

Listing 9.14   Adding a value to an immutable tree

```
public static Tree<T> Insert<T>(this Tree<T> tree, T value)
   => tree.Match(
      Leaf: _ => Branch(tree, Leaf(value)),
      Branch: (l, r) => Branch(l, r.Insert(value)));
```

As usual, the code uses pattern matching. If the tree is a leaf, it creates a branch whose two children are the leaf itself, and a new leaf with the inserted value; if it's a branch, it inserts the new value into the right subtree.

For example, if you start with a tree containing {1, 2, 3, 7} and insert the value 9, the result would be as shown in figure 9.7. As you can see, the new tree shares large portions of its structure with the original tree. This is an example of the more general idea of *structure sharing*; that is, the updated collection shares as much of its structure as possible with the original collection.

How many new items are created to insert an item into a tree? As many as it takes to reach a leaf. If you start with a balanced tree with n elements,[11] an insert involves the creation of $\log n + 2$ objects, which is very reasonable.[12]

---

[11] A tree is balanced if all paths from the root to a leaf have the same length, or differ at most by one.

[12] The base of the log will be the arity of the tree: how many children each node has. A real-world implementation of a tree underlying a list representation may have an arity of 32, so that after inserting 1 million objects, your tree may still only have a depth of 2 or 3 levels.

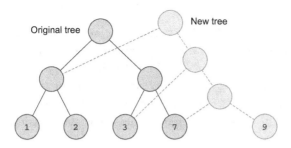

Original tree

New tree

Figure 9.7 The tree with the added value shares parts of the structure with the original tree.

Of course, the implementation in listing 9.14 would eventually lead to a very imbalanced tree, because it always adds elements to the right. To guarantee efficient inserts, we'd need to refine the tree representation to include a self-balancing mechanism. This is certainly possible, but beyond the scope of this introduction.

Developing efficient functional data structures is a vast and fascinating topic, of which we've only scratched the surface.[13] Nonetheless, in this section you've gained some insight into the inner workings of functional data structures and the idea of structure sharing, which allows immutable data structures to be safe and perform well.

Functional programs may incur some performance penalty for copying data rather than updating it in-place, but imperative programs may have to introduce locking and defensive copies to ensure correctness. As a result, functional programs tend to perform better in many scenarios. For most practical applications, however, performance isn't the critical concern, but rather the greater reliability that you gain by embracing immutability.

Exercises

1 Lists—implement functions to work with the singly linked `List` defined in this chapter:
   a `InsertAt` inserts an item at the given index.
   b `RemoveAt` removes the item at the given index.
   c `TakeWhile` takes a predicate and traverses the list, yielding all items until it finds one that fails the predicate.
   d `DropWhile` works similarly, but excludes all items at the front of the list.
   e What's the complexity of these four functions? How many new objects are required to create the new list?
   f `TakeWhile` and `DropWhile` are useful when working with a list that's sorted and you'd like to get all items greater or smaller than some value. Write implementations that take an `IEnumerable` rather than a `List`.

---

[13] The reference book on the subject is *Purely Functional Data Structures* by Chris Okasaki (Cambridge University Press, 1999). Unfortunately the code samples are in Standard ML.

2 Trees:

  a Is it possible to define `Bind` for the binary tree implementation shown in this chapter? If so, implement `Bind`; otherwise explain why it's not possible. (Hint: start by writing the signature, and then sketch a binary tree and how you could apply a tree-returning function to each value in the tree.)

  b Implement a `LabelTree` type, where each node has a label of type `string` and a list of subtrees. This could be used to model a typical navigation tree or a category tree in a website.

  c Imagine you need to add localization to your navigation tree. You're given a `LabelTree` where the value of each label is a key, and a dictionary that maps keys to translations in one of the languages that your site must support. You need to compute the localized navigation/category tree. (Hint: define `Map` for `LabelTree`.)

  d Unit test the preceding implementation.

Summary

- The FP paradigm discourages state mutation, preventing several drawbacks associated with state mutation, such as lack of thread safety, coupling, and impurity.

- Things that don't change are represented with immutable objects.

- In FP, things that change are also represented with immutable objects; these immutable snapshots represent an entity's state at a given point. Change is represented by creating a new snapshot with the desired changes.

- Enforcing immutability in C# is doable, but laborious; using immutability by convention, or modeling domain objects in F# are alternatives worth considering.

- Like objects, collections should also be immutable, so that existing collections are never altered, but rather new collections are created with the desired changes.

- Immutable collections can be safe as well as efficient, because an updated version shares much of its structure with the original collection without affecting it.

Event sourcing:
a functional approach
to persistence

10

This chapter covers

- Thinking functionally about persisted data
- Event sourcing concepts and implementation
- Architecture of event-sourced systems

In the last chapter, you saw that in FP we avoid mutating state, especially global state. Did I mention that the database is also state, so it too should be immutable? What? Yes, didn't you see this one coming? A database is, conceptually, just a data structure. Whether it's stored in memory or on disk is ultimately just an implementation detail.

You saw how functional data structures, although immutable, can "evolve." That is, you can create new "states" or new "views" of any given structure, which are built upon, but don't alter, the original structure. This idea, which we explored with respect to objects, lists, and trees, naturally applies to in-memory data just as to stored data, and this is how our applications can represent change without mutation, even at the database level.

There are currently two approaches to this idea of *append-only* data storage:

- *Assertion-based*—Treats the DB as an ever-growing collection of *facts* that are true at a given point in time
- *Event-based*—Treats the DB as an ever-growing collection of events that occur at given points in time

In both cases, data is never updated or deleted, only appended.[1] I'll compare these two approaches in more detail at the end of the chapter, but most of the chapter will be spent discussing the event-based approach, usually referred to as *event sourcing* (ES). This is because it's easier to understand and to implement using various kinds of backing storage, and its adoption in the .NET community so far has been much wider.

10.1   *Thinking functionally about data storage*

Many server applications today are inherently *stateless*; that is, when they receive a request, they retrieve the required data from the database, do some processing, and persist the relevant changes (see figure 10.1). A vast majority of server applications follow this approach.

Indeed, this approach has proven effective precisely because state is such a major source of complexity. If you can get the data out of thin air, as it were, when you need it, then a lot of difficult problems go away. This is, in essence, what stateless server processes do.

This also means that it's relatively

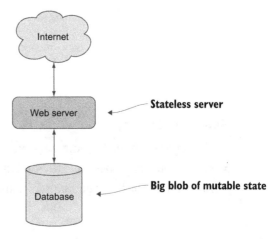

Figure 10.1   So-called stateless servers usually rely on a big blob of mutable data called the DB.

easy to avoid state mutation in a stateless server: just create new, updated versions of the data, and persist those to the database. But we're fooling ourselves if we think that we're developing functionally, if values in the DB are being updated or deleted in the process. Whenever we develop an application with a CRUD approach—that is, updating stored data in-place—we're essentially using the DB as a big blob of global mutable state.

10.1.1   *Why data storage should be append-only*

Relational databases have been in use for some 40 years. They were conceived in a time when disk space was scarce, so using it efficiently was paramount. Typically, only

---

[1]   The traditional functions of a relational DB are the CRUD operations: create, read, update, and delete. The functional approach to data storage is CRA: create, read, append.

the "current state" was stored. When a customer changed address, the old address was overwritten with the new one—a mindset we still have today, even though it's now become completely obsolete.

Today, in the age of big data, the tables are turned: storage is cheap, and data is valuable. Overwriting data is like throwing money out the window. Say that a customer removes an item from their shopping basket: what do you do? Do you delete a row in the database? If you do, you've just deleted valuable information that might be useful in determining why certain items aren't selling as expected. Maybe customers often abandon certain items mid-purchase and replace them with cheaper items from the suggestions list. If you delete the data, you can never run this sort of analysis.

This is why the idea of *append-only* storage has gained traction: never delete or overwrite any data, and only append new data. (For example, think about the version control system you use to store your code: does it overwrite existing code when you commit new changes?)

Append-only storage has another great virtue: it eliminates the problem of database contention. DB engines internally use locks to ensure that concurrent connections modifying the same cells don't conflict with each other. For instance, imagine you have an e-commerce site, and there's a rush of purchases for one particular product. If the inventory count for that product is modeled as a value in a DB cell that's updated as orders are placed, that puts contention on that cell, making database access inefficient. An append-only approach, such as event sourcing, eliminates this problem.

Let's see what event sourcing looks like.

10.1.2 *Relax, and forget about storing state*

We're overly concerned with representing state. In fact, we take it for granted that we must persist state. But this tacit assumption is unfounded: it's just the effect of relational databases being prevalent for half a century.

An important idea in chapter 9 was the relation of states to entities. *States* are snapshots of an entity at a given time; conversely, an *entity* is a sequence of logically related states. *State transitions* cause a new state to be associated with the entity, or, more intuitively, cause the entity to go from one state to the next.

For example, your bank account is in one state now, and it will be in a different state tomorrow as the result of some *events*, like deposits, withdrawals, or interest charges, that cause the account to transition from one state into the next. This is illustrated in figure 10.2.

In relational databases, we tend to only store the latest state of an entity, overwriting previous states. When we really need to know about the past, we often use history tables, in which we store *all* snapshots. This approach is inefficient, because we're duplicating all the data that hasn't changed between snapshots, and it's ineffective, because we must run complicated logic to compare two states if we want to figure out what caused the changes.

Event sourcing (ES) turns things around: it shifts the focus from states to state transitions. Instead of storing data about the states, it stores data about the events: it's

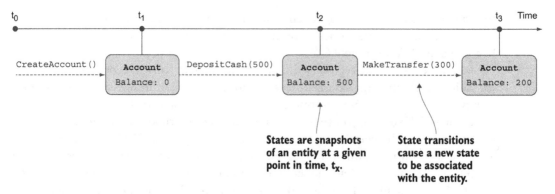

Figure 10.2   An entity as a sequence of logically related states

always possible to reconstruct the current state of an entity by "replaying" all the events that affected the entity.

Figure 10.3 is the same as the previous one, but the focus has changed. We don't want to focus on state: *state is secondary*. In fact, an entity's state is (literally) a function of its event history.

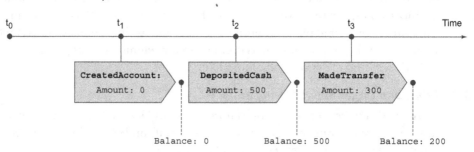

Figure 10.3   Shifting the focus from states to state transitions

It's difficult, given two states, to figure out what event may have caused the transition, but it's easy to figure out the new state, given an event and the previous state. So in ES, we persist data that captures details about events, not states.

10.2   *Event sourcing basics*

Next, we'll look at how we can apply these ideas in practice, illustrating them through our BOC scenario. You'll see how

- *Events* can be represented as simple, immutable data objects capturing details of what happened.
- *States* can also be represented as immutable data objects, although they may have a more complex structure than events.
- *State transitions* can be represented as functions that take a state and an event, and produce a new state.

Finally, you'll see how you can recreate an entity's state from its event history.

10.2.1 *Representing events*

Events are really simple, and they *should* be really simple. They're just plain data objects that capture the *minimum* amount of information required to faithfully represent what happened. For example, here are some events that represent things that may affect a bank account.

Listing 10.1 Some events affecting a bank account

```
public abstract class Event
{
    public Guid EntityId { get; }                    Identifies the affected
    public DateTime Timestamp { get; }               entity (in this case, an
}                                                    account)

public sealed class CreatedAccount : Event
{
    public CurrencyCode Currency { get; }
}

public sealed class DepositedCash : Event
{
    public decimal Amount { get; }
    public Guid BranchId { get; }
}

public sealed class DebitedTransfer : Event
{
    public string Beneficiary { get; }
    public string Iban { get; }
    public string Bic { get; }

    public decimal DebitedAmount { get; }
    public string Reference { get; }
}
```

The preceding events are only a subset of the events that might affect an account (most obviously, we're missing cash withdrawals and credited transfers), but they're representative enough that, with these examples, you could figure out how any other event would be handled.

Events should be treated as being immutable: they represent things that happened in the past, and there's no changing the past. They are persisted to storage, so they must also be serializable.

10.2.2 *Persisting events*

If you look at the sample events in listing 10.1 with a view to persisting them to a DB, you'll immediately notice that all the events have a different structure—different fields—so you can't store them in a fixed-format structure like a relational table.

There are various options for storing events. In order of preference, you should consider using the following:

- A specialized event DB such as Event Store (https://geteventstore.com).
- A document database such as Redis, MongoDB, and others. These storage systems make no assumptions about the structure of the data they store.
- A traditional relational DB such as SQL Server.

 EVENT STORE VS. EVENT STORE   Whatever storage you use to persist your events is generally referred to as an *event store*. Don't confuse this with Event Store (always capitalized in this chapter), which is a specific product that includes an event store and much related functionality.

If you opt to store events in a relational DB, you'll need an events table with some header columns such as `EntityId` and `Timestamp`, which you'll need in order to query the event history of an entity (sorted, and potentially filtered by timestamp). The event payload is serialized into a JSON string and stored into a wide column, as illustrated in table 10.1.

Table 10.1   Event data can be stored in a relational DB table.

EntityId	Timestamp	EventType	Data
abcd	2016-07-22 12:40	CreatedAccount	{ "Currency": "EUR" }
abcd	2016-07-30 13:25	DepositedCash	{ "Amount": 500, "BranchId": "BOCLHAYMCKT" }
abcd	2016-08-03 10:33	DebitedTransfer	{ "DebitedAmount": 300, "Beneficiary": "Rose Stephens", ...}

All three storage options are viable; it just depends on your requirements and existing infrastructure. If most of your data is already in a relational DB, and you only want to event source some entities, then using that same DB may make sense, because it would involve less operational overhead.

10.2.3 Representing state

We spent much of chapter 9 discussing how to represent state, so we're already in a pretty good position. But now we must ask the question, if we're using events for persistence, what exactly is the purpose of these states or snapshots? It turns out that they are needed for various completely independent purposes:

- We need snapshots to make decisions on how to process commands. For example, if we receive a command that we should make a transfer, and the account is frozen or has an insufficient balance, then we must reject the command.
- We also need snapshots to display to users. I'll refer to these as *view models*.[2]

---

[2] Running complex analytics on data stored as events can be inefficient, so you may also decide to store snapshots for this reason. These snapshots are called *projections* and are updated as the events occur, to make the data available for querying in an efficient format. They're not fundamentally different from view models—more precisely, you can think of a view model as a projection—so I won't deal with projections specifically in this book.

Let's start with the first type of snapshot. We need an object that will capture *just* what we need in order to make decisions about how to handle commands. The following listing shows such an object that models the account state.

Listing 10.2 A simplified model of the entity state

```
public sealed class AccountState
{
    public AccountStatus Status { get; }
    public CurrencyCode Currency { get; }
    public decimal Balance { get; }
    public decimal AllowedOverdraft { get; }

    public AccountState WithStatus(AccountStatus newStatus) // ...

    public AccountState Debit(decimal amount)
        => Credit(-amount);

    public AccountState Credit(decimal amount)
        => new AccountState(
            Balance: this.Balance + amount,
            Currency: this.Currency,
            Status: this.Status,
            AllowedOverdraft: this.AllowedOverdraft
        );
}
```

This is our usual, dumb, immutable data object with read-only properties, some copy methods such as `WithStatus`, and the more meaningfully named `Debit` and `Credit` methods, which are also just copy methods and contain no business logic.

You'll notice that this is somewhat simplified compared to the examples shown in the last chapter. For instance, I don't have a list of transactions because I'm assuming that the current balance and the account status are enough to make decisions about how to handle any commands. Transactions may be shown to the user, but they're not required when processing commands.

10.2.4 *An interlude on pattern matching*

Before we move on, we must take a detour to discuss *pattern matching*. We want to have different behavior depending on the *type* of event that has occurred, but C# lacks good support for this; hence the digression. If you want to stay focused on ES, skip ahead to section 10.2.5 and come back to this section later.

C#'S INCIPIENT SUPPORT FOR PATTERN MATCHING

Pattern matching is a language feature that allows you to execute different code depending on the "shape" of some data—most importantly, its type. It's a staple of functional languages. You can think of the classic `switch` statement as a very limited form of pattern matching, because you can only match on the exact *value* of an expression. What if you want to match on the *type* of an expression?

For example, suppose you have the following simple domain:

```
enum Ripeness { Green, Yellow, Brown }

abstract class Reward { }

class Peanut : Reward { }
class Banana : Reward { public Ripeness Ripeness; }
```

Up to C# 6, computing a description of a given `Reward` had to be done as follows.

Listing 10.3   Matching on the type of an expression in C# 6

```
string Describe(Reward reward)
{
   Peanut peanut = reward as Peanut;
   if (peanut != null)
      return "It's a peanut";

   Banana banana = reward as Banana;
   if (banana != null)
      return $"It's a {banana.Ripeness} banana";

   return "It's a reward I don't know or care about";
}
```

For such a simple operation, this is incredibly tedious and noisy. C# 7 introduces some limited support for pattern matching, so that the preceding code could be abridged as follows.

Listing 10.4   Matching on type in C# 7 with `is`

```
string Describe(Reward reward)
{
   if (reward is Peanut _)
      return "It's a peanut";

   else if (reward is Banana banana)
      return $"It's a {banana.Ripeness} banana";

   return "It's a reward I don't know or care about";
}
```

Or, alternatively, using the `switch` statement as follows.

Listing 10.5   Matching on type in C# 7 with `switch`

```
string Describe(Reward reward)
{
   switch (reward)
   {
```

```
   case Peanut _:
      return "It's a peanut";
   case Banana banana:
      return $"It's a {banana.Ripeness} banana";
   default:
      return "It's a reward I don't know or care about";
   }
}
```

This is still fairly awkward, especially because in FP we'd like to use expressions, whereas both if and switch expect statements in each branch.

A CUSTOM SOLUTION FOR EXPRESSION-BASED PATTERN MATCHING

Improvements to pattern matching are planned for future versions of C#,[3] but I don't want to wait that long, so I've included in LaYumba.Functional a Pattern class to help out. Using this implementation, the previous function can be rewritten as follows.

> **Listing 10.6 A custom `Pattern` class enabling expression-based pattern matching**

The generic parameter specifies the type that will be returned when calling `Match`.

```
string Describe(Reward reward)
   => new Pattern<string>            ◄───
   {
      (Peanut _) => "It's a peanut",
      (Banana b) => $"It's a {b.Ripeness} banana"
   }
   .Default("It's a reward I don't know or care about")   ◄───
   .Match(reward);                   ◄───
```

A list of functions; the first one with a matching type will be evaluated.

Supplies the value on which to match

Optionally add a default value or handler.

This isn't as good as first-class language support, but it's still an improvement. You first set up the functions that handle each case (internally, Pattern is essentially a list of functions, so I'm using list initializer syntax). You can optionally call Default to provide a default value, or handler, to use if no matching function is found. Finally, you use Match to supply the value to match on; this will evaluate the first function whose input type matches the type of the given value.

There's also a non-generic version of Pattern, in which Match returns dynamic. You could use this in the preceding example by simply omitting <string>, making the syntax a bit cleaner still.

Note that all the Match methods you've seen so far (for Option, Either, List, Tree, and so on) simply mimic what you'd be able to do with pattern matching in a language that supports it. Defining such methods makes sense when you know from the start all the cases you'll need to handle (for instance, Option can only be Some or None). By

---

[3] Documentation is currently available on https://github.com/dotnet/roslyn/blob/master/docs/features/patterns.md.

contrast, the `Pattern` class is useful for types that are open for inheritance, like `Event` or `Reward`, where you can envisage adding new subclasses as the system evolves.

MATCHING ON THE STRUCTURE OF A LIST

Sometimes it's useful to match not only on the type in question, but on its inner structure. For example, you may want to execute different code depending on whether a list is empty or not. You saw how to do this with the functional linked list, for which we defined `Match` to use different handlers for the `Empty` and `Cons` cases. As a reminder, here's an example of using `Match` to compute the length of a list:

```
public static int Length<T>(this List<T> list)
    => list.Match(
        () => 0,
        (_, tail) => 1 + tail.Length());
```

A `Match` method with the same semantics can be defined to work for any `IEnumerable` and can be implemented as follows:

> Calls the `Otherwise` handler with the list's head and tail if it's not empty

```
public static R Match<T, R>(this IEnumerable<T> list
    , Func<R> Empty, Func<T, IEnumerable<T>, R> Otherwise)
    => list.Head()                        Calls the Empty handler
        .Match(                           if the list is empty
            None: () => Empty(),     ←
            Some: (head) => Otherwise(head, list.Skip(1))    ←
        );
```

Head returns None if the list is empty; otherwise the head of the list wrapped in a Some.

```
public static Option<T> Head<T>(this IEnumerable<T> list)
{
    var enumerator = list.GetEnumerator();
    return enumerator.MoveNext()
        ? Some(enumerator.Current) : None;
}
```

Here `Match` takes a handler for the case in which the `IEnumerable` is empty, and another handler accepting its head and tail. You'll see an example of using this when computing an entity's state from its event history—an entity whose history is an empty list doesn't exist, so it should receive special treatment.

With these pattern matching utilities in place, let's go back to discussing ES.

10.2.5 *Representing state transitions*

Now let's see how states and events are combined in state transitions. Once you have a state and an event, you can compute the next state by *applying* the event to the state. This computation is called a *state transition*, and it's a function whose signature has this general form:

```
state → event → state
```

In other words, "Give me a state and an event, and I'll compute the new state after the event." Particularized for our scenario, this signature becomes

```
AccountState → Event → AccountState
```

Here, `Event` is the base class from which all our events derive, so an implementation must pattern match on the *type* of the event and then compute a new `AccountState` with the relevant changes.

There's also one special state transition, which is when an account is first created. In that case we have an event, but no prior state, so the signature is in this form:

```
event → state
```

The following listing shows the implementation for our scenario.

Listing 10.7 Modeling state transitions

```
public static class Account
{
    public static AccountState Create(CreatedAccount evt)      ◁─┐  CreatedAccount
        => new AccountState                                        is a special case,
            (                                                      because there is no
                Currency: evt.Currency,                            prior state.
                Status: AccountStatus.Active
            );

    public static AccountState Apply(this AccountState account, Event evt)
        => new Pattern
        {
            (DepositedCash e) => account.Credit(e.Amount),
            (DebitedTransfer e) => account.Debit(e.DebitedAmount),
            (FrozeAccount _) => account.WithStatus(AccountStatus.Frozen),
        }
        .Match(evt);
}
```

**Calls the relevant transition
depending on the type of the event**

The first method is the special case of creation: it takes a `CreatedAccount` event and creates a new `AccountState` populated with values from the event. Here we also have some business logic: we say that an account is `Active` as soon as it's created.

The `Apply` method is the more general formulation of a state transition, and it will process all other types of events, pattern matching on the event type: if the event is `FrozeAccount`, we return a new state that has status `Frozen`; if the event is `Deposited-Cash`, we call `Credit`, which returns a new state that has the balance increased accordingly; and so on. In a real application, you'd have many more types of events here.

10.2.6 *Reconstructing the current state from past events*

Now that you've seen how to represent states and events, and how to combine them with state transitions, you're ready to see how an entity's current state can be computed from the history of events that affected that entity in the past.

Listing 10.8 Recovering the present state of an entity from its event history

Given the history of events

```
public static Option<AccountState> From(IEnumerable<Event> history)
    => history.Match(
        Empty: () => None,
        Otherwise: (created, otherEvents) => Some(
            otherEvents.Aggregate(
                seed: Account.Create((CreatedAccount)created),
                func: (state, evt) => state.Apply(evt))));
```

Applies each subsequent event

Creates a new account from the first event, and uses it as an accumulator

---

Let's look at the signature first. We're taking a sequence of events: the entity's history. This is the list of events you get from the DB when you query all events for a given `EntityID`. I'm assuming that the sequence is sorted: events that happened first should be at the top of the list. You must enforce this when you retrieve events from the database, and this often comes for free: because events are persisted as they occur, they're appended in order, and this ordering is normally preserved when they're retrieved.

The desired return value is an `AccountState`, but here it's wrapped in an `Option`. This is where the previously discussed implementation of `Match` for `IEnumerable` comes in handy. If the history is empty, which means that there's no recorded history of that entity, the entity doesn't exist in the system, so the code returns `None`. Otherwise the sequence must contain a `CreatedAccount` at the head of the list, with the tail containing all following events. In this case, the code creates the initial state from the `CreatedAccount` event and uses that as an accumulator to `Aggregate`, which applies all subsequent events to the state, finally obtaining the current state.

Notice that if you wanted to see not the *current* state of the account, but its state at any point in the past, this can be done trivially by evaluating the very same function but filtering to exclude events past the desired date. For this reason, event sourcing is a very valuable model when you need an audit trail and to see how an entity has changed through time.

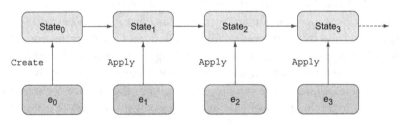

Figure 10.4 Recovering the present state of an entity from its event history

Now that you've seen how event sourcing offers a viable, append-only model for persistence, from which present or past states can be easily computed, let's see what an event-sourced system looks like from a high-level architectural point of view.

10.3 Architecture of an event-sourced system

The data flows in an event-sourced system are different from those in a traditional system, where data is backed up by a relational store. As figure 10.5 shows, in CRUD-oriented systems the program deals in entities, or, better, in states. States are saved in the DB, states are retrieved by the server, and states are sent to the client. The transformations between the "model" (the data stored in the DB) and the "view model" (the data sent to the client) are often very minor.

In an event-sourced system, things are quite different. What we persist is events. But users won't want to see an event log, so the data that we surface for the users' consumption must be structured in a meaningful way. For this reason, an event-sourced system can be split neatly into two separate parts:

- *The command side*—This side has the job of *writing* data, which consists mainly of validating commands received from users. Valid commands will result in events being persisted and propagated.
- *The query side*—This side has the job of *reading* data. View models are dictated by what you want to show on the client, and the query side must populate those view models from the stored events. Optionally, the query side can also publish notifications to the client when new events cause the views to change.

This natural split between the command and query sides results in smaller, more focused components. It also gives you flexibility: the command and query sides can be

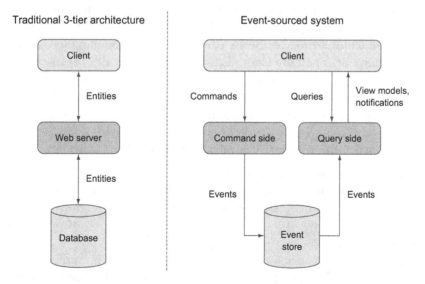

Figure 10.5 High-level comparison of data flows in a traditional vs. event-sourced system.

completely separate applications and can therefore be scaled and deployed independently. This is advantageous when you think that the load on the query side is likely to be much greater than on the command side. For example, think about how little data you post when you visit a site like Twitter or Facebook, compared to the amount of data you retrieve.

Conversely, on the command side, you may need to synchronize writes to prevent concurrent changes. This is much more easily accomplished if there's a single instance of the command side. So this separation (which goes by the name of CQRS, for command/query responsibility segregation), allows you to easily scale the data-intensive query side to satisfy demand, while keeping fewer or perhaps even a single instance of the command side.

The command and query sides don't *have* to be separate applications. Both can live in the same application. But if you use event sourcing, there will still be an internal separation between the two sides. Let's see how you could go about implementing them, starting with the command side.

10.3.1 *Handling commands*

Commands are, if you like, the earliest source of data. Commands are sent to your application by users (or by other systems) and are handled by the command side, which must do the following:

- Validate the command
- Turn the command into an event
- Persist the event and publish it to interested parties

Let's start by comparing commands and events, which are similar yet distinct:

- *Commands* are requests from a user or other application. It's possible for a command to be disobeyed or disregarded for some reason. Maybe the command fails validation, or maybe the system crashes while handling it. Commands are named in the imperative form, such as `MakeTransfer` or `FreezeAccount`.
- *Events*, in contrast, can't fail because they've already happened. They're named in the past tense, such as `DebitedTransfer` or `FrozeAccount`. I am specifically considering events that cause state transitions, and therefore must be persisted. If you have other, more transient events in your system that need not be persisted, make sure you clearly distinguish between them.

Other than that, commands and events *generally* capture the same information, and creating an event from a command is just a matter of copying field by field (sometimes with some variations). An event directly affects a single entity, but events are broadcast within your system, so they may trigger the creation of other events that affect other entities.

Next, let's look at the main workflow on the command side, illustrated in figure 10.6.

For simplicity, I'll temporarily disregard validation as well as error handling. This will allow us to concentrate on the essentials of the data flow.

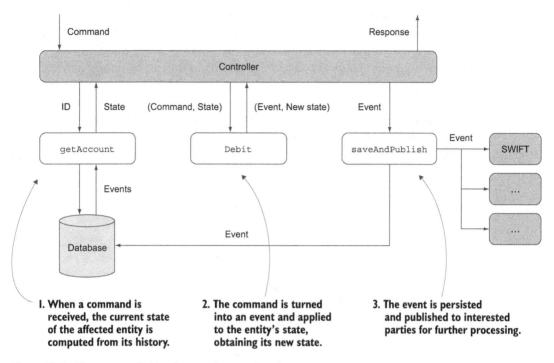

1. When a command is received, the current state of the affected entity is computed from its history.

2. The command is turned into an event and applied to the entity's state, obtaining its new state.

3. The event is persisted and published to interested parties for further processing.

Figure 10.6 The command side of an event-sourced system

The following listing shows the entry point and main workflow of the command side.

Listing 10.9 Top-level command-handling workflow

```
public class MakeTransferController : Controller
{
    Func<Guid, AccountState> getAccount;                    Handles receiving a command
    Action<Event> saveAndPublish;

    public IActionResult MakeTransfer([FromBody] MakeTransfer cmd)
    {
        var account = getAccount(cmd.DebitedAccountId);      Retrieves the account

        var (evt, newState) = account.Debit(cmd);            Performs the state transition;
                                                             returns a tuple with the event
        saveAndPublish(evt);                                 and the new state

        return Ok(new { Balance = newState.Balance });       Returns information to the
    }                                                        user about the new state
}
```

Persists the event and publishes to interested parties

Let's look at the dependencies first (assume they're injected in the constructor). We have getAccount, which will retrieve the current state of the affected account (computed from its event history, as you've seen earlier). We then have saveAndPublish, which will persist the given event to storage, and publish it to any interested parties.

Now for the MakeTransfer method. It receives a command to make a transfer and uses the getAccount function to retrieve the state of the account to be debited. It then feeds the retrieved account state and the command to the Debit function (invoked as an extension method). This will convert the command into an event and compute the new state of the account.

Debit returns a tuple containing both the created event and the account's new state. The code then uses C# 7 syntax (see the "Tuples in C# 7" sidebar) to destructure this tuple into its two elements: the created event, which is passed to saveAndPublish, and the account's new state, which is used to populate the response that's sent back to the client.

Next, let's look at the Debit function:

```
public static class Account
{
    public static (Event Event, AccountState NewState) Debit
        (this AccountState state, MakeTransfer transfer)
    {
        Event evt = transfer.ToEvent();
        AccountState newState = state.Apply(evt);

        return (evt, newState);
    }
}
```

Translates the command into an event → (annotation pointing to `Event evt = transfer.ToEvent();`)

Computes the new state ← (annotation pointing to `AccountState newState = state.Apply(evt);`)

Debit converts the command into an event,[4] and feeds that event, along with the new state, to the Apply function to obtain the account's new state. Notice that this is the very same Apply function that's used when computing the account's current state from its event history; this ensures that state transitions are consistent, regardless of whether the event is just occurring now or has occurred in the past and is being replayed.

Tuples in C# 7

There's no *conceptual* difference between tuples in C# 7 and tuples as we've had them since C# 4, but there are important differences in terms of performance and usability.

The old tuples have unattractive syntax: to access their elements, you must use properties called Item1, Item2, and so on. With C# 7 comes new lightweight syntax for creating and consuming tuples, similar to the syntax found in many other languages:

---

[4] Other authors on ES would allow for a command to be translated into several events at this point, but I find this tends to add complexity without any real benefit. Instead, I find that a command should be translated into a single event; when this event is then published, downstream event handlers can create other events, affecting the same, but more frequently other, entities.

(continued)

Declares tuple as the
method's return type

```
(string, string, int) GetAuthorInfo()          ◄─┐   Creates a
    => ("Enrico", "Buonanno", 40);              ◄─┘   tuple literal

var (first, last, age) = GetAuthorInfo();       ◄─┐   Tuples can be
first // => "Enrico"                               │   deconstructed.
age   // => 40
```

Furthermore, you can assign meaningful names to the elements of a tuple, so that you can query them as you would fields or properties, as in the following example:

```
(string First, string Last, int Age) GetAuthorInfo()
    => ("Enrico", "Buonanno", 40);

var info = GetAuthorInfo();
info.First // => "Enrico"
info.Age   // => 40
```

Apart from the new syntax, the underlying implementation of tuples has also changed. The old tuples are backed by the `System.Tuple` classes, which are immutable reference types. The new tuples are backed by the `System.ValueTuple` structs. Being structs, they're copied when passed between functions, yet they're mutable, so you can update their members within methods—a compromise between the expected immutability of tuples and performance considerations.

Note that the techniques shown here in no way *require* that you use C# 7 or the new tuple implementation. If you're on an older version of C#, you can still use the old `System.Tuple` and pay a penalty in terms of readability.

10.3.2 Handling events

Where do we actually send the money to the recipient? That's done as part of `saveAndPublish`: the newly created event should be propagated to interested parties. A dedicated service should subscribe to these events and send the money to the receiving bank (via SWIFT or another inter-bank platform) as appropriate. Several other subscribers may consume the same event for other reasons, such as recomputing the bank's cash reserve, sending a toast notification to the client's phone, and so on.

This may throw some light on why the function is called `saveAndPublish`: both things should happen atomically. If the process saves the event and then crashes before all subscribers were able to handle the event, the system may be left in an inconsistent state. For example, the account may be debited but the money not sent to SWIFT.

How this atomicity is achieved is somewhat intricate and strictly depends on the infrastructure you're targeting (both for storage and for event propagation). For instance, if you use Event Store, you can take advantage of *durable* subscriptions to

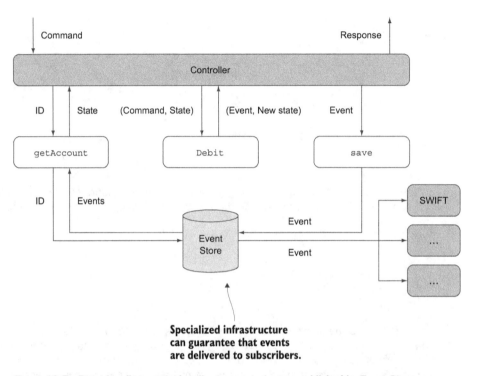

Figure 10.7 Event handlers can subscribe to event streams published by Event Store.

event streams, which guarantee that the event is delivered *at least once* to the subscriber (that's the meaning of "durable" in this context).

So, by using Event Store, you could simplify the logic in saveAndPublish to only save the event. Event handlers then subscribe to Event Store's event streams, as shown in figure 10.7.

10.3.3 Adding validation

Let's now add validation so that the command is only accepted and turned into an event if the current state of the account allows it.

Listing 10.10   Ensuring only valid transitions take place

```
public static class Account
{
    public static Validation<(Event, AccountState)> Debit
        (this AccountState account, MakeTransfer transfer)
    {
        if (account.Status != AccountStatus.Active)
            return Errors.AccountNotActive;

        if (account.Balance - transfer.Amount < account.AllowedOverdraft)
            return Errors.InsufficientBalance;
```

```
        Event evt = transfer.ToEvent();
        AccountState newState = account.Apply(evt);

        return (evt, newState);
    }
}
```

Here `Debit` performs some account-specific validation, so the return type is wrapped in a `Validation`. Only if all goes well does it return the event-new state tuple. Otherwise it returns a validation error. (Note that in either case, the returned value is implicitly lifted into a `Validation` in the appropriate state.)

With this in place, let's revisit the main workflow, adding validation.

Listing 10.11 Command handling, with validation

```
public class MakeTransferController : Controller
{
    Func<MakeTransfer, Validation<MakeTransfer>> validate;
    Func<Guid, AccountState> getAccount;
    Action<Event> saveAndPublish;

    public IActionResult MakeTransfer([FromBody] MakeTransfer cmd)
        => validate(cmd)
            .Bind(t => getAccount(t.DebitedAccountId).Debit(t))
            .Do(result => saveAndPublish(result.Item1))
            .Match<IActionResult>(
                Invalid: errs => BadRequest(new { Errors = errs }),
                Valid: result => Ok(new { Balance = result.Item2.Balance }));
}
```

This listing has a new dependency, `validate`, which should perform some more general validation of the command, such as ensuring that the IBAN and BIC codes are in the right format, and the like. This will have to be combined with the account-specific validation that happens in `Debit`, and naturally this is done with `Bind`.

The next step of the workflow, which involves calling `saveAndPublish`, happens inside a `Do` function. `Do` is similar to `ForEach` in that it takes a side-effecting function. But whereas `ForEach` "throws away" the inner value, `Do` passes the value along, like this:

```
public static Validation<T> Do<T>
    (this Validation<T> val, Action<T> action)
{
    val.ForEach(action);
    return val;
}
```

This enables us to have the value available in the subsequent call to `Match`, the final step in the workflow, where we send an appropriate response to the client, depending on the outcome of the validation.

This revised version adds validation, but no exception handling: getAccount and saveAndPublish perform IO, so they could both fail. To express this, we'd have to combine Validation with another effect, such as Exceptional. You'll see how this can be achieved in chapter 14.

You should now have a pretty good idea of how the command side of an event-sourced system works. Let's now look at the query side.

10.3.4 Creating views of the data from events

We'll again start our exploration from the client. The client displays data in the format that's best suited for the user's needs, and the server is meant to provide data that appears in these views—the view models.

Let's take a bank account statement as a typical view of a bank account. It will contain a list of transactions that occurred within a given period (let's assume that periods coincide with calendar months), as well as the balance at the start and at the end of the period. Figure 10.8 shows an example.

Your summary for:		July 2016	
Starting Balance		**550**	

Transactions

Date	Description	Credited	Debited
2016-07-03	Cash deposit	200	-
2016-07-10	Transfer to Rose Stephens	-	350
2016-07-03	Direct debit payment to Electro	-	65

| **End Balance** | | **335** | |

Figure 10.8   Example structure of a bank statement

Next, let's define the structure of the view model: the objects containing the data used to populate the bank statement. We'll have a parent object, AccountStatement, with a list of Transactions.

Listing 10.12   The view model for a bank statement

```
public class AccountStatement
{
    public int Month { get; }
    public int Year { get; }

    public decimal StartingBalance { get; }
```

```
   public decimal EndBalance { get; }
   public IEnumerable<Transaction> Transactions { get; }
}

public class Transaction
{
   public DateTime Date { get; }
   public decimal DebitedAmount { get; }
   public decimal CreditedAmount { get; }
   public string Description { get; }
}
```

Next we need to populate this data from the event history of a given account. Notice that we need the *full* history of events. The following listing shows how we can calculate the starting and ending balance for the statement period.

Listing 10.13 Calculating start and end balance

```
public class AccountStatement
{
   public decimal StartingBalance { get; }
   public decimal EndBalance { get; }

   public AccountStatement(int month, int year, IEnumerable<Event> events)
   {
      var startOfPeriod = new DateTime(year, month, 1);
      var endOfPeriod = startOfPeriod.AddMonths(1);

      var eventsBeforePeriod = events
         .TakeWhile(e => e.Timestamp < startOfPeriod);
      var eventsInPeriod = events
         .SkipWhile(e => e.Timestamp < startOfPeriod)
         .TakeWhile(e => endOfPeriod < e.Timestamp);

      StartingBalance = eventsBeforePeriod.Aggregate(0m, BalanceReducer);
      EndBalance = eventsInPeriod.Aggregate(StartingBalance, BalanceReducer);
   }

   decimal BalanceReducer(decimal bal, Event evt)
      => new Pattern
      {
         (DepositedCash e) => bal + e.Amount,          │ Events that affect
         (DebitedTransfer e) => bal - e.DebitedAmount, │ the balance
      }
      .Default(bal)          ◁──┐ Other events don't affect the
      .Match(evt);              │ balance, so this default clause
}                              │ returns the running balance.
```

Just as we used `Aggregate` to compute the state on the command side, we can use it here to compute the data we need for the query. We can calculate the starting balance by aggregating all events up to the start of the statement period by using 0 as a seed value and a reducer function that increments or decrements the balance, depending on what the event was and how it affected the balance.

Not all events affect the balance; hence the call to `Default`, which will return `bal`, the running balance, if the event is of a different type than the ones listed in the `Pattern` initializer. For the end balance, the same logic can be used, including the events that occurred within the statement period.

Now for the list of transactions. Some events involve a transaction; others don't. Let's begin by adding some methods to construct a `Transaction` from an `Event`:

```
public class Transaction
{
   public Transaction(DebitedTransfer e)
   {
      this.DebitedAmount = e.DebitedAmount;
      Description = $"Transfer to {e.Bic}/{e.Iban}; Ref: {e.Reference}";
      Date = e.Timestamp.Date;
   }

   public Transaction(DepositedCash e)
   {
      this.CreditedAmount = e.Amount;
      Description = $"Deposit at {e.BranchId}";
      Date = e.Timestamp.Date;
   }
}
```

We now need to create the list of `Transactions` for the period. To do this, we need to "map" all events that occurred in the period to the corresponding transactions. It's not quite as simple as using `Map` on the list of events, though, because we need to filter out events that don't involve a transaction. To do this, we can instead `Bind` an `Option`-returning function that only returns `Some<Transaction>` for events that do involve a transaction (remember from section 4.5 that `Bind` filters out the `None`s from the result list).

Listing 10.14   Populating the list of transactions on the statement

```
public class AccountStatement
{
   public AccountStatement(int month, int year, IEnumerable<Event> events)
   {
      var startOfPeriod = new DateTime(year, month, 1);
      var endOfPeriod = startOfPeriod.AddMonths(1);

      var eventsDuringPeriod = events
         .SkipWhile(e => e.Timestamp < startOfPeriod)
         .TakeWhile(e => endOfPeriod < e.Timestamp);

      Transactions = eventsDuringPeriod.Bind(CreateTransaction);
   }
```

```
Option<Transaction> CreateTransaction(Event evt)
   => new Pattern<Option<Transaction>>
   {
      (DepositedCash e) => new Transaction(e),
      (DebitedTransfer e) => new Transaction(e),
   }
   .Default(None)
   .Match(evt);
}
```

Creates a `Transaction`
from each event

Returns `None` for events that
don't involve a transaction

As you can see, populating a view model from a list of events requires some work and a bit of thinking. The data transformations involved can usually be performed through the usual `Map`, `Bind`, and `Aggregate` functions. View models stay centered on the user experience, and are completely decoupled from the underlying representation.

Populating a view model can be computationally intensive if it involves processing a large number of events, so some optimization is often required to avoid recomputing a view model every time it's required. One such optimization is for the query side to cache the current version for every view model, and update it as new events are received. In this case, the query side subscribes to events published by the command side, and upon receiving these, updates the cached version and optionally publishes the updated view model to connected clients.

As you can see, if you want an event-sourced model with the performance characteristics of a relational database (or better), some extra work is required to precompute and maintain view models. Some more sophisticated optimizations involve a dedicated DB for the query side, where data is stored in an optimized format for querying. For example, if you need to query views with arbitrary filters, this can be a relational DB. This "query model" is always a by-product of past events, so that the event store acts as a "source of truth."

10.4 Comparing different approaches to immutable storage

In this chapter you've had a fairly complete overview of ES, an *event-based approach* to data storage. You've seen why it's a functional technique at heart and how storing data about state transitions, rather than state, provides some important benefits. The other approach I mentioned in the opening of the chapter is the *assertion-based approach*. This is more like the relational model in the sense that you still define entities and attributes, which are essentially like rows and columns in a relational DB. (For example, you could define a "Person" entity with an "Email" attribute.)

You modify this DB through *assertions*—things like "starting now, the 'Email' attribute of the 'Person' with id 123 has value 'jobl@manning.com'." In the future, this attribute may become associated with a different value, but the fact that it was associated with the value "jobl@manning.com" within a particular time range is never forgotten, overwritten, or destroyed. In this model, the DB becomes an ever-growing collection of facts.

You can then query the DB in much the same manner that you would a relational DB, but you get to specify whether you want to query the current state or the state at any point in time.

With both the assertion-based and event-based approaches, you get the following:

- An audit trail, making it possible to query the state of an entity at any point in time
- No database contention, because no data is ever overwritten

These benefits are inherent in the fact that both approaches embrace immutability. Let's look at some other factors that may influence your choice between these two approaches.

10.4.1 Datomic vs. Event Store

The assertion-based approach really only has one embodiment, Datomic (http://www.datomic.com/), which, apart from the principles discussed here, implements other interesting design decisions that give it good characteristics in terms of performance and scalability. Datomic is a proprietary product with a free version that's limited in terms of scalability. It would be an arduous task to roll out your own implementation.

Implementing an event-sourced system, on the other hand, is relatively simple: most of what's required was covered in this chapter. You can write an effective implementation using any DB—either NoSQL or relational—as underlying storage. For a large-scale application, it still pays to use a DB specifically designed for ES such as Event Store, which is open source.[5] In short, if you want an assertion-based approach, you pretty much *have* to use Datomic; with ES, you *may* need or choose to use Event Store.

Event Store was developed in .NET, it provides a .NET client for communicating with the store via TCP, and the project has good visibility in the .NET community. Datomic was developed in Clojure, so interoperability with .NET isn't as good.[6] These aspects have tilted the scales in favor of Event Store, and partly as a result of that we've seen much wider adoption of ES—whether using Event Store or not—among .NET users.

10.4.2 How event-driven is your domain?

The most important consideration when deciding on any technology is the specific requirements of your domain: some applications are intrinsically event-driven, and others aren't.

How can you assess whether ES is a good fit? First, look at what you consider "events" in your domain; how important are they? Second, see if there's a natural difference between the sort of data being provided and the data being consumed by the parties involved.

---

[5] Although Event Store is particularly attractive for .NET users, it's not the only database designed around event streams. Another stack built on the same principles is Apache Kafka, which manages event streams, and Samza, a framework for maintaining view models computed from these streams.

[6] As of early 2017, it's possible to connect to Datomic via a RESTful API. This API is considered legacy (but will continue to be supported), and there's no native client for .NET.

Consider, for example, the domain of online auctions: a typical event would be when a client places a bid on an item. This event triggers changes: the client becomes the high bidder, and the value for the next bid is raised. Another important event is when the hammer comes down: the high bidder is bound to purchase the item, which is no longer for sale, and so on. This domain is definitely event-driven.

Furthermore, the data consumed by clients tends to be in a completely different shape from the data they produce: most clients produce single bids, but they may consume data containing the details of an item for sale, the history of bids placed so far on an item, or the list of items they purchased. So there's already a natural decoupling between user actions (commands) and the data they consume (queries). ES is a very natural fit for this domain.

By contrast, imagine an application enabling an insurance provider to manage its products. What events can you think of? A new policy can be created, or it can be retired, or some parameter can be modified…but, wait, these are essentially the CRUD operations! You still require an audit log, because modifying the characteristics of a product may affect thousands of contracts once the modification comes into effect. This is a much better fit for an assertion-based DB.

Immutable data storage is an area to watch for future developments, as both approaches to immutable storage provide important responses to the needs and challenges of modern applications.

Summary

- Thinking functionally about data also encompasses storage. Instead of mutating stored data, consider the database as a big immutable collection: you can append new data, but never overwrite existing data.
- There are two main approaches to immutable storage:
    - *Event-based*—The DB is an ever-growing collection of events.
    - *Assertion-based*—The DB is an ever-growing collection of facts.
- Event sourcing means persisting event data as events occur. The state of an entity need not be stored, because it can always be computed as the "sum" of all events that affected the entity.
- An event-sourced system naturally separates the concerns of reading and writing data, enabling a CQRS architecture that separates between
    - The command side, where commands are received, validated, and turned into events that are persisted and published.
    - The query side, where events are combined to create view models, which are served to clients and, optionally, cached for better performance.
- Event-sourced systems have several main components:
    - *Commands*—Simple, immutable data objects encapsulating a request from a client program.
    - *Events*—Simple, immutable data objects capturing what happened.

- *States*—Data objects representing the state of an entity at a certain point in time.
- *State transitions*—Functions that take a state and an event, and produce a new state.
- *View models*—Data objects for populating views. They're computed from events.
- *Event handlers*—These subscribe to events to perform business logic (on the command side) or to update view models (on the query side).

Part 3

Advanced techniques

This part tackles the complex topics of state management, asynchrony, and concurrency.

Chapter 11 discusses the benefits of lazy evaluation and how lazy computations can be composed. This is a general pattern for which you'll see several practical uses.

Chapter 12 shows how you can implement stateful programs without state mutation, and how stateful computations can also be composed.

Chapter 13 deals with asynchronous computations, and with how asynchrony can be combined with other effects discussed in previous parts of the book. This leads to the wider concern of combining several monadic effects—still an open topic of research in FP.

Asynchronous streams are even more general than asynchronous values, and they're discussed in chapter 14, along with Rx, a framework for working with streams.

Finally, chapter 15 introduces message-passing concurrency, a style of lock-free concurrency that can be used when writing stateful concurrent programs.

Each chapter in part 3 introduces important techniques that have the potential to completely alter the way you think about writing software. Many of these topics are too vast to be discussed comprehensively, so these chapters aim to provide an introduction and a starting point for further exploration.

Lazy computations, continuations, and the beauty of monadic composition

This chapter covers

- Lazy computations
- Exception handling with `Try`
- Monadically composing functions
- Escaping the pyramid of doom with continuations

In this chapter, you'll first learn why it's sometimes desirable to define *lazy computations*; that is, functions that may or may not be executed. You'll then see how these functions can be composed with other functions, independently of their execution.

Once you've got your feet wet with lazy computations, which are just plain functions, you'll see how the same techniques can be extended to computations that have some useful effects other than laziness. Namely, you'll learn how to use the

Try delegate to safely run code that may throw an exception, and how to compose several Trys. You'll then learn how to compose functions that take a callback without ending up in "callback hell."

What holds all these techniques together is that, in all cases, you're treating functions as *things* that have certain specific characteristics, and you can compose them independently of their execution. This requires quite a leap in abstraction, but the result is quite powerful.

The contents of this chapter are challenging, so don't be discouraged if you don't get it all on your first reading.

11.1   *The virtue of laziness*

Laziness in computing means deferring a computation until its result is needed. This is beneficial when the computation is expensive and its result may not be needed.

To introduce the idea of laziness, consider the following example of a method that randomly picks one of two given elements. You can try it out in the REPL:

```
var rand = new Random();

T Pick<T>(T l, T r) =>
    rand.NextDouble() < 0.5 ? l : r;

Pick(1 + 2, 3 + 4) // => 3, or 7
```

The interesting thing to point out here is that when you invoke Pick, both the expressions 1 + 2 and 3 + 4 are evaluated, even though only one of them is needed in the end.[1] So, the program is performing some unnecessary computation; this is suboptimal and should be avoided if the computation is expensive enough.

To prevent this, we could rewrite Pick to take not two values, but two lazy computations instead; that is, functions that can produce the required values:

```
T Pick<T>(Func<T> l, Func<T> r) =>
    (rand.NextDouble() < 0.5 ? l : r)();

Pick(() => 1 + 2, () => 3 + 4) // => 3, or 7
```

Pick now first chooses between the two functions and then evaluates one of them. As a result, only one computation is performed.

In summary, if you're not sure whether a value will be required, and it may be expensive to compute it, pass the value lazily by wrapping it in a function that will compute the value.

Next, you'll see how such a lazy API can be beneficial when working with Option.

---

[1] This is because C# is a language with strict or eager evaluation—expressions are evaluated as soon as they're bound to a variable. Although strict evaluation is more common, there are languages—notably Haskell— that use lazy evaluation, so that expressions are evaluated only as needed.

11.1.1 *Lazy APIs for working with Option*

The `Option` API provides a couple of examples that nicely illustrate how laziness can be useful: namely, when you want to use a value only when the `Option` is in the `None` state.

PROVIDING A FALLBACK OPTION

`Or Else` is a convenience function that allows you to combine two `Option`s. It yields the left `Option` if it's `Some`; otherwise it falls back to the right `Option`:

```
public static Option<T> OrElse<T>
   (this Option<T> left, Option<T> right)
   => left.Match(
      () => right,
      (_) => left);
```

For example, say you define a repository that looks items up from a cache, failing which it goes to the DB:

```
interface IRepository<T> { Option<T> Lookup(Guid id); }

class CachingRepository<T> : IRepository<T>
{
   IDictionary<Guid, T> cache;
   IRepository<T> db;

   public Option<T> Lookup(Guid id)
      => cache.Lookup(id).OrElse(db.Lookup(id));
}
```

Can you see the problem in the preceding code? Because `OrElse` is always called, its argument is always evaluated, meaning that you're going to the DB even if the item is found in the cache, defeating the purpose of the cache altogether!

This can be solved by using laziness. For such scenarios, I've defined an overload of `OrElse` taking not a fallback `Option` but a function that will be evaluated if necessary to produce the fallback `Option`:

```
public static Option<T> OrElse<T>
   (this Option<T> opt, Func<Option<T>> fallback)
   => opt.Match(
      () => fallback(),
      (_) => opt);
```

In this implementation, the `fallback` function will only be evaluated if `opt` is `None` (compare this to the previously shown overload, where the fallback option, `right`, is always evaluated). You can accordingly fix the implementation of the caching repository as follows:

```
public Option<T> Lookup(Guid id)
   => cache.Lookup(id).OrElse(() => db.Lookup(id));
```

Now, if the cache lookup returns Some, OrElse will still be called, but db.Lookup won't, achieving the desired behavior.

As you can see, all that's required to make the evaluation of an expression lazy is, instead of providing an expression, providing a function that will evaluate to that expression. Instead of a T, provide a Func<T>.

PROVIDING A DEFAULT VALUE

GetOrElse is a similar function that allows you to get the inner value of an Option, specifying a default value to use if it's None. For instance, you may need to look up a value from configuration, and use a default value instead if no value is specified:

```
string DefaultApiRoot => "localhost:8000";

string GetApiRoot(IConfigurationRoot config)
   => config.Lookup("ApiRoot").GetOrElse(DefaultApiRoot);
```

Assume that Lookup returns a duly populated Option whose state depends on whether the value was specified in configuration. Notice that the DefaultApiRoot property is evaluated regardless of the state of the Option.

In this case that's OK, because it simply returns a constant value. But if Default-ApiRoot involved an expensive computation, you'd prefer to only perform it if needed by passing the default value lazily. This is why I've also provided two overloads of GetOrElse:

```
public static T GetOrElse<T>(this Option<T> opt, T defaultValue)
   => opt.Match(
      () => defaultValue,
      (t) => t);

public static T GetOrElse<T>(this Option<T> opt, Func<T> fallback)
   => opt.Match(
      () => fallback(),
      (t) => t);
```

The first overload takes a regular fallback value, T, which will be evaluated whenever GetOrElse is called. The second overload takes a Func<T>: a function that will be evaluated only when necessary.

 WHEN SHOULD AN API TAKE VALUES LAZILY?   In general, whenever a function may not use some of its arguments, those arguments should be specified as lazy computations.

You may choose to provide two overloads, taking a value for the argument, or a lazy computation. Then the client code can decide on the most appropriate overload to call:

- If computing the value is expensive enough, pass the value lazily (more efficient).
- If the cost of computing the value is negligible, pass the value (more readable).

11.1.2 *Composing lazy computations*

In the rest of this chapter, you'll see how lazy computations can be composed, and why doing so is a powerful technique. We'll start with the plain-vanilla lazy computation Func<T>, and then move on to lazy computations that include some useful effects such as handling errors or state.

You've seen that Func<T> is a lazy computation that can be invoked to obtain a T. It turns out that Func<T> is a functor over T. Remember, a functor is something that has an inner value, over which you can Map a function. How is that possible? The functors you've seen so far are all "containers" of some sort. How can a function possibly be a container, and what's its inner value?

Well, you can think of a function as containing its "potential" result. If, say, Option<T> "maybe-contains" some value of type T, you can say that Func<T> "potentially contains" some value of type T or, perhaps more accurately, contains the potential to produce a value of type T. So a function's inner value is the value it will yield when it's evaluated.

You may know the tale of Aladdin's magic lamp. When rubbed, it would produce a powerful genie. Clearly, such a lamp could have the power to contain anything: put a genie into it, and you can rub it to get the genie back out; put your grandma in it, and you can rub it to get grandma back. And you can think of it as a functor: map a "turn blue" function onto the lamp, and whenever you rub the lamp, you'll get the contents of the lamp, turned blue. Func<T> is such a container, where rubbing is function invocation.

In reality, you know that a functor must expose a Map method with a suitable signature, so if you follow the pattern to define Map, you'll have this:

- An input functor of type () → T; that is, a function that can be called to generate a T. Let's call it f.
- A function to be mapped, of type T → R. Let's call it g.
- An expected result of type () → R; that is, a function that can be called to generate an R.

The implementation is quite simple: invoke f to obtain a T, and then pass it to g to obtain an R, as illustrated in figure 11.1. Listing 11.1 shows the corresponding code.

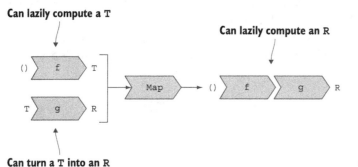

Can lazily compute a T

Can lazily compute an R

Can turn a T into an R

Figure 11.1 Definition of Map for Func<T>

Listing 11.1 Definition of `Map` for `Func<T>`

```
public static Func<R> Map<T, R>
   (this Func<T> f, Func<T, R> g)
   => () => g(f());
```

Notice that `Map` doesn't invoke `f`: it takes a lazily evaluated `T` and returns a lazily evaluated `R`. Also notice that the implementation is just function composition.

To see this in action, open the REPL, import `LaYumba.Functional` as usual, and type the following:

```
Func<string> lazyGrandma = () => "grandma";
Func<string, string> turnBlue = s => $"blue {s}";
Func<string> lazyGrandmaBlue = lazyGrandma.Map(turnBlue);

lazyGrandmaBlue() // => "blue grandma"
```

To better understand the laziness of the whole computation, you can bake some debug statements in:

```
Func<string> lazyGrandma = () =>
{
   WriteLine("getting grandma...");
   return "grandma";
};

Func<string, string> turnBlue = s =>
{
   WriteLine("turning blue...");
   return $"blue {s}";
};
```
None of the functions are evaluated yet.
```
var lazyGrandmaBlue = lazyGrandma.Map(turnBlue);
```

```
lazyGrandmaBlue()
// prints: getting grandma...
//         turning blue...
// => "blue grandma"
```
All previously composed functions are evaluated now.

As you can see, the functions `lazyGrandma` and `turnBlue` aren't invoked until the last line. This shows that you can build up arbitrarily complex logic without executing anything until you decide to fire things off.

Once you've thoroughly understood the preceding examples, experimented in the REPL, and understood the definition of `Map`, it will be easy to understand the definition of `Bind`.

Listing 11.2 Definition of `Bind` for `Func<T>`

```
public static Func<R> Bind<T, R>
   (this Func<T> f, Func<T, Func<R>> g)
   => () => g(f())();
```

Bind returns a function that, when evaluated, will evaluate f to get a T. Apply g to it to get a Func<R>, and evaluate it to get the resulting R.

This is all very interesting, but how useful is it exactly? Well, because functions are already built into the language, being able to treat Func as a monad might not give you a lot. On the other hand, now that you know you can compose functions monadically, you can bake some effects into how those functions behave. You'll see an example of this next.

11.2 *Exception handling with Try*

In chapter 6, I showed how you could go from an Exception-based API to a functional one by catching exceptions and returning them in an Exceptional—a structure that can hold either an exception or a successful result.

For instance, if you want to safely create a Uri from a string, you could write a method as follows:

```
Exceptional<Uri> CreateUri(string uri)
{
    try { return new Uri(uri); }
    catch (Exception ex) { return ex; }
}
```

This works, but should you do this for every method that can throw an exception? Surely, at the third method, you'll start to feel that all this trying and catching is boilerplate. Could we abstract it away?

11.2.1 *Representing computations that may fail*

Indeed we can, with Try—a delegate representing the operation that may throw an exception. It's defined as follows:

```
public delegate Exceptional<T> Try<T>();
```

Try<T> is simply a delegate you can use to represent a computation that normally returns a T but may throw an exception instead. Notice that its type is () → T, the same as (or compatible with) Func<T>. It's just a lazy computation, but we're adding some semantic meaning by calling it Try; this conveys that the evaluation may throw an exception.

Defining Try as a separate type allows you to define extension methods specific to Try, most importantly Run, which safely invokes it, and returns a suitably populated Exceptional:

```
public static Exceptional<T> Run<T>(this Try<T> @try)
{
    try { return @try(); }
    catch (Exception ex) { return ex; }
}
```

Run does the try/catch ceremony once and for all, so you don't ever have to write a try/catch statement again. Test it for yourself by typing the following into the REPL:

```
Try<Uri> CreateUri(string uri) => () => new Uri(uri);

CreateUri("http://github.com").Run()
// => Success(http://github.com/)

CreateUri("rubbish").Run()
// => Exception(Invalid URI: The format of the URI could not be determined.)
```

Notice how this allows you to define CreateUri without any boilerplate, but when you invoke it with Run, the result is correctly wrapped in an Exceptional. You now have functional error-handling without side effects and without boilerplate.

As a shorthand notation, if you didn't want to define CreateUri as a dedicated function, you could use the Try function (defined on F), which simply transforms a Func<T> into a Try<T>:

```
Try(() => new Uri("http://google.com")).Run()
// => Success(http://google.com/)
```

11.2.2 *Safely extracting information from a JSON object*

Now comes the interesting part—the reason why it's important that you can compose lazy computations. If you have two (or more) computations that may fail, you can monadically compose them into a single computation that may fail.

For example, imagine you have a string representing an object in JSON format with the following structure:

```
{
  'Site': 'github',
  'Uri': 'http://github.com'
}
```

You want to define a method that creates a Uri from the value in the "Uri" field of the JSON object. An unsafe way to do this would be as follows.

Listing 11.3   Unsafely extracting data from a JSON object

```
using Newtonsoft.Json.Linq;

Uri ExtractUri(string json)
{
    JObject jObj = JObject.Parse(json);        ⟵  Deserializes the string
    string uri = jObj["Uri"];                      into a JObject
    return new Uri(uri);        ⟵  Creates a Uri
}                                   object from it
```

Extracts the string value of the Uri attribute

Both the `Uri` constructor and `JObject.Parse` will throw an exception if their input isn't well-formed. (The indexer on `JObject` returns `null` if the requested field isn't present, and this will in turn cause the `Uri` constructor to throw an exception.)

Let's use `Try` to make the implementation safe. We can start by modeling the operations that can fail with `Try`, as follows:

```
Try<JObject> Parse(string s) => () => JObject.Parse(s);
Try<Uri> CreateUri(string uri) => () => new Uri(uri);
```

The way you compose several operations that return a `Try` is (as with any other "container") by using `Bind`. We'll look at its definition in a moment. For now, trust that it works, and let's use it to define a method that combines the two preceding operations into another `Try`-returning function:

```
Try<Uri> ExtractUri(string json)
   => Parse(json)
        .Bind(jObj => CreateUri((string)jObj["Uri"]));
```

This works, but it's not particularly readable. The `LaYumba.Functional` library includes the implementation of the LINQ query pattern (see the sidebar on the LINQ query pattern) for `Try` and all other included monads, so we can improve readability by using a LINQ expression instead.

Listing 11.4 Safely extracting data from a JSON object

```
Try<Uri> ExtractUri(string json) =>
   from jObj in Parse(json)
   let uriStr = (string)jObj["Uri"]
   from uri in CreateUri(uriStr)
   select uri;
```

Extracts the `Uri` field as a string

Deserializes the string into a `JObject`

Creates a `Uri` from its string representation

Let's feed a few sample values to `ExtractUri` to see that it works as intended:

```
ExtractUri("{'Uri': 'http://github.com'}").Run()
// => Success(http://github.com/)

ExtractUri("blah!").Run()
// => Exception(Unexpected character encountered while parsing value: b...)

ExtractUri("{}").Run()
// => Exception(Value cannot be null.\r\nParameter name: uriString)

ExtractUri("{'Uri': 'rubbish'}").Run()
// => Exception(Invalid URI: The format of the URI could not be determined.)
```

Remember, everything happens lazily. When you evaluate the expression `ExtractUri("{}")`, you just get a `Try` that will eventually perform some computation. Nothing happens until you call `Run`.

11.2.3 Composing computations that may fail

Now that you've seen how to use `Bind` to compose several computations that may fail, let's look under the hood and see how `Bind` is defined for `Try`.

Remember that a `Try<T>` is just like a `Func<T>`, for which we know that invocation may throw an exception. So let's start by quickly looking at `Bind` for `Func` again:

```
public static Func<R> Bind<T, R>
    (this Func<T> f, Func<T, Func<R>> g)
    => () => g(f())();
```

A cavalier way of describing this code is that it first invokes `f` and then `g`. Now we need to adapt this to work with `Try`. First, replacing `Func` with `Try` will give us the correct signature. (This is often half of the work because, for the core functions, if the implementation type checks, it usually works.) Second, because invoking a `Try` directly may throw an exception, we need to use `Run` instead. Finally, we don't want to run the second function if the first function fails.

Listing 11.5 Definition of `Bind` for `Try<T>`

```
public static Try<R> Bind<T, R>
    (this Try<T> @try, Func<T, Try<R>> f)
    => ()
    => @try.Run().Match(
        Exception: ex => ex,
        Success: t => f(t).Run());
```

If the first `Try` fails, doesn't execute the second one →

← **Uses `Run` to safely execute each `Try`**

`Bind` takes a `Try` and a `Try`-returning function `f`, and returns a function that, when invoked, will run the `Try` and, if it succeeds, run `f` on the result to obtain another `Try`, which is also run.

If we can define `Bind`, we can always define `Map`, which is usually simpler. I suggest you define `Map` as an exercise.

A reminder on the LINQ query pattern

A fundamental idea of this chapter is that you can use `Bind` to sequence computations, and for this reason I'll be showing the implementations of `Bind`.

In order to use LINQ expressions with monadic types—in this case, `Try`—you additionally need to implement the LINQ query pattern, which I discussed in section 8.4.2. Here's a reminder of how to do this:

- Alias `Map` as `Select`.
- Alias `Bind` as `SelectMany`.
- Define an additional overload of `SelectMany` that takes a binary projection function. This additional overload can be defined in terms of `Map` and `Bind`, although a more efficient implementation can usually be defined.

I won't clutter up this chapter by showing all these method implementations, which are available in the code samples. By now you have all the tools to understand them.

11.2.4 *Monadic composition: what does it mean?*

In this chapter and the next, you'll often read about "monadically composing" computations. That sounds complicated, but it really isn't, so let's take the mystery out of it.

First, let's recap "normal" function composition, which I covered in chapter 5. Suppose you have two functions:

```
f : A → B
g : B → C
```

You can compose them by simply piping the output of f into g, obtaining a function A → C.

Now imagine you have the following functions:

```
f' : A → Try<B>
g' : B → Try<C>
```

These functions obviously don't compose, because f' returns a Try<B>, whereas g' expects a B, but it's fairly clear that you may want to combine them by "extracting" the B from the Try<B> and feeding it to g'. This is monadic composition, and it's exactly what Bind for Try does, as you've seen.

In other words, monadic composition is a way to combine functions that's more general than function composition and involves some logic dictating how the functions are composed. This logic is captured in the Bind function.

There are several variations on this pattern. Imagine the following functions:

```
f" : A → (B, K)
g" : B → (C, K)
```

Could we compose these into a new function of type A → (C, K)? Given an A, it's easy to compute a C: run f" on the A, extract the B from the resulting tuple, and feed it to g". In the process, we've computed two K's, so what should we do with them? If there's a way to combine two K's into a single K, then we could return the combined K. For example, if K is a list, we could return all elements from both lists. Functions in the preceding form can be monadically composed if K is of a suitable type.[2]

The functions for which I'll demonstrate monadic composition in this book are listed in table 11.1, but there are many more possible variations.

Table 11.1 Monadically composable computations demonstrated in this book

Delegate	Signature	Section	Scenario
Try<T>	() → T	11.2	Exception handling
Middleware<T>	(T → R) → R	11.3	Adding behavior before or after a given function

---

[2] This is referred to as the *writer monad* in the literature, and types for which two instances can always be combined into one are called *monoids*.

Table 11.1   Monadically composable computations demonstrated in this book (continued)

Delegate	Signature	Section	Scenario
`Generator<T>`	`int → (T, int)`	12.2	Generating random data
`StatefulComputation<S, T>`	`S → (T, S)`	12.3	Keeping state between computations

11.3   Creating a middleware pipeline for DB access

In this section, I'll start by showing how using HOFs in some cases leads to deeply nested callbacks, a problem commonly referred to as "callback hell," or "the pyramid of doom." I'll use DB access as the specific scenario to illustrate this problem and show how you can leverage the LINQ query pattern to create flat, monadic workflows instead.

This section contains advanced material that isn't required to understand the following chapters, in case you want to skip ahead.

11.3.1   Composing functions that perform setup/teardown

In chapter 1, you saw that you can use a function that performs some setup and teardown and is parameterized with another function to be invoked in between. An example of this was a function that manages a DB connection, and that's parameterized with a function that uses the connection to interact with the DB:

```
public static R Connect<R>
    (ConnectionString connString, Func<SqlConnection, R> f)
{
    using (var conn = new SqlConnection(connString))
    {
        conn.Open();
        return f(conn);
    }
}
```

This function can be consumed in client code like so:

```
public void Log(LogMessage message)
    => Connect(connString, c => c.Execute("sp_create_log"
        , message, commandType: CommandType.StoredProcedure));
```

Let's define a similar function that can be used to log a message before and after an operation:

```
public static T Trace<T>(ILogger log, string op, Func<T> f)
{
    log.LogTrace($"Entering {op}");
    T t = f();
    log.LogTrace($"Leaving {op}");
    return t;
}
```

If you wanted to leverage both functions—opening/closing a connection, and tracing entering/leaving a block—you'd write something like the following.

Listing 11.6   Nested callbacks are hard to read

```
public void Log(LogMessage message)
    => Instrumentation.Trace("CreateLog"
        , () => ConnectionHelper.Connect(connString
            , c => c.Execute("sp_create_log"
                , message, commandType: CommandType.StoredProcedure)));
```

This is starting to become hard to read. What if you wanted some other setup of work to be done as well? For every HOF you add, your callbacks are nested one level deeper, making the code harder to understand. This is what's commonly referred to as "the pyramid of doom."

Instead, what we'd ideally like to have is a clean way to compose a *middleware pipe-line*, as illustrated in figure 11.2. That is, we want to add some behavior (like connection management, diagnostics, and so on) to each trip to the DB. Conceptually, this is similar to the middleware pipeline for handling requests in ASP.NET Core.

In a normal, *linear* function pipeline, the output of each function is piped into the next function, so that a function has no control of what happens downstream. A middleware pipeline, on the other hand, is U-shaped: each function passes some data along, but it also receives some data on the way out, so to speak. As a result, each function is able to perform some operations before *and* after the functions downstream.

I'm going to call each of these functions or blocks a *middleware*. We want to be able to nicely compose such middleware pipelines: add logging, add timing, and so on. But because each middleware must take a callback function as an input argument

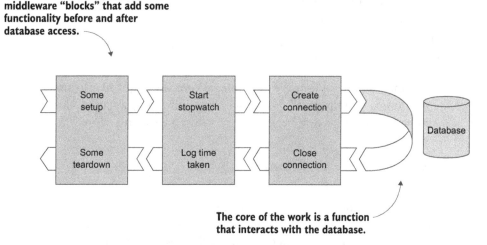

You want to compose a pipeline from middleware "blocks" that add some functionality before and after database access.

The core of the work is a function that interacts with the database.

Figure 11.2   A middleware pipeline for accessing the DB

(otherwise, it can't intervene after the callback has returned), how can we escape the pyramid of doom?

11.3.2 *A recipe against the pyramid of doom*

It turns out that one way we can look at Bind is as a recipe against the pyramid of doom. For instance, you may remember how in chapter 6 we used Bind to combine several Either-returning functions:

```
WakeUpEarly()
    .Bind(ShopForIngredients)
    .Bind(CookRecipe)
    .Match(
        Left: PlanB,
        Right: EnjoyTogether);
```

If you expand the calls to Bind, the preceding code looks like this:

```
WakeUpEarly().Match(
    Left: planB,
    Right: u => ShopForIngredients(u).Match(
        Left: planB,
        Right: ingr = CookRecipe(ingr).Match(
            Left: planB,
            Right: EnjoyTogether)));
```

You can see that Bind effectively enables us to escape the pyramid of doom in this case—the same would apply to Option, and so on. But can we define Bind for our middleware functions?

11.3.3 *Capturing the essence of a middleware function*

To answer this question, let's look at the signatures of our middleware functions and see if there's a pattern that we can identify and capture in an abstract way. These are the functions we've seen so far:

```
Connect : ConnectionString → (SqlConnection → R) → R
Trace : ILogger → string → (() → R) → R
```

Let's imagine a couple more examples where we might like to use middleware. We could use a timing middleware that logs how long an operation has taken, and another middleware that begins and commits a DB transaction. The signatures would look like this:

```
Time : ILogger → string → (() → R) → R
Transact : SqlConnection → (SqlTransaction → R) → R
```

Time has the same signature as Trace: it takes a logger and a string (the name of the operation that's being timed) and the function being timed. Transact is similar to Connect, but it takes a connection that will be used to create a transaction and a function that consumes the transaction.

Now that we have four reasonable use cases, let's see if there's a pattern in the signatures:

```
ConnectionString → (SqlConnection → R) → R
ILogger → string → (() → R) → R
SqlConnection → (SqlTransaction → R) → R
```

Each function has some parameters that are specific to the functionality it exposes, but there's definitely a pattern. If we abstract away these specific parameters (which we could provide with partial application) and only concentrate on the arguments shown in bold font, all the functions have a signature in this form:

```
(T → R) → R
```

That is, they all take a callback function—although in this context it's usually called a *continuation*—that produces an R, and they return an R—presumably the very R returned by the continuation, or a modified version of it. So the essence of a middleware function is that it takes a continuation of type T → R, supplies a T to it to obtain an R, and returns an R, as shown in figure 11.3.

Let's capture this essence with a delegate:

```
// (T → dynamic) → dynamic
public delegate dynamic Middleware<T>(Func<T, dynamic> cont);
```

But wait. Why is it returning dynamic, rather than R?

The problem is that T (the input to the continuation) and R (its output) are not known at the same time. For example, suppose you want to create a Middleware instance from a function such as Connect, which has signature

```
public static R Connect<R>(ConnectionString connString
    , Func<SqlConnection, R> func) // ...
```

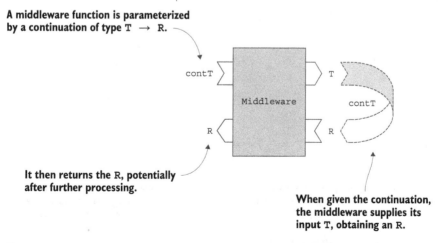

A middleware function is parameterized by a continuation of type T → R.

It then returns the R, potentially after further processing.

When given the continuation, the middleware supplies its input T, obtaining an R.

Figure 11.3 A single middleware function

The continuation accepted by Connect takes a SqlConnection as input, so we can use Connect to define a Middleware<SqlConnection>. That means the T type variable in Middleware<T> resolves to SqlConnection, but we don't yet know what the given continuation will yield, so we can't yet resolve the R type variable in Connect<R>.

Unfortunately, C# doesn't allow us to "partially apply" type variables; hence, dynamic. So although conceptually we're thinking of combining HOFs of this type

```
(T → R) → R
```

we're modeling them as follows:

```
(T → dynamic) → dynamic
```

Later you'll see that you can still work with Middleware without compromising on type safety.

The interesting—and mind-bending—thing is that Middleware<T> is a monad over T, where, remember, T is the type of the *input* argument taken by the continuation that is given to the middleware function. This seems counterintuitive. A monad over T is usually something that "contains" a T, or some Ts. But this still applies here: if a function has the signature (T → R) → R, then it can provide a T to the given function T → R, so it must "contain" or somehow be able to produce a T.

11.3.4 *Implementing the query pattern for middleware*

It's time to learn how to combine two middleware blocks with Bind. Essentially, Bind attaches a downstream middleware block to a pipeline, as shown in figure 11.4.

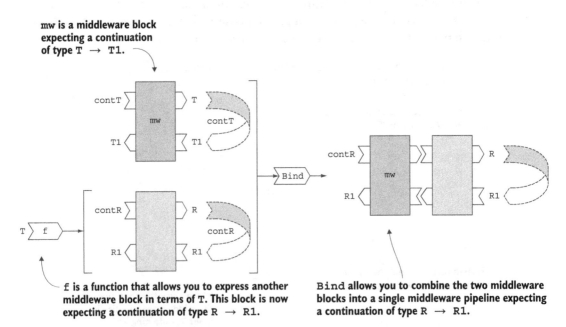

mw is a middleware block expecting a continuation of type T → T1.

f is a function that allows you to express another middleware block in terms of T. This block is now expecting a continuation of type R → R1.

Bind allows you to combine the two middleware blocks into a single middleware pipeline expecting a continuation of type R → R1.

Figure 11.4 Bind adds a middleware block to the pipeline.

The implementation of Bind is simple to write, but not easy to fully grasp:

```
public static Middleware<R> Bind<T, R>
    (this Middleware<T> mw, Func<T, Middleware<R>> f)
    => cont
    => mw(t => f(t)(cont));
```

We have a Middleware<T> expecting a continuation of type (T → dynamic). We then have a function, f, that takes a T and produces a Middleware<R>, expecting a continuation of type (R → dynamic). What we get as a result is a Middleware<R> that, when supplied a continuation, cont, will run the initial middleware, giving it as continuation a function that will run the binder function f to obtain the second middleware, to which it will pass cont. Don't worry if this doesn't fully make sense at this point.

Let's look at Map now:

```
public static Middleware<R> Map<T, R>
    (this Middleware<T> mw, Func<T, R> f)
    => cont
    => mw(t => cont(f(t)));
```

Map takes a Middleware<T> and a function f from T to R. The middleware knows how to create a T and supply it to a continuation that takes a T. By applying f, it now knows how to create an R and supply it to a continuation that takes an R. You can visualize Map as adding a transformation T → R before the continuation, or alternatively, as adding a new setup/teardown block to the pipeline, performing a transformation as the setup and just passing the result along as the teardown, as shown in figure 11.5.

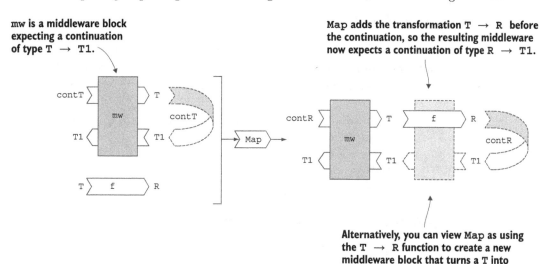

mw is a middleware block expecting a continuation of type T → T1.

Map adds the transformation T → R before the continuation, so the resulting middleware now expects a continuation of type R → T1.

Alternatively, you can view Map as using the T → R function to create a new middleware block that turns a T into an R on the way in, and just passes the result along on the way out.

Figure 11.5 Map adds a transformation to the pipeline.

Finally, once we've composed the desired pipeline, we can run the whole pipeline by passing a continuation:

```
Middleware<A> mw;
Func<A, B> cont;

dynamic exp1 = mw(cont);
```

The preceding code shows that if you have a `Middleware<A>` and a continuation function cont of type A → B, you can directly supply the continuation to the middleware.

There's still a small crease to iron out. Notice that when we provide the continuation, we get a dynamic back, where we really expect a B. To maintain type safety, we can define a Run function that runs the pipeline with the identity function as continuation:

```
public static T Run<T>(this Middleware<T> mw)
   => (T)mw(t => t);
```

Because mw is a `Middleware<T>` (that is, mw can create a T and provide it to its continuation) and because the continuation in this case is the identity function, we know that the continuation produces a T, so we can confidently cast the result of running the middleware to T.

When we want to run a pipeline, instead of directly providing the continuation, we can use Map to map the continuation, and then call Run:

```
Middleware<A> mw;
Func<A, B> cont;

B exp2 = mw.Map(cont).Run()
```

Here we map our continuation, A → B, onto our `Middleware<A>`, obtaining a `Middleware<B>`, and then run it (with the identity function) to obtain a B. Notice that exp2 from this snippet is identical to exp1 from the previous one,[3] but we've regained type safety.

Let's put this all to work by refactoring DbLogger to use Middleware, rather than HOFs:

```
public class DbLogger
{
    Middleware<SqlConnection> Connect;

    public DbLogger(ConnectionString connString)
    {
        Connect = f => ConnectionHelper.Connect(connString, f);
```

---

[3] This is because when computing exp2, we first compute mw.Map(cont), which composes cont with the continuation that will eventually be given, and then by calling Run we provide the identity function as continuation. The resulting continuation is the composition of cont and identity, which is exactly the same as providing cont as the continuation.

```
   }

   public void Log(LogMessage message) => (
      from conn in Connect
      select conn.Execute("sp_create_log", message
         , commandType: CommandType.StoredProcedure)
   ).Run();
```

In the constructor, we essentially use partial application to bake the connection string into the `Connect` function, which now has the right signature to be used as a `Middleware<SqlConnection>`.

In the `Log` method, we create a pipeline that has a single middleware block, which creates the DB connection. We can then use LINQ syntax to refer to `conn`, the connection that will be available when the pipeline will be run, when calling `Execute`, the main operation that will interact with the DB.

Of course, we could have written `Log` more concisely by just passing a callback to `Connect`. But the whole point here is to avoid callbacks. As we add more blocks to the pipeline, we'll be able to do this by just adding `from` clauses to our LINQ comprehension. You'll see this next.

11.3.5 *Adding middleware that times the operation*

Suppose we have a DB operation that sometimes takes longer than expected, so we'd like to add another middleware that logs how long the DB access operation took. For this, we could define the following HOF:

```
public static class Instrumentation
{
   public static T Time<T>(ILogger log, string op, Func<T> f)
   {
      var sw = new Stopwatch();
      sw.Start();

      T t = f();

      sw.Stop();
      log.LogDebug($"{op} took {sw.ElapsedMilliseconds}ms");
      return t;
   }
}
```

`Time` takes three arguments: a logger, to which it will log the diagnostic message; `op`, the name of the operation being performed, which will be included in the logged message; and a function representing the operation whose duration is being timed.

There's a slight problem, because `Time` takes a `Func<T>` (a function with *no* input arguments), whereas we defined the continuations accepted by our middleware to be in the form T → dynamic; that is, there should always be an input parameter. We can bridge the gap with `Unit`, as usual, but this time on the input side. For this, I've defined an adapter function that converts a function taking `Unit` to a function taking no arguments:

```
public static Func<T> ToNullary<T>(this Func<Unit, T> f)
    => () => f(Unit());
```

With this in place, we can enrich our pipeline with a block for logging the time taken for DB access.

Listing 11.7   A two-block middleware pipeline combining timing and connection management

```
public class DbLogger
{
    Middleware<SqlConnection> Connect;
    Func<string, Middleware<Unit>> Time;

    public DbLogger(ConnectionString connString, ILogger log)
    {
        Connect = f => ConnectionHelper.Connect(connString, f);
        Time = op => f => Instrumentation.Time(log, op, f.ToNullary());
    }

    public void DeleteOldLogs() => (
        from _    in Time("DeleteOldLogs")
        from conn in Connect
        select conn.Execute
            ( "DELETE [Logs] WHERE [Timestamp] < @upTo"
            , new { upTo = 7.Days().Ago() })
    ).Run();
}
```

Once we've wrapped the call to `Instrumentation.Time` in a `Middleware`, we can use it in the pipeline by adding an additional `from` clause. Notice that the `_` variable will be assigned the `Unit` value returned by `Time`. You can disregard it, but LINQ syntax doesn't allow you to omit it.

11.3.6   *Adding middleware that manages a DB transaction*

As a final example, let's add one more type of middleware that manages a DB transaction. We can abstract simple transaction management into a HOF like this:

```
public static R Transact<R>
    (SqlConnection conn, Func<SqlTransaction, R> f)
{
    R r = default(R);
    using (var tran = conn.BeginTransaction())
    {
        r = f(tran);
        tran.Commit();
    }
    return r;
}
```

`Transact` takes a connection and a function, `f`, that consumes the transaction. Presumably, `f` involves multiple actions against the DB, which we want to be performed atomically. As an effect of `using`, the transaction will be rolled back if an exception is thrown by `f`.

Here's an example of integrating `Transact` into a pipeline.

Listing 11.8   A pipeline that provides connection and transaction management

```
public class Orders
{
    ConnectionString connString;        ◁——— Should be injected

    Middleware<SqlConnection> Connect                              ◁┐  Adapters to turn
        => f => ConnectionHelper.Connect(connString, f);           │  existing HOFs into
                                                                    │  Middleware
    Middleware<SqlTransaction> Transact(SqlConnection conn)   ◁────┘
        => f => ConnectionHelper.Transact(conn, f);

    public void DeleteOrder(Guid id)
        => DeleteOrder(new { Id = id }).Run();

    SqlTemplate deleteLines = "DELETE OrderLines WHERE OrderId = @Id";
    SqlTemplate deleteOrder = "DELETE Orders WHERE OrderId = @Id";

    Middleware<int> DeleteOrder(object param) =>
        from conn in Connect
        from tran in Transact(conn)
        select conn.Execute(deleteLines, param, tran)
            + conn.Execute(deleteOrder, param, tran);
}
```

Look at our pipeline now: we have a block that creates the connection, and another block that uses it to create a transaction. Within the `select` clause, we have two DB actions that use the connection and the transaction, and which as a result will be executed atomically. Because `Execute` returns an `int` (the number of affected rows), we can just use + to combine the two operations.

As you've already seen in previous chapters, the `Guid` of the order being deleted is used to populate the `Id` field of a `param` object, and as a result it will replace the `@Id` token of the SQL template strings.

Once the middleware functions are set up, adding or removing a step from the pipeline is a one-line change. If you're logging timing information, do you only want to time the DB actions, or also the time taken to acquire the connection? Whatever the case, you can change that by simply changing the order of middleware in the pipeline:

**Acquiring the connection counts
toward the time that will be logged.**

```
from _ in Time("slowQuery")      ◁——┐
from conn in Connect
select conn.Execute(mySlowQuery)
```

Only the DB action is timed.

```
from conn in Connect
from _ in Time("slowQuery")      ◁——┐
select conn.Execute(mySlowQuery)
```

The flat layout of LINQ queries makes it easy to see and change the order of the middleware functions. And, of course, this solution avoids the pyramid of doom. Although I've used the idea of middleware and the somewhat specific scenario of DB access to illustrate it, the concept of continuations is wider and applies to any function in this form:[4]

```
(T → R) → R
```

This also means that we could have avoided defining a custom delegate `Middleware`. The definitions of `Map`, `Bind`, and `Run` have nothing specific to this scenario, and we could have used `Func<Func<T, dynamic> dynamic>` instead of `Middleware<T>`. This might even save a few lines of code, because it removes the need for creating delegates of the correct type. I opted for `Middleware` as a more explicit, domain-specific abstraction, but that's a personal preference.

`Middleware`, as well as the other delegate-based monads `Try` and `StatefulComputation` you saw earlier in the chapter, illustrates how computations that can be composed monadically provide powerful and expressive constructs, allowing us to elegantly address general problems like exception handling or state passing, and more specific scenarios like middleware pipelines and others that we'll address in chapter 12.

Summary

- Laziness means deferring a computation until its result is needed. It's especially useful when the result may not be required in the end.
- Lazy computations can be composed to create more complex computations that can then be triggered as needed.
- When dealing with an exception-based API, you can use the `Try` delegate type. The `Run` function safely executes the code in the `Try` and returns the result wrapped in an `Exceptional`.
- HOFs in the form $(T \rightarrow R) \rightarrow R$ (that is, functions that take a callback or *continuation*) can also be composed monadically, enabling you to use flat LINQ expressions rather than deeply nested callbacks.

---

[4] In the literature, this is known as *the continuation monad*, which again is a misnomer, because the monad here isn't the continuation, but the computation that takes a continuation as input.

Stateful programs
and stateful computations

This chapter covers

- What makes a program stateful?
- Writing stateful programs without mutating state
- Generating random structures
- Composing stateful computations

Since chapter 1, I've been preaching against state mutation as a side effect that should be avoided at almost any cost, and you've seen several examples of refactoring programs to avoid state mutation. In this chapter you'll see how the functional approach works when there's a *requirement* for the program to be stateful.

But what's a stateful program exactly? It's a program whose behavior differs, depending on past inputs or events.[1] By analogy, if somebody says "Good morning," you'll probably mindlessly greet them in return. If that person immediately says

[1] This means that a program may be considered stateful/stateless depending on where you draw the program boundary. You may have a stateless server that uses a DB to keep state. If you consider both as one program, it's stateful; if you consider the server in isolation, it's stateless.

"Good morning" again, your reaction will certainly differ: why in the world would somebody say "Good morning" twice in a row? A stateless program, on the other hand, would keep answering "Good morning" just as mindlessly as before, because it has no notion of past inputs. Every time is like the first time.

In this chapter, you'll see how two apparently contradictory ideas—keeping state in memory, and avoiding state mutation—can be reconciled in a stateful functional program. You'll then see how functions that handle state can be composed, using the techniques you learned in chapter 11.

12.1 Programs that manage state

In this section, you'll see a very simple command-line program that enables the user to get foreign exchange rates (FX rates). A sample interaction with the program would be as follows (bold letters indicate user input):

```
Enter a currency pair like 'EURUSD', or 'q' to quit
usdeur
fetching rate...
0.9162
gbpusd
fetching rate...
1.2248
q
```

An initial *stateless* implementation is shown in the following listing.

Listing 12.1   Stateless implementation of a simple program to look up FX rates

```
public class Program
{
    public static void Main()
    {
        WriteLine("Enter a currency pair like 'EURUSD', or 'q' to quit");
```

```
        for (string input; (input = ReadLine().ToUpper()) != "Q";)
          WriteLine(Yahoo.GetRate(input));
    }
}

static class Yahoo
{
    public static decimal GetRate(string ccyPair)
    {
        WriteLine($"fetching rate...");
        var uri = $"http://finance.yahoo.com/d/quotes.csv?f=l1&s={ccyPair}=X";
        var request = new HttpClient().GetStringAsync(uri);
        return decimal.Parse(request.Result.Trim());
    }
}
```

You can pretty much ignore the implementation details of the Yahoo class. We only care about the fact that its GetRate function takes a currency pair identifier such as "EURUSD" (for Euro/US Dollar) and returns the exchange rate.

The program works, but if you ask it for the same pair n times in a row, it will perform an HTTP request every time. There are several reasons why you might like to limit the number of unnecessary requests—performance, network use, or cost incurred per request. Next, we'll introduce an in-memory cache to avoid looking up rates we've already retrieved.

12.1.1 Maintaining a cache of retrieved resources

We want to store rates in a cache when they're retrieved, and only make HTTP requests for rates we haven't seen before, as shown in figure 12.1.

Of course, as functional programmers, we want to do this without state mutation. What will be the type of the program's state? A dictionary would be a natural choice,

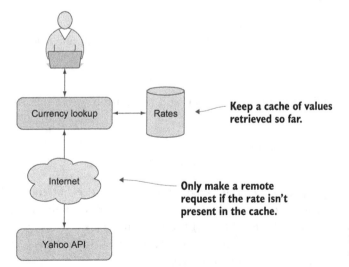

Figure 12.1 Keeping a cache of previously retrieved rates

mapping the pair identifier (such as "EURUSD") to the retrieved exchange rate. Just to make sure we don't mutate it, let's make it an immutable dictionary: `Immutable-Dictionary<string, decimal>`. And because that's quite an ugly type, we'll alias it as `Rates` to make the code less verbose.

Here's an implementation that stores already-retrieved rates in the cache, and only calls the remote API if the rate wasn't previously retrieved.

> **Listing 12.2   Stateful implementation keeping a cache of rates, without state mutation**

```
using Rates = ImmutableDictionary<string, decimal>          Creates a readable name
                                                            for the object representing
public class Program                                        the program state
{
    public static void Main()
    {
        WriteLine("Enter a currency pair like 'EURUSD', or 'q' to quit");
        MainRec(Rates.Empty);
    }                                        Main simply sets up an
                                             initial state and passes
    static void MainRec(Rates cache)         control to MainRec.
    {
        var input = ReadLine().ToUpper();
        if (input == "Q") return;

        var (rate, newState) = GetRate(input, cache);       Gets a result, as well
        WriteLine(rate);                                    as the new state
        MainRec(newState);            Recursively calls itself
    }                                 with the new state

    static (decimal, Rates) GetRate(string ccyPair, Rates cache)
    {
        if (cache.ContainsKey(ccyPair))
            return (cache[ccyPair], cache);

        var rate = Yahoo.GetRate(ccyPair);
        return (rate, cache.Add(ccyPair, rate));       Returns a tuple with
    }                                                  the retrieved rate and the
}                                                      updated state of the program
```

Look at the signature of the `GetRate` function, and compare it with `Yahoo.GetRate`, which it uses:

```
Yahoo.GetRate   : string → decimal
Program.GetRate : string → Rates → (decimal, Rates)
```

If `Yahoo.GetRate` is the stateless version, `Program.GetRate` is the stateful version: it takes, along with the requested currency pair, the current state of the program; it returns, along with the result, the new state of the program. This is the key to writing stateful applications without mutation: if global variables can't be mutated, you must pass state around via arguments and return values.

Let's now move up to `MainRec` (for recursive), which contains the basic control flow of the program. The thing to note here is that it takes as an input parameter the current state of the program, which it will pass on to `GetRate` to retrieve the new state (along with the rate, which is printed). It ends by calling itself with the new state.

Finally, `Main` does nothing other than calling `MainRec` with the initial state of the program, which is an empty cache. You can view the entire program execution as a loop with `MainRec` recursively calling itself, passing the current version of the state as a parameter.

Note that, although there are no global variables in the program, it's still a stateful program. The program keeps some state in memory, which affects how the program operates.

Generally speaking, recursion is a risky business in C#, as it can blow the stack if more than about 10,000 recursive calls are made. If you wanted to avoid the recursive definition, you could use a loop instead, and `Main` could be rewritten as follows.

Listing 12.3 Converting a recursive function to a loop with a local mutable variable

```
public static void Main()
{
    WriteLine("Enter a currency pair like 'EURUSD', or 'q' to quit");
    var state = Rates.Empty;                    ⟵ The initial state

    for (string input; (input = ReadLine().ToUpper()) != "Q";)
    {
        var (rate, newState) = GetRate(input, state);
        state = newState;              ⟵ Reassigns the state variable
        WriteLine(rate);                 for the next iteration
    }
}
```

Here, instead of the recursive call, we keep a local, mutable variable, `state`, which is reassigned to the new state as needed. We're not mutating any global state, so the fundamental idea still holds.

For the remaining examples, I'll stick to the recursive version, which I think is clearer.

12.1.2 Refactoring for testability and error handling

You've seen how you can create a stateful program that doesn't require mutation. Before we move on, I'll take advantage of this fairly complete example to illustrate some of the concepts introduced earlier in the book around testability and error handling.

You'll notice that although there are no side effects in terms of state mutation, there are I/O side effects everywhere, so the program isn't at all testable. We can refactor `GetRate` to take the function performing the HTTP request as an input argument, following the pattern explained in chapter 2:

```
static (decimal, Rates) GetRate
   (Func<string, decimal> getRate, string ccyPair, Rates cache)
{
   if (cache.ContainsKey(ccyPair))
      return (cache[ccyPair], cache);
   var rate = getRate(ccyPair);
   return (rate, cache.Add(ccyPair, rate));
}
```

Now GetRate has no side effects other than those that may occur by calling the given delegate, getRate. As a result, it's easy to unit test this function by providing a delegate with a predictable behavior. You can probably see how MainRec could likewise be brought under test by injecting functions to invoke for I/O.

Next, there's no error handling at all: if you enter the name of a currency pair that doesn't exist, the program just crashes. Let's put Try to good use. First, we'll enrich Yahoo with a method returning a Try:

```
static class Yahoo
{
   public static Try<decimal> TryGetRate(string ccyPair)
      => () => GetRate(ccyPair);
}
```

TryGetRate does nothing other than wrap the unsafe call to GetRate in a Try. Our main class's GetRate method must now change its signature to take not a function returning a decimal, but a Try<decimal>. Accordingly, its return type will also be wrapped in a Try. Here's the signature before and after:

```
before : (string → decimal) → string → (decimal, Rates)
after  : (string → Try<decimal>) → string → Try<(decimal, Rates)>
```

The refactored implementation is shown in the following listing.

> **Listing 12.4 The program refactored to use `Try` for error handling**

```
public class Program
{
   public static void Main()
      => MainRec("Enter a currency pair like 'EURUSD', or 'q' to quit"
         , Rates.Empty);

   static void MainRec(string message, Rates cache)
   {
      WriteLine(message);
      var input = ReadLine().ToUpper();
      if (input == "Q") return;

      GetRate(Yahoo.TryGetRate, input, cache) .Run().Match(
         ex => MainRec($"Error: {ex.Message}", cache),
         result => MainRec(result.Rate.ToString(), result.NewState));
   }
```

```
static Try<(decimal Rate, Rates NewState)> GetRate
  (Func<string, Try<decimal>> getRate, string ccyPair, Rates cache)
{
  if (cache.ContainsKey(ccyPair))
    return Try(() => (cache[ccyPair], cache));
  else return from rate in getRate(ccyPair)
    select (rate, cache.Add(ccyPair, rate));
}
}
```

Notice how we were able to add testability and error handling in a relatively painless way, without puffing up the implementation with interfaces, `try`/`catch` blocks, and so on. Instead, we have more powerful function signatures, and more explicit relations between functions via parameter passing.

12.1.3 Stateful computations

As you've seen in this section, if you want to handle state functionally—that is, without state mutation—state must be made available to functions as an input argument, and functions that affect the state must return the updated state as part of their result. The remaining part of this chapter focuses on *stateful computations*, which are functions that interact with some state.

 DEFINITION *Stateful computations* are functions that take a state (as well as, potentially, other arguments), and return a new state (along with, potentially, a return value). They're also called state transitions.

Stateful computations may appear both in stateful and stateless programs. You've already seen a few examples: in the previous scenario, `GetRate` is a stateful computation because it takes some state (the cache) along with a currency pair, and returns the updated state along with the requested rate. In chapter 10, the static `Account` class contained only stateful computations, each taking an `AccountState` (along with a command) and returning a new `AccountState` (along with an event to store), although in this case things were slightly complicated by the result being wrapped in a `Validation`.

If you want to combine several stateful computations, the process of always passing the state into a function, extracting it from the result, and passing it to the next function can become quite tedious. Fortunately, stateful computations can be composed monadically, in a way that hides the state-passing, as you'll see next. The rest of this chapter contains advanced material, which is not required to understand the following chapters, in case you decide to skip ahead.

12.2 A language for generating random data

Random data has many legitimate practical uses, including property-based testing (which I discussed in chapter 8), load testing (where you generate lots of random data and then bombard your system and see how it holds up), and simulation algorithms

like Monte Carlo. In this context, I'm mainly interested in presenting random generation as a very good and fairly simple example of how stateful computations compose.

To get started, type the following into the REPL:

```
var r = new Random(100);
r.Next() // => 2080427802
r.Next() // => 341851734
r.Next() // => 1431988776
```

Since you're explicitly passing the value 100 as a seed for the random generator, you should
get *exactly* the same results. As you can see, it's not that random after all. It's next to impossible to get real randomness with our current computers; instead, random generators use
a scrambling algorithm to deterministically produce an output that *looks* random. Typically,
you don't want to get the same sequence of values every time, so a Random instance is usually
initialized without an explicit seed, in which case the current time is used.

So, if Random is deterministic, how does it produce a different output every time
you call Next? The answer is that Random is stateful: every time you call Next, the state
of the instance changes, so that the following call to Next will yield a new value. In
other words, Next has side effects: although Next produces an int as its explicit output, there's an implicit input (the current state of the Random instance) that determines the output, and another implicit output, the new state of the Random, that will
determine the output of the following call to Next.

We're going to create a side-effect-free random generator, where all inputs and
outputs are explicit. Generating a number value is a stateful computation, because it
requires a seed, and it must also generate a new seed to be used in the next generation. We don't want to only generate integers, but values of any type, so the type of a
generator function can be captured with the following delegate:

```
public delegate (T Value, int Seed) Generator<T>(int seed);
```

That is, a Generator<T> is a stateful computation that takes an int value as a seed (the
state), and returns a tuple consisting of the generated T and a new seed, which can be
used to generate a subsequent value. The standard arrow-notation signature of a
Generator<T> is

```
int → (T, int)
```

To run a generator, we can define the following Run methods:

```
public static T Run<T>(this Generator<T> gen, int seed)
   => gen(seed).Value;

public static T Run<T>(this Generator<T> gen)
   => gen(Environment.TickCount).Value;
```

The first overload runs the generator with the given seed and just returns the
generated value, disregarding the state. The second overload uses the clock to get a

different seed value each time it's called (it's therefore impure and not testable, unlike the first overload).

Next, let's create some generators.

12.2.1 *Generating random integers*

The basic building block we need is a generator that scrambles the seed value into a new int. Here's one possible implementation.

Listing 12.5   A stateful computation returning a pseudo-random number

```
public static Generator<int> NextInt = (seed) =>
{
    seed ^= seed >> 13;
    seed ^= seed << 18;
    int result = seed & 0x7fffffff;
    return (result, result);
};
```

This is a generator that, when given a seed, scrambles it to obtain another integer that *looks* unrelated.[2] It then returns that value both as a result value, and as a seed to be used in the following computation.

Things start to get exciting when you want to generate more complex values. It turns out that if you can generate a random int, you can generate random values for arbitrarily complex types. But let's start with baby steps: you know how to write a generator for an int; how could you write a generator for a *simpler* type, such as a Boolean?

12.2.2 *Generating other primitives*

Remember, a generator takes a seed and returns a new value (in this case, a generated Boolean), along with a new seed. The skeleton of a Generator<bool> would be as follows:

```
public static Generator<bool> NextBool = (seed) =>
{
    bool result = // ???
    int newSeed = // ???
    return (result, newSeed);
};
```

How can we go about it? We already have a generator for an int, so we can generate an int and return true/false depending on whether the generated int is even/odd, while taking advantage of the new seed computed when generating the int. Essentially, we're using NextInt, transforming the resulting int into a bool and reusing the seed, as illustrated in figure 12.2.

---

[2] The specifics of the algorithm are irrelevant for the purposes of this discussion. There are many algorithms for generating pseudo-random numbers.

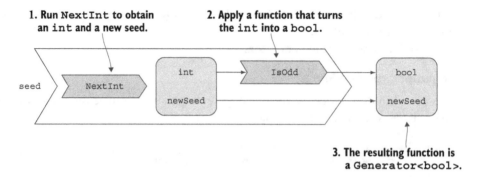

Figure 12.2   Using the NextInt generator to generate a Boolean

The implementation is as follows:

```
public static Generator<bool> NextBool = (seed) =>
{
    var (i, newSeed) = NextInt(seed);
    return (i % 2 == 0, newSeed);
};
```

Now let's think of this differently. What we're doing here is effectively *mapping* a function that turns an int into a bool, while reusing the new seed returned by the existing NextInt generator. We can generalize this pattern to define Map: if you have a Generator<T> and a function f : T → R, you can obtain a Generator<R> by running the generator to obtain a T and a new seed, then applying f to obtain an R, and returning it along with the new seed.

In code, the implementation of Map/Select looks like this.

Listing 12.6   Definition of Map for Generator<T>

Map **returns a generator that, when given a seed...**

... **will run the given generator, gen, to obtain a T and a new seed...**

```
public static Generator<R> Map<T, R>
    (this Generator<T> gen, Func<T, R> f)
    => seed =>
    {
        var (t, newSeed) = gen(seed);
        return (f(t), newSeed);
    };
```

... **then use f to turn the T into an R, which is returned along with the new seed.**

We can now define generators for types that carry less information than an int, such as bool or char, much more concisely, as in the following listing.

Listing 12.7   Building upon NextInt to generate other types

Generates an int...

```
public static Generator<bool> NextBool =>
    from i in NextInt
    select i % 2 == 0;
```

◄—— ... **returns whether it's even**

```
public static Generator<char> NextChar =>
    from i in NextInt
    select (char)(i % (char.MaxValue + 1));
```

That's much more readable because we don't have to explicitly worry about the seed, and we can read the code in terms of "generate an int, and return whether it's even."

12.2.3 Generating complex structures

Now let's move on and see how we can generate more complex values. Let's try to generate a pair of integers. We'd have to write something like this:

```
public static Generator<(int, int)> PairOfInts = (seed0) =>
{
    var (a, seed1) = NextInt(seed0);
    var (b, seed2) = NextInt(seed1);
    return ((a, b), seed2);
};
```

Here you see that, for each stateful computation (or for each time we generate a random value), we need to extract the state (the newly created seed) and pass it on to the next computation. This is rather noisy. Fortunately we can do away with the explicit state-passing by composing the generators with a LINQ expression.

Listing 12.8 Defining a function that generates a pair of random integers

```
                 public static Generator<(int, int)> PairOfInts =>
Generates            from a in NextInt
an int and           from b in NextInt
calls it a           select (a, b);
                 Returns the pair of a and b
```
Generates another int and calls it b

This is much more readable, but under the covers it's the same as before. This works because I've defined an implementation of `Bind/SelectMany` that takes care of "threading the state"; that is, passing it from one computation to the next. Graphically, `Bind` works as shown in figure 12.3. Listing 12.9 shows the corresponding code.

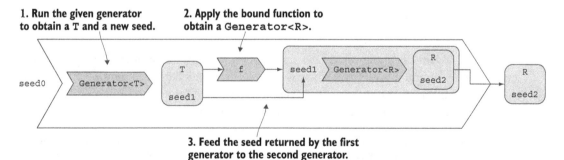

1. Run the given generator to obtain a T and a new seed.

2. Apply the bound function to obtain a Generator<R>.

3. Feed the seed returned by the first generator to the second generator.

Figure 12.3 Definition of `Bind` for `Generator<T>`

Listing 12.9   Definition of Bind for Generator<T>

```
public static Generator<R> Bind<T, R>
   (this Generator<T> gen, Func<T, Generator<R>> f)
   => seed0 =>
   {
       var (t, seed1) = gen(seed0);
       return f(t)(seed1);
   };
```

Now we have all the building blocks to generate arbitrarily complex types. Say we want to create an `Option<int>`. That's easy—generate a Boolean for the state of the `Option` and an `int` for the value:

```
public static Generator<Option<int>> OptionInt =>
   from some in NextBool
   from i in NextInt
   select some ? Some(i) : None;
```

This should look familiar: you saw some very similar code in chapter 9 when we were using FsCheck to define property tests, and we needed to provide a method for generating random `Options`. Indeed, FsCheck's random generator is defined along the same lines as this one.

Next we'll generate a sequence of ints. That's slightly more complex.

Listing 12.10   Generating a list of random numbers

```
public static Generator<IEnumerable<int>> IntList
   => from empty in NextBool
      from list in empty ? Empty : NonEmpty
      select list;

static Generator<IEnumerable<int>> Empty
   => Generator.Return(Enumerable.Empty<int>());

static Generator<IEnumerable<int>> NonEmpty
   => from head in NextInt
      from tail in IntList
      select List(head).Concat(tail);

public static Generator<T> Return<T>(T value)
   => seed => (value, seed);
```

Let's start with the top-level `IntList`: we generate a random Boolean to tell us if the sequence should be empty.[3] If so, we use `Empty`, which is a generator that always returns an empty sequence; otherwise, we return a non-empty sequence by calling `NonEmpty`. This generates an `int` as the first element and a random sequence to follow

---

[3] This means that, statistically, half the generated lists will be empty, a quarter of the lists will have one element, and so on, so this generator is very unlikely to produce a long list. You can follow a different approach and generate a random length first, presumably within a given range, and then populate the values. As this shows, once you start to generate random data, it's important to define parameters that govern the random generation.

it. Note that `Empty` uses the `Return` function for `Generator`, which lifts a value into a generator that always returns that value and doesn't affect the state it's given.

What about generating a string? A string is essentially a sequence of characters, so we can just generate a list of `int`s, convert each `int` to a `char`, and build a string from the resulting sequence of characters. As you can see, we follow this approach to generate a language for combining generators of various types into generators for arbitrarily complex types.

12.3 *A general pattern for stateful computations*

There are many other scenarios in which we may want to compose several stateful computations—other than generating random values. For this, we can use a more general delegate, `StatefulComputation`:

```
delegate (T Value, S State) StatefulComputation<S, T>(S state);
```

A `StatefulComputation<T>` is a function in this form:

```
S → (T, S)
```

`T` is the function's result value, and `S` is the state.[4]

You can compare this to the signature of `Generator<T>` to see how similar they are:

```
StatefulComputation<T> : S   → (T, S)
Generator<T>           : int → (T, int)
```

With `Generator`, the state that gets passed in and out is always an `int`; with the more general `StatefulComputation`, the state could be of an arbitrary type `S`. Thus we can define `Map` and `Bind` in the same way (the only difference being the additional type parameter), and let them take care of "threading" the state between one computation and the next.

In chapter 9 we discussed trees, and you saw how you could define a `Map` function that creates a new tree, where each element is the result of applying a function to each value in the original tree. Imagine that you now want to assign a number to each element, as shown in figure 12.4.

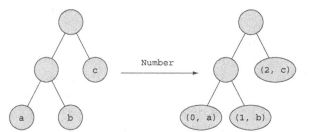

Figure 12.4 Numbering each element in a tree

---

[4] In FP lingo, this is called *the state monad*. This is a truly terrible name to describe a *function* that takes some state as an argument. This unfortunate name is probably the greatest hurdle to understanding it.

This operation is similar to Map, in the sense that you must still traverse the tree and apply a function to each element, but you must now hold some state—a counter value—that needs to be used to label each leaf and be incremented.

Let's start by defining a Numbered<T> class that wraps a T and a number (the constructor is omitted for brevity):

```
public class Numbered<T>
{
    public int Number { get; }
    public T Value { get; }
}
```

This means the operation we're trying to model can be expressed as a function from Tree<T> to Tree<Numbered<T>>.

To start with, here's an implementation that traverses the tree, explicitly passing the state around.

Listing 12.11   Numbering the leaves of a tree by explicitly passing a counter value

```
using LaYumba.Functional.Data.BinaryTree;

public Tree<Numbered<T>> Number<T>(Tree<T> tree)          Calls the stateful overload,
   => Number(tree, 0).Tree;                               passing 0 as initial state

(Tree<Numbered<T>> Tree, int Count) Number<T>(Tree<T> tree, int count)
   => tree.Match(

       Leaf: t =>
          (
                                                          Labels this leaf with
             Tree.Leaf(new Numbered<T>(t, count)),        the current count
             count + 1
          ),                       Returns the incremented
                                   count as the new state
       Branch: (l, r) =>                                  Recursively calls
       {                                                  Number on the
          var (left, count1) = Number(l, count);          left and right
          var (right, count2) = Number(r, count1);        subtrees
          return (Tree.Branch(left, right)), count2);
       });                         Returns the new tree
                                   with the updated count
```

We start the computation with a count of 0. The numbering function simply matches on the type of tree. If it's a leaf, then it contains a T, so Number returns the result/new-state pair containing as the result a Numbered<T> (wrapping the T and the current count) and as the new state the incremented counter. If it's a branch, then we recursively call Number on the left and right subtrees. Because each of these operations returns an updated state, we must thread the state along and return it in the result value.

Although I find the preceding solution satisfactory, it's true that manually passing state along introduces some noise. We can get rid of that by refactoring the code to use the `StatefulComputation` delegate instead.

We'll start by defining a simple stateful computation that takes an `int` (the state, which in this case is the counter), and returns the counter as the value, and the incremented state as the new state:

```
static StatefulComputation<int, int> GetAndIncrement
   = count => (count, count + 1);

GetAndIncrement(0) // => (0, 1)
GetAndIncrement(6) // => (6, 7)
```

Remember, a stateful computation returns both a *value* and a *new state*. GetAndIncrement returns the incremented counter as the *new state*, and the current counter value as the returned *value*. (This is what "gets" the state; that is, it makes the state the inner value of the computation. You can now refer to it in a LINQ expression and assign it to `count` in the following code.) Now we can rewrite our tree numbering function as follows.

Listing 12.12 Numbering the leaves of a tree using LINQ to take care of passing the state

```
StatefulComputation<int, Tree<Numbered<T>>> Number<T>(Tree<T> tree)
   => tree.Match(

   Leaf: t =>
      from count in GetAndIncrement          <──  Assigns the current count to the
      select Tree.Leaf(new Numbered<T>(t, count)),  <──┐   count variable, while assigning the
                                                        │   incremented count to the state
   Branch: (left, right) =>
      from newLeft in Number(left)
      from newRight in Number(right)
      select Tree.Branch(newLeft, newRight));
```

The result is a new leaf containing the original leaf value, numbered with the current count.

As you can see, when you're composing a sequence of several stateful computations, as in the Branch case, LINQ can really improve readability. Otherwise, I find that passing the state around explicitly is clearer. Note that the preceding function returns a computation, which does nothing until it's given an input state:

```
Number(tree).Run(0)
```

Although stateful computations are ubiquitous, the need to chain several computations isn't as frequent. It does crop up often in certain areas, though, such as simulations or parsers. A functional parser, for example, is usually modeled as a function that takes a string (the state), consumes part of the string, and produces a result consisting of a structured representation of what's been parsed and the remainder of the string that's left to parse (the new state).

Summary

- When writing stateful programs, you can avoid changing state as a side effect by always passing the state explicitly as part of a function's input and output.
- Stateful computations are functions in the form $S \rightarrow (T, S)$. That is, they take some state and return a value as well as an updated state.
- Stateful computations can be composed monadically, to reduce the syntactic burden of passing the state from one computation to the next.

Working with
asynchronous computations

13

This chapter covers

- Using `Task` to represent asynchronous computations
- Composing asynchronous operations sequentially and in parallel
- Traversables: handling lists of elevated types
- Combining the effects of different monads

In today's world of distributed applications, many operations are performed asynchronously. A program may begin some operation that takes a relatively long time, such as requesting data from another application, but it won't sit idle, waiting for that operation to complete. Instead, it will go on to do other work and resume the operation once the data has been received.

Asynchrony certainly is the bread and butter of today's programmer. I waited until this late in the book to deal with it because it adds a level of complexity, which I wanted to postpone in order to make the ideas presented so far more approachable.

Asynchronous operations are represented in C# using `Tasks`, and in the first half of this chapter you'll see that `Task<T>` is not so different from other containers, such as `Option<T>`, `Try<T>`, and so on.

As our list of containers keeps growing, we'll inevitably hit the problem of combining different containers. If you have a list of Tasks that you want to execute, how can you instead get a single Task that will complete when all the operations have completed? If you have a value of type Task<Validation<T>>, how do you compose it with a function, T → Task<R>, with the least amount of type noise? The second part of this chapter will show you how to deal with these more complex, stacked types.

13.1 *Asynchronous computations*

In this section, I'll start by introducing the need for asynchrony and how Task is used to model the asynchronous delivery of a value. You'll then see that Task<T> is just another container for a T, like Option and the others you've seen, and therefore supports operations like Map and Bind.

We'll then address some frequently recurring concerns when working with Tasks: combining several asynchronous operations, handling failure, performing multiple retries, and running tasks in parallel.

13.1.1 *The need for asynchrony*

Some operations take longer than others—massively longer! Whereas the time required to perform a typical computer instruction is in the order of nanoseconds, I/O operations such as reading from the filesystem or making a network request are in the order of milliseconds, or even seconds.

To get a better grasp on how big the difference is, let's scale things up to something more human: if an in-memory instruction such as adding two numbers took about a second, then a typical I/O operation could take months or years. And, just as in real life you can wait a few seconds at the water cooler while your cup is filled, you wouldn't wait around at the bank for weeks while your mortgage application is processed. Instead, you'd file your application, go back to your daily life, and expect to be notified of the result in the future.

This is the idea behind asynchronous computations: kick off an operation that takes a long time, move on to doing other work, and then come back once the operation has completed.

13.1.2 *Representing asynchronous operations with Task*

The main tool for working with asynchronous computations since C# 4 is the Task-Based Asynchronous Pattern.[1] In a nutshell, here's what it consists of:

- Use `Task` and `Task<T>` to represent asynchronous operations.
- Use the `await` keyword to await the `Task`, which frees the current thread to do other work, while the asynchronous operation completes.

For instance, consider the code you saw in section 12.1 that gets an exchange rate from the Yahoo API (slightly refactored to highlight how `Task` is used in this case).

Listing 13.1 Blocking the current thread while a network call completes

```
static class Yahoo
{
    public static decimal GetRate(string ccyPair)
    {
        var task = new HttpClient().GetStringAsync(QueryFor(ccyPair));
        var body = task.Result;                    ⟵  Calling Result blocks the
        return decimal.Parse(body.Trim());             thread until the operation
    }                                                  completes.
    static string QueryFor(string ccyPair)
        => $"http://finance.yahoo.com/d/quotes.csv?f=l1&s={ccyPair}=X";
}
```

In this code, the current thread pauses and waits for the result to be received from the remote API. This is OK for a simple console application, but it would be unacceptable for most real-world applications, whether client or server. There's no need to block a thread while waiting for a network call to complete.

---

[1] I assume you're already familiar with it. If not, you'll find ample documentation on MSDN by searching for "Task-Based Asynchronous Pattern."

You can refactor this code to perform the request asynchronously, as follows.

```
public static async Task<decimal> GetRate(string ccyPair)
{
    var s = await new HttpClient().GetStringAsync(QueryFor(ccyPair));
    return decimal.Parse(s.Trim());
}
```

Notice the changes:

- The method now returns not a decimal, but a Task<decimal>.
- await suspends the current context (freeing the thread to do other work), which is resumed when the asynchronous operation has completed and its result is available.
- You have to mark the method async. This is just noise and was added to allow backward compatibility when await was added to the language.

 NAMING CONVENTIONS   I strongly advise *against* naming Task-returning methods with the -Async suffix.[2]

So far, no surprises. Now let's look at Task<T> from a more functional point of view.

13.1.3 *Task as a container for a future value*

Given the perspective we've been building up in this book, it's natural to look at Task<T> as just another container of T. If Option<T> can be seen as a box that *may* contain a T, and Func<T> as a container that can be run to get a T, then Task<T> can be seen as a box within which a T will materialize at some time. So Task<T> can be seen as a construct that adds the effect of asynchrony.

> **TASK VS. TASK<T>**   Again, there's a vexing dichotomy between the non-generic Task and the generic Task<T>: asynchronous operations that yield void, and some type T, respectively.
>
> In what follows, I'll always use a return value (at least Unit), so even if I write Task for brevity, you should take it to mean Task<T>.

To put this idea of a Task as a container into code, I've defined its Return, Map, and Bind functions, effectively making Task<T> a monad over T.

---

[2] This unfortunate convention was proposed by Microsoft in the early days of async. For one thing, you don't name methods that return a string with a special -Str suffix, do you? So why would you with Task? The idea behind the convention was, I believe, to facilitate disambiguation in APIs that expose both synchronous and asynchronous variants of the same operation. But this leads to bad design: if there's a reason for a method to be asynchronous, then using the synchronous variant is suboptimal. An API should encourage doing the right thing by only exposing the asynchronous variant. If both variants are exposed, then, if anything, the synchronous version should be labeled with the -Sync suffix, which should stick out like an eyesore. Good design makes it easy to do the right thing, so forcing longer, noisier names for the asynchronous variant is bad design.

Listing 13.3 Map and Bind can be defined trivially in terms of await

```
public static partial class F
{
    public static Task<T> Async<T>(T t)
        => Task.FromResult(t);

    public static async Task<R> Map<T, R>
        (this Task<T> task, Func<T, R> f)
        => f(await task);

    public static async Task<R> Bind<T, R>
        (this Task<T> task, Func<T, Task<R>> f)
         => await f(await task);
}
```

I'll use `Async` as the `Return` function for `Task`, which lifts a `T` into a `Task<T>`. It's just a shorthand for .NET's `Task.FromResult` method.

Notice how easy it is to define `Map` and `Bind` with the `await` keyword. Why is it so easy? Remember, `Map` *extracts* the inner value(s) from a container, applies the given function, and wraps the result back up into a container. But this unwrapping and wrapping is exactly what the `await` language feature does: it extracts the `Task`'s inner value (that is, the value the operation returns when it completes), and when a method contains an `await`, its result is automatically wrapped in a `Task`.[3] All that's left for `Map` to do is to apply the given function to the awaited value.

`Bind` is similar. It awaits the given `Task<T>`, and when this completes, the resulting `T` can be supplied to the bound function. This in turn returns a `Task<R>`, which must also be awaited before the desired result of type `R` is obtained.

I've implemented the LINQ query pattern for `Task` along the same lines, so you can rewrite the `GetRate` function using a LINQ comprehension.

Listing 13.4 Using LINQ comprehensions with Tasks

```
public static Task<decimal> GetRate(string ccyPair) =>
    from s in new HttpClient().GetStringAsync(QueryFor(ccyPair))
    select decimal.Parse(s.Trim());

public static async Task<decimal> GetRate(string ccyPair)
{
    var s = await new HttpClient().GetStringAsync(QueryFor(ccyPair));
    return decimal.Parse(s.Trim());
}
```

Listing 13.4 shows the implementation with LINQ and the implementation with `await` to stress their similarity. In the version that uses LINQ, the `from` clause takes the inner value of the `Task` and binds it to the variable `s` (more generally, when you see a clause

---

[3] `await` works not only with `Task`, but any *awaitable*; that is, any value for which a `GetAwaiter`(instance or extension) method returning an `INotifyCompletion` is defined.

like `from s in m`, you can read it as, "extract the inner value of `m` and call it `s`, then…");
this is exactly what `await` does. The difference is that `await` is specific to `Task`,
whereas LINQ can be used with any monad.

Lazy vs. asynchronous computations

Lazy and asynchronous computations both allow you to write code that "runs in the
future." That is, at a certain point your program defines what to do with a value `T`
returned by a lazy computation `Func<T>` or an asynchronous computation `Task<T>`,
but those instructions are then executed at a later point. There are also important
differences between the two.

From the point of view of the code that defines the computation

- Creating a lazy computation (like a `Func`, `Try`, `StatefulComputation`, and so
  on) doesn't start the computation. In fact, it *does* nothing (no side effects).
- Creating a `Task` *does* kick off an asynchronous computation.

From the point of view of the code consuming the computed result

- The code consuming a lazy value *decides* when to run the computation,
  obtaining the computed value.
- The code consuming an asynchronous value has no control over when it will
  receive the computed value.

13.1.4 *Handling failure*

I mentioned that `Task<T>` can be seen as a construct that adds the effect of asynchrony. In fact, it *also* captures error handling. Because asynchronous operations are,
most frequently, I/O operations, there's a high chance of something going wrong, and
fortunately `Task<T>` also has error handling, via the `Status` and `Exception` properties.

This is important. Imagine that you have a synchronous computation and are using
`Exceptional<T>` to model a computation that may fail. If you now want to make the computation asynchronous, you don't need a `Task<Exceptional<T>>`, but only a `Task<T>`.

To see some examples of how various asynchronous computations can be composed, let's look at some slightly more complex variations on the scenario of retrieving exchange rates.

Imagine that your company has purchased a subscription with CurrencyLayer, a
company providing good quality exchange rate data (that is, data with a small delay
compared to the market) via an API. If, for some reason, a call to CurrencyLayer's API
fails, you want to fall back to the good old Yahoo API (whose rates are less timely, but
still good enough for use as a fallback).

First, assume you define two classes encapsulating access to the APIs:

```
public static class Yahoo
{
    public static Task<decimal> GetRate(string ccyPair) => //...
}
```

```
public static class CurrencyLayer
{
    public static Task<decimal> GetRate(string ccyPair) => //...
}
```

The implementation for Yahoo is the same as you've seen in listing 13.2; Currency-Layer is implemented along the same lines, but adapted to CurrencyLayer's API.

The interesting part is combining the two calls to GetRate. For this kind of task, you can use the OrElse function, which takes a task and a fallback to use in case the task fails (the idea is similar to the OrElse defined for Option in chapter 11).

```
                    public static Task<T> OrElse<T>
                        (this Task<T> task, Func<Task<T>> fallback)
                    => task.ContinueWith(t =>
                            t.Status == TaskStatus.Faulted
                              ? fallback()
    Flattens a                : Async(t.Result)
Task<Task<T>>          )
 into a Task<T>     .Unwrap();
```

Notice that OrElse assumes that a Task either fails or succeeds. In reality, C# Tasks also support cancellation, but this feature is rarely used and complicates the API, so I won't deal with cancellation here.

You can now use this as follows:

```
CurrencyLayer.GetRate(ccyPair)
    .OrElse(() => Yahoo.GetRate(ccyPair))
```

The result is a new Task that will produce the value returned by CurrencyLayer if the operation was successful, and otherwise the value returned by Yahoo.

There is, of course, always the possibility that *both* calls fail—if, say, the network is down. So we also need a function to specify what to do when a task fails. I'll call it Recover:

```
public static Task<T> Recover<T>
    (this Task<T> task, Func<Exception, T> fallback)
    => task.ContinueWith(t =>
        t.Status == TaskStatus.Faulted
            ? fallback(t.Exception)
            : t.Result);
```

You can use Recover as follows:

```
Yahoo
    .GetRate("USDEUR")
    .Map(rate => $"The rate is {rate}")
    .Recover(ex => $"Error fetching rate: {ex.Message}")
```

Recover is something you'd typically use at the end of a workflow to specify what to do if an error occurred somewhere along the way. In other words, you can use Recover in the same way you'd use Match for things like Option or Either. But Match works synchronously; a Task doesn't have anything to match on because its status isn't available until some point in the future, so technically Recover is more like Map for the faulted case (you can confirm this by looking at its signature).

It's also reasonable to define an overload of Map that takes a handler for both the success and failure cases:

```
public static Task<R> Map<T, R>
    (this Task<T> task, Func<Exception, R> Faulted, Func<T, R> Completed)
=> task.ContinueWith(t =>
        t.Status == TaskStatus.Faulted
            ? Faulted(t.Exception)
            : Completed(t.Result));
```

This could then be used as follows:

```
Yahoo.GetRate("USDEUR").Map(
    Faulted: ex => $"Error fetching rate: {ex.Message}",
    Completed: rate => $"The rate is {rate}")
```

13.1.5 *An HTTP API for currency conversion*

Let's put it all together by writing an API controller that allows clients to convert an amount from one currency to another. A sample interaction with this API is as follows:

```
$ curl http://localhost:5000/convert/1000/USD/to/EUR -s
896.9000

$ curl http://localhost:5000/convert/1000/USD/to/JPY -s
103089.0000

$ curl http://localhost:5000/convert/1000/XXX/to/XXX -s
{"message":"An unexpected error has occurred"}
```

That is, you can call the API on a route such as "convert/1000/USD/to/EUR" to find out how many euros are equivalent to 1000 US dollars. Here's the implementation:

```
[HttpGet("convert/{amount}/{from}/to/{to}")]
public Task<IActionResult> Convert
    (decimal amount, string from, string to)
=> CurrencyLayer.GetRate(from + to)                      ┐ Fall back to a
    .OrElse(() => Yahoo.GetRate(from + to))    ◄────────┘ secondary API
    .Map(rate => amount * rate)
    .Map(
        Faulted: ex => StatusCode(500, Errors.UnexpectedError),   ◄──────┐
        Completed: result => Ok(result) as IActionResult);                │
                                                                          │
                           Specify what to do in case of failure ─────────┘
```

When the application gets a request, it calls the CurrencyLayer API to get the relevant rate. If this fails, it calls the Yahoo API. Once it has a rate, it uses it to calculate the equivalent amount in the target currency. Finally, it maps a successful result to a 200 and failure to a 500.

You may remember from chapter 6 that once you're in the elevated world, you should stay in it for as long as possible. This is all the more true of `Task`: being in the world of `Task` means writing code that runs in the future, so leaving the elevated world in this case means blocking the thread and waiting for the future to catch up. We hardly ever want to do that.

Note that the controller method returns `Task<IActionResult>`. That is, ASP.NET will send the response to the client when the `Task` has run to completion, and you don't need to worry about when this will take place. You *never* need to leave the elevated world of `Task` in this case.

13.1.6 If it fails, try a few more times

When remote operations, such as a call to an HTTP API, fail, the reasons for failure are often transient: maybe there's a glitch in connectivity, or the remote server is being restarted. In other words, an operation that fails once may succeed if you retry a few seconds or minutes later.

The need to retry when an operation fails is a common requirement when dealing with third-party APIs over whose health you have no control. Here's one simple and elegant solution that performs an asynchronous operation, retrying for a specified number of times if it fails.

Listing 13.5 Retrying with exponential backoff

```
public static Task<T> Retry<T>
    (int retries, int delayMillis, Func<Task<T>> start)
    => retries == 0
        ? start()
        : start().OrElse(() =>
            from _ in Task.Delay(delayMillis)
            from t in Retry(retries - 1, delayMillis * 2, start)
            select t);
```

Last attempt →

If the attempt fails, wait for a while, and then retry.

To use it, simply wrap the function performing the remote operation in an invocation to the `Retry` function:

```
Retry(10, 1000, () => Yahoo.GetRate("GBPUSD"))
```

This specifies that the operation should be retried at most 10 times, with an initial delay of one second between attempts. The last argument is the operation to perform, specified lazily because invoking the function kicks off the task.

Notice that `Retry` is recursive: if the operation fails, it waits for the specified interval and then retries the same operation, decreasing the number of retries left, and doubling the interval to wait the next time around (a retry strategy known as exponential backoff).

13.1.7 *Running asynchronous operations in parallel*

Because `Task` is used to represent operations that take time, it's only natural that you may want to execute them in parallel when possible. Imagine you want to check prices offered by different airlines. Assume you have several classes encapsulating access to the airlines' APIs, each implementing the `Airline` interface:

```
interface Airline
{
   Task<IEnumerable<Flight>> Flights(string from, string to, DateTime on);
   Task<Flight> BestFare(string from, string to, DateTime on);
}
```

`Flights` gets you all the flights offered by the airline for a given route and date, whereas `BestFare` only gets you the cheapest flight. The flight details are queried via a remote API, so naturally the results are wrapped in a `Task`.

Now imagine for a second that we're back in the 90s, and you're interested in touring Europe on a shoestring. You'd need to look at the only two low-cost airlines on the market: EasyJet and Ryanair. You could then find the best price offered between two airports on a given date like so:

```
Airline ryanair;
Airline easyjet;

Task<Flight> BestFareM(string @from, string to, DateTime @on)
   => from r in ryanair.BestFare(@from, to, @on)
      from e in easyjet.BestFare(@from, to, @on)
      select r.Price < e.Price ? r : e;
```

This works, but can you see the catch? Because LINQ queries are monadic, `easyjet` `.BestFare` will only be called *after* `ryanair.BestFare` has completed (you'll see why in a moment). But why wait? After all, the two calls are completely independent, so there's no reason we can't make the calls in parallel.

You may remember from chapter 8 that when you have independent computations, you can use applicatives. The following listing shows `Apply` defined for `Task`, which again is implemented rather trivially in terms of `await`.

Listing 13.6   Implementation of `Apply` for `Task`

```
public static async Task<R> Apply<T, R>
   (this Task<Func<T, R>> f, Task<T> arg)
   => (await f)(await arg);

public static Task<Func<T2, R>> Apply<T1, T2, R>
   (this Task<Func<T1, T2, R>> f, Task<T1> arg)
   => Apply(f.Map(F.Curry), arg);
```

As with other containers, the important overload is the first one (where a unary function is wrapped in a container), and overloads for greater arities can be defined by just currying that function. As with `Map` and `Bind`, the implementation simply uses the `await` keyword to reference the `Task`'s inner value. `Apply` awaits the wrapped function, awaits the wrapped argument, and applies the function to the argument; the result is wrapped in a task automatically as a result of using `await`.

So you can rewrite the preceding computation using `Apply`, as follows.

Listing 13.7 Performing two `Tasks` in parallel with `Apply`

```
Task<Flight> BestFareA(string from, string to, DateTime on)
   => Async(PickCheaper)
      .Apply(ryanair.BestFare(from, to, on))
      .Apply(easyjet.BestFare(from, to, on));

static Func<Flight, Flight, Flight> PickCheaper
   = (l, r) => l.Price < r.Price ? l : r;
```

In this version, the two calls to `BestFare` are kicked off independently, so they run in parallel, and the total time needed for `BestFareA` to complete is determined by the time required for the longer of the API calls to complete— not their sum.

To get a better understanding of why this is, compare `Apply` with `Bind`:

Listing 13.8 `Bind` runs tasks sequentially, `Apply` in parallel

```
public static async Task<R> Bind<T, R>
   (this Task<T> task, Func<T, Task<R>> f)
   => await f(await task);

public static async Task<R> Apply<T, R>
   (this Task<Func<T, R>> f, Task<T> arg)
   => (await f)(await arg);
```

`Bind` first awaits the given `Task<T>`, and only then evaluates the function starting the second task. It runs the tasks sequentially and can't do otherwise because a value for `T` is required in order to create the second task.

`Apply`, on the other hand, takes two `Tasks`, meaning that both tasks have been started. With this in mind, let's revisit this code:

```
Async(PickCheaper)
   .Apply(ryanair.BestFare(from, to, on))
   .Apply(easyjet.BestFare(from, to, on));
```

When you call `Apply` the first time (with the Ryanair task), it *immediately* returns a new `Task`, without waiting for the Ryanair task to complete (that's the behavior of the `await` inside `Apply`). Then the program immediately goes on to create the EasyJet task. As a result, both tasks run in parallel.

In other words, the difference in behavior between Bind and Apply is dictated by their signatures:

- With Bind, the first Task must be awaited in order to create the second task, so it should be used when the creation of a Task depends on the return value of another.
- With Apply, both tasks are provided by the caller, so you should use it when the tasks can be started independently.

Now let's flash-forward to today: low costs have multiplied, and traditional airlines compete with them on price. We now have not two, but a long list of airlines whose offers we should take into account. To tackle this more complex scenario, we'll need a new tool: Traverse, which I'll introduce next.

The rest of this chapter contains advanced material that's not required to understand the following chapters, in case you decide to skip ahead.

13.2 *Traversables: working with lists of elevated values*

Traverse is one of the slightly more esoteric core functions in FP, and it allows you to work with lists of elevated values. It's probably easiest to approach through an example.

Imagine a very simple command-line application that reads a comma-separated list of numbers entered by the user, and returns the sum of all the given numbers. We could start along these lines:

```
using Double = LaYumba.Functional.Double;
using String = LaYumba.Functional.String;

var input = Console.ReadLine();

var nums = input.Split(',')      // Array<string>
   .Map(String.Trim)            // IEnumerable<string>
   .Map(Double.Parse);          // IEnumerable<Option<double>>
```

Exposes a static Trim function ⟶

Exposes an Option-returning function for parsing a double ⟵

We split the input string to get an array of strings, and remove any whitespace with Trim. We can then map onto this list the parsing function Double.Parse, which has signature string → Option<double>. As a result, we get an IEnumerable<Option<double>>.

Instead, what we really want is an Option<IEnumerable<double>>, which should be None if *any* of the numbers failed to parse, in which case we can warn the user to correct their input.[4] We saw that Map will yield a type where the effects are stacked up in the opposite order than the one we need.

This is a common enough scenario that there's a specific function called Traverse to address it, and a type for which Traverse can be defined is called a *traversable*. Figure 13.1 shows the relation between Map and Traverse.

---

[4] You may remember from chapter 4 that we could use Bind instead of Map to filter out all the None values, and only add up the numbers that were successfully parsed. That's not desirable for this scenario: we'd be silently removing values that the user probably mistyped in error, effectively giving an incorrect result.

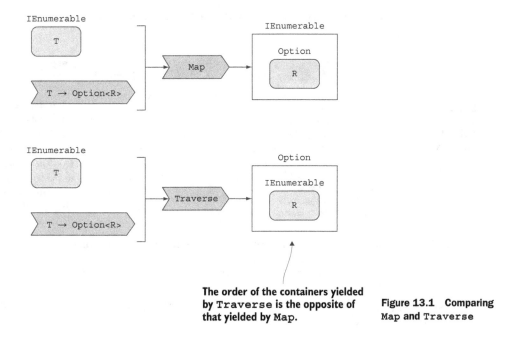

The order of the containers yielded by `Traverse` is the opposite of that yielded by `Map`.

Figure 13.1 Comparing `Map` and `Traverse`

Let's generalize the idea of a traversable:

- We have a "traversable" structure of Ts, so let's indicate this with Tr<T>. In this example it's IEnumerable<string>.
- We have a world-crossing function, f : T → A<R>, where A must be at least an applicative. In this example it's Double.Parse, which has type string → Option<double>.
- We want to obtain an A<Tr<R>>.

The general signature for Traverse should be

```
Tr<T>  →  (T  →  A<R>)  →  A<Tr<R>>
```

Particularized for this example, it looks like this:

```
IEnumerable<T>  →  (T  →  Option<R>)  →  Option<IEnumerable<R>>
```

13.2.1 *Validating a list of values with monadic Traverse*

Let's see how we could go about implementing Traverse with the preceding signature. If you look at the top-level types in the signature, you'll see that we start with a list and end up with a single value. Remember, we reduce lists to a single value using Aggregate, which was covered in section 7.6.

Aggregate takes an accumulator and a reducer function, which combines each element in the list with the accumulator. The accumulator will be returned as the result if the list is empty. This is easy; we just create an empty IEnumerable and lift it into an Option using Some.

Listing 13.9 Monadic Traverse with an Option-returning function

Extracts the
accumulated
list of Rs from
the Option

```
public static Option<IEnumerable<R>> Traverse<T, R>
  (this IEnumerable<T> ts, Func<T, Option<R>> f)
  => ts.Aggregate(
    seed: Some(Enumerable.Empty<R>()),
    func: (optRs, t) => from rs in optRs
                        from r in f(t)
                        select rs.Append(r));
```

If the traversable
is empty, lifts an
empty instance

Applies the function to
the current element, and
extracts the value from
the resulting Option

Appends the value
to the list, and lifts
the resulting list
into an Option

Now let's look at the reducer function—that's the interesting bit. Its type is

```
Option<IEnumerable<R>> → T → Option<IEnumerable<R>>
```

When we apply the function f to the value t, we get an Option<R>. After that, we must satisfy the signature:

```
Option<IEnumerable<R>> → Option<R> → Option<IEnumerable<R>>
```

Let's simplify this for a moment by removing the Option from each element:

```
IEnumerable<R> → R → IEnumerable<R>
```

Now it becomes clear that the problem is that of appending a single R to an IEnumerable<R>, yielding an IEnumerable<R> with all the elements traversed so far. The appending should happen within the elevated world of Option, since all the values are wrapped in an Option. As you learned in chapter 8, we can apply functions in the elevated world in the applicative or the monadic way. Here we use the monadic flow.

We're now ready to go back to the scenario of parsing a comma-separated list of numbers typed by the user. We can put Traverse to use and implement the program as follows.

Listing 13.10 Safely parses and sums a comma-separated list of numbers

```
using Double = LaYumba.Functional.Double;
using String = LaYumba.Functional.String;

public static void Main()
{
    var input = Console.ReadLine();
    var result = Process(input);
    Console.WriteLine(result);
}
```

```
static string Process(string input)
   => input.Split(',')            // Array<string>
      .Map(String.Trim)           // IEnumerable<string>
      .Traverse(Double.Parse)     // Option<IEnumerable<double>>
      .Map(Enumerable.Sum)        // Option<double>
      .Match(
         () => "Some of your inputs could not be parsed",
         (sum) => $"The sum is {sum}");
```

In the preceding listing, `Main` performs the I/O, and all the logic is in the `Process` function.

Let's test it to see the behavior:

```
Process("1, 2, 3")
// => "The sum is 6"

Process("one, two, 3")
// => "Some of your inputs could not be parsed"
```

13.2.2 *Harvesting validation errors with applicative Traverse*

Let's improve the error handling so we can tell the user *which* values are wrong. For that, we need `Validation`, which can contain a list of errors. This means we'll also need an implementation of `Traverse` that takes a list of values and a `Validation`-returning function.

We can start by adapting the implementation that takes an `Option`-returning function.

> **Listing 13.11 Monadic `Traverse` with a `Validation`-returning function**

```
public static Validation<IEnumerable<R>> TraverseM<T, R>
   (this IEnumerable<T> ts, Func<T, Validation<R>> f)
   => ts.Aggregate(
      seed: Valid(Enumerable.Empty<R>()),
      func: (valRs, t) => from rs in valRs
                          from r in f(t)
                          select rs.Append(r));
```

The preceding implementation is identical to the implementation that takes an `Option`-returning function except for the signature and the fact that the `Return` function being used is `Valid` instead of `Some`. This duplication is due to the lack of an abstraction common to both `Option` and `Validation`.[5]

Notice that I've called the function `TraverseM` (for monadic) because the implementation is monadic: if one item fails validation, the validation function won't be called for any of the subsequent items.

---

[5] The reasons for this were discussed in chapter 4, in the "Why is functor not an interface?" sidebar.

If, instead, we want errors to accumulate, we should use the applicative flow. We can therefore define `TraverseA` (for applicative) with the same signature, but using the applicative flow.

Listing 13.12 Applicative `Traverse` with a `Validation`-returning function

```
static Func<IEnumerable<T>, T, IEnumerable<T>> Append<T>()
   => (ts, t) => ts.Append(t);

public static Validation<IEnumerable<R>> TraverseA<T, R>
   (this IEnumerable<T> ts, Func<T, Validation<R>> f)
   => ts.Aggregate(
      seed: Valid(Enumerable.Empty<R>()),
      func: (valRs, t) => Valid(Append<R>())
                            .Apply(valRs)
                            .Apply(f(t)));

public static Validation<IEnumerable<R>> Traverse<T, R>
   (this IEnumerable<T> list, Func<T, Validation<R>> f)
   => TraverseA(list, f);
```

If the traversable is empty, just lifts an empty instance

Lifts the `Append` function, particularized for `R`

Applies it to the accumulator

Applies `f` to the current element to get an `R`; this is the second argument to which `Append` is applied

`Traverse` defaults to the applicative implementation.

The implementation of `TraverseA` is very similar to `TraverseM`, except that in the reducer function, the appending is done with the applicative, rather than monadic, flow. As a result, the validation function `f` will be called for *each* `T` in `ts`, and all validation errors will accumulate in the resulting `Validation`.

Because this is the behavior we usually want with `Validation`, I've defined `Traverse` to point to the applicative implementation `TraverseA`, but there's still scope for having `TraverseM` if you want a short-circuiting behavior.

We can now refactor the program to use `Validation`.

Listing 13.13 Program that safely parses and sums a comma-separated list of numbers

```
static Validation<double> Validate(string s)
   => Double.Parse(s).Match(
      () => Error($"'{s}' is not a valid number"),
      (d) => Valid(d));

static string Process(string input)
   => input.Split(',')          // Array<string>
      .Map(String.Trim)         // IEnumerable<string>
      .Traverse(Validate)       // Validation<IEnumerable<double>>
      .Map(Enumerable.Sum)      // Validation<double>
      .Match(
         errs => string.Join(", ", errs),
         sum => $"The sum is {sum}");
```

The `Main` method is the same as before. If we test the `Process` function, we now get this:

```
Process("1, 2, 3")
// => "The sum is 6"

Process("one, two, 3")
// => "'one' is not a valid number, 'two' is not a valid number"
```

As you can see, in the second example the validation errors have accumulated as we traversed the list of inputs. If we change to use the monadic implementation, `TraverseM`, we'll only get the first error.

13.2.3 *Applying multiple validators to a single value*

The preceding example demonstrates how to apply a single validation function to a list of values you want to validate. What about the case in which you have a single value to validate and many validation functions?

We tackled such a scenario in section 7.6.3, where we had a request object to validate, and a list of validators, each of which checks that certain conditions for validity are met. We had to jump through a few hoops to get a validation behavior where multiple errors were combined in the result.

Now that you know about using `Traverse` with a `Validation`-returning function, we can write a more elegant solution to this problem. Remember that we were using a delegate to capture a function performing validation:

```
// T → Validation<T>
public delegate Validation<T> Validator<T>(T t);
```

The idea is to have a single `Validator` function that combines the validation of a list of `Validators`, harvesting all errors. With `Traverse`, defining such a function is simple.

Listing 13.14 Aggregating errors from multiple validators

```
public static Validator<T> HarvestErrors<T>
   (params Validator<T>[] validators)
   => t
   => validators
      .Traverse(validate => validate(t))
      .Map(_ => t);
```

Here, `Traverse` returns a `Validation<IEnumerable<T>>`, collecting all the errors. If there are no errors, the inner value, of type `IEnumerable<T>`, will contain as many instances of the input value `t` as there are validators. The subsequent call to `Map` disregards this `IEnumerable` and replaces it with the original object being validated. Here's an example of using `HarvestErrors` in practice:

```
Validator<string> ShouldBeLowerCase
   = s => (s == s.ToLower())
      ? Valid(s)
      : Error($"{s} should be lower case");

Validator<string> ShouldBeOfLength(int n)
   => s => (s.Length == n)
      ? Valid(s)
      : Error($"{s} should be of length {n}");

Validator<string> ValidateCountryCode
   = HarvestErrors(ShouldBeLowerCase, ShouldBeOfLength(2));

ValidateCountryCode("us")
// => Valid(us)

ValidateCountryCode("US")
// => Invalid([US should be lower case])

ValidateCountryCode("USA")
// => Invalid([USA should be lower case, USA should be of length 2])
```

13.2.4 *Using Traverse with Task to await multiple results*

Traverse works with Task much as it does with Validation. We can define TraverseA, which uses the applicative flow and runs all tasks in parallel, TraverseM, which uses the monadic flow and runs the tasks sequentially, and Traverse, which defaults to TraverseA, because running in parallel is usually preferable.

Given a list of long-running operations, we can use Traverse to obtain a single Task that we can use to await all the results.

Let's use this in our scenario of searching for flight fares. Remember, we have a list of airlines, and each airline's flights can be queried with a method that returns a Task<IEnumerable<Flight>>. This time, imagine we want to get not just the cheapest flight, but all flights for the desired date, sorted by price.

Notice what happens if we use Map:

```
IEnumerable<Airline> airlines;

IEnumerable<Task<IEnumerable<Flight>>> flights =
   airlines.Map(a => a.Flights(from, to, on));
```

We end up with an IEnumerable<Task<IEnumerable<Flight>>>—this isn't at all what we want!

With Traverse, instead, we'll end up with a Task<IEnumerable<IEnumerable <Flight>>>; that is, a *single* task that will complete when *all* airlines have been queried (and will fail if any query fails). The task's inner value is a list of lists (one list for each airline), which can then be flattened and sorted to get our list of results sorted by price:

```
async Task<IEnumerable<Flight>> Search(IEnumerable<Airline> airlines
   , string from, string to, DateTime on)
{
```

```
var flights = await airlines.Traverse(a => a.Flights(from, to, on));
return flights.Flatten().OrderBy(f => f.Price);
}
```

`Flatten` is simply a convenience function that calls `Bind` with the identity function, hence flattening the nested `IEnumerable` into a single list of flights from all airlines, which are then sorted by price.

Most of the time you'll want the parallel behavior, so I've defined `Traverse` to be the same as `TraverseA`. But if you have, say, 100 tasks, and the second one fails, then the whole task fails. Using monadic traverse in this case would save you from running 98 tasks that would still be kicked off when using applicative traverse. The implementation you choose depends on the use case, and this is the reason for including both.

Let's look at one final variation on this example. In real life, you probably don't want your search to fail if one of perhaps dozens of queries to a third-party API fails. Imagine you want to display the best results available—like on many price comparison websites. If a provider's API is down, results from that provider won't be available, but we still want to see results from all the others.

The change is easy—we can use the previously defined `Recover` function, so that *each* query returns an empty list of flights if the remote query fails:

```
async Task<IEnumerable<Flight>> Search(IEnumerable<Airline> airlines
, string from, string to, DateTime on)
{
    var flights = await airlines
        .Traverse(a => a.Flights(from, to, on)
                        .Recover(ex => Enumerable.Empty<Flight>()));

    return flights.Flatten().OrderBy(f => f.Price);
}
```

Here we have a function that queries several APIs in parallel, disregards any failures, and aggregates all the successful results into a single list sorted by price. I find this a great example of how composing core functions—like `Traverse`, `Bind`, and others—allows you to specify rich behavior with little code and effort.

13.2.5 *Defining Traverse for single-value structures*

So far you've seen how to use `Traverse` with an `IEnumerable` and a function that returns an `Option`, `Validation`, `Task`, or any other applicative. It turns out that `Traverse` is even more general. That is, `IEnumerable` isn't the only traversable structure out there; you can define `Traverse` for many of the constructs you've seen in the book.

If we take a nuts and bolts approach, we can see `Traverse` as a utility that stacks effects up the opposite way as when performing `Map`:

```
Map      : Tr<T> → (T → A<R>) → Tr<A<R>>
Traverse : Tr<T> → (T → A<R>) → A<Tr<R>>
```

So if we have a function that returns an applicative A, Map returns a type with the A on the inside, whereas Traverse returns a type with the A on the outside.

For example, in chapter 6 we had a scenario in which we used Map to combine a Validation-returning function with an Exceptional-returning function. The code went along these lines:

```
Func<BookTransfer, Validation<BookTransfer>> validate;
Func<BookTransfer, Exceptional<Unit>> save;

public Validation<Exceptional<Unit>> Handle(BookTransfer request)
   => validate(request).Map(save);
```

What if, for some reason, we wanted to return an Exceptional<Validation<Unit>> instead? Well, now you know the trick: just replace Map with Traverse!

```
public Exceptional<Validation<Unit>> Handle(BookTransfer request)
   => validate(request).Traverse(save);
```

But can we make Validation traversable? The answer is yes. Remember that we can view Option as a list with at most one element. The same goes for Either, Validation, and Exceptional: the success case can be treated as a traversable with a single element; the failure case as empty.

In the preceding scenario, we'd need to define Traverse for Validation, given an Exceptional-returning function.

Listing 13.15 Making Validation traversable

```
public static Exceptional<Validation<R>> Traverse<T, R>
   (this Validation<T> valT, Func<T, Exceptional<R>> f)
   => valT.Match(
      Invalid: errs => Exceptional(Invalid<R>(errs)),
      Valid: t => f(t).Map(Valid));
```

The base case is if the Validation is Invalid; that's analogous to the empty list case. Here we just create a value of the required output type, *preserving* the validation errors. If the Validation is Valid, that means we should "traverse" the single element it contains, identified by t. We apply the Exception-returning function f to it to get an Exceptional<R>, and then we Map the Valid function on it, which will lift the inner value r into a Validation<R>, giving us the required output type, Exceptional<Validation<R>>.

You can follow this scheme to define Traverse for the other one-or-no-value effects. Notice that once you have Traverse, if you have, say, a Validation <Exceptional<T>> and want to reverse the order of the effects, you could just use Traverse with the identity function.

In summary, Traverse is useful not just to handle lists of elevated values, but more generally whenever you have stacked effects. As you encode your application's requirements through `Option`, `Validation`, and others, `Traverse` is one of the tools you can use to ensure that the types don't get the better of you.

13.3 Combining asynchrony and validation (or any other two monadic effects)

Most enterprise applications are distributed and depend on a number of external systems, so much if not most of your code may run in an asynchronous context. If you want to use constructs like `Option` or `Validation`, soon enough you'll be dealing with `Task<Option<T>>`, `Task<Validation<T>>`, `Validation<Task<T>>`, and so on.

13.3.1 The problem of stacked monads

These nested types can be difficult to work with. When you work within one monad, such as `Option`, everything is fine, because you can use `Bind` to compose several `Option`-returning computations. But what if you have a function that returns an `Option<Task<T>>` and another function of type T → `Option<R>`? How can you combine them? And how would you use an `Option<Task<T>>` with a function of type T → `Task<Option<R>>`?

We can refer to this more generally as the problem of *stacked monads*. In order to illustrate this problem and how it can be addressed, let's revisit one of the examples from chapter 10. The following listing shows a skeletal version of the controller that handles API requests to make a transfer.

Listing 13.16 Skeleton of the `MakeTransfer` command handler

```
public class MakeTransferController : Controller
{
    Func<Guid, AccountState> getAccount;          Dependencies
    Action<Event> saveAndPublish;

    public IActionResult MakeTransfer([FromBody] MakeTransfer cmd)
    {
        var account = getAccount(cmd.DebitedAccountId);   ⟵── Retrieves the account

        var (evt, newState) = account.Debit(cmd);   ⟵┐ Performs the state transition,
                                                      │ producing an event and a new state
        saveAndPublish(evt);

        return Ok(new { Balance = newState.Balance });   ⟵┐ Returns information to the
    }                                                     │ user about the new state
}
```

Persists the event and publishes to interested parties (annotation pointing to `saveAndPublish(evt);`)

The preceding code will serve as an outline, and next you'll see how to add asynchrony and validation. I'm assuming that the dependencies (the functions to retrieve an account and save an event) are injected in the constructor.

First, we'll add a new dependency to perform validation on the `MakeTransfer` command. Its signature will be

```
validate : MakeTransfer → Validation<MakeTransfer>
```

Next, we need to revise the signatures of the existing dependencies. When we retrieve the current state of an account, that operation will hit the database. We want to make it asynchronous, so the result type should be wrapped in a `Task`. Furthermore, errors may occur in connecting to the DB. Fortunately, `Task` already captures this. Finally, there's the possibility that the account doesn't exist— that is, no events were ever recorded for the given ID—so the result should also be wrapped in an `Option`. The full signature will be

```
getAccount : Guid → Task<Option<AccountState>>
```

Saving and publishing an event should also be asynchronous, so that the signature will be

```
saveAndPublish : Event → Task
```

Finally, remember that `Account.Debit` will also return its result wrapped in a `Validation`:

```
Account.Debit : AccountState → MakeTransfer
                    → Validation<(Event, AccountState)>
```

Now let's write a skeleton of the command handler with all these effects in place:

```
public class MakeTransferController : Controller
{
    Func<MakeTransfer, Validation<MakeTransfer>> validate;
    Func<Guid, Task<Option<AccountState>>> getAccount;
    Func<Event, Task> saveAndPublish;

    public Task<IActionResult> MakeTransfer([FromBody] MakeTransfer command)
    {
        Task<Validation<AccountState>> outcome = // TODO...

        return outcome.Map(
            Faulted: ex => StatusCode(500, Errors.UnexpectedError),
            Completed: val => val.Match<IActionResult>(
                Invalid: errs => BadRequest(new { Errors = errs }),
                Valid: newState => Ok(new { Balance = newState.Balance })));
    }
}
```

So far we've just listed the dependencies with the new signatures, established that the main workflow will return a `Task<Validation<AccountState>>`, and mapped its possible states to appropriately populated HTTP responses. Now comes the real work: how do we put together the functions we need to consume?

13.3.2 *Reducing the number of effects*

First, we'll need a couple of adapters. Notice that `getAccount` returns an `Option`, meaning we should cater for the case in which no account is found. What does it *mean* if there's no account? It means the command is incorrectly populated, so we can map

None to a `Validation` with an appropriate error. Hence, we can write an adapter function like this:

```
Func<Guid, Task<Option<AccountState>>> getAccount;

Func<Guid, Task<Validation<AccountState>>> GetAccount
   => id
   => getAccount(id)
      .Map(opt => opt.ToValidation(() => Errors.UnknownAccountId(id)));
```

`ToValidation` is a helper method that turns an `Option<T>` into a `Validation<T>`, using the inner value from the `Option` in the `Some` case and using the provided function to create a `Validation` in the `Invalid` state in the `None` case. This doesn't solve all our problems, but at least now we're only dealing with two monads: `Task` and `Validation`.

Second, `saveAndPublish` returns a `Task`, which doesn't have an inner value, so it won't compose well. Let's write an adapter that will return a `Task<Unit>` instead:

```
Func<Event, Task> saveAndPublish;

Func<Event, Task<Unit>> SaveAndPublish
   => async e =>
   {
      await saveAndPublish(e);
      return Unit();
   };
```

Let's look again at the functions we must compose in order to get our desired outcome:

```
validate : MakeTransfer → Validation<MakeTransfer>
GetAccount : Guid → Task<Validation<AccountState>>
Account.Debit : AccountState → MakeTransfer
                    → Validation<(Event, AccountState)>
SaveAndPublish : Event → Task<Unit>
```

If we used `Map` the whole way through, we'd get a result type of `Validation<Task<Validation<Validation<Task<Unit>>>>>`. We could use `Bind` to flatten the adjacent `Validation`s, but that would still leave us with a stack of four monads. We'd then have to use a sophisticated combination of calls to `Traverse` to change the order of monads, and `Bind` to flatten them. Honestly, I tried. It took me about half an hour to figure it out, and the result was very cryptic, and not something you'd be keen to ever refactor!

We have to look for a better way. Ideally, we'd like to write something like this:

```
from cmd in validate(command)
from acc in GetAccount(cmd.DebitedAccountId)
from result in Account.Debit(acc, cmd)
from _ in SaveAndPublish(result.Event)
select result.NewState
```

We'd then have some underlying implementations of Select and SelectMany that figure out how to combine the types together. Unfortunately, this can't be achieved in a general-enough way: add too many overloads of SelectMany, and this will cause overload resolution to fail. The good news is that we can have a close approximation. You'll see this next.

13.3.3 *LINQ expressions with a monad stack*

We can implement Bind and the LINQ query pattern for a specific monad stack—in this case, Task<Validation<T>>.[6] This allows us to compose several functions that return a Task<Validation<>> within a LINQ expression. With this in mind, we can adapt our existing functions to this type by following these rules:

- If we have a Task<Validation<T>> (or a function that returns such a type), then there's nothing to do. That's the monad we're working in.
- If we have a Validation<T>, we can use the Async function to lift it into a Task, obtaining a Task<Validation<T>>.
- If we have a Task<T>, we can map the Valid function onto it to again obtain Task<Validation<T>>.
- If we have a Validation<Task<T>>, we can call Traverse with the identity function to swap the containers around.

So our previous query needs to be modified as follows:

```
from cmd in Async(validate(command))
from acc in GetAccount(cmd.DebitedAccountId)
from result in Async(Account.Debit(acc, cmd))
from _ in SaveAndPublish(result.Event).Map(Valid)
select result.NewState;
```

This will work, as long as the appropriate implementations of Select and SelectMany for Task<Validation<T>> are defined. As you can see, the resulting code is still reasonably clean and easy to understand and refactor. We just had to add a few calls to Async and Map(Valid) to make the types line up. The complete implementation (barring the adapter functions) is as follows.

> **Listing 13.17 The command handler, refactored to include asynchrony and validation**

```
public class MakeTransferController : Controller
{
    Func<MakeTransfer, Validation<MakeTransfer>> validate;
    Func<Guid, Task<Validation<AccountState>>> GetAccount;
    Func<Event, Task<Unit>> SaveAndPublish;
```

---

[6] I won't show the implementation, which is included in the code samples. This really is library code, not code that a library user should worry about. You may also ask whether an implementation is required for every stack of monads, and indeed this is the case, given the pattern-based approach we've been following in the book.

```
public Task<IActionResult> MakeTransfer([FromBody] MakeTransfer command)
{
    Task<Validation<AccountState>> outcome =
        from cmd in Async(validate(command))
        from acc in GetAccount(cmd.DebitedAccountId)
        from result in Async(Account.Debit(acc, cmd))
        from _ in SaveAndPublish(result.Event).Map(Valid)
        select result.NewState;

    return outcome.Map(
        Faulted: ex => StatusCode(500, Errors.UnexpectedError),
        Completed: val => val.Match<IActionResult>(
            Invalid: errs => BadRequest(new { Errors = errs }),
            Valid: newState => Ok(new { Balance = newState.Balance })));
    }
}
```

In summary, although monads are very nice and pleasant to work with in the context of a single monadic type, things get more complicated when you need to combine several monadic effects.[7] Keep this in mind, and limit the nesting of different monads to what you really need. For instance, once we simplified things in the previous example by mapping Option to Validation, we only had to deal with two stacked monads, not three. Similarly, if you have a Task<Try<T>>, you can probably reduce it to a Task<T>, because Task can capture any exceptions raised when running the Try. Finally, if you find yourself always using a stack of two monads, you can write a new type that encapsulates both effects into that single type. For example, Task encapsulates both asynchrony and error handling.

Summary

- Task<T> represents a computation that will asynchronously deliver a T.
- Tasks should be used whenever the underlying operation may have significant latency, such as most I/O operations.
- Task-returning functions can be composed with Map, Bind, and several other combinators to specify error handling or multiple retries.
- If Tasks are independent, they can be run in parallel. You can use Task as an applicative, and providing several Tasks with Apply runs them in parallel.
- If you have two monads, A and B, you may like to stack them up in values like A<B<T>>, to combine the effects of each monad.
- Traverse can be used to invert the order of monads in the stack.
- Implementing the query pattern for such a stack allows you to combine As, Bs, and A<B<>>s with relative ease.
- Still, stacked monads tend to be cumbersome, so use them sparingly.

---

[7] Note that this isn't just the case in C#, but even in functional languages. Even in Haskell, where monads are used everywhere, stacked monads are usually dealt with via rather clunky "monad transformers." A more promising approach is called "composable effects," and it has first-class support in a very niche functional language called Idris. It's possible that languages of the future won't just have syntax optimized for monads, such as LINQ, but also syntax optimized for monad stacks.

Data streams and the Reactive Extensions

This chapter covers

- Using IObservable to represent data streams
- Creating, transforming, and combining IObservables
- Knowing when you should use IObservable

In chapter 13, you gained a good understanding of asynchronous values—values that are received at some point in the future. What about a *series* of asynchronous values? For example, say you have an event-sourced system like the one in chapter 10; how can you model the stream of events that are produced and define downstream processing of those events? For example, say you want to recompute an account's balance with every transaction, and send a notification if it becomes negative?

The IObservable interface provides an abstraction to represent such event streams. And not just event streams, but more generally *data streams*, where the values in the stream could be, say, stock quotes, byte chunks being read from a file, successive states of an entity, and so on. Really, anything that constitutes a sequence of logically related values in time can be thought of as a data stream.

In this chapter, you'll learn what IObservables are, and how to use the *Reactive Extensions* (Rx) to create, transform, and combine IObservables. We'll also discuss what sort of scenarios benefit from using IObservable.

Rx is a set of libraries for working with IObservables—much like LINQ provides utilities for working with IEnumerables. Rx is a very rich framework, so thorough coverage is beyond the scope of this chapter; instead, we'll just look at some basic features and applications of IObservable and at how it relates to other abstractions we've covered so far.

14.1 Representing data streams with IObservable

If you think of an array as a sequence of values in space (space in memory, that is), then you can think of IObservable as a sequence of values in time:

- With an IEnumerable, you can enumerate its values at your leisure.
- With an IObservable, you can observe the values as they come.

Table 14.1 shows how IObservable relates to other abstractions.

Table 14.1 How IObservable compares with other abstractions

	Synchronous	Asynchronous
Single value	T	Task<T>
Multiple values	IEnumerable<T>	IObservable<T>

IObservable is like an IEnumerable, in that it contains several values, and it's like a Task, in that values are delivered asynchronously. IObservable is therefore more general than both: you can view IEnumerable as a special case of IObservable that produces all its values synchronously; you can think of Task as a special case of IObservable that produces a single value.

14.1.1 A sequence of values in time

The easiest way to develop an intuition about IObservable is through *marble diagrams*, a few examples of which are shown in figure 14.1. Marble diagrams represent the values in the stream. Each IObservable is represented with an arrow, representing time, and marbles, representing values that are produced by the IObservable.

The image illustrates that an IObservable can actually produce three different kinds of messages:

- OnNext signals a new value, so if your IObservable represents a stream of events, OnNext will be fired when an event is ready to be consumed. This is an IObservable's most important message, and often the only one you'll be interested in.
- OnCompleted signals that the IObservable is done and will signal no more values.
- OnError signals that an error has occurred and provides the relevant Exception.

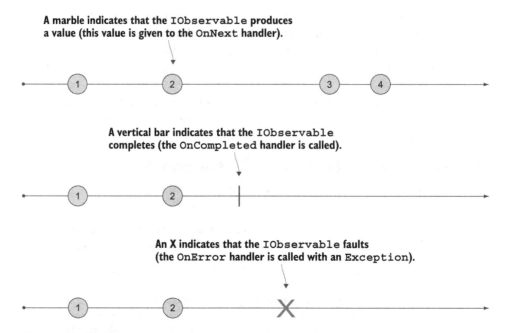

A marble indicates that the `IObservable` produces a value (this value is given to the `OnNext` handler).

A vertical bar indicates that the `IObservable` completes (the `OnCompleted` handler is called).

An X indicates that the `IObservable` faults (the `OnError` handler is called with an `Exception`).

Figure 14.1   Marble diagrams provide an intuitive way to understand `IObservable`s.

The `IObservable` contract

The `IObservable` contract specifies that an `IObservable` should produce messages according to the following grammar:

```
OnNext* (OnCompleted|OnError)?
```

That is, an `IObservable` can produce an arbitrary number of `T`'s (`OnNext`), possibly followed by a single value indicating either successful completion (`OnCompleted`) or an error (`OnError`).

This means that there are three possibilities in terms of completion. An `IObservable` can

- Never complete
- Complete normally, with a completion message
- Complete abnormally, in which case it produces an `Exception`

An `IObservable` *never* produces any values after it's completed, *regardless* of whether it completes normally or with an error.

14.1.2 *Subscribing to an IObservable*

Observ-*ables* work in tandem with observ-*ers*. Simply put,

- Observables produce values
- Observers consume them

If you want to consume the messages produced by an `IObservable`, you can create an observer and associate it with an `IObservable` via the `Subscribe` method. The simplest way to do this is by providing a callback that will handle the values produced by the `IObservable`, like so:

Exposes the IObservable interface →
```
using System;
using System.Reactive.Linq;

IObservable<int> nums = //...

nums.Subscribe(Console.WriteLine);
```
← **Exposes the Subscribe extension method used below**

So when I say that `nums` "produces" an `int` value, all I really mean is that it calls the given function (in this case, `Console.WriteLine`) with the value. The result of the preceding code is that whenever `nums` produces an `int`, it's printed out.

I find the naming a bit confusing; you'd expect an `IObservable` to have an `Observe` method, but instead it's called `Subscribe`. Basically, you can think of the two as synonyms: an "observer" is a subscriber, and in order to "observe" an observable, you subscribe to it.

What about the other types of messages an `IObservable` can produce? You can provide handlers for those as well. For instance, the following listing shows a convenience method that attaches an observer to an `IObservable`; this observer will simply print some diagnostic messages whenever the `IObservable` signals. We'll use this method later for debugging.

Listing 14.1 Subscribing to the messages produced by an `IObservable`

```
using static System.Console;

public static IDisposable Trace<T>
   (this IObservable<T> source, string name)
   => source.Subscribe(
      onNext: t => WriteLine($"{name} -> {t}"),
      onError: ex => WriteLine($"{name} ERROR: {ex.Message}"),
      onCompleted: () => WriteLine($"{name} END"));
```

`Subscribe` actually takes three handlers (all are optional arguments), to handle the different messages that an `IObservable<T>` can produce. It should be clear why the handlers are optional: if you don't expect an `IObservable` to ever complete, there's no point providing an `onComplete` handler.

A more OO option for subscribing is to call `Subscribe` with an `IObserver`,[1] an interface that, unsurprisingly, exposes `OnNext`, `OnError`, and `OnCompleted` methods.

Also notice that `Subscribe` returns an `IDisposable` (the subscription). By disposing it, you unsubscribe.

---

[1] This is the method defined on the `IObservable` interface. The overload that takes the callbacks is an extension method.

In this section you've seen some of the basic concepts and terminology around `IObservable`. It's a lot to absorb, but don't worry; things will become clearer as you see some examples. These are the basic ideas to keep in mind:

- Observables produce values; observers consume them.
- You associate an observer with an observable by using `Subscribe`.
- An observable produces a value by calling the observer's `OnNext` handler.

14.2   Creating IObservables

You now know how to consume the data in a stream by subscribing to an `IObservable`. But how do you get an `IObservable` in the first place? The `IObservable` and `IObserver` interfaces are included in .NET Standard, but if you want to create or perform many other operations on `IObservable`s, you'll typically use the Reactive Extensions (Rx) by installing the `System.Reactive` package.[2]

The recommended way to create `IObservable`s is by using several dedicated methods included in the static `Observable`, and we'll explore them next. I recommend you follow along in the REPL when possible.

14.2.1   Creating a timer

A timer can be modeled with an `IObservable` that signals at regular intervals. We can represent it with a marble diagram as follows:

This is a good way to start experimenting with `IObservable`s because it's simple but does include the element of time.

You create a timer with `Observable.Interval`.

> **Listing 14.2   Creating an `IObservable` that signals every second**

```
using System.Reactive.Linq;

var oneSec = TimeSpan.FromSeconds(1);
IObservable<long> ticks = Observable.Interval(oneSec);
```

Here we define `ticks` as an `IObservable` that will begin signaling after one second, producing a `long` counter value that increments every second, starting at 0. Notice I said "will begin" signaling? The resulting `IObservable` is lazy, so unless there's a subscriber, nothing will actually be done. Why talk, if nobody's listening?

---

[2] Rx includes several libraries. The main library, `System.Reactive`, bundles the packages you'll most commonly need: `System.Reactive.Interfaces`, `System.Reactive.Core`, `System.Reactive.Linq`, and `System.Reactive.PlatformServices`. There are several other packages that are useful in more specialized scenarios, such as if you're using Windows forms.

If we want to see some tangible results, we need to *subscribe* to the `IObservable`. We can do this with the `Trace` method defined earlier:

```
ticks.Trace("ticks");
```

At this point, you'll start to see the following messages appear in the console, one second apart:

```
ticks -> 0
ticks -> 1
ticks -> 2
ticks -> 3
ticks -> 4
...
```

Because this `IObservable` never completes, you'll have to reset the REPL to stop the noise—sorry!

14.2.2 *Using Subject to tell an IObservable when it should signal*

Another way to create an `IObservable` is by instantiating a `Subject`, which is an `IObservable` that you can imperatively tell to produce a value that it will in turn push to its observers. For example, the following program turns inputs from the console into values signaled by a `Subject`.

Listing 14.3   Modeling user inputs as a stream

```
using System.Reactive.Subjects;

public static void Main()
{
    var inputs = new Subject<string>();          ◁—— Creates a Subject

    using (inputs.Trace("inputs"))               ◁—— Subscribes to the Subject
    {
        for (string input; (input = ReadLine()) != "q";)
            inputs.OnNext(input);

        inputs.OnCompleted();                     ◁┐ Tells the Subject to
    }                                                │ signal completion
}
```

Tells the Subject to produce a value, which it will push to its observers → `inputs.OnNext(input);`

Leaving the using block disposes the subscription. → `}`

Every time the user types in some input, the code pushes that value to the `Subject` by calling its `OnNext` method. When the user types "q", the code exits the `for` loop and calls the `Subject`'s `OnCompleted` method, signaling that the stream has ended. Here we've subscribed to the stream of inputs using the `Trace` method defined in 14.1, so we'll get a diagnostic message printed for each user input.

An interaction with the program looks like this (user inputs in bold):

```
hello
inputs -> hello
world
inputs -> world
q
inputs END
```

14.2.3 Creating IObservables from callback-based subscriptions

If your system subscribes to an external data source, such as a message queue, event broker, or publisher/subscriber, you can model that data source as an `IObservable`.

For example, Redis can be used as a publisher/subscriber, and the following listing shows how you can use `Observable.Create` to create an `IObservable` from the callback-based `Subscribe` methods that allows you to subscribe to messages published to Redis.

> **Listing 14.4 Creating an `IObservable` from messages published to Redis**

`Create` takes an observer, so the given function will only be called when a subscription is being made.

Converts from the callback-based implementation of `Subscribe` to values produced by the `IObservable`

```
using StackExchange.Redis;
using System.Reactive.Linq;

ConnectionMultiplexer redis = ConnectionMultiplexer.Connect("localhost");

IObservable<RedisValue> RedisNotifications(RedisChannel channel)
    => Observable.Create<RedisValue>(observer =>
    {
        var sub = redis.GetSubscriber();
        sub.Subscribe(channel, (_, value) => observer.OnNext(value));
        return () => sub.Unsubscribe(channel);
    });
```

Returns a function that will be called when the subscription is disposed

The preceding method returns an `IObservable` that will produce the values received from Redis on the given channel. You could use this as follows:

Gets an `IObservable` that signals when messages are published on the "weather" channel

```
RedisChannel weather = "weather";

var weatherUpdates = RedisNotifications(weather);
weatherUpdates.Subscribe(
    onNext: val => WriteLine($"It's {val} out there"));

redis.GetDatabase(0).Publish(weather, "stormy");
// prints: It's stormy out there
```

Subscribes to the `IObservable`

Publishing a value causes `weatherUpdates` to signal, and the `onNext` handler is called as a result.

AVOID USING `Subject` `Subject` works *imperatively* (you tell a `Subject` when to fire), and this goes somewhat counter to the *reactive* philosophy of Rx (you specify how to react to certain things when they happen).

For this reason, it's recommended that you avoid `Subjects` whenever possible, and instead use other methods, such as `Observable.Create`. For example, as an exercise, try to rewrite the code in listing 14.3, using `Observable.Create` to create an `IObservable` of user inputs.

14.2.4 Creating IObservables from simpler structures

I said that `IObservable<T>` is more general than a value T, a `Task<T>`, or an `IEnumerable<T>`, so let's see how each of these can be "promoted" to an `IObservable`. This becomes useful if you want to combine one of these less powerful structures with an `IObservable`.

`Return` allows you to lift a single value into an `IObservable` that looks like this:

That is, it immediately produces the value and then completes. Here's an example:

```
IObservable<string> justHello = Observable.Return("hello");
justHello.Trace("justHello");

// prints: justHello -> hello
//         justHello END
```

`Return` takes a value, T, and lifts it into an `IObservable<T>`. This is the first container where the `Return` function is actually called `Return`!

Let's see about creating an `IObservable` from a single asynchronous value—a `Task`. Here, we have an `IObservable` that looks like this:

That is, after some time we'll get a single value, immediately followed by the signal for completion. In code, it looks like this:

```
Observable.FromAsync(() => Yahoo.GetRate("USDEUR"))
    .Trace("singleUsdEur");

// prints: singleUsdEur -> 0.92
//         singleUsdEur END
```

Finally, an `IObservable` created from an `IEnumerable` looks like this:

That is, it immediately produces all the values in the `IEnumerable`, and completes:

```
IEnumerable<char> e = new[] { 'a', 'b', 'c' };
IObservable<char> chars = e.ToObservable();
chars.Trace("chars");

// prints: chars -> a
//         chars -> b
//         chars -> c
//         chars END
```

You've now seen many—but not all—methods for creating `IObservable`s. You may end up creating `IObservable`s in other ways; for example, in Windows application development you can turn UI events such as mouse clicks into event streams by using `Observable.FromEvent` and `FromEventPattern`.

Now that you know about creating and subscribing to `IObservable`, let's move on to the most fascinating area: transforming and combining different streams.

14.3 *Transforming and combining data streams*

The power of using streams comes from the many ways in which you can combine them and define new streams based on existing ones. Rather than dealing with individual values in a stream (like in most event-driven designs), you deal with the stream as a whole.

Rx offers *a lot* of functions (often called *operators*) to transform and combine `IObservable`s in a variety of ways. I'll discuss the most commonly used ones, and add a few operators of my own. You'll recognize the typical traits of a functional API: purity and composability.

14.3.1 *Stream transformations*

You can create new observables by transforming an existing observable in some way. One of the simplest operations is mapping. This is achieved with the `Select` method, which works—as with any other "container"—by applying the given function to each element in the stream, as shown in figure 14.2.

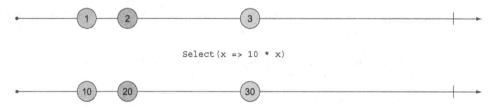

Figure 14.2   `Select` maps a function onto a stream.

Here's some code that creates a timer and then maps a simple function on it:

```
var oneSec = TimeSpan.FromSeconds(1);
var ticks = Observable.Interval(oneSec);

ticks.Select(n => n * 10)
   .Trace("ticksX10");
```

We're attaching an observer on the last line, with the `Trace` method, so the preceding code will cause the following messages to be printed every second:

```
ticksX10 -> 0
ticksX10 -> 10
ticksX10 -> 20
ticksX10 -> 30
ticksX10 -> 40
...
```

Because `Select` follows the LINQ query pattern, we can write the same thing using LINQ:

```
from n in ticks select n * 10
```

Using `Select`, we can rewrite our simple program that checks exchange rates (first introduced in listing 12.1) in terms of observables:

```
public static void Main()
{
    var inputs = new Subject<string>();          ◁── The stream of values
                                                      entered by the user
    var rates = from pair in inputs
                select Yahoo.GetRate(pair).Result;     ┐ Maps user inputs to the
                                                         corresponding retrieved
    using (inputs.Trace("inputs"))                      values
    using (rates.Trace("rates"))
        for (string input; (input = ReadLine().ToUpper()) != "Q";)
            inputs.OnNext(input);
}
```

**Subscribes to both streams
to produce debug messages**

Here, `inputs` represents the stream of currency pairs entered by the user, and in `rates` we map those pairs to the corresponding values retrieved from the Yahoo API. We're subscribing to both observables with the usual `Trace` method, so an interaction with this program could be as follows:

```
eurusd
inputs -> EURUSD
rates -> 1.0852
chfusd
inputs -> CHFUSD
rates -> 1.0114
```

Notice, however, that we're calling `Result` to wait for the remote query in `GetRate` to complete. In a real application, we wouldn't want to block a thread, so how could we avoid that?

We saw that a `Task` can easily be promoted to an `IObservable`, so we could generate an `IObservable` of `IObservables`. Sound familiar? Bind! We can use `SelectMany` instead of `Select`, which will flatten the result into a single `IObservable`. We can therefore rewrite the definition of the `rates` stream as follows:

```
var rates = inputs.SelectMany
    (pair => Observable.FromAsync(() => Yahoo.GetRate(pair)));
```

`Observable.FromAsync` promotes the `Task` returned by `GetRate` to an `IObservable`, and `SelectMany` flattens all these `IObservables` into a single `IObservable`.

Because it's always possible to promote a `Task` to an `IObservable`, an overload of `SelectMany` exists that does just that (this is similar to how we overloaded `Bind` to work with an `IEnumerable` and an `Option`-returning function in chapter 4). This means we can avoid explicitly calling `FromAsync` and return a `Task` instead. Furthermore, we can use a LINQ query:

```
var rates =
    from pair in inputs
    from rate in Yahoo.GetRate(pair)
    select rate;
```

The program thus modified will work the same way as before, but without the blocking call to `Result`.

`IObservable` also supports many of the other operations that are supported by `IEnumerable`, such as filtering with `Where`, `Take` (takes the first *n* values), `Skip`, `First`, and so on.

14.3.2 *Combining and partitioning streams*

There are also many operators that allow you to combine two streams into a single one. For example, `Concat` produces all the values of one `IObservable`, followed by all the values in another, as shown in figure 14.3.

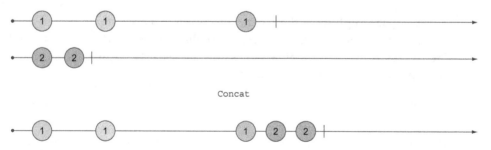

Figure 14.3 `Concat` waits for an `IObservable` to complete and then produces elements from the other `IObservable`.

For instance, in our exchange rate lookup, we have an observable called `rates` with the retrieved rates. If we want an observable of all the messages the program should output to the console, this must include the retrieved rates, but also an initial message prompting the user for some input. We can lift this single message into an `IObservable` with `Return` and then use `Concat` to combine it with the other messages:

```
IObservable<decimal> rates = //...

IObservable<string> outputs = Observable
    .Return("Enter a currency pair like 'EURUSD', or 'q' to quit")
    .Concat(rates.Select(Decimal.ToString));
```

In fact, the need to provide a starting value for an `IObservable` is so common that there's a dedicated function, `StartWith`. The preceding code is equivalent to this:

```
var outputs = rates.Select(Decimal.ToString)
    .StartWith("Enter a currency pair like 'EURUSD', or 'q' to quit");
```

Whereas `Concat` waits for the left `IObservable` to complete before producing values from the right observable, `Merge` combines values from two `IObservables` without delay, as shown in figure 14.4.

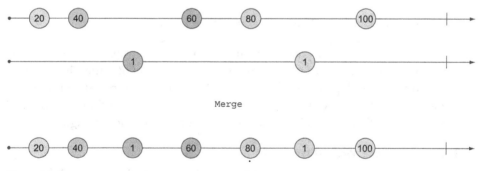

Figure 14.4 **Merge merges two `IObservables` into one.**

For example, if you have a stream of valid values and one of error messages, you could combine them with `Merge` as follows:

```
IObservable<decimal> rates = //...
IObservable<string> errors = //...

var outputs = rates.Select(Decimal.ToString)
    .Merge(errors);
```

Just as you might want to merge values from different streams, the opposite operation—partitioning a stream according to some criterion—is also often useful. Figure 14.5 illustrates this.

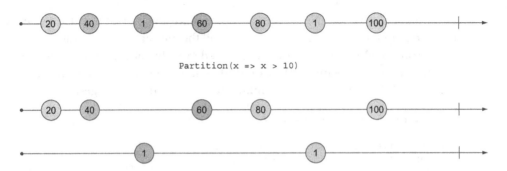

Figure 14.5   Partitioning an `IObservable` according to a predicate

This is one of many cases in which C# 7 tuple syntax facilitates working with `IObservable` effectively. `Partition` is defined as follows:

```
public static (IObservable<T> Passed, IObservable<T> Failed)
   Partition<T>(this IObservable<T> ts, Func<T, bool> predicate)
   => ( Passed: from t in ts where predicate(t) select t
      , Failed: from t in ts where !predicate(t) select t );
```

It can be used in client code like this:

```
var (evens, odds) = ticks.Partition(x => x % 2 == 0);
```

Partitioning an `IObservable` of values is roughly equivalent to an `if` when dealing with a single value, so it's useful when you have a stream of values that you want to process differently, depending on some condition. For example, if you have a stream of messages and some criterion for validation, you can partition the stream into two streams of valid and invalid messages, and process them accordingly.

14.3.3   *Error handling with IObservable*

Error handling when working with `IObservable` works differently from what you might expect. In most programs, an uncaught exception either causes the whole application to crash, or causes the processing of a single message/request to fail, while subsequent requests work fine. To illustrate how things work differently in Rx, consider this version of our program for looking up exchange rates:

```
public static void Main()
{
    var inputs = new Subject<string>();

    var rates =
        from pair in inputs
        from rate in Yahoo.GetRate(pair)
        select rate;
```

```
        var outputs = from r in rates select r.ToString();

        using (inputs.Trace("inputs"))
        using (rates.Trace("rates"))
        using (outputs.Trace("outputs"))
            for (string input; (input = ReadLine().ToUpper()) != "Q";)
                inputs.OnNext(input);
}
```

The program captures three streams, each dependent on another (outputs is defined in terms of rates, and rates is defined in terms of inputs, as shown in figure 14.6), and we're printing diagnostic messages for all of them with Trace.

Now look what happens if you break the program by passing an invalid currency pair:

Figure 14.6   Simple dataflow between three IObservables

```
eurusd
inputs -> EURUSD
rates -> 1.0852
outputs -> 1.0852
chfusd
inputs -> CHFUSD
rates -> 1.0114
outputs -> 1.0114
xxx
inputs -> XXX
rates ERROR: Input string was not in a correct format.
outputs ERROR: Input string was not in a correct format.
chfusd
inputs -> CHFUSD
eurusd
inputs -> EURUSD
```

What this shows is that once rates errors, it never signals again (as specified in the IObservable contract). As a result, everything downstream is also "dead." But IObservables upstream of the failed one are fine: inputs is still signaling, as would any other IObservables defined in terms of inputs.

To prevent your system from going into such a state, where a "branch" of the dataflow dies, while the remaining graph keeps functioning, you can use the techniques you learned for functional error handling.

To do this, you can use a helper function I've defined in the LaYumba.Functional library, which allows you to safely apply a Task-returning function to each element in a stream. The result will be a pair of streams: a stream of successfully computed values, and a stream of exceptions.

Listing 14.5   Safely performing a `Task` and returning two streams

Converts each `Task<R>` to a `Task<Exceptional<R>>` to get a stream of `Exceptionals`

```
public static (IObservable<R> Completed, IObservable<Exception> Faulted)
   Safely<T, R>(this IObservable<T> ts, Func<T, Task<R>> f)
   => ts
      .SelectMany(t => f(t).Map(
         Faulted: ex => ex,
         Completed: r => Exceptional(r)))
      .Partition();

static (IObservable<T> Successes, IObservable<Exception> Exceptions)
   Partition<T>(this IObservable<Exceptional<T>> excTs)
{
   bool IsSuccess(Exceptional<T> ex)
      => ex.Match(_ => false, _ => true);

   T ValueOrDefault(Exceptional<T> ex)
      => ex.Match(exc => default(T), t => t);

   Exception ExceptionOrDefault(Exceptional<T> ex)
      => ex.Match(exc => exc, _ => default(Exception));

   return (
      Successes: excTs
         .Where(IsSuccess)
         .Select(ValueOrDefault),
      Exceptions: excTs
         .Where(e => !IsSuccess(e))
         .Select(ExceptionOrDefault)
   );
}
```

Partitions a stream of `Exceptionals` into successfully computed values and exceptions

For each `T` in the given stream, we apply the `Task`-returning function `f`. We then use the binary overload of `Map` defined in chapter 13 to convert each resulting `Task<R>` to a `Task<Exceptional<R>>`. This is where we gain safety: instead of an inner value `R` that will throw an exception when it's accessed, we have an `Exceptional<R>` in the appropriate state. `SelectMany` flattens away the `Tasks` in the stream and returns a stream of `Exceptionals`. We can then partition this in successes and exceptions.

With this in place, we can refactor our program to handle errors more gracefully:

```
var (rates, errors) = inputs.Safely(Yahoo.GetRate);
```

14.3.4   *Putting it all together*

Let's showcase the various techniques you've learned in this section by refactoring the exchange rates lookup program to safely handle errors, and without the debug information.

Listing 14.6 The program refactored to safely handle errors

```
public static void Main()
{
    var inputs = new Subject<string>();

    var (rates, errors) = inputs.Safely(Yahoo.GetRate);

    var outputs = rates
        .Select(Decimal.ToString)
        .Merge(errors.Select(ex => ex.Message))
        .StartWith("Enter a currency pair like 'EURUSD', or 'q' to quit");

    using (outputs.Subscribe(WriteLine))
        for (string input; (input = ReadLine().ToUpper()) != "Q";)
            inputs.OnNext(input);
}
```

The dataflow diagram in figure 14.7 shows the various IObservables involved, and how they depend on one another.

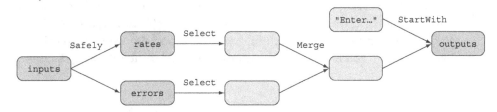

Figure 14.7 Dataflow with a separate branch for handling errors

Notice how Safely allows us to create two branches, each of which can be processed independently until a uniform representation for both cases is obtained and they can be merged. Also take note of the three parts of a program that uses IObservables:

1 *Set up the data sources*—In our case: inputs, which requires a Subject; and the single value "Enter…"
2 *Process the data*—This is where functions like Select, Merge, and so on are used.
3 *Consume the results*—Observers consume the most downstream IObservables; in this case: outputs.

14.4 *Implementing logic that spans multiple events*

So far I've mostly aimed at familiarizing you with IObservables and the many operators that can be used with them. For this, I've used familiar examples like the exchange rates lookup. After all, given that you can promote any value T, Task<T>, or IEnumerable<T> to an IObservable<T>, you could pretty much write all of your code in terms of IObservables! But should you?

The answer, of course, is "probably not." The area in which IObservable and Rx really shine is when you can use them to write stateful programs without any explicit state manipulation. By "stateful programs," I mean programs in which events aren't treated independently; past events influence how new events are treated. In this section, you'll see a few such examples.

14.4.1 *Detecting sequences of pressed keys*

At some point, you've probably written an event handler that listens to a user's keypresses and performs some actions based on what key and key modifiers were pressed. A callback-based approach is satisfactory for many cases, but what if you want to listen to a specific *sequence* of keypresses? For example, say you want to implement some behavior when the user presses the combination Alt-K-B.

In this case, pressing Alt-B should lead to different behavior, based on whether it was shortly preceded by the leading Alt-K, so keypresses can't be treated independently. If you have a callback-based mechanism that deals with single keypressed events, you effectively need to set in motion a state machine when the user presses Alt-K, and then wait for the possible Alt-B that will follow, reverting to the previous state if no Alt-B is received in time. It's actually pretty complicated!

With `IObservable`, this can be solved much more elegantly. Let's assume that we have a stream of keypress events, `keys`. We're looking for two events—Alt-K and Alt-B—that happen on that same stream in quick succession. In order to do this, we need to explore how to combine a stream with itself. Consider the following diagram:

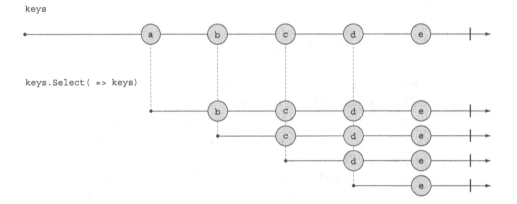

It's important to understand this diagram. The expression `keys.Select(_ => keys)` yields a new `IObservable` that maps each value produced by `keys` to `keys` itself. So when `keys` produces its first value, *a*, this new `IObservable` produces an `IObservable` that has *all following values* in `keys`. When `keys` produces its second value, *b*, the new `IObservable` produces another `IObservable` that has all the values that follow *b*, and so on.[3]

---

[3] Imagine what `keys.Select(_ => keys)` would look like if `keys` were an `IEnumerable`: for each value, you'd be taking the whole `IEnumerable`, so in the end you'd have an `IEnumerable` containing *n* replicas of `keys` (*n* being the length of `keys`). With `IObservable`, the behavior is different because of the element of time, so when you say "give me `keys`," what you really get is "all values `keys` will produce in the future."

Looking at the types can also help clarify this:

```
keys                      : IObservable<KeyInfo>
_ => keys                 : KeyInfo → IObservable<KeyInfo>
keys.Select(_ => keys)    : IObservable<IObservable<KeyInfo>>
```

If we use `SelectMany` instead, all these values are flattened into a single stream:

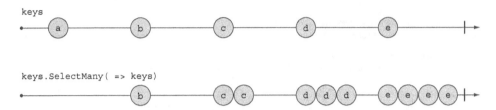

Of course, if we're looking for *two* consecutive keypresses, we don't need *all* values that follow an item, but just the next one. So instead of mapping each value to the whole `IObservable`, let's reduce it to the first item with `Take`:

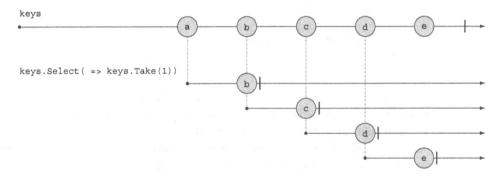

We're getting close. Now, let's make the following changes:

- Instead of ignoring the current value, pair it with the following value.
- Use `SelectMany` to obtain a single `IObservable`.
- Use LINQ syntax.

The resulting expression pairs each value in an `IObservable` with the previously emitted value:

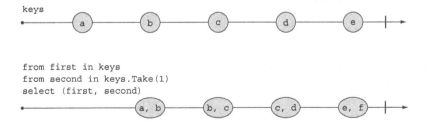

This is a pretty useful function in its own right, and I'll call it `PairWithPrevious`. We'll use it later.

But for this particular scenario, we only want pairs to be created if they're sufficiently close in time. This can be achieved easily: in addition to taking only the next value with `Take(1)`, we only take values within a timespan, using an overload of `Take` that takes a `TimeSpan`. The solution is shown in the following listing.

Listing 14.7   Detecting when the user presses the Alt-K-B key sequence

```
IObservable<ConsoleKeyInfo> keys = //...
var halfSec = TimeSpan.FromMilliseconds(500);

var keysAlt = keys
   .Where(key => key.Modifiers.HasFlag(ConsoleModifiers.Alt));

var twoKeyCombis =
   from first in keysAlt
   from second in keysAlt.Take(halfSec).Take(1)        For any keypress, pairs it with
   select (First: first, Second: second);             the next keypress that occurs
                                                       within a half-second
var altKB =
   from pair in twoKeyCombis
   where pair.First.Key == ConsoleKey.K
      && pair.Second.Key == ConsoleKey.B
   select Unit();
```

As you can see, the solution is simple and elegant, and you can apply this approach to recognize more complex patterns within sequences of events—all without explicitly keeping track of state and introducing side effects!

You've probably also realized that coming up with such a solution isn't necessarily easy. It takes a while to get familiar with `IObservable` and its many operators, and develop an understanding of how to use them.

14.4.2 *Reacting to multiple event sources*

Imagine we have a bank account denominated in euros, and we'd like to keep track of its value in US dollars. Both changes in balance and changes in the exchange rate cause the dollar balance to change. To react to changes from different streams, we could use `CombineLatest`, which takes the latest values from two observables, whenever one of them signals, as shown in figure 14.8.

Its usage would be as follows:

```
IObservable<decimal> balance = //...
IObservable<decimal> eurUsdRate = //...

var balanceInUsd = balance.CombineLatest(eurUsdRate
   , (bal, rate) => bal * rate);
```

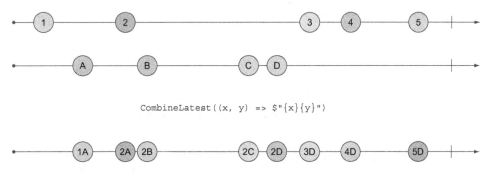

Figure 14.8 `CombineLatest` **signals whenever one of two** `IObservables` **signals.**

This works, but it doesn't take into account the fact that the exchange rate is much more volatile than the account balance. In fact, if exchange rates come from the FX market, there may well be dozens or hundreds of tiny movements every second! Surely this level of detail isn't required for a private client who wants to keep an eye on their finances. Reacting to each change in exchange rate would flood the client with unwanted notifications.

This is an example of an `IObservable` producing too much data (see the sidebar on backpressure). For this, we can use `Sample`, an operator that takes an `IObservable` that acts as a data source, and another `IObservable` that signals *when* values should be produced. `Sample` is illustrated in figure 14.9.

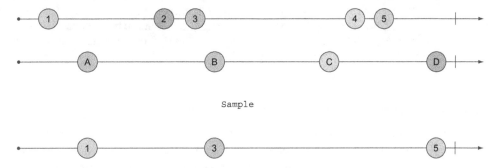

Figure 14.9 `Sample` **produces the values from a "source" stream whenever a "sampler" stream signals.**

In this scenario, we can create an `IObservable` that signals at 10 minute intervals, and use it to sample the stream of exchange rates.

Listing 14.8   Sampling a value from an `IObservable` **every 10 minutes**

```
IObservable<decimal> balance = //...
IObservable<decimal> eurUsdRate = //...

var tenMins = TimeStamp.FromMinutes(10);
```

```
var sampler = Observable.Interval(tenMins);
var eurUsdSampled = eurUsdRate.Sample(sampler);

var balanceInUsd = balance.CombineLatest(eurUsdSampled
    , (bal, rate) => bal * rate);
```

Both `CombineLatest` and `Sample` are cases in which our logic spans multiple events, and Rx allows us to do so without explicitly keeping any state.

Backpressure: when an `IObservable` produces data too quickly

When you iterate over the items in an `IEnumerable`, you're "pulling" or requesting items, so you can process them at your own pace. With `IObservable`, items are "pushed" to you (the consuming code). If an `IObservable` produces values more rapidly than they can be consumed by the subscribed observers, this can cause excessive *backpressure*, causing strain to your system.

To ease backpressure, Rx provides several operators:

- `Throttle`
- `Sample`
- `Buffer`
- `Window`
- `Debounce`

Each has a different behavior and several overloads, so we won't discuss them in detail. The point is that with these operators, you can easily and declaratively implement logic like, "I want to consume items in batches of 10 at a time," or "if a cluster of values come in quick succession, I only want to consume the last one." Implementing such logic in a callback-based solution, where each value is received independently, would require you to manually keep some state.

14.4.3 Notifying when an account becomes overdrawn

For a final, more business-oriented example, imagine that, in the context of the BOC application, we consume a stream of all transactions that affect bank accounts, and we want to send clients a notification if their account's balance becomes negative.

An account's balance is the sum of all the transactions that have affected it, so at any point, given a list of past `Transactions` for an account, you could compute its current balance using `Aggregate`. There is an `Aggregate` function for `IObservable`; it waits for an `IObservable` to complete, and aggregates all the values it produces into a single value.

But this isn't what we need: we don't want to wait for the sequence to complete, but to know the balance with every `Transaction` received. For this, we can use `Scan` (see figure 14.10), which is similar to `Aggregate` but aggregates all previous values with every new value that is produced.

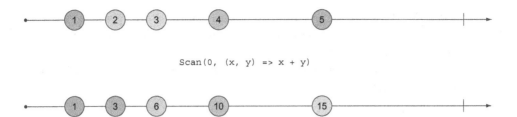

Figure 14.10 Scan **aggregates all values produced so far.**

As a result, we can effectively use Scan to keep state. Given an IObservable of Transactions affecting a bank account, we can use Scan to add up the amounts of all past transactions as they happen, obtaining an IObservable that signals with the new balance whenever the account balance changes:

```
IObservable<Transaction> transactions = //... decimal initialBalance = 0;

IObservable<decimal> balance = transactions.Scan(initialBalance
    , (bal, trans) => bal + trans.Amount);
```

Now that we have a stream of values representing an account's current balance, we need to single out what changes in balance cause the account to "dip into the red," going from positive to negative.

For this, we need to look at changes in the balance, and we can do this with Pair-WithPrevious, which signals the current value, together with the previously emitted value. We've discussed this before, but here it is again for reference:

```
// ----1-------2---------3--------4------>
//
//           PairWithPrevious
//
// -----------(1,2)-----(2,3)----(3,4)-->
//
public static IObservable<(T Previous, T Current)>
    PairWithPrevious<T>(this IObservable<T> source)
    => from first in source
        from second in source.Take(1)
        select (Previous: first, Current: second);
```

This is one of many examples of custom operations that can be defined in terms of existing operations. It's also an example of how you can use ASCII marble diagrams to document your code.

We can now use this to signal when an account dips into the red as follows:

```
IObservable<Unit> dipsIntoTheRed =
    from bal in balance.PairWithPrevious()
    where bal.Previous >= 0
        && bal.Current < 0
    select Unit();
```

Now let's make things a bit closer to the real world. If your system receives a stream of transactions, this will probably include transactions for all accounts. Therefore, we must group them by account ID in order to correctly compute the balance. GroupBy works for IObservable similarly to how it does for IEnumerable, but it returns a stream of streams.

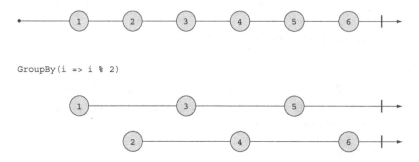

GroupBy(i => i % 2)

Let's rewrite the code, assuming an initial stream of transactions for all accounts.

Listing 14.9   Signalling whenever an account becomes overdrawn

```
IObservable<Transaction> transactions = //...          Includes transactions
                                                        from all accounts

IObservable<Guid> dipsIntoRed = transactions
    .GroupBy(t => t.AccountId)
    .Select(DipsIntoTheRed)                Applies the transformation
    .MergeAll();                           to each grouped observable

static IObservable<Guid> DipsIntoTheRed
    (IGroupedObservable<Guid, Transaction> transactions)
    {
        Guid accountId = transactions.Key;
        decimal initialBalance = 0;

        var balance = transactions.Scan(initialBalance
            , (bal, trans) => bal + trans.Amount);

        return from bal in balance.PairWithPrevious()
               where bal.Previous >= 0
                   && bal.Current < 0
               select accountId;              Signals the ID of the
    }                                         offending account

public static IObservable<T> MergeAll<T>
    (this IObservable<IObservable<T>> source)
    => source.SelectMany(x => x);
```

Groups by account ID — *Flattens back into a single observable*

Now we're starting with a stream of Transactions for all accounts, and we end up with a stream of Guids that will signal whenever an account dips into the red, with the Guid identifying the offending account. Notice how this program is effectively keeping track of the balances of all accounts, without the need for us to do any explicit state manipulation.

14.5 When should you use IObservable?

In this chapter, you've seen how you can use IObservable to represent data streams, and Rx to create and manipulate IObservables. There are many details and features of Rx that we haven't discussed at all,[4] but we've still covered enough ground for you to start using IObservables and to further explore the features of Rx as needed.

As you've seen, having an abstraction that captures a data stream enables you to detect patterns and specify logic that spans across multiple events, within the same stream or across different streams. This is where I'd recommend using IObservable. The corollary is that, if your events can be handled independently, then you probably shouldn't use IObservables, because using them will probably reduce the readability of your code.

A very important thing to keep in mind is that because OnNext has no return value, an IObservable can only push data downstream, and never receives any data back. Hence, IObservables are best combined into *one-directional data flows*. For instance, if you read events from a queue and write some data into a DB as a result, IObservable can be a good fit. Likewise if you have a server that communicates with web clients via WebSockets, where messages are exchanged between client and server in a fire-and-forget fashion. On the other hand, IObservables are not well-suited to a request-response model such as HTTP. You could model the received requests as a stream and compute a stream of responses, but you'd then have no easy way to tie these responses back to the original requests.

Finally, if you have complex synchronization patterns that can't be captured with the operators in Rx, and you need more fine-grained control over how messages are sequenced and processed, you may find the building blocks in the System.DataFlow namespace (based on in-memory queues) more appropriate.

Summary

- IObservable<T> represents a *stream* of Ts: a sequence of values in time.
- An IObservable produces messages according to the grammar
  OnNext* (OnCompleted|OnError)?.
- Writing a program with IObservables involves three steps:
  - Create IObservables using the methods in System.Reactive.Linq.Observable.
  - Transform and combine IObservables using the operators in Rx, or other operators you may define.
  - Subscribe to and consume the values produced by the IObservable.
  - Associate an observer to an IObservable with Subscribe.

---

[4] To give you an idea of what was not covered, there are many more operators along with important implementation details of Rx: schedulers (which determine how calls to observers are dispatched), *hot* vs. *cold* observables (not all observables are lazy), and Subjects with different behaviors, for example.

- Remove an observer by disposing of the subscription returned by `Subscribe`.
- Separate side effects (in observers) from logic (in stream transformations).
- When deciding on whether to use `IObservable`, consider the following:
  - `IObservable` allows you to specify logic that spans multiple events.
  - `IObservable` is good for modeling unidirectional data flows, not request-response.

An introduction to message-passing concurrency

This chapter covers

- Why shared mutable state is sometimes required
- Understanding message-passing concurrency
- Programming with agents in C#
- Hiding agent-based implementations behind conventional APIs

Every seasoned developer has some first-hand experience of how difficult it can be to deal with problems such as deadlocks and race conditions. These are the hard problems that can arise in concurrent programs that involve shared mutable state ("shared," that is, between processes that execute concurrently).

This is why, throughout this book, you've seen many examples of how to solve problems *without* making recourse to shared mutable state. Indeed, my recommendation is to avoid shared mutable state *whenever possible*, and FP provides an excellent paradigm for doing so.

In this chapter, you'll see why it's not always possible to avoid shared mutable state, and what strategies there are to synchronize access to shared mutable state. We'll then concentrate on one of these strategies: *agent-based concurrency*, a style of concurrent programming that relies on message-passing between *agents* that "own" some state that they access in a single-threaded way. Programming with agents is popular with F# programmers, but you'll see that it's perfectly doable in C#.

15.1 The need for shared mutable state

It's generally possible to avoid shared mutable state when designing parallel algorithms. For instance, if you have a computationally intensive problem that you'd like to parallelize, you can usually break the data set or the tasks down in such a way that several threads compute an intermediate result *independently*. Hence, these threads can do their work independently, without the need to share any state among themselves. Finally, another thread may compute the final result by combining all the intermediate results.

The problem, however, is that avoiding shared mutable state isn't always possible. Although it can generally be achieved in the case of parallel computations, it's much more difficult if the source of concurrency is multithreading. For example, imagine a multithreaded application, such as a server application handling requests on multiple threads, that needs to do the following:

- Keep an application-wide counter, so that unique, *sequential* account numbers can be generated
- Cache some resources in memory to improve efficiency
- Represent real-world entities, like items for sale, trades, contracts, and so on, ensuring that you don't sell the same (unique, real-world) item twice, just because two concurrent requests to buy it have been received

In such scenarios, it's essentially a requirement to share mutable state between the many threads that the server application uses to more efficiently handle requests. To prevent concurrent access from leading to data inconsistencies, you need to ensure the state can't be accessed (or, at least, updated) concurrently by different threads. That is, you need to *synchronize* access to shared mutable state.

In mainstream programming, this synchronization is usually achieved using locks. Locks define critical sections of the code that can only be entered by one thread at a time. When one thread enters a critical section, it blocks other threads from entering it.

Functional programmers tend to avoid using locks and resort instead to alternative techniques:

- *Compare-and-swap* (CAS)—CAS allows you to atomically read and update a single value; this can be done in C# using the `Interlocked.CompareExchange` methods.
- *Software transactional memory* (STM)—STM allows you to update mutable state within *transactions*, which offers some interesting guarantees about how these updates take place:

- Each thread performs a transaction in *isolation*; that is, it sees a view of the program state that is unaffected by transactions that occur concurrently on other threads.
- Transactions are then committed *atomically*; that is, either all changes succeed, or none.[1]
- If a transaction fails because another, concurrent transaction has modified the data, it will be retried with a fresh view of the data.

- *Message-passing concurrency*—The idea of this approach is that you set up lightweight *processes* that have exclusive ownership of mutable state. Communication between processes is via message-passing, and processes handle messages sequentially, hence preventing concurrent access to their state. There are two main embodiments of this approach:

  - *The actor model*—This is most famously implemented at Ericsson in conjunction with the Erlang language (but implementations for other languages, including C#, abound), in which processes are called "actors," and they can be distributed across different processes and machines.
  - *Agent-based concurrency*—This is inspired by the actor model, but it's much simpler, because processes, called *agents*, only exist within one application.

CAS only allows you to deal with a single value, so it only provides an effective solution for a very limited number of scenarios. STM is an important paradigm for in-process concurrency, and it's particularly popular among Clojure and Haskell developers because these languages come with a compelling and battle-tested implementation of STM. Unfortunately, no comparable implementation of STM exists for C#.

For these reasons, I'll concentrate on message-passing concurrency in the rest of this chapter, and especially agent-based concurrency. You'll later see how agents and actors differ in more detail. Let's begin by looking at message-passing concurrency as a programming model.

15.2 Understanding message-passing concurrency

You can think of an agent (or actor; the fundamental idea is the same) as a process that has exclusive ownership of some mutable state. Communication between actors is via message passing, so that the state can never be accessed from outside of the actor. Furthermore, incoming messages are processed sequentially, so that concurrent state updates can never take place.

---

[1] In fact, there are several different strategies for implementing STM, with different characteristics. Some implementations also enforce *consistency*, meaning that it's possible to enforce invariants that a transaction can't violate. Do these properties—atomicity, consistency, isolation—sound familiar? That's because they are three of the ACID properties guaranteed by many databases—the last one being *durability*, which of course does not apply to STM, which applies to data in memory.

Figure 15.1 illustrates an agent: a process that runs in a loop. It has an inbox, in which messages are queued, and it has some state. When a message is dequeued and processed, the agent typically does some of the following:

- Perform side effects
- Send messages to other agents
- Create other agents
- Compute its new state

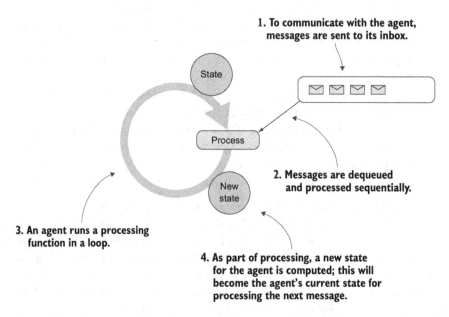

1. To communicate with the agent, messages are sent to its inbox.

State

Process

2. Messages are dequeued and processed sequentially.

New state

3. An agent runs a processing function in a loop.

4. As part of processing, a new state for the agent is computed; this will become the agent's current state for processing the next message.

Figure 15.1   An agent consists of a message inbox and a processing loop.

The new state will be used as the current state at the next iteration, when the following message is processed.

Let's begin with an idealized, almost pseudo-code implementation of an agent, as I've just described. Look at this code in detail and see how each part corresponds to what's depicted in figure 15.1.

Listing 15.1   Idealized implementation of an agent

```
public sealed class Agent<State, Msg>          Uses a concurrent queue
{                                              as a message inbox
    BlockingCollection<Msg> inbox
        = new BlockingCollection<Msg>(new ConcurrentQueue<Msg>());

    public void Tell(Msg message) => inbox.Add(message);

    public Agent(State initialState               Telling a message to the agent
        , Func<State, Msg, State> process)        enqueues the message
```

Creates an agent by providing an initial state and a processing function

```
{
    void Loop(State state)
    {
        Msg message = inbox.Take();
        State newState = process(state, message);
        Loop(newState);
    }

    Task.Run(() => Loop(initialState));
}
}
```

Loops with the new state → `Loop(newState);`

Dequeues a message as soon as it's available → `Msg message = inbox.Take();`

Processes the message, determining the new state of the agent → `State newState = process(state, message);`

Actor runs in its own process → `Task.Run(() => Loop(initialState));`

There are several interesting things to point out here. First, notice that there are only two public members. So only two interactions with an agent are allowed:

- You can create (or *start*) an agent.
- You can tell it a message, which simply enqueues the message in the agent's inbox.

More complex interactions can be defined from these primitive operations.

Let's now look at the processing loop, encoded in the Loop function. This dequeues the first message from the inbox (or waits until a message becomes available) and processes it using the agent's processing function and its current state. It thus obtains the agent's new state, which will be used in the next execution of the loop.

Notice that the implementation is side-effect free—apart from any side effects that may occur when calling the given processing function. The way changes in state are captured is by always passing the state as an argument to the Loop function (a technique you already saw in chapter 12).

Notice also that this implementation assumes that State must be an immutable type; otherwise, it could be shared by the process function and updated arbitrarily outside of the scope of the agent's processing loop. As a result, the state only "appears" to be mutable because a new version of the state is used with each invocation of Loop.

Finally, take a moment to look at the signature for the constructor. Does it remind you of anything? Compare it with Enumerable.Aggregate—can you see that it's essentially the same? The current state of an agent is the result of reducing all the messages it's received so far, using the initial state as an accumulator value, and the processing function as a reducer. It's a fold in time over the stream of messages received by the agent.

This implementation is elegant, and it would work well in a language with tail-call elimination, but not in C#, so we'll need to make some changes for a stack-safe implementation. Furthermore, we can also dispense with many of the low-level details by using existing functionality in .NET. We'll look at this next.

15.2.1 *Implementing agents in C#*

.NET has an implementation of agents called MailboxProcessor, but it was designed for use from F# and is very awkward to use from C#. And although the preceding implementation is useful for understanding the idea, it's not optimal. Instead, in the coming examples I'll use the following, more practical implementation of an agent, which is included in LaYumba.Functional.

Listing 15.2   Implementation of an agent that builds upon `Dataflow.ActionBlock`

```
using System.Threading.Tasks.Dataflow;

public interface Agent<Msg>
{
    void Tell(Msg message);
}

class StatefulAgent<State, Msg> : Agent<Msg>
{
    private State state;
    private readonly ActionBlock<Msg> actionBlock;

    public StatefulAgent(State initialState
        , Func<State, Msg, State> process)
    {
        state = initialState;

        actionBlock = new ActionBlock<Msg>(msg =>
        {
            var newState = process(state, msg);
            state = newState;
        }
    }

    public void Tell(Msg message)
        => actionBlock.Post(message);
}
```

Assigns the result to the stored state

Processes the message with the current state

Queueing and processing messages is managed by the `ActionBlock`.

Here I've replaced the recursive call (which could lead to stack overflow) with a single mutable variable `state` that keeps track of the agent's state and is reassigned as each message is processed. Although this is a side effect, messages are processed sequentially, therefore preventing concurrent writes.

I've also dispensed with the details of managing the queue and process by using `ActionBlock`, one of the building blocks in .NET's `Dataflow` library. An `ActionBlock` contains a buffer (by default, unbounded in size) that will act as the agent's inbox, and that only allows a fixed number of threads to enter the block (by default, a single thread), ensuring messages are processed sequentially.

`State` should still be an immutable type (otherwise, as previously pointed out, it could be shared by the `process` function and mutated outside the scope of the `ActionBlock`). If this is observed, the code is thread-safe.

From the point of view of the client code, nothing has changed: we still only have two public members with the same signatures as before. The reason for the `Agent<Msg>` interface is twofold:

- From the point of view of the client code consuming an agent, you can only tell it messages, so by using the interface we avoid exposing the type parameter for the state. After all, the type of the state is an implementation detail of the agent.
- You can envisage other implementations, such as stateless agents, or agents that persist their state.

Finally, here are some convenience methods for easily creating agents:

```
public static class Agent
{
    public static Agent<Msg> Start<State, Msg>
        ( State initialState
        , Func<State, Msg, State> process)
        => new StatefulAgent<State, Msg>(initialState, process);

    public static Agent<Msg> Start<Msg>(Action<Msg> action)
        => new StatelessAgent<Msg>(action);
}
```

The first overload simply creates an agent with the given arguments. The second takes an action and is used to create a *stateless agent*: an agent that processes messages sequentially but doesn't keep any state. (The implementation is trivial, as it just creates an `ActionBlock` with the given `Action`.) We can also define agents with an asynchronous processing function/action; I've omitted the overloads for brevity, but the full implementation is in the code samples. Next, we'll get started using agents.

15.2.2 Getting started with agents

Let's look at some simple examples of using agents. We'll build a couple of simple agents that interact as shown in figure 15.2.

We'll start with a really simple, stateless agent that takes a message of type `string` and just prints it out. You can follow along in the REPL:

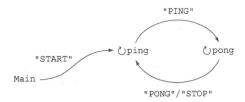

Figure 15.2 Simple interaction between agents by exchanging messages

```
Agent<string> logger = Agent.Start((string msg) => WriteLine(msg));

logger.Tell("Agent X");
// prints: Agent X
```

Next, let's define the ping and pong agents that interact with the logger and with each other:

```
Agent<string> ping, pong = null;

ping = Agent.Start((string msg) =>
{
    if (msg == "STOP") return;
```

```
    logger.Tell($"Received '{msg}'; Sending 'PING'");
    Task.Delay(500).Wait();
    pong.Tell("PING");
});

pong = Agent.Start(0, (int count, string msg) =>
{
    int newCount = count + 1;
    string nextMsg = (newCount < 5) ? "PONG" : "STOP";

    logger.Tell($"Received '{msg}' #{newCount}; Sending '{nextMsg}'");
    Task.Delay(500).Wait();
    ping.Tell(nextMsg);

    return newCount;
});

ping.Tell("START");
```

Here, we define two additional agents. ping is stateless; it sends a message to the logger agent and a "PING" message to the pong agent, unless the message it's told is "STOP", in which case it does nothing. It's quite common for an agent to have different behavior depending on the message; that is, to interpret the message as a command.

Now let's see a stateful agent: pong. The implementation is quite similar to ping: it sends "PONG" to ping, but it also keeps a counter as state that is incremented with every message, so after five messages it can send a "STOP" message instead.

The whole ping-pong is set in motion when we send the initial "START" message to ping on the last line. Running the program causes the following to be printed:

```
Received 'START'; Sending 'PING'
Received 'PING' #1; Sending 'PONG'
Received 'PONG'; Sending 'PING'
Received 'PING' #2; Sending 'PONG'
Received 'PONG'; Sending 'PING'
Received 'PING' #3; Sending 'PONG'
Received 'PONG'; Sending 'PING'
Received 'PING' #4; Sending 'PONG'
Received 'PONG'; Sending 'PING'
Received 'PING' #5; Sending 'STOP'
```

Now that you've seen some simple agents interact, it's time to move on to something closer to real-world requirements.

15.2.3   *Using agents to handle concurrent requests*

Let's go back to the scenario of a service that provides exchange rates. The service should retrieve rates from the Yahoo API and cache them. In our previous implementation, the interaction was via the command line, so that requests necessarily came in one by one.

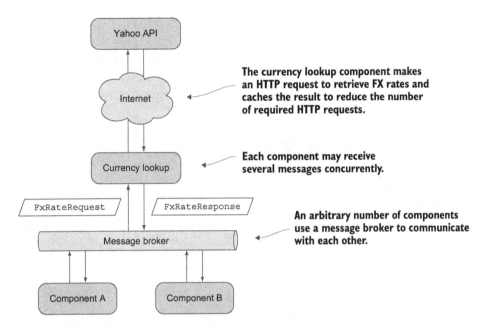

Figure 15.3   A system in which several requests may be received concurrently

Let's change that. Let's imagine that the service is part of a larger system, and that other components may request rates via a message broker, as illustrated in figure 15.3.

Components communicate with each other by sending messages via the message broker. To communicate with the currency lookup service, the following messages are defined:

```
public sealed class FxRateRequest
{
    public string CcyPair { get; set; }
    public string Sender { get; set; }
}

public sealed class FxRateResponse
{
    public string CcyPair { get; set; }
    public decimal Rate { get; set; }
    public string Recipient { get; set; }
}
```

The currency pair whose rate is being requested

The sender and recipient fields are used by the message broker to correctly route messages.

We'll assume that the message broker is multithreaded; that is, our service may receive multiple requests on different threads at exactly the same time.

In this case, sharing state between threads is a requirement: if we had a different cache for every thread, that would be suboptimal. So we need to synchronize write access to the cache, ensuring that only a single thread can write values to the cache at any given time.

Next, we'll see how we can use agents to achieve this. First, we'll need a bit of setup code, defining the interaction with the message broker. This is shown in the following listing. Note that the code isn't specific to any particular message broker; we just need to be able to subscribe to it to receive requests, and to use it to send responses. (The code samples include an implementation of `MessageBroker` that uses Redis as its underlying transport.)

Listing 15.3   Setting up the handling of requests received from the message broker

An agent that will process the requests and use the previously defined agent to send the response

An agent that will send responses

```
public static void SetUp(MessageBroker broker)
{
    Agent<FxRateResponse> sendResponse = Agent.Start(
        (FxRateResponse res) => broker.Send(res.Recipient, res));

    Agent<FxRateRequest> processRequest = StartReqProcessor(sendResponse);

    broker.Subscribe<FxRateRequest>("FxRates", processRequest.Tell);
}
```

When a request is received, passes it to the processing agent

---

Starting at the bottom, we subscribe to receive requests, providing a callback to handle the request. This callback (which will be called on multiple threads) simply passes the request to the processing agent, which is defined on the previous line. Hence, although requests are received on multiple threads, they'll be immediately queued up in the processing agent's inbox and processed sequentially.

Does this mean that processing is now single-threaded, and we lose any benefit of multithreading? Not necessarily! If the processing agent did *all* the processing, that would indeed be the case. Instead, let's take a more granular approach: we can have an agent for each currency pair in charge of fetching and storing the rate for its particular pair. The request-processing agent will just be in charge of managing these per-currency-pair agents and delegating the work to them, as in figure 15.4.

Let's look at the definitions of the agents. We'll start with the higher level request-processing agent in charge of creating and delegating work to per-currency-pair agents.

Listing 15.4   A coordinating agent routes requests to a per-currency-pair agent

```
using CcyAgents = ImmutableDictionary<string, Agent<string>>;

static Agent<FxRateRequest> StartReqProcessor
    (Agent<FxRateResponse> sendResponse)

    => Agent.Start(CcyAgents.Empty
        , (CcyAgents state, FxRateRequest request) =>
```

```
{
    string ccyPair = request.CcyPair;

    Agent<string> agent = state
        .Lookup(ccyPair)
        .GetOrElse(() => StartAgentFor(ccyPair, sendResponse));

    agent.Tell(request.Sender);
    return state.Add(ccyPair, agent);
});
```

If required, starts a new agent for the requested currency pair

Passes the request to the agent in charge of the pair

Requests received from the message broker are handled by a request processing agent.

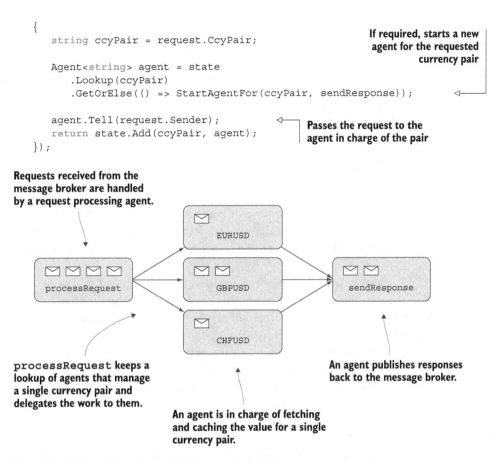

processRequest keeps a lookup of agents that manage a single currency pair and delegates the work to them.

An agent is in charge of fetching and caching the value for a single currency pair.

An agent publishes responses back to the message broker.

Figure 15.4 Breaking up the work between agents that can run concurrently

As you can see, the request-processing agent holds not a cache of values, but of agents—one for each currency pair. It starts those agents as needed and forwards the requests to them.

The benefit of this solution is that requests for one currency, say GBPUSD, won't impact requests for another, say EURUSD. On the other hand, if you get several requests for GBPUSD at the same time, only one remote request will be made to fetch that rate, while other requests are queued.

Finally, here's the definition of the agent that manages the rate for a single currency pair.

Listing 15.5 An agent that manages lookup and storage of an FX rate for a currency pair

```
static Agent<string> StartAgentFor
    (string ccyPair, Agent<FxRateResponse> sendResponse)
    => Agent.Start<Option<decimal>, string>(None
        , async (optRate, recipient) =>
```

```
{
    decimal rate = await optRate.Map(Async)        │ If required, fetches the
        .GetOrElse(() => Yahoo.GetRate(ccyPair));  ◁─┘ rate from the remote API

    sendResponse.Tell(new FxRateResponse    ◁──── Sends the response
    {
        CcyPair = ccyPair,
        Rate = rate,
        Recipient = recipient,
    });

    return Some(rate);
});
```

This agent's state is the rate for a single pair wrapped in an `Option`, because when it's first created the rate isn't available yet. It decides whether a remote lookup is required, so you could easily improve this to fetch the rate if the cached value is expired.

To keep the example simple, I've avoided the question of expiry, as well as error handling. I'm also assuming that sending the request to the message broker is a fire-and-forget operation with minimal latency, so that it's OK to have a single agent performing it.

The main point of the example is that using agents, with their sequential processing of messages, can be quite efficient. It does, however, require a mental shift, both from the functional approach we've been pursuing in this book, and from the traditional approach of using locks.

15.2.4 *Agents vs. actors*

Agents and actors are closely related. In both cases, a single thread processes messages sequentially and communicates with other actors/agents by sending them messages. There are also important differences:

- Agents run within a single process, whereas actors are designed for distributed systems. In the examples we've looked at so far, a reference to an agent refers to a specific instance in the current process. References to actors, on the other hand, are location-transparent; that is, when you have a reference to an actor, that actor may be running in the same process or on another process, possibly on a remote machine. So a reference to an agent is a pointer, whereas a reference to an actor is an ID that the actor model implementation will use to route messages across processes as appropriate.

- Most implementations of the actor model cater for error handling through *supervisor* actors that monitor a supervised actor and take action when it faults. This allows us to nicely separate happy-path logic from error handling and makes it possible to create very robust systems. There's no counterpart of this with agents.

- An agent's state should be immutable and never shared outside the scope of the agent. In our implementation, however, there's nothing stopping an inexperienced developer from creating an agent whose state is mutable, and from passing that mutable state to other functions, thus allowing that state to be changed from outside the scope of the agent. With actors, messages are serialized, so this should never occur.

As you can see, although the fundamental idea behind agents and actors is the same, the actor model is richer and more complex. You should only consider using the actor model if you require coordination of concurrent operations across different applications or machines; otherwise, the operational and setup cost would be unjustified, and you should rely on agents instead.

Although I was able to implement an actor with just a few lines of code, implementing the actor model is much more complex. So if you want to use actors, you'll probably use one of several implementations of the actor model for .NET:

- *Orleans* (https://dotnetfoundation.org/orleans) is Microsoft's take on the actor model. It has a distinctly object-oriented feel. The underlying philosophy is that less experienced developers can interact with actors (called "grains") as though they were local objects, without being exposed to any additional complexities specific to the actor model. Orleans takes care of managing the grains' lifecycle, meaning that their state is kept in memory or persisted to storage automatically. Persistence can be to a variety of media, including SQL Server and cloud storage on Azure.

- *Akka.NET* (http://getakka.net/) is a community-driven port of the Akka framework popular with Scala developers. It predates Orleans and is much more explicit about its message-driven nature, so the barrier to entry is higher. A variety of options are available for message transport and persistence of the actors' state.

- *echo* (https://github.com/louthy/echo-process) is the implementation that stays closest to Erlang. It's the most lightweight option, both in terms of syntax and configuration: you can create an actor (called a "process") with a function, like we did with agents, or you can use an interface-based approach (which reads more naturally if you need to handle different kinds of messages). Message transport across application domains and persistence are done with Redis only, out of the box, but you can implement adapters to target a different infrastructure.

All these actor model implementations differ both in terminology and in important technical details, so it's difficult to offer a description of *the* actor model without being somewhat specific to one implementation. This is one of the reasons why I've opted to illustrate the fundamental ideas of message-passing concurrency with a simple implementation of agents. You can carry these principles over to actor-based programming, but you'll need to learn other principles, such as error handling with supervisors, and the guarantees for message delivery offered by the specific implementation you're using.

15.3 *Functional APIs, agent-based implementations*

Is agent-based programming even functional? Although agents and actors were developed in the context of functional languages (remember, in our idealized implementation an agent was side-effect free), agent-based programming differs starkly from the functional techniques you've seen throughout this book:

- You tell an agent a message, and this is usually interpreted as a command, so the semantics are rather imperative.
- An agent often performs a side effect, or tells a message to another agent, which will in turn perform a side effect.
- Most importantly, telling an agent a message returns no data, so you can't compose tell operations into pipelines the way you can with functions.
- FP separates logic from data; agents contain data and at least some logic in the processing function.

As a result, agent-based programming *feels* very different from FP as you've seen it so far, so that it's debatable whether or not agent-based concurrency is actually a functional technique. If you think it's not (as I'm inclined to), then you must conclude that FP is not very good at *certain types* of concurrency (that is, where shared mutable state can't be avoided) and it needs to be complemented with a different paradigm, such as agent-based programming or the actor model.

With agents, it's easy to program *unidirectional data flows*: the data always flows forward (to the next agent), and no data is ever returned. In the face of this, we have two choices:

- Embrace the idea of unidirectional data flow, and write your applications in this style. In this approach, if you had clients connecting to a server, you wouldn't use a request-response model like HTTP, but rather a message-based protocol, such as WebSockets or a message broker. This is a viable approach, especially if your domain is event-driven enough that you already have a messaging infrastructure in place.
- Hide the agent-specific details behind a more conventional API. This implies that agents should be able to return a response to a message sender. In this approach, agents are used as concurrency primitives that are implementation details (just as locks are) and that should not dictate the program's design. We'll explore this approach next.

15.3.1 *Agents as implementation details*

The first thing we need is a way to get a reply from an agent, a "return value" of sorts. Imagine that a sender creates a message that includes a "handle" that it can wait on. It then tells the message to an agent, which will signal a result on that handle, making it available to the sender. With this, we can effectively have two-way communication on top of the fire-and-forget `Tell` protocol.

`TaskCompletionSource` provides a suitable handle for this purpose: the sender can create a `TaskCompletionSource`, add it to the message payload, and await its `Task`. The agent will do its work and set the result on the `TaskCompletionSource` when ready. Doing this manually for every message for which you want a response would be tedious, so instead I've included in my `LaYumba.Functional` library a beefed-up agent that takes care of all this wiring. I won't include the implementation details here, but the interface definition is as follows:

```
public interface Agent<Msg, Reply>
{
    Task<Reply> Tell(Msg message);
}
```

Notice that this is a completely new interface, with not one but two generic arguments: the type of messages that the agent accepts, and the type that it replies with. Telling a message of type `Msg` to this agent will return a `Task<Reply>`.

To start an agent of this type, we'll use a processing function of type

$$State \rightarrow Msg \rightarrow (State, Reply)$$

or

$$State \rightarrow Msg \rightarrow Task<(State, Reply)>$$

That is, a function that, given the agent's current state and the received message, computes not only the agent's new state, but also a reply to be returned to the sender.

Let's look at a very simple example—an agent that keeps a counter and can be told to increment the counter, but that also returns the counter's new value:

```
var counter = Agent.Start(0
   , (int state, int msg) =>
   {
       var newState = state + msg;
       return (newState, newState);         ◁─── Returns the new state to
   });                                              be stored and the reply
                                                    to the sender
```

You can now consume this agent like this:

```
var newCount = await counter.Tell(1);
newCount // => 1
newCount = await counter.Tell(1);
newCount // => 2
```

Notice that `Tell` returns a `Task<int>`, so the caller can just await the reply, as with any asynchronous function. Essentially, you can use this agent as a thread-safe, stateful, asynchronous version of a function of type `Msg` → `Reply`:

- Thread safe, because it internally uses an `ActionBlock` that processes one message at a time.
- Stateful, because the state kept by the agent can change as a result of processing a message.
- Asynchronous, because your message may have to wait while the agent processes other messages in its queue.

This means that, compared to using locks, you're not only gaining in safety (no deadlocks) but also in performance (locks block the current thread, whereas `await` frees the thread to do other work).

15.3.2   *Hiding agents behind a conventional API*

Now that we have a mechanism for two-way communication in place, we can improve the API by hiding the specifics of agent-based programming. For example, in the case of a counter, we could define a `Counter` class as follows.

Listing 15.6   Hiding an agent-based implementation behind a public API

```
public sealed class Counter
{
    readonly Agent<int, int> counter =          The agent is just an
        Agent.Start(0, (int state, int msg) =>   implementation detail.
            {
                var newState = state + msg;
                return (newState, newState);
            });

    public int IncrementBy(int by)              Public interface
        => counter.Tell(by).Result;              of the Counter
}
```

Now a consumer of `Counter` can be blissfully unaware of its agent-based implementation. A typical interaction would look like this:

```
var counter = new Counter();
var newCount = counter.IncrementBy(10);
newCount // => 10
```

Notice that, because agents are asynchronous, *as a rule* you should expose any value that's computed with agents wrapped in a `Task`. In the preceding example, I'm making an exception to the rule by using the blocking call to `Result` and exposing a synchronous API. That's because incrementing a counter is such a fast operation that, even with high contention, latency should be minimal.

15.4 Message-passing concurrency in LOB applications

In LOB applications, the need to synchronize access to some shared state usually arises from the fact that entities in the application represent real-world entities, and we need to ensure that concurrent access doesn't leave them in an invalid state or otherwise break business rules. For example, two concurrent requests to purchase a particular item shouldn't result in that item being sold twice. Similarly, concurrent moves in a multiplayer game shouldn't lead to an invalid state of the game.

Let's see how this would play out in our banking scenario. We need to ensure that when different transactions (debits, credits, transfers) happen concurrently, they don't leave the account in an invalid state. Does this mean we need to synchronize access to the account data? Not necessarily! Let's see what happens if we don't take any special measures with respect to concurrency.

Imagine an account with a balance of 1,000. An automated direct debit payment occurs, causing 800 to be debited from the account. Concurrently, a transfer of 200 is requested, so that the amount of 200 is also debited. If we use the event-sourced approach shown so far in this book, we get the following result:

- The direct debit request will cause an event to be created, capturing a debit of 800, and the caller will receive an updated state with a balance of 200.
- The transfer request will likewise cause an event to be created, capturing a debit of 200, and the caller will receive an updated state with a balance of 800.
- Whenever the account is loaded next, its state is computed from all past events, so that its state will correctly have a balance of 0.
- As new events are published, any clients that subscribe to updates can reflect those changes in state. (For example, the client device on which the transfer request was made can be notified when the direct debit has taken place, so that the account balance shown to the user is always up to date.)

In short, if you use immutable objects and event sourcing, you don't get any inconsistent data as a result of concurrent updates, and this is another important benefit of event sourcing. But let's now change the requirements slightly. Assume that each account has a maximum allowed overdraft; that is, there's a business requirement that any account can never be overdraft beyond a certain amount.

Imagine, like before, we have the following:

- An account with a balance of 1000, and a maximum overdraft of 500
- A direct debit payment of 800
- Concurrently, a transfer request, also for 800

If you don't synchronize access to the account data, both requests will succeed, leading to the account having an overdraft of 600, violating our business requirement that the overdraft should never be over 500. To enforce the maximum allowed overdraft, we need to synchronize the execution of actions that modify the account balance, so that one of the concurrent requests in this scenario should fail.

Next, you'll see how to achieve this using actors.

15.4.1 *Using an agent to synchronize access to account data*

To ensure that the account data can't be affected concurrently by different requests, we can associate an agent with each account. Notice that agents are lightweight enough that it's OK to have thousands or even millions of them. Also notice that I'm assuming there's a single server process through which accounts can be affected. If this weren't the case, you'd need to use an implementation of the actor model instead; the gist of the following implementation would still be valid.

To associate an agent with an account, we'll define an `AccountProcess` class with an agent-based implementation. This means we're now using three classes to represent accounts:

- `AccountState`—An immutable class that represents the *state* of an account at a given moment in time
- `Account`—A static class that only contains pure functions used to calculate state transitions
- `AccountProcess`—An agent-based implementation that tracks the current state of an account and handles any commands that affect the account's state

You've seen implementations of `Account` and `AccountState` in chapter 10, and those don't need to change. Let's look at `AccountProcess` next.

Listing 15.7   Sequential processing of commands that affect an account

```
using Result = Validation<(Event Event, AccountState NewState)>;

public class AccountProcess
{
    Agent<Command, Result> agent;

    public AccountProcess(AccountState initialState
        , Func<Event, Task<Unit>> saveAndPublish)
    {
        agent = Agent.Start(initialState
            , async (AccountState state, Command cmd) =>
            {
                Result result = new Pattern
                {
                    (MakeTransfer transfer) => state.Debit(transfer),
                    (FreezeAccount freeze) => state.Freeze(freeze),
                }
                .Match(cmd);

                await result.Traverse(tpl => saveAndPublish(tpl.Event));
                var newState = result.Map(tpl => tpl.NewState).GetOrElse(state);
                return (newState, result);
            });
    }

    public Task<Result> Handle(Command cmd)
        => agent.Tell(cmd);
}
```

Persists the event within the block, so that the agent doesn't process new messages in a non-persisted state

Uses pure functions to calculate the result of the command

All commands are queued-up and processed sequentially.

Each instance of `AccountProcess` internally holds an agent, so all commands that affect the account can be processed sequentially. Let's look at the body of the agent: first, we calculate the result of the command, given the command and the current state. This is done using pure, static functions only.

The result, remember, is a `Validation` with an inner value including the resulting `Event` and the new account state. If the result is `Valid`, we proceed to save and publish the created event (the check is done as part of `Traverse`).

It's important to note that persistence happens *within* the processing function. That is, the agent shouldn't update its state and start processing new messages before it has successfully persisted the event representing its current state transition. (Otherwise, persisting the event could fail, leading to a mismatch between the agent's state and the state captured by the persisted events.)

Finally, we return the account's updated state (which will be used when processing subsequent commands) and the result of the command. This result includes both the new state and the created event, wrapped in a `Validation`. This makes it easy to send back to the client the details of the success and result of this request.

Notice how agents (and actors) complect state, behavior, and persistence (as such, they have been labeled "more object-oriented than objects"). In this implementation, I'm injecting a function for persisting the events, whereas most implementations of the actor model include some configurable mechanism for persisting an actor's state.

15.4.2 Keeping a registry of accounts

We now have an `AccountProcess` that can process commands applicable to a specific account in a thread-safe manner. But when we get a command via a brand new controller, how can we get the instance of `AccountProcess` for the relevant account? And how do we ensure that we never accidentally create two `AccountProcesses` for the same account?

What we need is a single, application-wide registry that will hold all live `Account-Processes`. It will need to manage their creation and serve them by ID, so that a controller can get an `AccountProcess` simply by providing the account ID that it's received as part of a request.

Actor model implementations have such a registry built in, allowing you to register any particular actor against an arbitrary ID. In our case, we'll build our own simple registry.

> **Listing 15.8 A registry for storing and managing the creation of `AccountProcesses`**

```
using AccountsCache = ImmutableDictionary<Guid, AccountProcess>;

public class AccountRegistry
{
    Agent<Guid, Option<AccountProcess>> agent;
```

```
public AccountRegistry
    ( Func<Guid, Task<Option<AccountState>>> loadState
    , Func<Event, Task<Unit>> saveAndPublish)
{
    this.agent = Agent.Start(AccountsCache.Empty
        , async (AccountsCache cache, Guid id) =>
        {
            AccountProcess account;
            if (cache.TryGetValue(id, out account))
                return (cache, Some(account));

            var optAccount = await loadState(id);

            return optAccount.Map(accState =>
            {
                var process = new AccountProcess(accState, saveAndPublish);
                return (cache.Add(id, process), Some(process));
            })
            .GetOrElse(() => (cache, (Option<AccountProcess>)None));
        });
}

public Task<Option<AccountProcess>> Lookup(Guid id)
    => agent.Tell(id);
}
```

> **If the `AccountProcess` is not in the cache, loads the current state from the DB**

> **Creates an `AccountProcess` with the retrieved state**

In this implementation, we have a single agent that manages a cache where all live instances of `AccountProcess` are kept. If no `AccountProcess` is found for the given ID, the account's current state is retrieved from the DB and used to create a new `Account-Process`, which is added to the cache. Notice that, as usual, the `loadState` function returns a `Task<Option<AccountState>>` to acknowledge that the operation is asynchronous and that no data may be found for a given ID.

Before you read on, go through the implementation again. Can you see any problems with this approach? Let's see: loading the account state from the DB is done *within* the agent body; is that warranted? This means that reading the state for account *x* will block another thread that's interested in account *y*. That's certainly suboptimal!

15.4.3 *An agent is not an object*

This is the kind of schoolboy error that's common when you're getting used to programming with agents or actors. Although agents and actors are similar to objects, you can't think of them as such. The error in listing 15.8 is that we're conceptually giving the agent the "responsibility" of providing the caller with the requested `AgentProcess`, and this has given us a suboptimal solution.

Instead, agents should only have the responsibility of managing some state. The agent in question manages a dictionary, so we can call it to look up an item, or to add a new item, but going to the DB to retrieve data is a relatively slow operation that's not directly pertinent to managing the cache of `AgentProcesses`.

With this in mind, let's think of an alternative solution. A thread that wants to get hold of an `AgentProcess` for an account with a given ID should do the following:

1 Ask the agent to look up the ID.
2 If no `AgentProcess` is stored, retrieve the current `AccountState`.
3 Ask the agent to create and register a new `AgentProcess` with the given state and ID.

This means that we need to go to the agent twice, so we need two different message types to specify what we want the agent to do.

> **Listing 15.9 Different types of message can be required to convey the caller's intention**

```
public class AccountRegistry
{
    abstract class Msg { public Guid Id { get; set; } }
    class LookupMsg : Msg { }
    class RegisterMsg : Msg
    {
        public AccountState AccountState { get; set; }
    }
}
```

I've defined these message types as inner classes because they're only used within the `AccountRegistry` class to communicate with its agent.

We can now define the `Lookup` method, which constitutes the `AccountRegistry`'s public API, and is therefore executed on the caller's thread, as follows:

```
public class AccountRegistry
{
    Agent<Msg, Option<Account>> agent;
    Func<Guid, Task<Option<AccountState>>> loadState;

    public Task<Option<Account>> Lookup(Guid id)
        => agent                                          ← Tells the agent to
            .Tell(new LookupMsg { Id = id })                look up the given ID
            .OrElse(() =>
                from state in loadState(id)
                from result in agent.Tell(new RegisterMsg  ← Tells the agent to
                {                                             register a new
                    Id = id,                                  process with the
                    AccountState = state                      given state and ID
                })
                select result);
    }
}
```

If the lookup fails, the state is loaded in the calling thread.

It first asks the agent to look up the ID; if the lookup fails, then the state is retrieved from the DB. Note that this is done on the calling thread, leaving the agent free to handle other messages. Finally a second message is sent to the agent asking it to create and register an `AccountProcess` with the given account state and ID.

Notice that everything happens within the `Task<Option<>>` stack, because this is the type returned both by `loadState` and by `Tell`. Even `OrElse` here resolves to an overload I've defined on `Task<Option<T>>`, which executes the given fallback function if the `Task` has faulted *or* if the inner `Option` is `None`.

All that's left to show is the definition of the agent in the `AccountRegistry`'s constructor.

Listing 15.10   Revised definition of the agent for storing a registry of `AccountProcesses`

```
using AccountsCache = ImmutableDictionary<Guid, Agents.Account>;

public class AccountRegistry
{
    Agent<Msg, Option<Account>> agent;
    Func<Guid, Task<Option<AccountState>>> loadState;

    public AccountRegistry(Func<Guid, Task<Option<AccountState>>> loadState
      , Func<Event, Task<Unit>> saveAndPublish)
    {
        this.loadState = loadState;

        this.agent = Agent.Start(AccountsCache.Empty
          , (AccountsCache cache, Msg msg) =>

            new Pattern<(AccountsCache, Option<Account>)>
            {
                (LookupMsg m) => (cache, cache.Lookup(m.Id)),

                (RegisterMsg m) => cache.Lookup(m.Id).Match(
                  Some: acc => (cache, Some(acc)),
                  None: () =>
                  {
                      var account = new Account(m.AccountState, saveAndPublish);
                      return (cache.Add(m.Id, account), Some(account));
                  })
            }
            .Match(msg));
    }
    public Task<Option<Account>> Lookup(Guid id) => // as above...
}
```

> The agent uses pattern matching to perform different actions depending on the message it's sent.

This implementation is slightly more complex, but more efficient, and it has given us the chance to see a common pitfall when programming with agents; namely, performing an expensive operation in the body of an agent that doesn't strictly require synchronized access to the agent's state.

On the other hand, in both proposed implementations, once an `AccountProcess` is created, it's never terminated; it will persist events to the DB to keep the stored version in sync with the in-memory state, but we read from the DB at most once. Is this a good thing, or bad? Of course, it depends on how much data you'll eventually have in memory and how much memory you have available. It's potentially a huge optimization, because access to in-memory data is orders of magnitude faster than access to the DB. The ability to keep all your data in memory is one of the big draws of the actor model: because actors can be distributed across machines, there's no effective limit on the amount of memory you can use, and accessing memory (even over the network) is much faster than accessing even a local DB.

15.4.4 Putting it all together

With the previous building blocks in place, our implementation for the API controller can remain fairly similar to what we had so far:

Injects a function to get an `AccountProcess` by ID

```
public class MakeTransferController : Controller
{
    Func<MakeTransfer, Validation<MakeTransfer>> Validate;
    Func<Guid, Task<Validation<AccountProcess>>> GetAccount;

    public MakeTransferController
        ( Func<Guid, Task<Option<AccountProcess>>> getAccount
        , Func<MakeTransfer, Validation<MakeTransfer>> validate)
    {
        Validate = validate;
        GetAccount = id => getAccount(id)
            .Map(opt => opt.ToValidation(() => Errors.UnknownAccountId(id)));    ⟵
    }

    public Task<IActionResult> MakeTransfer([FromBody] MakeTransfer command)
    {
        Task<Validation<AccountState>> outcome =
            from cmd in Async(Validate(command))
            from accountProcess in GetAccount(cmd.DebitedAccountId)
            from result in accountProcess.Handle(cmd)
            select result.NewState;

        return outcome.Map(
            Faulted: ex => StatusCode(500, Errors.UnexpectedError),
            Completed: val => val.Match<IActionResult>(
                Invalid: errs => BadRequest(new { Errors = errs }),
                Valid: newState => Ok(new { Balance = newState.Balance })));
    }
}
```

Changes from `Task<Option<>>` to `Task<Validation<>>`

The `AccountProcess` handles the command, updating the account state and persisting/publishing the corresponding event.

We now depend on one function for validating the command, and one for retrieving the `AccountProcess`—this will be the `Lookup` method exposed by the `AccountRegistry`. We use a simple adapter to translate from `Task<Option<>>` to `Task<Validation<>>`, so that we have a uniform monad stack and can present the client with meaningful error messages if the command's account ID is incorrectly populated.

The main change, compared to the version in chapter 10, is that the result tuple is only returned for feedback, whereas persisting and publishing the event happens when we submit the command to the AccountProcess's Handle method. This, as you've seen, is required to prevent concurrent modifications to the account's state, which could violate business rules such as limiting the account's maximal overdraft.

Finally, all that's left is wiring up the different pieces of the application, which in the case of a web application can be done in an IControllerActivator. The gist is as follows.

> **Listing 15.11   Wiring up the application components in an `IControllerActivator`**

```
public class ControllerActivator : IControllerActivator
{
   Func<Guid, Task<IEnumerable<Event>>> loadEvents;
   Func<Event, Task<Unit>> saveAndPublish;
   Func<MakeTransfer, Validation<MakeTransfer>> validate;

   Lazy<AccountRegistry> accountRegistry;

   public ControllerActivator()
   {
      accountRegistry = new Lazy<AccountRegistry>(() =>
         new AccountRegistry
            ( loadAccount: id => loadEvents(id).Map(Account.From)
            , saveAndPublish: saveAndPublish));
   }

   public object Create(ControllerContext context)
   {
      var type = context.ActionDescriptor.ControllerTypeInfo.AsType();
      if (type.Equals(typeof(MakeTransferController)))
         return new MakeTransferController
            ( getAccount: accountRegistry.Value.Lookup
            , validate: validate);

      throw new InvalidOperationException("Unexpected controller type");
   }
}
```

These functions should provide suitable implementations based on technology of choice and business requirements

A single instance of `AccountRegistry` will be lazily initialized.

A controller can get the `AccountProcess` it requires from the `AccountRegistry`.

I'm not including the implementation for the functions that read and write events to storage because they're so technology-specific and don't entail any particularly interesting logic. They're required to construct a single, application-wide AccountRegistry, whose Lookup function is provided to a controller, allowing it to get the AccountProcess it requires.

You've now seen all the main components of an end-to-end solution for handing a money transfer, with the added constraints of synchronized access to the account state.

Summary

- *Shared mutable state* that's accessed concurrently can cause difficult problems:
  - For this reason, it's best to avoid shared mutable state entirely, and this can often be achieved in parallel processing.
  - In other scenarios, notably in multithreaded applications that need to model real-world entities, shared mutable state is often required.
  - Access to shared mutable state must be serialized to avoid inconsistent changes to the data. This can be achieved using locks, but also using lock-free techniques.
- *Message-passing concurrency* is a technique that avoids locks by restricting state mutation to processes (actors/agents) that have exclusive ownership of some state, which they can access single-threadedly in reaction to messages they're sent.
- An actor/agent is a lightweight process featuring
  - An inbox, in which messages sent to it are queued up.
  - Some state, of which it has exclusive ownership.
  - A processing loop, in which it processes messages *sequentially*, taking actions such as creating and communicating with other agents, changing its state, and performing side effects.
- Agents and actors are fundamentally similar, but there are important differences:
  - Actors are distributed, whereas agents are local to a single process.
  - Unlike with agents, the actor model includes a model for error handling with *supervisor* actors that can take action if the supervised actor fails, resulting in very robust systems.
- Message-passing concurrency feels quite different from other FP techniques, mainly because FP works by composing functions, whereas actors/agents tend to work in a fire-and-forget fashion.
- It's possible to write high-level functional APIs with agent-based or actor-based implementations.

Epilogue: what next?

Congratulations on taking up the challenge of learning FP and making it to the end of the book! You're now familiar with all the fundamental concepts of FP, as well as several advanced techniques. I hope that you've enjoyed the book, and I encourage you to share your impressions through a review, social media, or just by talking with colleagues.

By way of goodbye, I want to give you some suggestions on where to look next if you'd like to take your exploration of FP further. Your next step would probably be to learn a functional language (or a few). C# is a multiparadigm language, so you can mix and match as you like. A functional language, on the other hand, will force you to use the functional approach throughout—for example, by not allowing any state mutation at all. You'll also find that functional languages have better syntactic support for the techniques presented in this book.

An additional benefit of learning a functional language is that it will allow you to take advantage of other learning resources: books, blogs, talks, and so on. Most learning material on FP available today has code samples in Haskell or Scala.

The natural choice would be to learn Haskell, which is the functional language of reference and a lingua franca among functional programmers. For this, I recommend you read *Learn You a Haskell for Great Good* by Miran Lipovaca (No Starch Press, 2011).[1] Another good way to learn Haskell is to do so while following Erik Meijer's MOOC on FP.[2]

Scala is a multiparadigm language with an emphasis on FP that runs on the Java virtual machine. As of today, Scala is your best chance at doing FP and getting paid for it, and the Scala community is the most active in addressing the question of how the ideas of FP (which tend to originate in academia) can best be put to work in

---

[1] You can read the full contents online for free at http://learnyouahaskell.com/, but do consider buying a copy to reward the author's hard work.

[2] Erik Meijer is, among other things, one of the main contributors to LINQ and Rx. His MOOC on FP is available on edX (https://www.edx.org/), and you can follow along in Haskell or one of several other languages.

industry. If you want to learn Scala, I recommend you do so by following Martin Odersky's MOOCs.[3]

Two younger functional languages I'm fond of are Elm and Elixir, both of which are supported by an enthusiastic user community and are gaining popularity, especially among startups. I hope to see these two languages gain wider adoption and recognition in the next few years.

Elm (http://elm-lang.org/) is a strongly typed, purely functional client-side language that compiles to JavaScript. The syntax is terse, similar to Haskell or F#, but the language and tooling are much more user-friendly. It includes a framework that takes care of managing state and performing side effects. As a result, the programmer only writes pure functions. Simply put, Elm puts any existing JavaScript framework to shame. If you're a full-stack web developer, consider using Elm for the front end.

Elixir (http://elixir-lang.org/) is a dynamically typed language that runs on the Erlang virtual machine (which is based on the actor model, discussed in chapter 15), and as such it's particularly well suited if your interest is in systems with a high degree of concurrency and you want to further explore message-passing concurrency.

There are many more functional and multiparadigm languages out there (sorry if I forgot to include your favorite!), each with its own appeal. But the ideas of FP that you've learned in this book are language-independent and will enable you to acquire a basic working knowledge of any functional language within a couple of days, or weeks at most. Also, don't forget to check out Manning's library, which has titles on all the languages I've just mentioned.

Goodbye.

---

[3]   Martin Odersky is the creator of Scala, and his MOOCs are available on Coursera (https://www.coursera.org/).

index